Walking and Mapping

Leonardo

Roger F. Malina, Executive Editor

Sean Cubitt, Editor-in-Chief

Information Arts: Intersections of Art, Science, and Technology, Stephen Wilson, 2002

Virtual Art: From Illusion to Immersion, Oliver Grau, 2003

Women, Art, and Technology, edited by Judy Malloy, 2003

Protocol: How Control Exists after Decentralization, Alexander R. Galloway, 2004

At a Distance: Precursors to Art and Activism on the Internet, edited by Annmarie Chandler and Norie Neumark, 2005

The Visual Mind II, edited by Michele Emmer, 2005

CODE: Collaborative Ownership and the Digital Economy, edited by Rishab Aiyer Ghosh, 2005

The Global Genome: Biotechnology, Politics, and Culture, Eugene Thacker, 2005

Media Ecologies: Materialist Energies in Art and Technoculture, Matthew Fuller, 2005

New Media Poetics: Contexts, Technotexts, and Theories, edited by Adalaide Morris and Thomas Swiss, 2006

Aesthetic Computing, edited by Paul A. Fishwick, 2006

Digital Performance: A History of New Media in Theater, Dance, Performance Art, and Installation, Steve Dixon, 2006

MediaArtHistories, edited by Oliver Grau, 2006

From Technological to Virtual Art, Frank Popper, 2007

META/DATA: A Digital Poetics, Mark Amerika, 2007

Signs of Life: Bio Art and Beyond, Eduardo Kac, 2007

The Hidden Sense: Synesthesia in Art and Science, Cretien van Campen, 2007

Closer: Performance, Technologies, Phenomenology, Susan Kozel, 2007

Video: The Reflexive Medium, Yvonne Spielmann, 2007

Software Studies: A Lexicon, Matthew Fuller, 2008

Tactical Biopolitics: Theory, Practice, and the Life Sciences, edited by Beatriz da Costa and Kavita Philip, 2008

White Heat and Cold Logic: British Computer Art 1960–1980, edited by Paul Brown, Charlie Gere, Nicholas Lambert, and Catherine Mason, 2008

Curating New Media Art, Beryl Graham and Sarah Cook, 2010

Green Light: Notes toward an Art of Evolution, George Gessert, 2010

Enfoldment and Infinity: An Islamic Genealogy of New Media Art, Laura U. Marks, 2010

Synthetics: Aspects of Art and Technology in Australia, 1956–1975, Stephen Jones, 2011

Hybrid Cultures: Japanese Media Arts in Dialogue with the West, Yvonne Spielmann, 2012

Walking and Mapping: Artists as Cartographers, Karen O'Rourke, 2013

See http://mitpress.mit.edu for a complete list of titles in this series.

Walking and Mapping

Artists as Cartographers

Karen O'Rourke

The MIT Press
Cambridge, Massachusetts
London, England

First MIT Press paperback edition, 2016

This book was set in Stone Serif and Stone Sans by Toppan Best-set Premedia Limited, Hong Kong.

Library of Congress Cataloging-in-Publication Data

O'Rourke, Karen.
Walking and mapping : artists as cartographers / Karen O'Rourke.
p. cm. — (Leonardo book series)
Includes bibliographical references and index.
ISBN 978-0-262-01850-0 (hardcover : alk. paper)--978-0-262-52895-5 (paperback)
1. Artists as cartographers. 2. Arts, Modern—20th century—Philosophy. 3. Arts, Modern—20th century—Philosophy. 4. Walking—Philosophy. I. Title.
NX175.O76 2013
700.9'04—dc23
2012020866

For Bernard

Contents

Series Foreword

Leonardo / International Society for the Arts, Sciences, and Technology (ISAST)

Leonardo, the International Society for the Arts, Sciences, and Technology, and the affiliated French organization Association Leonardo have some simple goals:

1. To document and make known the work of artists, researchers, and scholars interested in the ways that the contemporary arts interact with science and technology and
2. To create a forum and meeting places where artists, scientists, and engineers can meet, exchange ideas, and, where appropriate, collaborate.
3. To contribute, through the interaction of the arts and sciences, to the creation of the new culture that will be needed to transition to a sustainable planetary society

When the journal *Leonardo* was started some forty years ago, these creative disciplines existed in segregated institutional and social networks, a situation dramatized at that time by the "two cultures" debates initiated by C. P. Snow. Today we live in a different time of cross-disciplinary ferment, collaboration, and intellectual confrontation enabled by new hybrid organizations, new funding sponsors, and the shared tools of computers and the Internet. Above all, new generations of artist-researchers and researcher-artists are now at work individually and in collaborative teams bridging the art, science, and technology disciplines. For some of the hard problems in our society, we have no choice but to find new ways to couple the arts and sciences. Perhaps in our lifetime we will see the emergence of "new Leonardos," creative individuals or teams that will not only develop a meaningful art for our times but also drive new agendas in science and stimulate technological innovation that addresses today's human needs.

For more information on the activities of the Leonardo organizations and networks, please visit our Web sites at http://www.leonardo.info and http://www.olats.org.

Roger F. Malina
Executive Editor, Leonardo Publications

Preface

At the origin of this book were a number of maps. The first were the maps of my adopted city, Paris, that found their way into my CD-ROM, *Paris Réseau/Network*. Another project involved building a tool that allowed other people to map their itineraries. Its title reflected my ambition for it—*A Map Larger Than the Territory*.[1] It was intended as an urban form of tracking in which the footprints of past travelers, reactivated by contemporary practitioners, link past and present, real and virtual.

In his seminal lecture "The Author as Producer," (1934), Walter Benjamin claimed that new forms of mass communication—cinema, radio, advertising, the press—were breaking down traditional artistic genres and blurring professional distinctions. He held that, since the arts are grounded in the material structure of society, artists must revolutionize the means by which their work is produced and distributed. One way this can be accomplished is for authors to be involved in publishing.

We could say that Benjamin's wish has been more than fulfilled on the Internet. Social networking tools, blogs, and personal home pages have become a means for unprecedented numbers of authors to self-publish their works. But in an online world where everybody talks at once, is anyone listening?

Like the project out of which it evolved, this book offers a context for listening that brings together mappers and travelers, writers and readers, image makers and viewers. It is an occasion to develop a cross-cultural databank where another pedestrian's story can jog our memory, calling up places or events we had long forgotten. Following other paths encourages us to observe our own surroundings and gives us things to look for. From landmark to path, from itinerary to story, from narrative to network, we witness the creation of an emergent system—a dynamic, collectively drawn city map of a place that is embedded both in the streets of Kreuzberg, the Latin Quarter, or the Lower East Side and in a nebulous cyberspace.

The book confronts the itineraries of academics with Ph.D.s and self-taught do-it-yourself *bricoleurs*, geeks and social networkers, antiglobalization activists and researchers engaged in corporate R&D, scientists turned artists and artists squatting in science labs, sedentary mappers and nomads, those who began half a century ago and others fresh out of school. Each is capable of revealing an aspect of our collective imaginary. The details of their subjective itineraries take on more significance when confronted with others, and together with many other details, unique stories, and ordinary trips, they form a new entity—a dynamic whole that is greater than the sum of its parts.

The book/map with its multifarious itineraries and link networks holds up a mirror to our cities. The more a city favors diversity, the more lively it is. Versatile and abundant, it is a dynamic system that results largely from simple interactions between its inhabitants and their living spaces. Acting individually and interacting with others at a local level, they produce complex, collective behavior at a higher, global level. The map, like the city as a whole, forms an organized complex system made of "situations in which a half-dozen or even several dozen quantities are all varying simultaneously in subtly interconnected ways."[2] Both book and project focus on the interconnections—the ways these networks work.

Where can we find these interconnections? On the Web, I discovered experiments in psychogeography and a host of walking and mapping projects. Participating in festivals, workshops, and symposia (including the International Symposium on Electronic Art in Chicago (1997), ArtMedia in Paris (2002), the International Cultural Heritage Informatics Meeting in Berlin (2004), and Psy-Geo-Conflux in New York (2003), I met other artists who were seeking ways of "redefining the base map," as Alison Sant put it.[3]

Some chart "emotional GPS," while others call for "participatory mapping," "collective authoring," and "collaborative systems." Some adapt global positioning systems (GPS) for drawing, "elastic mapping," "annotating space," or creating hybrid "datascapes." Others use their legs for "speculative mapping," subvert lie detectors for "biomapping," invent wearable devices for "sousveillance." Artists are working with scientists, designers, and engineers. Some are themselves engineers, geographers, architects, and designers. Moving outside the museums and galleries of the art world, they practice neogeography, ubiquitous computing, existential technology, locative media, Web mapping, and augmented walking. Many of these experiments take the shape of one-time performances or workshops, and others are limited in time.

Acknowledgments

I would like to thank the artists and writers who inspired this book, and to all those who provided us with images of their work for publication. Special thanks to Janet Cardiff, Gavin Brown's enterprise, Wilfried Hou Je Bek, the Yvonne Lambert Gallery, Manu Luksch, and the Public Art Fund for providing documentation. I am grateful to Anne-Marie Duguet for telling me to write a book, and David-Olivier Lartigaud, who invited me to contribute a text to *Art++,* the volume he was preparing on "art-oriented programming." I develop here a number of the ideas first put forth in that article. This book benefited from the support of many people along the way: among them, Annick Bureaud, Sean Cubitt, Bernard Guelton, Roger Malina, Nicolas Thély, Isabelle Vodjdani, the late Steve Wilson, and Doug Sery, whose encouragement sustained me through the long and often painful process of writing. Warm thanks go to the anonymous reviewers whose comments gave me a glimpse of what the reader's experience might be and how I could improve it. Deborah Cantor-Adams, Katie Helke Dokshina, Mary Reilly, and Rosemary Winfield put skill and hard work into the daunting task of transforming the manuscript into a book.

My family has seen me through many years of walking and mapping. River Teyssèdre often accompanied me in the field and lent an ear to my stories, as did other Teyssèdres, Lewises, and O'Rourkes. Even 4,585 miles away, Eunice O'Rourke was always available to help, including last-minute proofreading. Maureen O'Rourke did some valuable fact-checking. I would like to thank all of them, and above all, Bernard Teyssèdre, who has been a source of inspiration for more than thirty years.

Introduction

Pedestrians and Cartographers

In Western civilization, the map has traditionally offered a bird's-eye view constructed from the vantage point of an ideal observer above the fray, like Michel de Certeau looking down over Manhattan from the top of the World Trade Center while pedestrians moved through the maze of streets below, unwittingly "writing the text of the city."[1]

When GPS technology came of age in the mid-1990s, artists had been using trajectories down here on earth to trace maps for many years. Today the convergence of global networks, online databases, and new tools for location-based mapping coincides with a renewed interest in walking as an art form. This book charts the cartographic jungle and maps the mappers, be they airborne or earthbound, surveyors, explorers, navigators or interlopers.

Walking is the way most of us make our way through the world most of the time, yet our gait is as personal as a fingerprint, and so are our multiple itineraries.[2] "Knowledge is grown along the myriad paths we take," writes Tim Ingold, it is "an improvisatory movement—of 'going along' or wayfaring—that is open-ended and knows no final destination."[3]

Picture a group of twenty-year-olds sauntering out of a train station during a railway strike. They have nowhere to go, and they are taking their time getting there. A walk can start with the pleasure of just moving—putting one foot in front of the other, ambling, laughing, shooting the breeze. Since the early 1950s, when Guy Debord and his friends wandered through Paris on day-long drifts, and the late 1960s, when Richard Long trampled a patch of grass in a field and snapped a photo of the result (*A Line Made by Walking*), contemporary artists have returned time and again to the walking motif, discovering that, no matter how many times it has been done, it is never done.

Like walking, mapping is an embodied experience carried out from a particular point of view that "makes possible both the finiteness of my perception and its opening out upon the complete world as a horizon of every perception."[4] Here it is considered as a way to locate ourselves in the world, allowing us to make sense of our situation and to act on it.

Mapping denotes a process that takes place every time a map of any kind is created—a drawing scribbled on the back of an envelope, a sequence of places or events etched in one's memory, an itinerary generated on the fly by an online route-finding service, or a projection prepared by a team of professional cartographers.

The environment to be mapped encompasses both the immediate, physical, often urban surroundings in which we walk, our own actions and perceptions as pedestrians, and the cultural or ideological filter through which we view this experience. "Surely this is exactly what the cognitive map is called upon to do in the narrower framework of daily life in the physical city," writes Fredric Jameson: "enable a situational representation on the part of the individual subject to that vaster and properly unrepresentable totality which is the ensemble of society's structures as a whole." Jameson advocates "an aesthetic of cognitive mapping," which he defines as "a pedagogical political culture which seeks to endow the individual subject with some new heightened sense of its place in the global system."[5]

Mapping is not only the object of our research; it also serves as its method. The situationists created maps to highlight the "psychogeographical contours" and "articulations" of modern cities, the "constant currents, fixed points and vortexes that strongly discourage entry into or exit from certain zones."[6] Their maps chart not the physical distances that separate two parts of a city but the influences that shape our experience of walking through it at street level. Because this mapping was at an early stage in its development, for Guy Debord its results were as imprecise as the first navigational charts: "The only difference is that it is no longer a matter of precisely delineating stable continents, but of changing architecture and urbanism."[7]

To show "psychogeographical pivotal points" in Paris, Debord and Asger Jorn cut up a street map, brought together districts that were miles apart in actual physical space, and added arrows representing the flow of atmospheres. Each map they produced was a collage on paper, an exploded yet synthetic view of a dynamic process. This book also attempts to capture a complex, evolving situation at a particular point in time.

Top-Down or Bottom-Up?

Computer programmers have two major approaches to developing large-scale applications. Top-down programming starts by considering the problem at a high level of generality and then progressively specifies it. Programmers proceed by successive refining until the level of abstraction coincides with that of the programming language.

In bottom-up programming, developers begin at the lowest level with the programming language and then increase their level of abstraction.

To reconcile pedestrians with cartographers, I combine both approaches. The book begins on the ground with a close study of an emblematic walking project and works its way up to a higher-angle view of what is involved. By alternating close study of a few characteristic projects and attempts to fit them into a broader picture, I aim to build a clear and highly differentiated map of a complex phenomenon.

This path recapitulates the history of modern cartography, which developed from the "rectilinear marking out of itineraries" that characterized the maps of antiquity by gradually incorporating more and more information.[8] Strikingly similar to today's computer-generated itinerary maps, medieval pilgrimage maps were aimed at facilitating action. Their instructions to pilgrims showed a path to take from one place to another, indicated stops to make, and noted distances in hours or days. A fifteenth-century Aztec map that describes the exodus of the Totomihuacas shows footprints and sketches of each day's meals, battles, and river crossings: it is as much history book as geographical map.[9] In Europe from the fifteenth to seventeenth centuries, the map gained autonomy, distinguishing itself from its constitutive narratives. The system of projection incorporated both tradition (Ptolemy's *Geographia* remained a model for subsequent cartography) and observation (such as navigators' portolan charts). The map became a theater.[10] In keeping with academic tradition, my first-person account is counterbalanced by the multiple voices of others—artists, scholars, and fellow mappers.

Choice of Artworks

The field has burgeoned over the past decade, so here I focus mainly on walkings and mappings I was able to experience firsthand. The corpus regroups works from several genres—performance, dance, writing, visual and sound arts, and cinema and video. Although the main focus is on the field of contemporary art, I have included projects not usually labeled art when they offer a fresh point of view and can otherwise contribute to the discussion. To give context and consistency to recent projects, I have related them to landmark works from the past half century.

Structure of the Book

The introductory chapters set the stage. Chapter 1 opens with a "thick description"[11] of an emblematic walk in which a group of people meet in a suburb of Orléans to map their surroundings by choosing their own landmarks and naming them. This experiment is grounded in the recent history of psychogeography and the "politics of applied pedestrianism" from the situationists to Reclaim the Streets. In what ways has walking contributed to the practice of culture-jamming?

Chapter 2 proceeds through a series of jump cuts. It begins by briefly evoking the biomechanics of walking before cutting to the Judson Church in New York in the early 1960s and the "dance of everyday language" where dancers explored ordinary movements of the body. It then fast-forwards, moving uptown to Central Park to take Janet Cardiff's audio tour *Her Long Black Hair* in the hopes of undergoing an experience that may or may not be art.

The next two chapters explore these questions from the artist's viewpoint. They deal with various methods artists have used to structure their walks: chapter 3 considers walks as objects seen from the outside, where the overall shape is important, and chapter 4 examines the use of instructions, protocols, and scores to create more open-ended walks.

Chapter 5 explores the ways in which mapping is involved when we move through space. When we navigate through artists' labyrinths, walking meets mapping through wayfaring and wayfinding.

Chapter 6 follows a few distinct trajectories (or lines made by walking) and reveals characteristic means of annotating space, and chapter 7 deals more generally with how movement, space, and time are envisioned or made visible in hybrid maps and datascapes.

Chapter 8 moves up another step to consider contemporary experiments in collaborative cartography using networked databases. Can collaborative mapping be a form of what Bertolt Brecht called *Umfunktionierung* (functional transformation)? After examining the various ways in which the maps can be linked up and what this fully networked model means for pedestrians today, in the last chapter, I attend to mapping "ways through."

1 Psychogeography: The Politics of Applied Pedestrianism

Drifting for an Hour in Orléans-La-Source

What the map cuts up, the story cuts across.
—Michel de Certeau[1]

Sunday, October 17, 2004: a "psychogeographic walk" with Wilfried Hou Je Bek was scheduled for 2 p.m. as part of Archilab, the Orléans architecture festival. He and I arrived a few minutes early, but across from the Bolière tram stop, several people were already waiting. Others arrived in small groups, until about twenty were gathered. The air was cool, and the sky overcast.

Wilfried Hou Je Bek handed us each a pencil, a small yellow card (figure 1.1), and a black and white map of the neighborhood. The card showed a four-item list that was designed to look like a software pull-down menu. It was a "walking algorithm." My card was printed with these instructions:

first right
first left
third right
repeat

A Psychogeographical Account of La-Source

Wilfried told us to walk for an hour following our algorithms. Every time we noticed something striking—an object, a street corner, a configuration of elements—we were to give it a name of our own invention that reflected the impression this place or phenomenon made on us.

We were not to look for names. It was up to them to find us. We had no cameras, no GPS, nothing to distract us—just pencil and paper.

A light wind, leaves rustling, chestnuts rolling off a sloped roof, in the distance the staccato rhythm of heels on the pavement. Another psychogeographer? Feet moving, fresh air, regular breathing that accelerated when I ran.

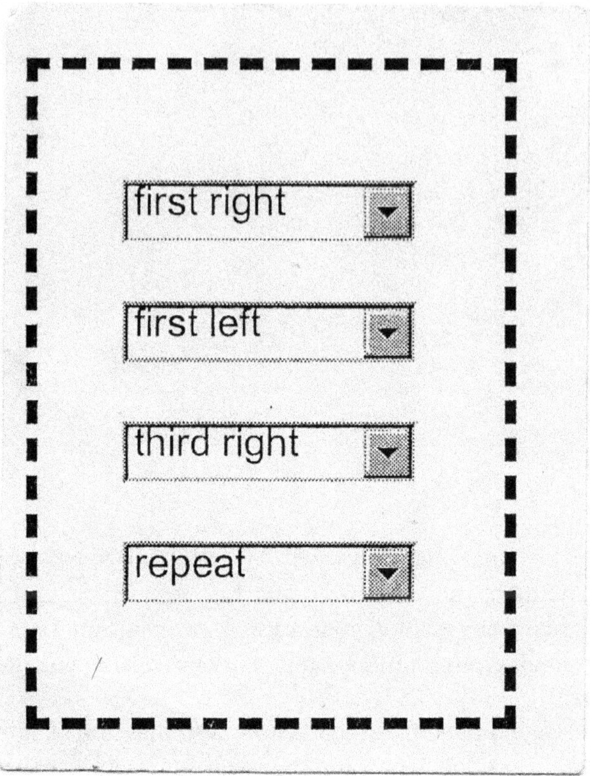

Figure 1.1
Wilfried Hou Je Bek, *Walk*, 2003–2004. The artist distributed yellow tickets with instructions for a walk in Orléans-la-Source. Participants gave names to the places they encountered as they followed the walking algorithm.

Armed with my instructions, I watched for crossroads I could identify and count. What exactly is a "first left"? Does this unmarked lane qualify, or should I wait for something more important? Another participant wrote that she entered "a false street where it has become very difficult to orient myself, I'm having a lot of trouble finding the third right."

I opted for the cul-de-sac, moving ahead slowly on the lookout for a marker or a nameable place. In one hour, in an area of about 400 meters, I eventually found sixteen of them and duly noted each one on the back of my map.

The first identifiable object was a monumental green "L" lying on its side in front of a school, the Collège La Bolière. A small girl passing in the street followed my gaze. "It's for playing," she declared in a tone that did not invite contradiction.

Farther on, I met up with "rusty doors: chestnuts on concrete." Then I stopped to contemplate the "modular beige boxes" across the street. Most of my names were attempts at description. I began with the quality that struck me first and then added other details, as if by stringing them together I might find in their accumulation the appropriate term. Once it was a cluster of street signs: Watteau, Cézanne, and Poussin huddled together like gossips near the intersection.

After a while, I realized that I was walking in circles, continually noting the same landmarks, hesitating at the same intersections. The program described an endless loop.

Bolière is an outlying area near the university campus. After a few minutes, I found myself in a development of tract homes that brought to mind an American archetype: "little identical suburban boxes which differ only in color and planting."[2] Here, the differences were a bit more pronounced. Many of the houses sat behind a hedge or a fence, their sloping A-roofs ready to ward off even the heaviest rain. On my map, I noted "keep out."

In Anglo-Saxon countries, wealthy city dwellers began emigrating to the outlying country in the eighteenth and nineteenth centuries, but only after World War II, middle-class families left the towns in droves and transformed suburban areas into the settlements we know today. In 1961, Lewis Mumford decried the conformity of the suburb: "the ultimate effect of the suburban escape in our time is, ironically, a low-grade uniform environment from which escape is impossible."[3] In the city centers, poverty and neglect were visible to all. By contrast, the suburb cultivated a false naïveté: it was a place where "one might live and die without marring the image of an innocent world, except when some shadow of evil fell over a column in the newspaper. . . . Here domesticity could flourish, forgetful of the exploitation on which so much of it was based. Here individuality could prosper, oblivious of the pervasive regimentation beyond. This was not merely a child-centered environment: it was based on a childish view of the world, in which reality was sacrificed to the pleasure principle."[4]

In Europe, many deplored the changes brought by the suburb: "In the older neighborhoods," wrote Constant in 1959, "the streets have degenerated into freeways, leisure activities are commercialized and denatured by tourism. Social relations become impossible there. The newly constructed neighborhoods have but two motifs, which dominate everything: driving by car and comfort at home."[5]

What about La-Source? Were its inhabitants as enamored of their pipes and slippers as their American counterparts? Did the small plots surrounding the individual dwellings reflect, as Robert Moses noted dryly, "not merely the rapacity of developers but the caution of owners, who do not want too much grass to cut and snow to shovel"?[6]

I was reminded of the California communities that photographer Bill Owens portrayed thirty years ago in his book *Suburbia*. The streets were planned for car traffic but did not seem unfriendly to pedestrians, not that I was likely to meet a little Richie fitted out with toy rifle and cowboy boots, cheerfully making his rounds on a Big Wheel.[7] In fact, I saw few people on foot and could only speculate on what went on behind the hedges.

Peeling the Onion

Founded in 1962, just a year after Mumford published his book, Orléans-La-Source was conceived as a "pilot town for the twenty-first century," part of a government plan to decentralize Paris. Grouping both small industries and the campus of the University of Orléans in a wooded area near the source of the Loiret River, it was intended to be the "French Oxford," a place where "princes would be pedestrians." In the city center designed by architect Louis Arretche, 7,500 apartments were built in twenty years.[8] Today, much of its population lives in low-cost housing, and newspapers refer to it as a working-class district.

The Bolière neighborhood harbors a school complex classified as a *zone d'education prioritaire* (ZEP) (prioritized education zone), a label given to "establishments concentrating the greatest difficulties," which qualify them for additional government funding. The Orléans board of education Web site lists these handicaps: "the proportion of underprivileged social categories, the results of the French tests given to sixth graders, the proportion of families with three children or more."[9]

Proportions? Categories? Results? Across the street, a construction of pale pink cinder blocks gazes back at me. Could these modest apartment buildings be part of the projects to which the town owed its recent notoriety? La Source briefly flickered through the headlines in 2005 during France's so-called suburban riots. The following year, another round of violence was feared when teenagers set fire to cars and dumpsters, throwing stones at vehicles parked near the police station.[10]

What did the organizers of Archilab have in mind when they picked this neighborhood? My fellow psychogeographers had their own ideas on the matter, noting details like "a forlorn Christmas wreath left on a street light," a "park with anything but trees, in front of a forest of buildings," "a bench to see nothing," and "a feeble attempt to make social housing cheerful with a bit of turquoise paint." The spot marked Lycée Voltaire on the official map was described by two people. The first wrote: "How can it be a ruin after only thirty years—I mean, treated like a ruin with this horrible pink and prisonlike [word I can't make out]? How can a pink foie-gras door mean "No entry!"? Don't go out either. That is a mystery." The second noted succinctly: "A prefabricated education," "'let me in'—'let me out.' Mussolinification of thought."[11]

The Avenue de la Bolière is known locally for its Sunday "rodeos." Motorcycle riders rear up on their hind wheels, speed side by side at over 100 MPH. Engines revving, tires screeching, neighbors grumbling. A member of our group noted a fence next to a roundabout: "looks like a car crashed into it."

Not far away is the Bolière 3 mall, with a Champion supermarket. In 2006, Babette, the head cashier, was fired for giving credit to customers, causing a general outcry. She recounts the time sixteen years ago when local companies first began downsizing: "a mother came in with her small daughter; she needed milk and diapers. She reimbursed the loan at the end of the month when she got her relief check," and Babette soon was "giving credit to 5 or 6 people each month, for 50 or 60 euros. Always for staples, jars of baby food, diapers, pasta, never alcohol."[12]

Toponym Territory

Our walk finished an hour later as arbitrarily as it had begun when the participants gave their annotated maps back to Wilfried Hou Je Bek. Nowadays, even flâneurs have to keep to a schedule. Our notations would be translated into a language of his invention, L-Expression, and visualized in a three-dimensional display for which the programming had been outsourced to artist Orkan Telhan in the United States. The results were presented on a plasma screen at the Archilab exhibition, *The Naked City*.

Before going our separate ways, we discussed how difficult it had been to find names. Although naming something can make us more acutely aware of the particular qualities of that thing,[13] our relationship with an environment is built over time. The visitors among us could not easily put a name on things we perceived confusedly. "On the tip of our tongues," the names slid off, and instead came paraphrases, descriptions, and approximations. However imprecise they may be as labels, these remarks give us a sense of place:

> "Fort Knox in the ghetto: money with nowhere to go." (facing the *Centre de Chèques Postaux*, local headquarters of the post office banking service)
>
> "A graffiti signs the blind wall of the shopping center: tpi (international penal court?)"
>
> "I arrive in an immense open space, a vacant lot divided in two: parking lot/basketball court. Around this space, buildings and iron bars. What urban developers call a *délaissé* [abandon] appears at the heart of another kind of abandon we don't usually name."

The stumbling block for people who are familiar with an area is a selective gaze that ignores everything but what is necessary for the task at hand. We see only what we expect to see. It takes a certain detachment to be able to look for one thing and find another fortuitously.

Wilfried Hou Je Bek maintains that "the ability to communicate about places in names you have yourself found the language for, the name of it reflecting the reason why it is named as it is, creates a strong emotional relationship with these objects. The survey of the names a community has given through the ages, will tell you about their collective history, it will relive past hopes and miseries, it will evoke mental maps of which some areas will be nearly abandoned, while elsewhere lots of names are in close proximity," which is why "the suppression of local names, in favor of gutless administrative ones [estranges] people from the world they live in."[14]

This seems to be the case everywhere in France, due to its highly centralized administration. Sifting through the archives of land registry in the Meuse valley near the German border, Patrick Beurard-Valdoye found that 90 percent of the toponyms from the Napoleonic era had disappeared. Over the years, successive administrations tended to regroup four or five plots of land into one, for which they retained only one name. He maintains that when we stop using a name, the place itself vanishes. In a poem-palimpsest composed entirely of obsolete toponyms, he conjures up long forgotten spots, such as Gringolet and Rebitorchon, simply by pronouncing their names.[15] This local memory is disappearing in many places. By interviewing elderly people in Palestine, geographer Kamal Abdul Fattah and his students were able to revive names of local wadis, springs, hillocks, and cliffs. The terms in Arabic, Canaanite, and Aramaic reflect the meaning these places had for the inhabitants.[16]

Indigenous Australian dreaming tracks are strings of toponyms that designate places in which members of a particular group have lived, represented as stages in the journey of their totemic ancestors. Each named place corresponds to a memory trace that is at once individual and collective, mythical and historic.[17] "No one who has not experienced Arunta landscape can appreciate the vivid reality of the myths," wrote Olive Pink in 1933: "The whole country through which we passed was apparently only mulga scrub, a few gum creeks, a low or high range here or there, or some open plains, yet it was made the scene of much activity by aboriginal history. . . . So vivid are the tales that the investigator has the feeling of an inhabited area with much activity around: people hurrying hither and thither."[18]

"To move forward we have to go backwards and start language anew. 'Right here Write now,'" says Wilfried Hou Je Bek. He put his own principle to work by dubbing the Orléans-La-Source experiment "psychogeonamics," a portmanteau name on which we can hang a host of others: *geonomics*, a theory that people own only what they create and therefore land and other natural resources belong to the community; *geodynamics*, "the study of the activity and forces inside the earth"; *onomastics*, "the study of the origin, form, meaning and use of names, especially proper names"[19]; and *nomic*, a game in which players propose "changes in the rules, debate the wisdom of changing them in that way, vote on the changes."[20] With our feet, we are continually writing the city, but can we read it?

Psychogeography: A Toolbox for Reading

"Psychogeography is the fact that you have an opinion about a space the moment you step into it. This has as much to do with the space as with our hardwired instincts to determine if it is safe," says Wilfried Hou Je Bek.[21] *Graphy* comes from the Greek *graphein* (to write), a decidedly polysemic word: if geographers "carve," "draw," or "write" the earth (*geos*), what about psychogeographers? The Latin prefix *psychē* (breath) adds a zest of soul to the mix, linking earth, mind and hand. Psychogeographic writing is an alternative way of reading the city. Wilfried Hou Je Bek calls it "the city-space cut-up." Just as William Burroughs and Brion Gysin cut and reorganized newspaper texts to reveal their implicit content, so too psychogeographers decode urban space by moving through it in unexpected ways.

Although the various practices gathered under the umbrella of psychogeography are ancient, the term itself was first used by members of the Lettrist International in the early 1950s. They described it as "a science of relations and ambiances" they were developing "to give play in the society of others [*le jeu de société*; literally, "the parlor game"] its true meaning: a society founded upon play. Nothing is more serious. Amusement is the royal privilege that must be made available to everyone."[22]

Writing in the Belgian surrealist journal *Les Lèvres Nues,* Guy-Ernest Debord attributes the term to an "illiterate Kabyle." Its vagueness appealed to the loosely organized group that adopted it to describe its various activities. Because geography deals with the impact of natural forces (such as climate and soil composition) "on the economic structures of a society, and thus on the corresponding conception that such a society can have of the world," wrote Debord, psychogeography should examine the "specific effects of the geographical environment . . . on the emotions and behavior of individuals."[23] To accomplish this ambitious investigation, he recommended drifting:

> The practice of de-familiarization and the choice of encounters, the sense of incompleteness and ephemerality, the love of speed transposed onto the plane of the mind, together with inventiveness and forgetting are among the elements of an ethics of drifting we have already begun to test in the poverty of the cities of our time.[24]

Contemporary practitioners take their cue from Debord, who proposed one of psychogeography's first genealogies. It began with Giovanni Piranesi's labyrinthine stairways and gathered Claude Lorrain, Jack the Ripper ("probably psycho-geographical in love"), Edgar Allan Poe, and André Breton (deemed "naively psycho-geographical in encounters"), among others.[25]

Each psychogeographer has his own list: Ralph Rumney's included "Renaissance architect Serlio, French garden designer Le Nôtre, and all builders of grottoes, follies and mazes"; Iain Sinclair turns to William Blake, "the Godfather of Psychogeography"; Rebecca Solnit makes a case for satirist John Gay, the author of *Trivia, or The Art of Walking the Streets of London* (1716); Wilfried Hou Je Bek singles out Horace Walpole, who, over a period of thirty years, transformed his Tudor mansion into a Gothic castle "meticulously designed to provoke a vast array of sensations in its visitors"; Merlin Coverly cites Robert Louis Stevenson's *The Strange Case of Dr. Jekyll and Mr. Hyde* for the way it depicts the seamy underside of the city as reflecting dark corners of the human psyche.[26]

Among the precursors found on nearly every list is opium-eater and peripatetic Thomas de Quincey: "On Saturday evenings," wrote de Quincey, "I have had the custom, after taking my opium, of wandering quite far, without worrying about the route or the distance" in search of an occult "Northwest Passage" allowing one to cross London unhampered.[27]

The Figure of the Flâneur

Charles Baudelaire's flâneur is often cited as a model for today's run of psychogeographer. Inspired by Edgar Allan Poe's story "The Man of the Crowd" and epitomized by Baudelaire's painter friend Constantin Guys, the flâneur was something of a dandy who ambled through the Paris arcades while ordinary people scurried to work all around him. Free from the pressures of the workaday world, he sought the random encounters that the city streets were always ready to offer. Guys, "the painter of modern life," was a man of the world whose domain was the crowd, "just as the air is the bird's and water that of the fish." He desired nothing more than to merge with the throng and to dwell in "the ebb and flow, the bustle, the fleeting and the infinite." The crowd was "[a]n enormous reservoir of electricity" that gave him the opportunity "to be away from home and yet to feel at home anywhere; to see the world, to be at the very center of the world, and yet to be unseen by the world" to the extent that the man himself has become a mirror, "a kaleidoscope endowed with consciousness," "an ego thirsting for the nonego and reflecting it at every moment in energies more vivid than life itself, always inconstant and fleeting."[28] Baudelaire completes this portrait in "The Crowds," one of the prose poems that comprise *Le Spleen de Paris*: "It is not given to everyone to be able to bathe in the multitude: enjoyment of the crowd is an art" that requires "a taste for dressing up and masque, a hatred for domesticity and a passion for travel. The solitary and thoughtful stroller derives a singular intoxication from this universal communion."[29]

In the 1930s, Walter Benjamin reappropriated Baudelaire's dandy for his own purposes, contrasting "the pedestrian who wedged himself into the crowd" with "the flâneur who demanded elbow room and was unwilling to forgo the life of the gentleman of leisure." He claimed that "Around 1840 it was briefly fashionable to take turtles for a walk in the arcades. The flâneurs liked to have the turtles set the pace for them" as a way of protesting against "the division of labor which makes people into specialists."[30]

In the tradition of Restif de la Bretonne, who wandered through Paris on the eve of the French Revolution (*Les nuits de Paris*, 1788–1794), Benjamin's contemporaries Louis Aragon (*Paris Peasant*, 1925), André Breton (*Nadja*, 1928), and Philippe Soupault (*Last Nights of Paris*, 1928) put to paper their citywide ramblings. Like Baudelaire ("Modernity is the transient, the fleeting, the contingent"),[31] they celebrated the inadvertent poetry of shop window displays, fleeting glances, elusive women, chance encounters, and mysterious pursuits.

Drifting through *New Babylon*: Montage and Metonymy

Drifting for members of the Lettrist International did not mean only walking. The adventure began during a transportation strike in the summer of 1953 on the platform at the Gare de Lyon, where the group was trying agit-prop. Failing to rally any of the stranded passengers to the strikers' cause, Guy Debord, Jean-Michel Mension, and their friends sauntered out of the station (or were they chased out?) and began flagging down cars.[32] Hitchhiking nonstop through Paris, they changed their destinations to fit that of the drivers. Their goal, as Debord noted facetiously, was to add to the confusion.[33]

Later, this "technique of rapid passage through varied ambiances" was accomplished on foot and by taxi, "depending on whether the goal [was] to study a terrain or to emotionally disorient oneself."[34] In "*Dérive* by the Mile," Michèle Bernstein argued in favor of replacing private transport in Paris by large numbers of low-cost taxis, which would be more conducive to recreational drifting. As they travel varying distances in a set time and follow an essentially random itinerary, taxis combine freedom of movement with automatic disorientation.[35]

Conversely, walking was better for close-up views that focus on the environment at hand.[36] The situationists prided themselves on detecting the "sudden change of ambiance in a street within the space of a few meters; the evident division of a city into zones of distinct psychic atmospheres."[37] It is a subjective science. When Guy Debord describes the urban ambiances that he and fellow lettrist Gil J. Wolman gathered while drifting through the north of Paris, his judgments are peremptory: here he sees a "repulsive *petit-bourgeois* landscape"; there he deems a staircase leading to a network of alleys to be "annoyingly picturesque"; farther on, he consecrates "the impressive rotunda by Claude-Nicolas Ledoux" as the center of an "important psychogeographic hub" because it is "a virtual ruin left in an incredible state of abandonment, whose charm is singularly enhanced by the curve of the elevated subway line that passes by at close distance."[38]

A drift could last as long as the drifters wanted it to—a whole day or, as Debord suggests, the time between two periods of sleep: "The maximum area of this spatial field does not extend beyond the entirety of a large city and its suburbs. At its minimum it can be limited to a small self-contained ambiance: a single neighborhood or even a single block of houses if it's interesting enough (the extreme case being a static-drift of an entire day within the Saint-Lazare train station)."[39]

It comprised both restless movement and alcohol-fueled talk. Speaking in Paris at the Palais de Tokyo in September 2003, Jean-Michel Mension described those early drifts as leading frequently from one neighborhood bar to another. It was not usually a solitary pursuit. Debord's and Wolman's drift began at 10 a.m. and finished at an unspecified time in the evening when the two drifters abruptly decided to put an end to it. On the way, they made a number of "stops—sometimes long, sometimes brief—at various bars patronized by the bargemen" on the right bank of the canal Saint-Denis, before arriving in a Spanish bar known as the Tavern of the Rebels.[40]

Architecture for Drifters

Members of the lettrist group[41] viewed drifting as part of a larger quest, which was outlined by Ivan Chtcheglov in his 1953 *Formulary for Unitary Urbanism*. Inveighing against "banalization," the mental illness of our time, he notes: "Everyone is hypnotized by production and conveniences: sewage system, elevator, bathroom, washing machine"—a state of affairs that arose out of the postwar struggle against poverty but "has overshot its ultimate goal." Instead of liberating people from worldly cares, he claims that the obsession with material comfort has enslaved his contemporaries to the point that "presented with the alternative of love or a garbage disposal unit, young people of all countries have chosen the garbage disposal unit." This is why he thought it necessary "to bring about a complete spiritual transformation by bringing to light forgotten desires and by creating entirely new ones. And by carrying out an intensive propaganda in favor of these desires."[42]

Chtcheglov goes on to portray the ideal city of the future in which drifting is the main activity of its inhabitants. Landscapes that change from one hour to the next will result in complete disorientation. All the other arts will be superseded by architecture, "the simplest means of *articulating* time and space, of *modulating* reality, of engendering dreams":

> Everyone will live in his own personal "'cathedral,'" so to speak. There will be rooms more conducive to dreams than any drug and houses where one cannot help but love. Others will be irresistibly alluring to travelers. . . . The districts of this city could correspond to the whole spectrum of diverse feelings that one encounters by chance in everyday life.[43]

The Dutch painter Constant later incorporated these ideals into his utopian city New Babylon, whose inhabitants, freed by automation from the obligation to work, could spend their days engaging in creative play.[44] Chtcheglov himself had second thoughts later, after several years in a psychiatric hospital. In "Letters from Afar," he likened the continual drift to free association in psychoanalysis. Too much of either threatened the unprotected individual with disintegration. He recommended it for a shorter period: "limited to Sundays for some people, up to one week average. A month, that's quite a bit. We drifted for three or four months in 1953–1954—that is the extreme limit. It's a miracle it didn't kill us."[45]

For Henri Lefebvre, the practice of drifting "revealed the growing fragmentation of the city." Industrial expansion in the nineteenth century had already begun to break the center of Paris into pieces. The Place des Vosges, a vestige of the aristocratic seventeenth-century city, was surrounded by newer bourgeois areas in the Marais, the Bastille, and the Faubourg Saint-Antoine. "We had a vision of a city that was more and more fragmented without its organic unity being completely shattered," said Lefebvre, and "Afterward, of course, the peripheries and the suburbs highlighted the problem. The experiment consisted of rendering different aspects or fragments of the city simultaneous, fragments that can only be seen successively." To accomplish this, Constant had the idea of using walkie-talkies to link up groups of drifters in spatially distant neighborhoods of the city. The drift took the form of narrative unfolding in several places at once by means of walkie-talkies: "you go along in any direction and recount what you see. . . . The goal was to attain a certain simultaneity . . . a synchronic history. That was the meaning of Unitary Urbanism: unify what has a certain unity, but a lost unity, a disappearing unity."[46]

The Demise of Unitary Urbanism

After 1960 and the development of urbanization and city planning (in France the urban planning code dates to 1961), the situationists abandoned the theory of unitary urbanism and the practice of structured drifting. The drift "had a precise meaning only for historic cities, like Amsterdam, that had to be renewed, transformed. But from the moment that the historic city exploded into peripheries, suburbs—like what happened in Paris and in all sorts of places, Los Angeles, San Francisco, wild extensions of the city—the theory of unitary urbanism lost any meaning."[47] For them, drifting would have been nonsensical in a new town like Orléans-La-Source.

Algorithmic Walking

The situationists reflected on what was for them a practice, unlike Wilfried Hou Je Bek, who began with the theory. His generation saw psychogeography as an "academic bon mot" that called for references to Michel Foucault, Antonio Negri, and Gilles Deleuze. It was not something you actually did. He decided to buck the trend: "I have always been into making walks—that is the real reason for psychogeography."[48]

So he and his friends began where the situationists left off in the newly built cities, following the method described in Guy Debord's "Theory of the Drift" (1956). In 2001, two groups of psychogeographers explored a neighborhood under construction in the new town of Leidsche Rijn ("the armpit of Utrecht," as Hou Je Bek put it) using a map of Rome "as some sort of randomiser." After agreeing to meet forty-five minutes later on the "Ponte Garibaldi," they set out to "rewire their perception of Leidsche Rijn"—This "way of manoeuvring" offered them "a pleasant afternoon" but, as Hou Je Bek concludes, it "was too strongly influenced by the limits of personal tastes, expectations and biases." They needed a more "objective method," since the psychogeographical effects were more likely to be stronger "if the route was as clear as possible."[49]

A solution came their way via the *Game of Life*, a cellular automata program developed by John Conway in 1970 that used stones on a Go board. In this game with simple rules (analogous to evolutionary patterns of bacteria populations), it was impossible to predict what would happen next: the only way to find out was to execute the program. Inspired by the *Game of Life*, which had been developed without a computer (to test his code, Conway had to update the patterns, one stone at a time), Wilfried Hou Je Bek came up with a set of rules to define a route that could be both endless and unpredictable. He notes that to succeed, these directions need both to "enslave" the participant, creating in him "the desire to find out where this all 'will lead to,'" and to enhance his "cognitive map with new images and experiences of the city."[50]

To measure the psychological effects of these strolls, he imagined a notational system that later developed into the psychogeographic markup language (PML) project.[51] Because the walking algorithm produces different results each time it is executed, it is a generative program. Groups of psychogeographers, each following a different set of instructions, can use it for experiments in collaborative cartography, as we had in Orléans-La-Source.

For him, walking is a process of self-education: "The psychogeography project started because I wanted to say something about cities. I had no idea what I would want to say, but that's what it started as—a systematic process of finding out. Slowly, while doing that, you build up enough understanding to be able to say something."[52]

Playful Pedestrianism

As unitary urbanism was winding down toward the end of the 1950s, other movements were gathering momentum in Europe and Japan. During the second Gutai[53] show in Tokyo (1956), Shiraga Kazuo dipped his feet in paint and walked over an expanse of canvas he had placed on the floor. Atsuko Tanaka walked through exhibition openings wearing her *Electric Dress*. Inspired by neon drugstore signs, the dress was a tangle of electric cords and light bulbs that lit up from time to time, like the electric impulses moving through the body. Akira Kanayama showed 150 meters of shoeprints and invented a four-wheel remote-control device filled with paint that automatically traced a meshwork of lines on the floor (*Remote-Control Paintings*, 1955).

While Guy Debord was oscillating between drifting and political activism, the decentralized Fluxus group was developing a kind of playful anarchy that was reminiscent of the dadaists. They wrote walking scores and organized tours in the city (such as *FreeFlux Tours* and *Fluxus Tour of Soho*).

Excursions, Tours and Mobile Galleries

The tradition of artist-led tours can be traced back to the *Excursions & Visits DADA*. At the instigation of André Breton, the dadaists planned a series of tours of "common places" like the Louvre, the Buttes Chaumont garden and the Gare Saint-Lazare. The *1st Visit* (and the last, too, it seems) was the Parisian church Saint-Julien-le-Pauvre.

The group's leaflets announced that "Thursday, 14 April, at 3 p.m., in the garden of St-Julien-le-Pauvre church, the dadaists passing through Paris, wanting to remedy the incompetence of suspicious tourist guides, have decided to inaugurate a series of visits to chosen places, particularly those that have really no reason to exist" (and were decorated with slogans such as "Cleanliness is the luxury of the poor man. Be dirty!," "You ought to trim your nose as you trim your hair," "Breasts should be washed like gloves," and "Distribution of silk stockings for 5.85").[54]

Intended to offend traditional aesthetic sensibilities and make the public aware of dada's militant antiart stance, the promised excursion failed to attract any takers other than the guides themselves. Photographs show them standing in the church garden under a forest of umbrellas, while André Breton reads from a paper.[55] As Hugo Ball said, "For us, art is not an end in itself . . . but it is an opportunity for the true perception and criticism of the times we live in."[56]

Like the visit to Saint-Julien-le-Pauvre, artists' tours often cast everyday sights in a new light. In 1962, after observing street vendors in Paris's Marais quarter illegally hawking "genuine cheap Swiss watches" *sous le manteau* (under the table; literally, "under the coat"), Robert Filliou found a subversive way to show art by peddling it "under the hat." The Galerie Légitime (Legitimate Gallery) with its *Couvre-Chef d'œuvre* (Masterpiece Hat) was born. In July 1962, an exhibition invitation was distributed: reminiscent of situationist maps, it showed an itinerary through Paris, with each stop marked with a time—from the Porte Saint-Denis at 4 a.m. to La Coupole at 9:30 p.m. The itinerant gallery, its owner, and the exhibiting artist (Ben Patterson) ambled through Paris, talking with people they met at the places noted on the flyer.[57] Filliou's itinerant gallery recalls Marcel Duchamp's *Boîtes-en-valise* (suitcases equipped with "samples" of his works) and his remark that the readymades were rendezvous at a certain time and place.

Walking blurs the borders between representing the world and designating oneself as a piece of it, between live art and object-based art. Artists moved from depicting places to pointing them out or demonstrating them, like André Breton quickly walking in and out of local cinema screenings in 1920s Paris.[58] And since the fabled nontour of Saint-Julien-le-Pauvre, they seem to be intent on taking us with them as well.

Walking Mathematically

Beginning in the early 1970s, Georges Perec examined his own relationship with lived spaces in books like *Especes d'espaces* (*Species of Spaces*) and *Tentative d'épuisement d'un lieu parisien* (*An Attempt to Exhaustively Describe a Parisian Place*),[59] in which he listed all the events he observed from a café table at the place Saint-Sulpice in Paris. He begins *Species of Spaces* by noting: "The subject of this book is not exactly the void but rather what there is around or inside it."[60] Positing that "To live is to go from one space to another, trying insofar as possible to not bump into things,"[61] the book itself moves from the space of the page ("Space begins in this way, with only words, signs traced on the blank page")[62] to that of the bed, the bedroom, the apartment, the building, the street, the quarter, the city, the countryside, the country, Europe, the world, and space, like a letter addressed by a child. Perec notes that he likes to walk in Paris, sometimes for an afternoon without a goal but "not really by chance" and sometimes by carefully preparing an itinerary. If he had the time, he would like to conceive and resolve problems like that of the bridges of Koenigsberg or "find a path crossing Paris from one end to the other, only taking streets beginning with the letter C."[63]

Fellow Oulipian, mathematician, scholar, and poet Jacques Roubaud "writes with his feet," using place names and arbitrarily concocted walks to help him mentally compose his poems and haibuns (a short literary form combining prose and haiku). He calls the process "sonnet-walking." The micro-haibun *Sonnet-walking* is composed of thirteen sonnets, each marking a stop on a trip in the United States (New York, Cambridge, Boston, Philadelphia, Cincinnati, Denver, and San Francisco), with intermediate sonnets describing the trip from one place to another. Another, composed in Tokyo, takes the shape of the Yamanote line circling the city. He stopped at each train station to explore the area on foot and compose poems.[64]

From Poaching to Protest: Walking the Cutting Edge

In the 1960s and early 1970s, visual artists explored unusual means of engaging with their everyday surroundings. In Amsterdam, Stanley Brouwn collected footprints of anonymous passers-by by putting sheets of paper on sidewalks. Later he handed paper to pedestrians in several European cities, asking them to draw a map showing how to get from wherever they were to the train station or the cathedral. He stamped these drawings *This Way Brouwn* and gathered them into an artist's book. The results show how different people see and convey spatial relationships. As maps, they depend on the particular context for which they were made.

Between 1970 and 1973, Adrian Piper made a series of unannounced street appearances in New York to which she gave the title *Catalysis* (figure 1.2). Catalysis is the change (often the increase) in the rate of a chemical reaction that is induced by a catalyst. The term *catalyst* is often used figuratively to designate someone or something that provokes change. She did not want her actions to be labeled guerrilla theater, streetworks, or happenings. To call them art would reduce their effect. For *Catalysis I*, she soaked her clothes in a mixture of vinegar, eggs, milk, and cod liver oil for a week

(a)
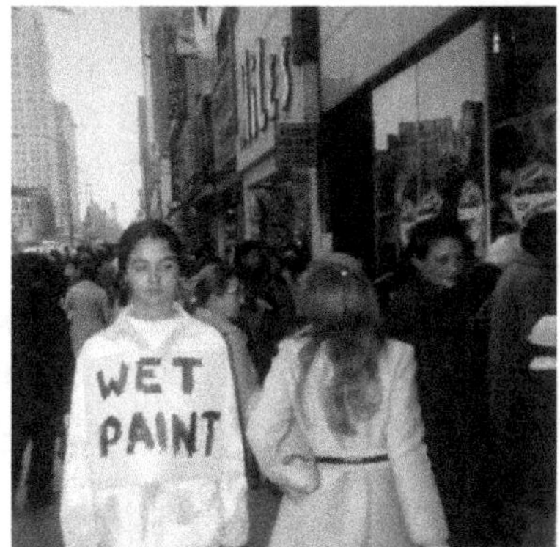

(b)
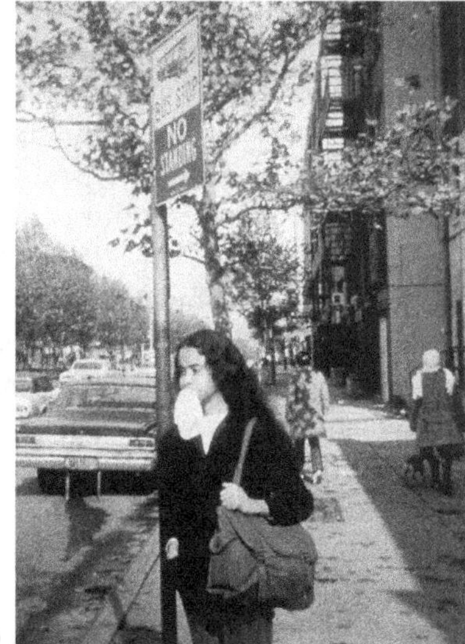

(c)
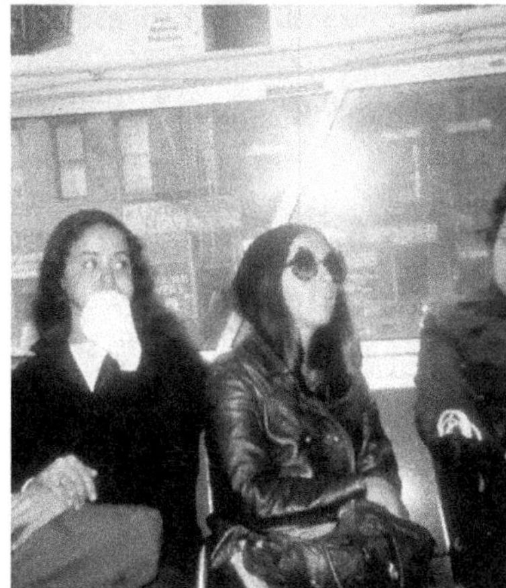

Figure 1.2

Adrian Piper, *Catalysis*, 1970. Performance documentation: black-and-white photographs, 16 in. × 16 in. (40.6 cm. × 40.6 cm.). A series of unannounced street appearances in New York. Photos: Rosemary Mayer. Collection of the Generali Foundation, Vienna. © Generali Foundation and APRA Foundation, Berlin. *a: Catalysis III*: The artist walks through Macy's department store to shop for gloves and sunglasses while wearing a sweatshirt covered with wet paint. *b:* The artist rides the bus with a towel hanging out her mouth.

and wore them on the subway during evening rush hour and in a bookstore on Saturday night. For *Catalysis III*, she strolled among racks of gloves and sunglasses at Macy's wearing a sweatshirt on which she spread a layer of sticky white paint and wrote *wet paint*. For *Catalysis IV*, she rode on a bus with a towel hanging out of her mouth.[65]

These actions, which express deliberate dislocation and alienation, have been interpreted as a socially charged critique of homelessness.[66] More basically, however, they explore the reactions of passers-by to destabilizing situations. Are New Yorkers as callous as they are said to be? In 1964, a young woman from the borough of Queens was stabbed to death in full view of many neighbors, whose lack of assistance led to many social psychological studies of the "bystander effect."[67]

By the time Taiwanese artist Tehching Hsieh carried out his third *One Year Performance*[68] (figure 1.3) in the streets of New York in 1981, the situation had changed considerably. This was the beginning of the Ronald Reagan presidency when a reaction against so-called big government led to decreased spending on public services.[69] As tax revenues declined, administrations across the United States cut back funding for social services, closed psychiatric wards in hospitals. There was a rise in the number of homeless people seeking refuge on the sidewalks, subway platforms and parks of New York.

For Hsieh, "art is not a career; it is my life"[70] and New York was the place he chose to live that life. After spending one year in solitary confinement in a self-made prison cell within his studio (1978–79) and another year punching a time clock every hour on the hour (1980–81), Hsieh issued a statement in which he resolved to "stay OUTDOORS for one year, never go inside" and "not go in to a building, subway, train, car, airplane, ship, cave, tent" from September 26, 1981 at 2 p.m. to September 26, 1982 at 2 p.m.[71] During that year, he moved around downtown New York on foot, slept on park benches, bought food in outdoor markets, made fires on the piers near the Brooklyn Bridge, and washed himself in fountains and fire hydrants. An illegal immigrant, he was not strictly speaking "homeless"—he had left home voluntarily—and did not have to rely on the street for his living. Locked in his cage, he could attain an inner freedom, yet outside, roaming around at will, he was "trapped . . . in a kind of restless, internal exile."[72] Always on his guard in public spaces, "because of the violence out there,"[73] he noted his journeys on maps and had friends take photographs. These radical experiments,[74] which have not been equaled since, engaged the artist in his everyday existence as a human being and offered the people he encountered the role of witness. As Hsieh puts it, "you have to make the art stronger than life so people can feel it."[75]

Boots Made for Walking

Others have stripped the genre to its essentials, devising spare but evocative performances. *Roadworks* was carried out in May 1985 by Mona Hatoum in the

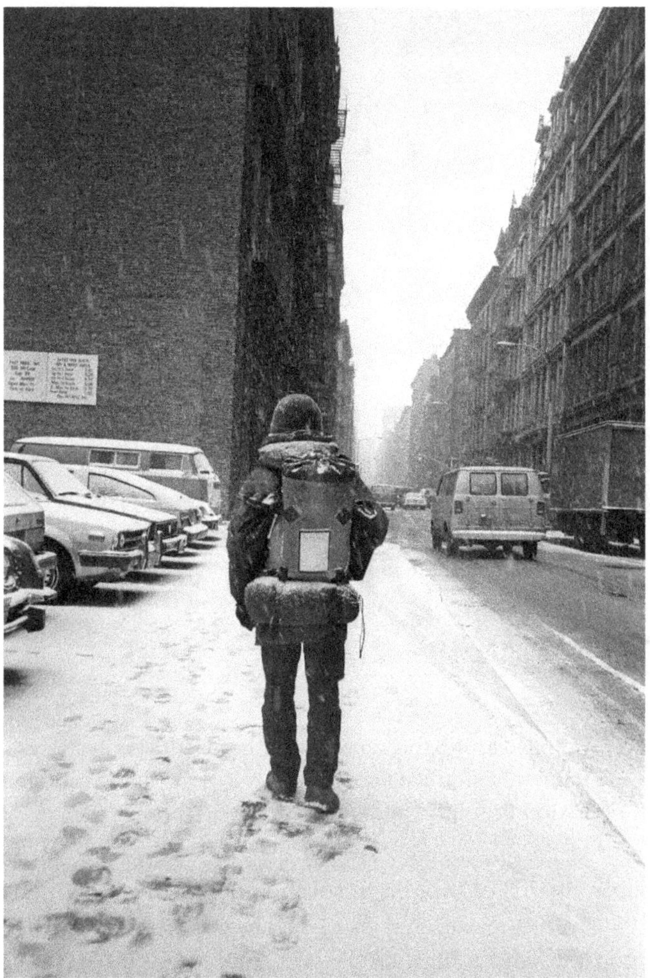

Figure 1.3
Tehching Hsieh, *One Year Performance 1981–1982*. The artist spent a year outdoors, moving around New York City with only a sleeping bag and a few other belongings. © Tehching Hsieh. Courtesy the artist and Sean Kelly Gallery, New York and the Gilbert and Lila Silverman Collection, Detroit.

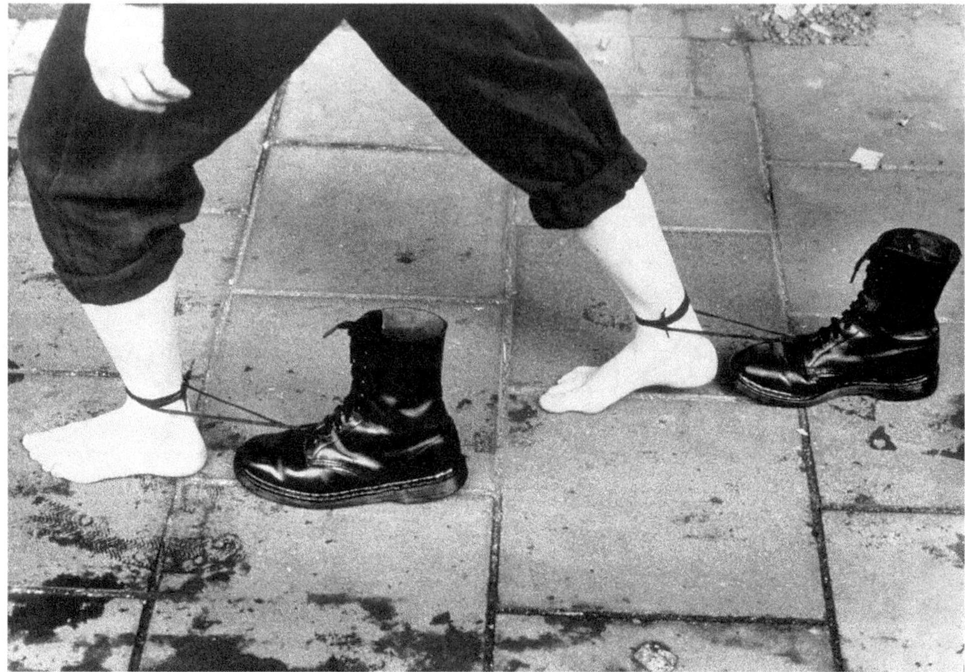

Figure 1.4
Mona Hatoum, *Roadworks*, 1985. Performance, Brixton, London. © the artist. Photo: Patrick Gilbert. Courtesy White Cube. Mona Hatoum performed *Roadworks* in May 1985 in the predominantly African Caribbean district of Brixton in south London.

predominantly African Caribbean district of Brixton in south London (figure 1.4). The site of violent riots in the 1980s, Brixton suffered from severe economic problems, unemployment, inadequate housing, and a high crime rate. Yet for the inhabitants, an increased police presence was not reassuring; indeed it felt like an army of occupation. In Brixton, bobbies had a reputation for brutality and for indiscriminately using their stop-and-search powers to target blacks and minorities. Later in 1985, during a nighttime raid in connection with a robbery, London police officers shot and paralyzed a Brixton woman. Coming after many instances of oppression by police, this accidental shooting triggered off a night of violence in which one person was killed.

In Brixton, Hatoum walked barefoot on a busy city sidewalk, a military-style boot (the kind worn by police officers and skinheads) tied to each ankle by its shoelaces.[76] The documentary video shows the artist moving laboriously past shopping carts, baby carriages, and market stalls. At first, we see only her feet pulling the boots as other pairs of shod feet pass quickly without pausing. When one oncoming pedestrian moves in and turns one of Hatoum's boots on its side, Hatoum stoops to stand it back up. The camera gradually moves out to show the action from other points of view. Some passers-by are startled, and others turn to gape or point her out to their companions. A group of men look on, chuckling. One of them says: "Does she know she's being followed?"[77]

This interplay of vulnerability and power has a particular significance in the United Kingdom, where walking is a national pastime. The Ramblers Association was created to promote "Britain's most popular outdoor recreation": "Walking is the most inclusive, sociable and sustainable means of transport, the closest thing to perfect exercise and the best way to access the outdoors."[78] Official maps in England and Wales record at least 225,000 kilometers of off-road public rights of way. Tourists meander through the foothills in the Lakes district, bird watching or pub crawling.

But walking also brings into play embedded class antagonisms. English tradition has long pitted aristocratic fox hunters against plebian foot travelers. Suspicion of pedestrians can be traced to sixteenth-century Britain, where they were suspected of vagrancy. After the enactment of the game laws in 1671, the pedestrian was seen as a potential poacher. His very existence was a threat to private property. Donna Landry argues that "walking means aligning oneself to some extent with a rebellious reclaiming of common rights, with the dream of liberal freedom, with the ideal of democracy."[79] In a country where common lands were being increasingly privatized and enclosed, the walker reclaimed the right to use public footpaths.

For those with the means to drive, walking was construed as a political statement that signified adhesion to the democratic principles of the Enlightenment. The young Samuel Coleridge and Joseph Hucks, gentlemen dressed as peasants, set off to walk from Cambridge to Wales: "By going amongst the Welsh populace disguised as a poor pedestrian, [Hucks] sought a different kind of experience. Pedestrianism was an expression of universal brotherhood, of solidarity with the laboring man. And the freedom to travel without carriages, horses, and servants, and to go wherever their feet might carry them, was a heady experience of freeborn liberty."[80] Mona Hatoum's performance suggests that more than a century after the abolition of slavery, this liberty may be illusory for those who have no choice but to travel on foot.

Taking his inspiration from the French situationists, Ewen Chardronnet sees psychogeography as a tool that can teach history, politics, and the theory of capitalism. In Paris, a city that sees about three thousand demonstrations every year, it means one thing to "start a demonstration moving from the Invalides (that is a symbol of Napoleon's grave) to Saint Michel (symbol of 1968)" and quite another to "go from Bastille Square (symbol of the French Revolution) to Nation Square (symbol of resistance to wars with Germany, Nation is on the east side of Paris, where invaders usually came in during wars). You can choose different places to pass through to stimulate the imaginations of the protesters and even provoke riots."[81]

At the time of Restif de la Bretonne, Place de Grève[82] facing the Paris Town Hall was the site of public executions. In 2009, a group of university professors made it the site of their protest against the French government's neoliberal university reforms. For six weeks, relaying each other night and day, marchers walked in a circle that they called *La ronde infinie des obstinés* (The Infinite Round of the Obstinate).

Reclaiming Public Space

Artists often choose to marry humor and political activism with walking. For the event *9 Evenings* in 1966, Öyvind Fahlström arranged for performers to carry signs through the streets of New York showing portraits of Chinese leader Mao Tse-tung and U.S. television comedian Bob Hope. This "odd couple" of media figures produces a cognitive dissonance that seems striking even today.

In 1966, Michelangelo Pistoletto made several large spheres of pressed newspapers that encapsulated the news from the period. The following year, Pistoletto and his wife rolled a two-meter *grande sfera di giornali* (great ball of newspapers) through the streets of Turin, inviting passers-by to play with it. This *Scultura da passeggio* (Walking Sculpture) was a way of engaging with the world outside museums and galleries (figure 1.5). The newspaper ball was one of Pistoletto's *oggetti in meno* (minus objects), of which he wrote:

> I feel that in my recent works I have entered the mirror and actively penetrated that dimension of time which was merely represented in the mirror-paintings. These recent works bear witness to the need to live and act in accordance with this dimension, i.e. in the light of the unrepeatable quality of each instant of time, each place, and thus of each "present" action. . . . My idea of evolution is also antievolutionary (like walking forward on a moving sidewalk that is going backward). Unlike the mirror paintings, my new objects do not represent: they are. Each individual work is a single word in a discussion which could last a lifetime and which is also a language closed in upon itself.[83]

Fred Forest cultivates the complicity of the general public through clearly delineated actions. He has been operating in the cracks between media since the late 1960s. Today, his playful hijacking of communication codes to show up dysfunctions in public institutions and his use of weapons provided by the mass media to criticize those same media might be called culture jamming. A former newspaper cartoonist, he began to experiment with the media as a way of thinking about "communication itself, its codes, its subversion, its ideological, symbolic and aesthetic foundations."[84]

For a series of projects called *Space Media*, Forest asked newspapers to print a small blank square that readers could fill in as they liked and send to the artist. The first, dubbed *150 cm² of Newspaper*, was printed in the French daily *Le Monde* on January 12, 1972. The eight hundred responses were exhibited at the Grand Palais. Ten days later, he appeared live on television with a request that viewers observe a moment of silence to "reflect on the meaning of their lives."

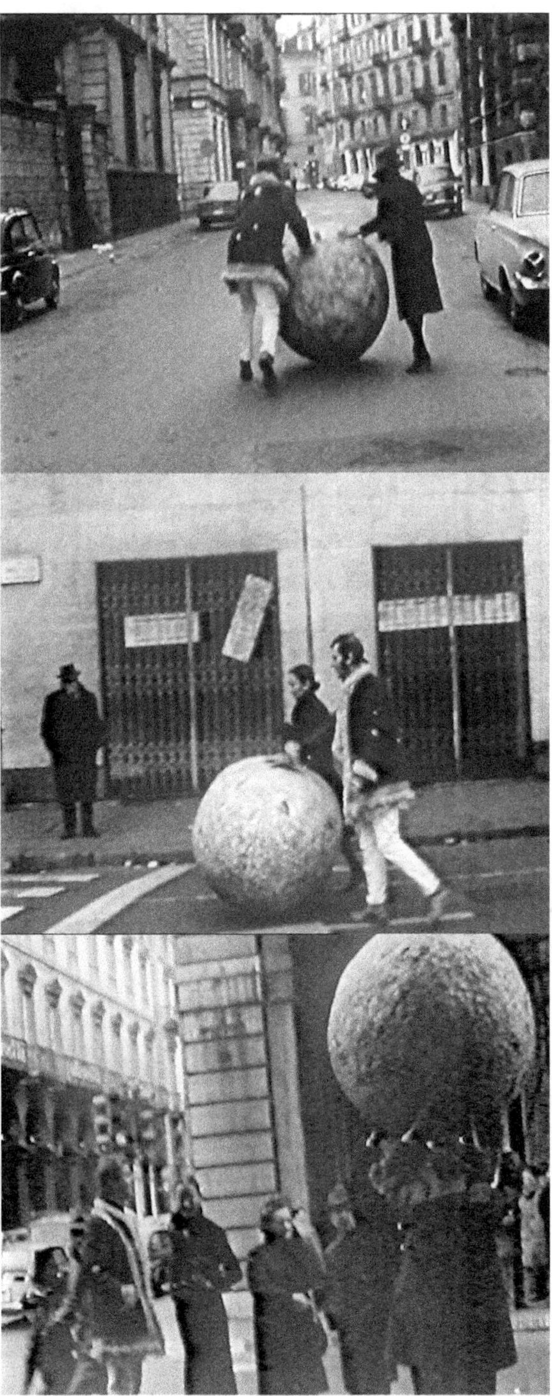

Figure 1.5
Michelangelo Pistoletto, *Walking Sculpture (Scultura da passeggio)*, 1967. Performance in the streets of Turin. Stills from the film by Ugo Nespolo, *Buongiorno Michelangelo*. Courtesy Cittadellarte-Fondazione Pistoletto, Biella.

After similar experiments in other European media, Forest was invited to participate in the twelfth São Paulo Biennial as part of the communication section curated by Vilém Flusser. Here was an opportunity to create a series of symbolic spaces for free expression. In defiance of Brazil's military junta in power at the time (albeit not one of Latin America's most repressive), he organized a nationwide call-in operation and published blank spaces in several newspapers. Every day, as they arrived, the public's responses were posted on the walls of Forest's stand at the Biennial. The local media responded enthusiastically.

The climax of the operation was a street demonstration in December 1972, *Hygiene of Art: The City Invaded by Blank Space*, that featured Forest and a group of marchers carrying blank signs (figure 1.6). Protest marches have long been joined by ordinary people to make their voices heard, but Forest's action was an example of sociological art that conflates protest and public relations. The operation was orchestrated with the help of curator Flusser's contacts in the Brazilian media. Instead of calling on dissidents or students who could have been arrested and tortured, Forest hired fifteen men to carry the signs. As professional sandwich-board

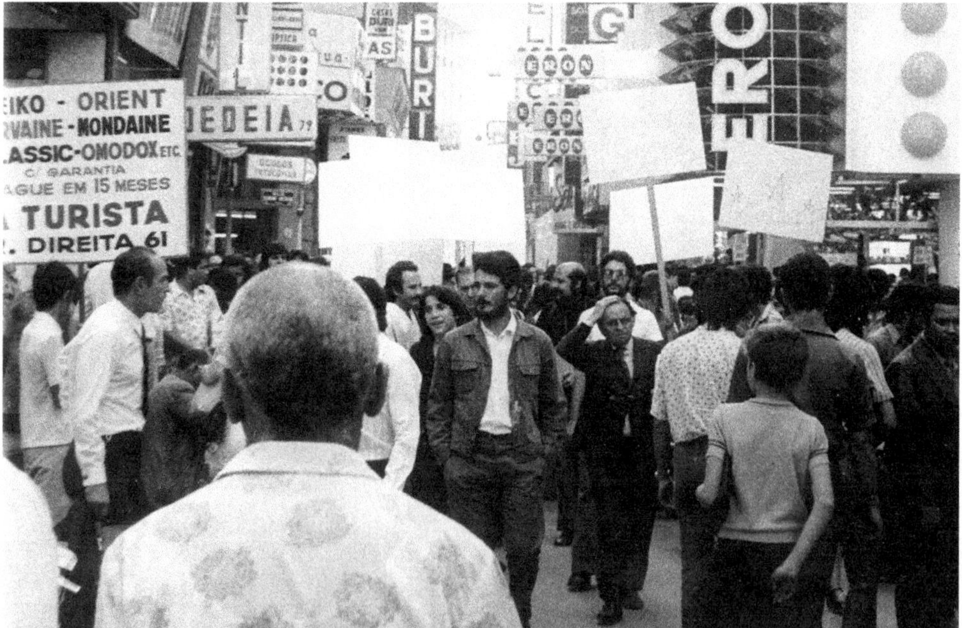

Figure 1.6
Fred Forest, *Hygiene of Art: The City Invaded by Blank Space*, 1973. Performance walk in the streets of São Paulo, Brazil, under the military dictatorship. The artist hired fifteen professional sandwich-board men to walk with him carrying blank signs.

men who work at street corners in the heart of São Paulo, they could not be held responsible for the content of their signs. The press published the itinerary of the march through the city center. Passers-by understood that the blank signs alluded to the censorship imposed by the regime. Although it was against the law for more than three people to congregate in the street, after fifteen minutes, recounts Forest, a hundred had joined the procession, and by the end, nearly two thousand were milling around. From their balconies, onlookers showered the marchers with ticker tape. The demonstration held up traffic for two hours, leading to the artist's arrest by the political police.

Although the march took place only two months after Augusto Pinochet's military coup d'état in neighboring Chile, Brazil was not Chile. Forest's arrest was abundantly reported in the local media, while foreign journalists noted laconically that "Brazilian police don't like freedom of expression."[85] Protected by his status as a foreign artist who had been officially invited by the Biennial, he was released after several hours of questioning.

Temporary Autonomous Zones

A number of culture jammers have cited the influence of Hakim Bey's *Temporary Autonomous Zone* (TAZ). Under the auspices of the Nietzschean Dionysus, "who will turn the world into a holiday," Bey called for the creation of temporary spaces that elude formal structures of control. A TAZ is located in a real time and space but depends on the Web "to bring it into being; crudely speaking one might say that the TAZ 'exists' in information- space as well as in the 'real world.'" The Web does not necessarily require computer technology. Groups can use both high- and low-tech means—word of mouth, phone trees, snail mail—to "construct an information webwork." The key to its utility is "the openness and horizontality of the structure."[86] In some ways, Forest's *Space Media* events prefigure the TAZ, yet participants in a TAZ are anonymous, and the experience is not documented, whereas his own "sociological art" relies on press coverage in which the artist himself figures prominently.

Reclaim the Streets is a collective that began in London in the early 1990s to advocate community ownership of public spaces by combining political activism with partying. It began with the occupation of Claremont Road in east London to prevent it from being destroyed to make way for a new link road. For six months, activists of all sorts—anarchists, ecologists, and squatters—joined forces to maintain the pressure through sit-ins, site invasions, and rave parties, which all received extensive media coverage.

The battle of Claremont Road was ultimately lost, but it served as a catalyst for a wider protest movement. During the 1990s, the group staged a number of nonviolent, festive street events to mark their opposition to cars and the corporate privatization of public space.[87] Protests in the form of "cheeky surprise actions" set up using phone trees and instant messaging spread quickly to other cities worldwide. In some cases, they were combined with antiglobalization actions. The 1999 protests in Seattle were echoed by similar events as far away as India and the Philippines, including Carnival against Capitalism, Seattle Solidarity Action, Reclaim the Future, Toxic Planet, Tube Party, No Blood for Oil, and Guerrilla Gardening.[88]

A similar spirit presided at the birth of the "free networks" movement in the next decade. Julian Priest, one of the founders of the London-based Consume the Net, sees the "digital media landscape" in England as a successor to "techno" culture "with its DIY bedroom music studios and self-organized parties." Locally, this situation resulted in part from the "unseen network effects" of London's orbital motorway, the M25, which was completed in 1986: "By connecting the edge of London's road network for the first time, a space was created for the emerging rave culture." Wireless free networking, which spread to other places from Berlin to San Francisco, was "an antidote to the commercial pipe dreams of telcos and investors, and with its focus on the ownership of infrastructure and local and co-operative action, it can be seen as a grounding of internet utopianism in something real, useful and manageable."[89]

The 1990s saw the development of other forms of activist art. "In the aftermath of the fall of the Berlin Wall, the term '*tactical media*' arose as a renaissance of media activism, blending old school political work, artists' engagement with new technologies," write David Garcia and Geert Lovink: "During the early nineties there was a growing awareness of gender issues, racism, postcolonial struggles, and the possible role that art could play in society."[90] Members of the collective Critical Art Ensemble define *tactical media* as "situational, ephemeral, and self-terminating. It encourages the use of any media that will engage a particular sociopolitical context in order to create molecular interventions and semiotic shocks that collectively could diminish the rising intensity of authoritarian culture."[91]

Walking Psychogeographically

Hakim Bey's intuition about the role of the Internet has been borne out by the rapid spread of psychogeography. Similar experiments in different places took place simultaneously and were quickly relayed by the Web as artists, architects, writers, teachers, and festival organizers caught the bug, spawning onsite mapping parties, dinnertime drifts, and haiku hikes.

The online publication of key situationist texts provided inspiration. Ken Knabb translated them into English and published them without copyright in 1981 and later online on his *Bureau of Public Secrets* Web site. Others appeared in Bill Brown's zine *Not Bored!* (started in 1983), "an autonomous, situationist-inspired, low-budget, irregularly published, photocopied journal. No copyrights, rights reserved, advertising or subscriptions."[92]

Psychogeography was popularized in Great Britain by the works of filmmaker Patrick Keiller (*London*, 1994) and writers Iain Sinclair (*Lights Out for the Territory*, 1997), Peter Ackroyd (*London: The Biography*, 2000), Will Self (*Psychogeography*, 2007), and Stewart Home ("The Psychogeography of Zeros and Ones," 1997), who in 1992 revived the London Psychogeographical Association.[93] Since the early 1990s, the Italian architecture group Stalker and artists Francis Alÿs and Gabriel Orozco have all used walking as a speculative tool.[94]

François Maspero would undoubtedly object to being called a psychogeographer.[95] His first-person account of a one-month trip on a suburban commuter train line, *Roissy Express: A Journey through the Paris Suburbs*, has inspired a number of French writers, who explore cracks in our "seamless" maps. Examples include François Bon, who recounted his weekly train trip from Paris to Nancy in *Paysage Fer*, to Philippe Vasset, who explored one by one all the blank spots on the official IGN map of Paris (*Un livre blanc*).[96]

Remaking the World?

What is psychogeography's legacy? In its diverse forms, it embodies the desire to renew language, social life, and oneself. For contemporary psychogeographers, the drift is purposeful; it can reveal the city's underlying structure. Sinclair aims for Jean-Jacques Rousseau's "alert reverie," a kind of double presence that is both in the here and now and in the imagination:

> Walking is the best way to explore and exploit the city; the changes, shifts, breaks in the cloud helmet, movement of light on water. Drifting purposefully is the recommended mode, trampling asphalted earth in alert reverie, allowing the fiction of an underlying pattern to assert itself. To the no-bullshit materialist this sounds suspiciously like *fin de siècle* decadence, a poetic of entropy—but the born-again flâneur is a stubborn creature, less interested in texture and fabric, eavesdropping on philosophical conversation pieces, than in noticing everything.[97]

In "Theory of the Drift," Debord proposed the idea of a "possible rendezvous" as a means of "behavioral disorientation." Here, a person is given an appointment at a particular time and place but has no idea if someone will be there to meet him or who that person is. Not knowing what to expect, he will study his surroundings and start conversations with passers-by: "He may meet no one, or he may even by chance meet the person who has arranged the 'possible rendezvous.' In any case, particularly if the time and place have been well chosen, his use of time will take an unexpected turn."[98]

Courting the unexpected is often combined with the unabashed apology of subjectivity. Stewart Home states: "For me photography is most alluring when both the person behind the lens and what is being photographed self-consciously manifest their subjectivity. Traveling across 'Britain' to discover 'America' is only one of the many ways in which such subjectivity might remake the world in both photographic and material form. . . . The psychogeographer . . . knows that the world cannot be recorded, it can only be remade."[99] "Remaking the world" is usually done in smoke-filled cafés. If these debates rarely lead to concrete action, what about walking?

2 A Form of Perception or a Form of Art?

The whole universe of science is built upon the world as directly experienced, and if we want to subject science itself to a rigorous scrutiny, and arrive at a precise assessment of its meaning and scope, we must begin by reawakening the basic experience of the world, of which science is the second-order expression.

—Maurice Merleau-Ponty, *Phenomenology of Perception*[1]

William Wordsworth used to walk in order to think or write, with phrases spoken adopting the cadence of feet on the ground. Jean-Jacques Rousseau could meditate only when walking: "When I stop I cease to think; my mind only works with my legs."[2] Friedrich Nietzsche was said to value only thoughts that come from walking, while Søren Kierkegaard spent his mornings strolling through Copenhagen, stopping briefly to chat with passers-by in the Ostergade or hail fishmongers in the Gammel Strand before returning home to put to paper what he had composed afoot: "Every day I walk myself into a state of well-being and walk away from every illness; I have walked myself into my best thoughts, and I know of no thought so burdensome that one cannot walk away from it."[3] As Saint Augustine put it, *solvitur ambulando* (it is solved by walking).

Walking and Falling

Robots have learned how to roll, dance, move up or down stairs and even hit a ball, but they are still clumsy when asked to move forward on two legs. Walking is not as simple as it looks.

In their table of contents for *La marche humaine: Kinésiologie dynamique, biomécanique et pathomécanique* (Human Walking: Dynamic, Biomechanical, and Pathmechanical Kinesiology), François Plas, Éric Viel, and Yves Blanc give us an idea of the complexity of this task.[4] The process known as the "double pendulum" combines muscular actions (the heel attacks the ground, the sole of the foot is pressed down flat, the heel takes off and is followed by the toes, the lower limbs move forward and then totally extend) and movements of the skeleton (the pelvis rotates vertically, shifting its weight to the free side, the knee flexes, the pelvis turns to the side, the lower limb rotates one way, the waist in the opposite direction). And this describes only the movement of a Western subject wearing city shoes and walking on level ground.

Bipedal walking mobilizes both a learned competency and involuntary input. A baby who totters across the living room for the first time sets into motion an innate motor program. His performance is played out by the abdominal and dorsal muscles and the osteoarticular system (feet, ankles, knees, legs, hips, arms, shoulders), which receive instructions by way of the peripheral nerves. Each participant responds by informing the nervous system of its state and position. In response to this sensory input, the brain modifies its command, immediately generating more feedback and further adjustments. For a long time, scientists believed that these movements were directed by a single control circuit in the brain. However, recent research has shown that walking involves several distinct networks.[5]

The workings of proprioception are visible in anyone who is learning a new movement skill. Toddlers wobble and sway as they correct their movements, gradually gaining in accuracy and fluidity. When the skill is finally acquired, it becomes automatic. Every time we take a step forward, we start to fall, then by swinging one arm and the opposite leg forward, we regain our balance and catch ourselves from falling. Walking literally embodies the process by which "the live being recurrently loses and reëstablishes equilibrium with his surroundings" (John Dewey).[6]

The ABCs of Movement

The Dance of Ordinary Language

In the early 1950s, San Francisco–based choreographer Anna Halprin developed the notion of task performance, the prescription and execution of improvisations based on everyday gestures. She was interested in the way movement arises from internal sensation. If you are aware of what is happening in your body, you notice that the bodily responses come straight from the nervous system. Responses can happen so quickly that you do not have time to prepare the next step: it is already there.[7]

Among Halprin's students were Simone Forti, Robert Morris, and Trisha Brown. When Forti moved to New York, she attended Robert Dunn's composition class from 1960 to 1962, where she met several dancers with whom she later formed the Judson Dance Theater. Dunn had been a student of John Cage at the New School for Social Research in the late 1950s. He encouraged participants in his Tuesday evening workshop to use constraints or predefined rules to produce new choreographic sequences.

The Judson group, which included Steve Paxton and Yvonne Rainer, explored the mechanics of everyday movements (walking, bending, carrying objects) and through them the fundamentals of motion—weight, verticality, speed, rhythm, balance, and imbalance. This "dance of ordinary language"[8] used methods derived from the sciences to explore basic physical phenomena. Its proponents renounced psychology and expressiveness to investigate experiential data. Yvonne Rainer set out these aims in her *NO Manifesto* from 1965:

> No to spectacle no to virtuosity no to transformations and magic and make believe no to glamor and transcendency of the star image no to the heroic no to the anti-heroic no to trash imagery no to involvement of performer or spectator no to style no to camp no to seduction of spectator by the wiles of the performer no to eccentricity no to moving or being moved.[9]

In her works of this period, the body was treated as an object. *We Shall Run* (1963) features twelve participants dressed in suits and ties, who dart back and forth across the stage for seven minutes.

Robert Morris was involved with Simone Forti, his first wife, in both the Halprin workshop and the Judson group. Influenced by Forti's use of "rules" to generate movement—she would employ "one set of things to generate results entirely different from the first set of intentions"—he began building objects to structure space.[10] Several of his early minimal works, like the 1961 *Column*, were made for dance performances.

These experiments crystallized the qualities of the Judson Dance Theater. Improvisation, chance procedures, and written scores all investigated the possibilities of ordinary movement—interdisciplinary border crossing and the "why not?" attitude. The Judson dancers gave themselves "time to explore, fail, get it right," as Trisha Brown put it. Forgoing the glazed look and robotic gestures of modern dance, performers looked and behaved like human beings who could be fat or thin, tall or short, trained or not. Blurring the distinctions between professionals and amateurs also meant that painters could dance and dancers could make movies.

In Steve Paxton's work *Satisfyin' Lover* (1967), forty-two participants[11] wearing street clothes walk from left to right, stop, stand or sit still, and then return, each at her own rhythm. In a note to performers, Paxton specified: "The pace is an easy walk, but not slow. Performance manner is serene and collected. This dance is about walking, standing, and sitting. Try to keep these elements clear and pure. The gaze is to be directed forward relative to the body, but should not be especially fixed. The mind should be at rest."[12]

Here the score given to each group of dancers is unambiguous, or so it seems. Members of each group walk across the stage one at a time, some pausing after a set number of paces and others sitting on chairs that face the audience. Asimina Chremos participated in the restaging of this dance in 2000 as part of *PastForward: The Influence of the Post-Moderns.*[13] She described lining up with forty other dancers to "walk down the hall, through the door, down the steps, past the security guard and onto the stage." When and at what point does "everyday life" segue into "art"?

I am #5 in line for *Satisfyin' Lover.* . . .

My score is:

Enter when #1 pauses
Walk to 1/5 across stage
Stand 20 seconds
Continue walk to exit.

My experience of doing this simple work so far, just walking on stage and standing and then walking, is that of being exposed. There's nothing to do but be yourself. A couple of previous performances, I've waited for my cue, entered, and then in the middle of counting start to think: did I walk too fast? Nancy asked us to be calm, relaxed. . . . am I calm? Oops, I'm thinking, not counting. . . . Breathe, sense the space, I remind myself. . . . I stand in the black space of the stage and try not to look directly into the light. . . . People pass by me; I feel as if I am receding. Then I'm done counting and I go. It's not the same walk I do upstairs to go down the hall, away from so many eyeballs.[14]

In 1972, Paxton instigated "a contemporary game" he called *Contact Improvisation* "as a means to explore the physical forces imposed on the body by gravity, by the physics of momentum, falling and lifting."[15] Paxton focused on breathing and becoming aware of one's bones and muscles to explore what he calls "a form of perception rather than a form of art": "I was trying to understand what makes integrity in movement. I thought I spied in CI a form arising from us rather than imposed upon us. It's a game that takes two people to win, so it doesn't create losers; it ignores gender, size, and other differences. It's about attending to your reflexes in a touch communication—faster than words, faster than conscious thinking."[16]

In Trisha Brown's pieces, dancers tried shifting and transferring weight, gravity, and weightlessness. They walked down a ladder (*Woman Walking down a Ladder*, 1973),[17] walked while suspended from a wall (*Walking on the Walls*, 1972),[18] and crawled over Manhattan rooftops (*Roof Piece*, 1971).

Man Walking down the Side of a Building was first performed in April 1970 by Jed Bark. Strapped into a mountain-climber's harness with his arms held tightly to his sides, he moved down the facade of a seven-story building at 80 Wooster Street in Manhattan. Out of the audience's view, an assistant on the roof gradually let out the rope to hold the dancer perpendicular. Brown described the process as a "natural activity under the stress of an unnatural setting. Gravity reneged. Vast scale. Clear order. You start at the top, walk straight down, stop at the bottom."[19]

In May 2006, this gravity-defying walk was reenacted in London: it took the performer less than five minutes to move slowly down the facade of the Tate Modern. Situating the body in the world meant the audience was faced with a kind of split perspective: no matter where they posted themselves, they could see only part of the performance. From the ground, they had to crane their necks to see the performer, while the man manipulating the rope was hidden from view; from the top floor, they could see the rope pulley but were unable to see the man who was walking on the facade.[20]

Repetitive Walking

In the 1960s, practitioners in every field explored repetitive forms. The experimental minimal music made famous by La Monte Young, Terry Riley, Steve Reich, and Philip Glass (the New York hypnotic school)[21] often involved the reiteration of motifs and phrases, using drone effects, phasing, and tape looping. Visual artists explored everyday rituals, cultivating obsessive, repetitious actions. From 1965 until his death in 2011, Roman Opalka counted and manually painted numbers as he spoke their names, from one to infinity. Each painting was called *Detail, OPALKA 1965 / 1 – ∞*. Since 1966, On Kawara has made paintings that bear only the date of their execution meticulously painted in white on a colored background (*Today* series). During the 1970s, he traced his daily itineraries on photocopied maps (*I went*), sent telegrams declaring *I am still alive*, and sent postcards on which he stamped the time at which he awoke on the day he posted the card (*I got up*). In an attempt to reconstitute ordinary moments of his childhood, Christian Boltanski produced photographs in which the artist mimed gestures he had made as a young child—sobbing, sliding down a bannister, throwing a pillow.[22]

For Bruce Nauman, the ritual meant making faces or pacing—to inventory the different ways he could walk around his studio, varying parameters like gait, rhythm, speed, angle, balance: "There was also the idea that if I was an artist and I was in the studio, then whatever I was doing in the studio must be art. Pacing around, for example."[23] So he borrowed a Portapak video camera to film himself *Playing a Note on the Violin While I Walk around the Studio* and *Walking in an Exaggerated Manner around the Perimeter of a Square*. The camera stood still in the middle of the room facing a wall. The videotape shows Nauman moving through the frame, disappearing, and reappearing, while in the background, the sounds of footsteps and violin playing continue.

In *Slow Angle Walk (Beckett Walk)* from 1968, he strode stiffly around the studio. Although earlier works were ten minutes long, *Slow Angle Walk* documents an hour of Nauman's antics in front of a camera posed on its side to make it look as if the artist were walking up the wall. As he explored various ways of keeping his balance, Nauman wavered and wobbled, turned, advanced with difficulty, crawled, rolled, and tripped, evoking the uncertain walk of the title character in Samuel Beckett's novel, *Molloy* (1951).[24] Says the former vagrant Molloy: "'and having heard' that when a man in a forest thinks he is going in a straight line, in reality he is going in a circle, I did my best to go in a circle, hoping in this way to go in a straight line. For I stopped being half-witted and became sly, whenever I took the trouble. And my head was a storehouse of useful knowledge. And if I did not go in a rigorously straight line, with my system of going in a circle, at least I did not go in a circle, and that was something."[25] Like the Judson dancers, Nauman used his body as an instrument to explore the limits of movements and the pull of gravity within the confines of the studio. He said he wanted to make art "that was just there all at once . . .like getting hit in the back of the neck. You never see it coming; it just knocks you down."[26] His videos manage to show space in time while also conveying a sense of "all at once." They are often shown as a continuous loop without beginning or end. The repetitive gestures and lack of any recognizable story line give even a casual viewer the impression after a few minutes that the work has been seen in its entirety, like a fractal in which every part reproduces the whole. In these pieces, he discovered that an effective way of structuring time was to make a work that was ongoing: "there wasn't a specific duration, so where this thing can just repeat and repeat and repeat, and you don't have to sit and watch the whole thing. . . . it became almost like an object that was there, that you could go back and visit whenever you wanted to."[27]

The 1960s were a period of experimentation when artists pushed limits, and boredom was one of those limits. During the same period, Andy Warhol was framing pieces of space-time, beginning with the six-hour opus *Sleep* (1963), and Michael Snow was exploring structure in films like *Wavelength* (1967), in which the camera takes forty-five minutes to zoom into a photo of waves tacked to a wall.

Nauman transposes into time the serial structures of the minimalists. As his contemporary Eva Hesse said: "If something is meaningful, maybe it's even more meaningful said ten times. . . . If something is absurd, it's much more greatly exaggerated, absurd, if it's repeated."[28] Repetition, especially if it builds to a high energy level, as it does in Sufi devotional music (Qawwali), can induce in viewers a hypnotic or ecstatic state of consciousness. Ecstasy comes from the ancient Greek *ἐκ-στασις* (*ek-stasis*) (to be or stand outside oneself, a removal to elsewhere). In Nauman's videos, however, the repetition creates no such build-up and, if anything, causes energy to be lost.

More than a decade later, Beckett himself made the television ballet *Quad I + II* (1982), which he called a "piece for four players, light and percussion."[29] Accompanied by relentless, polyrhythmical percussion, the cloaked performers in *Quad I* enter the square one by one, each stooped figure following its own itinerary, distinguishable from its fellows only by the color of its cowl. Yellow, red, blue, and white, the players scuttle around and through the square, tracing triangles with mathematical precision, smoothly avoiding one another as each skirts the center on the left. Then comes *Quad II*, the pared-down second act in black and white. The percussion has been reduced to what sounds like the footsteps of the four now identical ghostlike figures as they shuffle through their movements. All the way through, the figures move like automata. Although the piece is rather hypnotic to watch, there is no build-up: the pace is regular, even slowing in the second part, as if to suggest fatigue or winding down.

A Walk as an Experience

In his 1934 book *Art as Experience*, John Dewey argues that the task of aesthetics is "to restore the continuity between the refined experiences that are works of art and the everyday events, doings and sufferings that are universally recognized to constitute experience."[30] For the last century, artists have developed methods for bringing art and life into closer contact. Robert Filliou sums it up: "art is what makes life more interesting than art."[31]

Responsive Acts: Listen!

Dewey begins by looking for links between art and the everyday. How do works of art emerge out of ordinary experiences? What are "the factors and forces that favor the normal development of common human activities into matters of artistic value"?[32]

As a concert percussionist, Max Neuhaus witnessed "the gradual insertion of everyday sounds into the concert hall, from Russolo through Edgard Varèse and finally to John Cage, where live street sounds were brought directly into the hall." In Cage's silent piece, *4′33″* (1952), listeners were encouraged to pay attention to ordinary ambient sounds. Ironically, *4′33″* relies for its meaning on the concert hall context, with a seated ticket-holding audience that expects a pianist to perform. This method proved to be ineffective. Said Neuhaus: "the audience seemed more impressed with the scandal of 'ordinary' sounds placed in a 'sacred' place than with the sounds themselves." So he decided to take the experiment a step further: "Why limit listening to the concert hall? Instead of bringing these sounds into the hall, why not simply take the audience outside?" So in 1966, he brought twenty participants into the streets of New York to listen to the city, beginning at Avenue D and 14th Street. The word *listen* was stamped on their hands. Neuhaus recounted his first performance, carried out for a group of friends. Walking down 14th Street, they could hear "some spectacular massive rumbling" from a nearby power plant, and when they crossed a highway, they were accompanied by the sound of its "tirewash."[33] Later, he took them to his Lower East Side studio and played some of his percussion music. When invited to lead subsequent tours in other places, he made a point of saying nothing to encourage the audience to really listen to their surroundings. For the most part, they followed his example.

The idea is promising. But as someone twice removed from the events, I am left with more questions than answers: what did Neuhaus's tour groups take away from their experience?

"[R]eceptivity is not passivity," says Dewey. Nor is it mere recognition, which is perception arrested before it has time to develop so that it can serve some other purpose. In recognition, we fall back on a previously formed scheme. When we recognize a voice on the phone as a friend or a telemarketer, we greet one and hang up on the other. Recognition goes no further. Conversely, complete perception consists of "a series of responsive acts that accumulate toward objective fulfillment." It involves an act of reconstructive doing, in which consciousness becomes alive. This process requires the implicit cooperation of motor elements: "an act of perception proceeds by waves that extend serially throughout the entire organism." It entails "the going-out of energy in order to receive, not a withholding of energy. To steep ourselves in a subject matter, we have first to plunge into it."[34] I decided to take the plunge in New York.

Coming to Terms with Central Park

I began by going into Central Park through the wrong entrance. After collecting Janet Cardiff's audio guide, *Her Long Black Hair*, at the Public Art Fund on East 53rd Street, I entered the park as soon as I caught a glimpse of it, wandering for twenty-five minutes before locating the Jose Marti statue that stood opposite Sixth Avenue. After the merciless grid of city streets outside the park, here the winding paths were irregular and asymmetrical, like those of an English-style garden. Between 1858, when Central Park was started, until its completion in 1873, cartloads of depleted soil and rocks were dug up and replaced by fertile topsoil brought in from New Jersey. Hundreds of families were displaced to make room for over 4 million trees, shrubs, and plants.

Janet Cardiff's low voice in my ear interrupted my reverie: "I have some photographs to show you. Take out the first one. Number one, it says. It was 1965. Almost 40 years ago. Line up the image to the scene in front of us. It's taken from where we're sitting now. The tree is in blossom. Look at the Trump building back then . . . and the women's hats. They're all wearing them."[35]

Trumpets and tubas: is a brass band marching past as I study the seated audience in the photo (figure 2.1)? I had forgotten about pillbox hats with veils. The First Lady was wearing one of those in the Dallas motorcade on November 22, 1963.

"Put the picture away. I hope it doesn't rain again because I want you to walk with me." I look up: there is no band, just a couple of horse-drawn buggies with a cargo of tourists. "Get up. Go to the right. Walk past the statue. Try to walk to the sound of my footsteps so we can stay together. . . . And then down the stairs . . . all the way to the bottom."

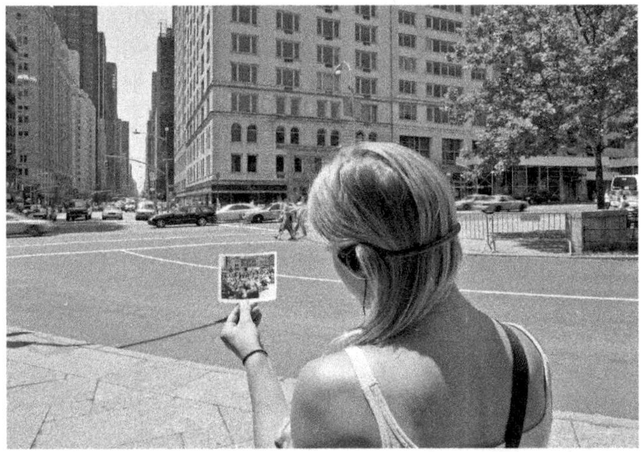

(a)

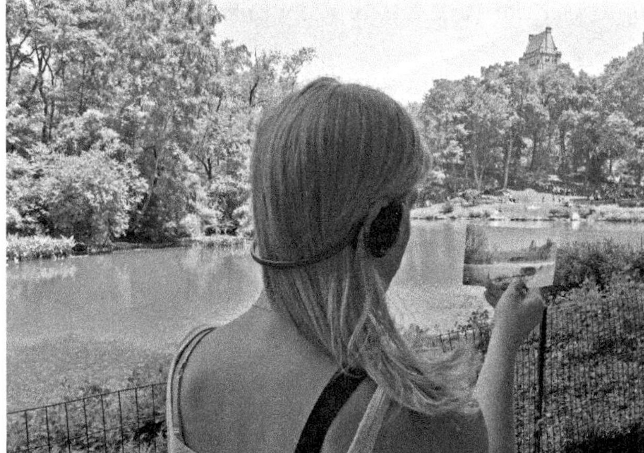

(b)

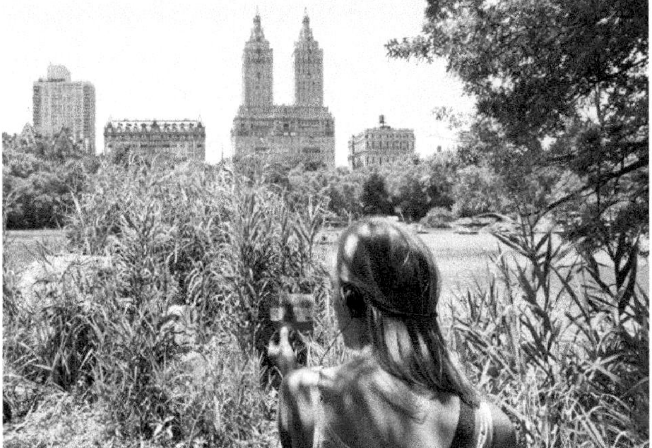

(c)

Figure 2.1
Janet Cardiff, *Her Long Black Hair*, 2004. Audio tour. Janet Cardiff designed the forty-six-minute audio tour for the Public Art Fund in New York City. Visitors to Central Park were given a compact disk player, a map, and a set of snapshots. While walking the route prescribed by the narrator, their experience was augmented by music, spoken text, and sound samples, many of which came from the site being explored. Courtesy of the artist; Luhring Augustine, New York; Galerie Barbara Weiss, Berlin; and Public Art Fund, New York. *a:* Trumpets and tubas, it sounds like a brass band is marching past. *b:* A snapshot made by Cardiff shows the pond frozen over, yet today is warm. *c:* Near the end of the walk, the narrator points out the Dakota building, where John Lennon lived and died. The found snapshot shows a woman with long black hair standing at this spot with her back to the photographer: "She's frozen by the camera, forever facing the lake."

Map, compact disk player in a bag with a shoulder strap, headset, photographs. These items, though neither heavy nor bulky, occupy my hands and monopolize my attention. It is hard to take notes, make sketches, or take photos while listening and looking. I decide not to try. Even so, I find myself stopping frequently, backtracking on the CD. My son had come with me, but we could not share the experience. If we had each taken an earphone, we would have missed the illusion of three-dimensional sound.

Is that someone sneaking up behind me? Cardiff told me not to look back, but I do so instinctively. No one. The sound of scissors makes me jump. She's cutting hair?

Reading over my notes later, I cannot always distinguish what I saw from what Cardiff's voice in my ear told me *she* could see: A man seated on a bench with all of his belongings in garbage bags, waiting for the park to close. If he had been there when I was, he would have had a long wait. Cardiff admitted to being a bit scared, "but it seems safe." A fleeting, involuntary image, almost a reflex in a woman walking alone. In 1989, a young woman jogging in Central Park was brutally raped and left for dead.

Later on the CD, after a chorus of "hellos," a phone rings:

Janet's voice: Hello?
Man's voice: Where are you?
J: In the park.
Man: Be careful.
J: Don't worry. There's lots of people around. What are you doing?
Man: I just had dinner.
J: Keep to the left.
Man: What?
J: I'm just recording. I'll phone you later, ok?

I noticed people lying on the grass, and Cardiff saw a couple kissing, or was it the contrary? One of her snapshots showed the pond frozen over. Today it was warm. By the time I left, the lawns were littered with sunbathers. She describes squatters walking on a tightrope. Pop!

> Do you hear that? They're shooting scavengers, the wild goats and pigs. They were supposed to eat the garbage in the city streets, but they keep coming into the park to eat the grass. So they have to shoot them.

Who are *they*, I wonder? The groundskeepers? The image is jarring. During the building of Central Park, "[t]he political quagmire was matched by the appearance of the park itself, which was rubbish-strewn, deep in mud, filled with recently vacated squatters' huts, and overrun with goats left behind by the squatters. Until they were eventually impounded, the rampant goats were a great nuisance, eating the foliage of the park's few trees."[36]

Charles Baudelaire portrayed the poet as a scavenger who extracts nuggets of art from the chaotic muck of ordinary life.[37] He knew Paris before Baron Haussman demolished great swathes of the city to make way for the *grands boulevards*. In the streets of New York, I did not see the dumpster divers who are often seen in Paris as they sift through detritus for food or salvageable objects. New York churches and libraries have begun to enforce antiloitering policies, relegating bag people to sidewalks and park benches. Some of the homeless camp in the subway and railroad tunnels, where they are virtually invisible. Cardiff's voice in my ear pointed out that during the Great Depression, Central Park housed over two thousand homeless: "Now many live underground in tunnels all over the city. Deep in the many layers, in some areas over ten stories deep."

"At this very moment . . . an organ-grinder in the street . . . wonderful." I strain to make out her words: "It is the accidental and insignificant things in life which are. . . . [The music gets louder. A child is wailing.] Kierkegaard wrote that. He was a walker. Every day for many hours, he would wander through the streets of Copenhagen."

At one point, the path is encumbered by children's strollers lined up in front of the zoo entrance. Negotiating my way around them, I pass the polar bears without a glance, so I need to rewind and turn back. Cardiff's voice tells me that the home range of a polar bear is an area the size of Iceland. There is still no bear. I hear thunder, and yet the sunlight feels warm on my head and arms. Are the bears in the zoo endangered too?

"Thunder. . . rain . . . hotel room . . . yesterday," says Cardiff's voice intermittently. "There are so many layers in front of my eyes." "I saw a woman fall to the ground. How can I really know what I've seen?"

The different layers shift, uncovering others. A lone saxophone player stands on the mall. The voice in my ear gives directions ("The bandstand should be on your right"), warns me sharply ("Watch out for the skaters"), comments ("The ice cream stand ruins the view of the bridge"), speculates on park dwellers that neither of us can see: "There's a whole other city beneath us. It's like in our minds. Deep layers that we only see in our dreams."

She points out The Dakota building, where John Lennon lived. Was Yoko Ono there with him when he was shot? she wonders. I squint at the skyline. She mentions a gondolier singing, but I see a couple of empty rowboats. Construction fences confuse the end of the walk, the path down to the lake, the woman in the snapshot:

> My words are here now, just as she was here. They'll disappear even though I try to keep them, record them, play them over and over in my attempts to hang onto time.
>
> I want you to do one last experiment. Match your breathing to mine.

Hard as I try, I cannot keep the rhythm. When I stop to catch my breath, the walk is over.

Artist's Experience and Viewer's Experience

John Dewey defines "*an* experience" as one in which "the material experienced runs its course to fulfillment."[38] This happens when we finish a job, solve a problem, or finish an activity like playing a game of chess or eating a meal. It happens when an action "is a whole with its own individualizing quality and self-sufficiency. It is *an* experience."[39] He opposes this to nonaesthetic experience in which we are not concerned with the outcome or the connection with previous events. We yield to outside pressure or evade; we do not complete what we started.[40] The enemies of the aesthetic are the humdrum, the slackness of loose ends. A walk can be an experience in this sense if it is complete. Janet Cardiff designed *Her Long Black Hair* as a whole. If I broke it off in the middle, would I then compromise its integrity? Although I was prevented by construction fences from reaching the edge of the water at the end of the walk, my greatest difficulty came from rewinding the recording. I did this several times. Then on the way back to the entrance, I listened to the beginning again to help me remember it. Although this is probably akin to the approach of professionals (musicians do not listen to music the way the rest of us do), it seemed somehow to minimize the experience. The experience should have to be completed at least once before we can analyze it.

An experience can also be distinguished from other experiences. It is composed of both disturbance and harmony: the passage from one to the other is the moment of "intensest life." If everything were entirely harmonious, it would be impossible to distinguish sleeping from waking. If it were only perturbed, with one interruption after the other, the odds would be too great: "In a world made after the pattern of ours, moments of fulfillment punctuate experience with rhythmically enjoyed intervals."[41] Taking in, responding to, a vital experience requires reconstruction, which may bring pain or pleasure—or both.

Doing/Undergoing: Two Sides to Every Story

Art involves both audience and artist engaging in "the intimate union of doing and undergoing" that makes an experience what it is: "To perceive, a beholder must *create* his own experience. This means ordering the elements into a whole. Just as the "artist selected, simplified, clarified, abridged and condensed according to his interest," writes Dewey,[42] so too the beholder. Both must extract what is significant. Moreover, this operation takes time. There is form because there is dynamic organization. It is a growth through the stages of inception, development, and fulfillment: "What distinguishes an experience as aesthetic is conversion of resistance and tensions . . . into a movement toward an inclusive and fulfilling close." He compares it to the advance of an army where "all gains from what has already been effected are periodically consolidated."[43]

The artist must find the right rhythm, neither too fast (the experience is diluted, "thin and confused") nor too slow (it "perishes of inanation"). The form of the whole is present in every part. The creator "is in process of completing at every stage of his work,"[44] as is the viewer or the listener. Aesthetic satisfaction must be intimately linked to the activity that gave rise to it: the qualities of the result organize the process of production. When the artist succeeds in incorporating the making into the outcome, the perceiver can appreciate the way the medium is being "used structurally" to create an aesthetic whole.

Can I as a listener incorporate the process into the result, since it is I who make the walk? The experience of making *Her Long Black Hair* is described in detail in *The Walk Book*. The audio walk is the medium with which Cardiff is most often associated. Although she is not the first to create a tour as an artwork (she mentions being influenced by Linda Montano's walking tours of San Francisco), she has extensively explored its possibilities.

She began working with sound in the early 1990s. During a residency at the Banff Centre in Alberta, she used a dictaphone to note her impressions as she wandered through a graveyard and stumbled onto the audio walk form after accidentally rewinding the tape. Playing it back to find where she had left off, she heard the sound of her footsteps, her spoken words, her breathing. She immediately began to walk with her "virtual body":[45] "I had found a way to be in two different places at once . . . to simulate space and time travel in a very simple way."[46]

Two weeks later, she produced her first audio work, *Forest Walk* (1991). Since then, she has created more than twenty-four walks for specific places in Europe and North America. Both *Janet Cardiff: The Walk Book* (written with Mirjam Schaub) and Cardiff's Web site offer excerpts from the soundtracks of her walks. Listening to them at the computer is like viewing reproductions of paintings. Isolated excerpts cannot replace perceiving the binaural sound in the setting for which it was conceived. These works are immersive and engage vision, smell, and proprioception as much as listening. Cardiff designed the forty-six-minute audio tour *Her Long Black Hair* for the Public Art Fund in New York City. It ran for a limited time in 2004 and then again in the summer of 2005. At kiosks set up at the entrance to Central Park, visitors were given a CD player, a map, and a set of snapshots. While walking the route prescribed by the narrator, they listened to music, spoken text, and sound samples, many of which come from the site being explored:

> The virtual recorded soundscape has to mimic the real physical one in order to create a new world as a seamless combination of the two. My voice gives directions but also relates thoughts and narrative elements, which instills in the listener a desire to continue and finish the walk.[47]

Wanting to "express the way our minds jump around all over the place," Cardiff has developed a nonlinear method of composition. She slows down the process of telling a story to build the intimacy that is necessary to create interest (and narrative tension) while still allowing the result to be open-ended.[48]

Begun at the instigation of curator Tom Eccles, *Her Long Black Hair* took six years to make. The artist searched New York to find a place that was quiet enough for the immersive experience she imagined: Manhattan lacks meandering side streets where the listener can be alone.[49] After settling on Central Park, she began filming there with a view to defining an itinerary. The route needed physicality and contrast, variety and texture (like a drawing, she notes, or a landscape), so she wanted to include both small and large spaces, quiet and noisy parts. It was important to "ground the listener's body physically."[50] Although the soundtrack overlays many layers of dialog, Cardiff eliminated the words whenever possible so the sounds themselves could produce the effects she wanted.

Narrative Threads

The recording is divided into six tracks, each one beginning at a place marked on the map—including the Jose Marti statue, the tunnel, the dog's statue and "the last bench facing gnarled tree and lamppost." These places play no structural part, says the artist, but are there only to help orient visitors and allow them to line up what they hear with visible landmarks.[51]

The title comes from a Baudelaire poem, "La chevelure" (The head of hair), which Cardiff quotes several times. The woman in the found photos also has "long dark hair." The narrative is fragmented, as in most of her other works. Cardiff weaves in several parallel stories, juxtaposing collective history (the digging of Central Park in the mid-nineteenth century, when "they uncovered human bones buried a hundred years before"), fiction (the flight of a runaway slave)[52], and mythology (Orpheus and Eurydice), with private memories (her own encounters while taping sounds in the park, fleeting memories of cutting her hair or watching her husband sleep). Other verbal images evoke Cardiff's themes of predilection—a friend whose mother abandoned him when he was small, three pedestrians, Kierkegaard in Copenhagen, Baudelaire in Paris, and a (fictive?) escaped slave in America. At times, Cardiff links the different strands of her narrative: "In 1850 while Harry Thomas made his epic nighttime journey across America, three months of walking, Baudelaire walked the streets of Paris. I like to imagine that at times their footsteps, lined up as if they walked together." To dramatize the experience, a low-pitched voice can be heard singing "Sometimes I feel like a motherless child" a cappella. Elsewhere, opera singers perform airs from Gluck's *Orfeo ed Euridice*.

When a couple asks her to photograph them on the bridge, she notes "A lot of photos have been taken from here. The camera tries over and over to capture it but it can't." Along with the map of the park, the visitor can consult a set of five snapshots—one made by Cardiff during a previous visit, the others found at a flea market. Three of these showed a young dark-haired woman posing in different areas of the park. Cardiff instructs us to stop at each of these locations.

She speculates about the woman and the photographer, her companion. "Why were there no photos of them together?" "We don't know if she's happy or sad, if they stayed together or walked home separately." At the end, before telling us to look at the last photo (where the woman turns her back to the camera), she whispers a bit melodramatically: "Don't look around. I think Orpheus's final glance must have been very much like a snapshot, burned into his retina forever."

A Dialectical Landscape?

In a 1973 essay titled "Frederick Law Olmsted and the Dialectical Landscape," Robert Smithson presents Olmsted, the creator of Central Park, as "America's first 'earthwork artist'."[53]A photograph of the site from 1858 showed that the land used for the park was already degraded, like the strip-mining regions Smithson had seen in 1972 in southeastern Ohio. He declared "the best sites for 'earth art' are sites that have been disrupted by industry, reckless urbanization, or nature's own devastation."[54]

Janet Cardiff's narrator takes a more traditional view: "Olmstead designed this park with the aesthetics of landscape painting in mind. There's a foreground of trees and grass with a winding lane. Then the rough texture of the rock contrasts with the lightness of the tree foliage." These remarks illustrate the way that the artist built her walk to follow the course of a stream that was covered over when the park was created. Like Smithson, she's interested in the multiple narrative layers that anchor her story in the site's past. Sometimes her attempts to create resonance sound strained: "The soldiers who fought during the Civil War could have walked along this path and seen this tree. . . . Perhaps beauty is linked to things that vanish. It's about our sadness at wanting it but not being able to catch it." At other times, simple details set off recognition. When she recounts coming to New York as an art student many years earlier, she adds: "I found everything beautiful then. I would take pictures of garbage on the street, sunlight hitting the concrete, mannequins in a store window. That's one reason I like walking through the city now—to come across those spontaneous moments of magic again." I remember photographing abandoned houses awaiting destruction; they had been ripped open to make way for a freeway. On their walls, several layers of peeling paper recapitulated the physical history of each room: flower prints lay exposed next to flaking paint and psychedelic patterns. Cardiff's sound collage produces a similar effect.

In the 1970s, when Central Park was thought to exemplify an outdated nineteenth-century picturesque aesthetic, "a static formalistic view of nature", Smithson maintained that "[a] park can no longer be seen as 'a thing-in-itself', but rather as a process of ongoing relationships existing in a physical region"[55] An "endless maze of relations and interconnections", it evolves continually and "nothing remains what or where it is."[56] His article begins with an epigraph, in which Olmstead recounts visiting the Parc des Buttes-Chaumont in Paris with the landscape architect who had designed it. When Olmstead complimented him on "the best piece of artificial planting of its age" he had ever seen, his interlocutor "smiled and said, 'Shall I confess that it is a result of neglect?'"[57] At the time Smithson was writing, New York City was on the verge of bankruptcy and Central Park showed signs of decline:

> In the spillway that pours out of the Wollman Memorial Ice Rink, I noticed a metal grocery cart and a trash basket half-submerged in the water. Further down, the spillway becomes a brook choked with mud and tin cans. The mud then spews under the Gapstow Bridge to become a muddy slough that inundates a good part of The Pond, leaving the rest of The Pond aswirl with oil slicks, sludge, and dixie cups.[58]

By the time Cardiff created her piece, the neglect had been displaced. The lawns in Central Park are now groomed for tourists, yet the homeless man sprawled on a bench evokes the underside of the city's prosperity. Smithson suggested dredging the mud and depositing it "on a site in the city that needs 'fill.' The transportation of mud would be followed from point of extraction to point of deposition. A consciousness of mud and the realms of sedimentation is necessary in order to understand the landscape as it exists."[59] Cardiff's sound-work evokes this sedimentation metaphorically—yet on site, in the real landscape.

Augmented Walking

To build her audio tours, Janet Cardiff "uses miniature microphones placed in the ears of a person. The result is an incredibly lifelike 3D reproduction of sound. Played back on a headset, it is almost as if the recorded events were taking place live." She records the main track and adds as many as eighteen tracks of layered sound effects, music, and voices.

Binaural sound is not new. In 1881, the *théâtrophone* allowed Parisian subscribers to listen to the opera from their homes using a telephone equipped with a special headset and small speakers for each ear. Proust was a subscriber. Forty years later, a Connecticut radio station tried a stereo experience, broadcasting sound for each ear on different frequencies. Listeners needed to have two radios.[60]

In 1930, Walter Ruttmann made a "movie for ears" that used only the sound track on a reel of film. *Wochenende* (Weekend) used sound effects to create mental images and enhance the narrative. It could be either broadcast on radio or projected as a movie without images. Shortly before the onset of World War II, Orson Welles's Mercury Theater on the Air staged a radio performance of H. G. Wells's 1898 novel *War of the Worlds* that was so effective that listeners felt they were "witnessing" an invasion of unidentified flying objects in Grover's Mill, New Jersey.[61]

These works differ fundamentally from Cardiff's, since their listeners stay still rather than moving through space. Her sound walks rely on the mode of perception associated with portable museum audio guides, which date to the cassette tape recorders of the early 1960s.[62] In the 1990s, museums adopted the computerized system Inform using CDs so that users could invent their own path through the exhibition.[63]

Janet Cardiff's walks revert to the earlier linear model, but the listener is not drawn into a structured narrative that moves toward a climax and denouement. Cardiff seems to flirt with narrative to give resonance to the audience's experience. The details are evocative, but the characters are only roughly sketched: the runaway slave flits through the story like the proverbial ghost. Even Cardiff herself is a more of a docent than a character. The intimate details do not add up to anything, unless it is that hair cutting is a form of violence on a par with shooting scavengers. Were it simply a story, the experience would be disappointing. It is not just a story.

One parallel might be surrealist novels. In Louis Aragon's *Paris Peasant* (1926) and André Breton's *Nadja* (1928), photographs are used to replace verbal descriptions just as Cardiff uses sound sampling to evoke events and places we cannot see. The awareness of space is exacerbated by precise indications (Breton gives addresses) that readers/listeners can match up to what they see on the street. It is a story that we perform.

Contemporary artists are often suspicious of straightforward storytelling, thinking it too easy to manipulate the audience. Directors who make films to be projected in darkened theaters have at their disposal a large panoply of rhetorical devices to shape moviegoers' experience. Although Cardiff uses artifice to ground her listeners' bodies in her narrative, she renounces complete authorial control over their sensory experience. *Her Long, Black Hair* depends for its dynamic on what Central Park brings to the mix. And this may change over time.

The Art of Walking

Richard Long was probably the first contemporary artist to see walking as an art form. Hamish Fulton, another British "walking artist," says: "The walking is the constant, the art medium is the variable"[64]

Many artists do projects that involve walking but not exclusively. Indeed, the art of walking has gathered practitioners from nearly every field insofar as it concerns all of us. Walking blurs the borders between the arts, between artist and audience.

The situationists imagined a total art that resembled architecture and was experienced by drifting. Walking structures experience. We perceive ourselves and our environment in interaction as we move along a path. We shape space as we go. Walking may be a form of architecture. Stalker, an Italian collective known for its walks within the landscape at the edges of cities, was founded by a group of architecture students. Francis Alÿs studied architecture. When Heath Bunting and Kayle Brandon take tours of fences and underground paths, they consider this joint practice to be "architectural" as it deals with space.[65]

Here While We Walk is an improvised sidewalk choreography executed by a group of silent participants who move within the limits of an elastic band (figure 2.2). I was among the dozen people led by Gustavo Ciríaco and Andrea Sonnberger through the

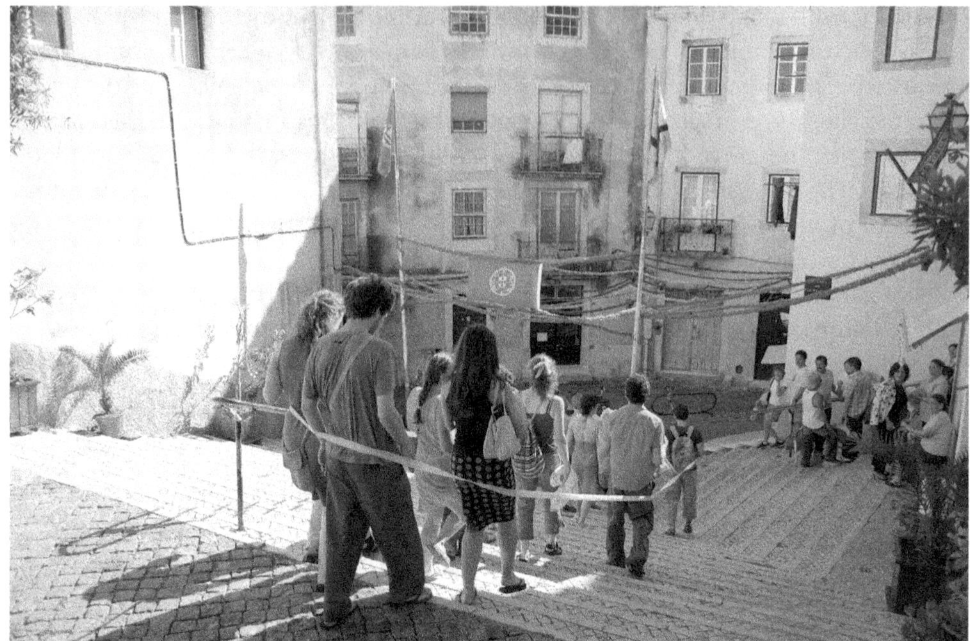
(a)

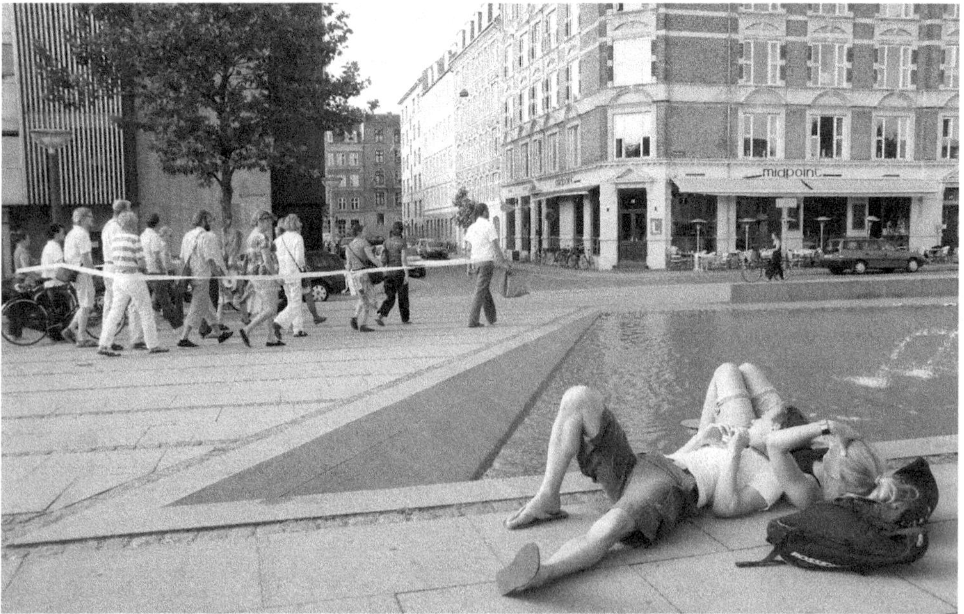

(b)

streets of Paris. The area we explored encompassed small side streets, a park, an expanse of open ground near a building project, and an industrial loading dock on the banks of the Seine.

Without speaking, the group formed a mobile architecture in which the individual parts worked together to create an overall shape, a fluid configuration that was arrived at by subtle negotiation. Both the walkers, who were busy concentrating on being "here" while we walked, and the passers-by, whose remarks were met by silence, perceived the urban landscape differently. Like a line of pupils on a class field trip or the dancers in *Satisfyin' Lover*, we learned to move through space collaboratively. Crossing busy streets, walking up and down steps, sharing the shifting space within the elastic band while keeping pace with each other, we produced a proprioceptive architecture that insiders and outsiders alike could feel as well as see. Were we on our way to becoming an army, swapping our individuality for a group identity? When the walk was over, as we stepped outside of the band, the artists handed us kites they had been carrying in a backpack. We watched the kites soar to the sky. Walking together structured our perception *here*, and as we moved along, the time we spent confined within the elastic band felt like *an* experience. It culminated in a collective letting go. As if birds were free.

◀ **Figure 2.2**
Gustavo Ciríaco and Andrea Sonnberger, *Here whilst we walk (Aqui enquanto caminhamos)*, 2006. A group of silent participants moves through the city streets within the limits of an elastic band. *a:* Walk in Lisbon, Portugal, 2006. Photograph: José Luís Neves. *b:* Walk in Copenhagen, 2009. Photograph: Torben Huss.

3 A Map, No Directions

August 5, 1997. Two pedestrians wearing jeans and t-shirts stand at the corner of Kenmare and Centre streets in the Nolita (north of Little Italy) neighborhood of lower Manhattan. It is 8 a.m., and the heat is already beginning to be felt. Using a compass as a guide, they will head for the Williamsburg Bridge, cross it, and make a beeline for Kennedy Airport in Queens.

In 1998, two others meet at Waltham Abbey south of London to embark on an odd pilgrimage. Starting at the Greenwich meridian, they plan to circumnavigate London's orbital motorway, all 125 miles of it, on foot.

In 2002, a third pair draws a circle on a map of Bristol. Under cover of night, armed with a pair of wire-cutters, they will follow the circle as closely as they can, cutting a path through all the fences they encounter.

That October in France, two adventurers sporting brand new hiking gear set out to walk a straight line from Nantes on the Atlantic coast to the Norman town of Caen. A month later they bundle up against the cold rain to hike from there to Metz in Lorraine near the German border.

Walking Protocols

A protocol is a rule, guideline, or document that specifies how an activity should be performed. In the natural sciences, it is a "predefined written procedural method in the design and implementation of experiments. . . . It should include safety, procedural, equipment, and reporting standards."[1] Other scientists should be able to reproduce the experiment later and obtain the same results.

In contemporary art, a protocol is a set of rules that an artist establishes to realize an artwork. It is a statement of intention and informs the viewer's understanding of the results. Defining objectives and methods in a preliminary document facilitates collaboration. Some prefer the terms *scenario, script,* or *score,* borrowed from the performing arts. Unlike its scientific counterpart, an artistic protocol may deliberately leave room for interpretation, thus making it possible for a work to be executed in more than one way or restaged by someone else.

Shaped Walks

Walking protocols usually begin with an idea—an itinerary, a figure or a method for calculating one's route. Sol LeWitt offered a radical formulation: "When an artist uses a conceptual form of art, it means that all of the planning and decisions are made beforehand and the execution is a perfunctory affair. The idea becomes a machine that makes the art."[2]

There can be a considerable difference between making all decisions in advance and leaving the details for later. Top-down planning can mean creating idea machines to execute instructions, but it can also take other forms. Sometimes artists determine the overall shape of a walk they intend to make without knowing beforehand how they will manage the details. A fervent practitioner of the *ars memoriae,* Jacques Roubaud often maps out walks following a series of locations in which he has placed memories. In *The Great Fire of London,* he writes:

> I find walking around at random unappealing, as did my teacher, Raymond Queneau. Even if I don't know where I'm going, because it's a place in the city or the scrubland or a foreign country where I've never been, I don't set out without some minimal knowledge of the locale I'll be traveling through, using a map, or city plan, or occasionally even photographs; I am not interested in virgin terrain. . . . This is why I have a very acute taste for obligatory routes whose itinerary is unpredictable insofar as I've never traveled it, but which becomes nevertheless necessary as soon as I've selected the rule or rules that will guide my steps. These rules can be very constraining, absurd, bizarre. . . . [E]scape is possible only through a sheer display of force, a clinamen.[3]

Richard Long has said that all of his projects begin with an idea.[4] He then looks for the most appropriate region in which to carry it out. He has made walks all over the world, including the Scottish highlands, the Himalayas, the Sahara Desert, and the Australian bush. After he has located a place, he buys a detailed map of the area and studies it closely to ensure that there are no topological features (a bog or a deep river, for instance) that might make him deviate from his planned route.[5]

Before setting out to walk, he draws the shape of the itinerary on the map. This preparatory stage helps him to follow the predefined figure in the landscape. If he has sufficient visibility, he can align himself visually with the topographical features indicated on the map. In most cases, he is able to work out the kinks in advance through careful map reading, but occasionally he has to deal with an unforeseen obstacle. On a straight twelve-hour walk across the Scottish highlands, the map showed a small cliff that turned out to be huge. The final artwork contains a hook in an otherwise straight line.[6]

To map out this kind of walk, a preliminary drawing is sufficient—a line, a circle, a series of arbitrary shapes (Daniel Buren's *7 Ballets in Manhattan*, 1975). An artist also can choose a destination—the town of Metz—or follow a preexisting route—a wall, a railway line, a motorway, a river, or the world's largest particle collider (Gianni Motti, *HIGGS, à la recherche de l'anti-Motti*, 2005).

Executing a Figure in the Landscape

The simplest of these protocols involves executing a recognizable figure in the landscape. La Monte Young's *Composition No. 10* (1960) is remarkable for its concision: "Draw a straight line and follow it." The line here is both map and path. This directive, he says, although impossible to carry out literally (it provides no end), has guided his life and work ever since. In another performance, he spent a whole evening drawing a line. What interested him in this process is that a line is "one of the more sparse, singular expressions of oneness." The line held particular interest "because it was continuous—it existed in time. A line is a potential of existing time. In graphs and scores one designates time as one dimension. Nonetheless, the actual drawing of the line did involve time, and it did involve a singular event."[7]

Richard Long's *A Walk of Four Hours and Four Circles* (1972) takes the form of four concentric circles superimposed on a detailed topographical map of Dartmoor (Devon). Long transposes the principle of John Cage's one-minute stories, which he had heard as a student at St. Martin's in London. In his lecture "Indeterminacy," Cage told sixty stories of varying word lengths that each lasted exactly one minute. Thus, a long story had to be told quickly, and a short one required drawing out each phrase to fit the format: "so it was about pace and time, rhythm and humor and formal ideas about time."[8]

Long sees walking as a "means to explore relationships between time, distance, geography and measurement."[9] How long does it take to walk a circle? One hour, responds Long in this work, whatever the circumference. The circles on the map show the four different distances he covered in each hour, transposing the temporal constraint into space. For each circle, he had to adjust his pace to fit the predefined path. The change in rhythm modifies the experience. A brisk pace lifts the walker into the air and propels him ahead. A slower gait allows for more contact between foot, shoe, and terrain, giving the senses more time to take in the surroundings—the sweeping view of the river valley, the smell of cut grass or cow dung, the humidity in the air, or the dryness of the soil. For desert-dwellers, walking rhythm is essential. The same journey can take one day or three, according to the season and number of waterholes on the way.[10]

In recent years artists like Heath Bunting and Kayle Brandon have paid tribute to Long's conceptual rigor, while bringing to the walk ideas of their own. When they

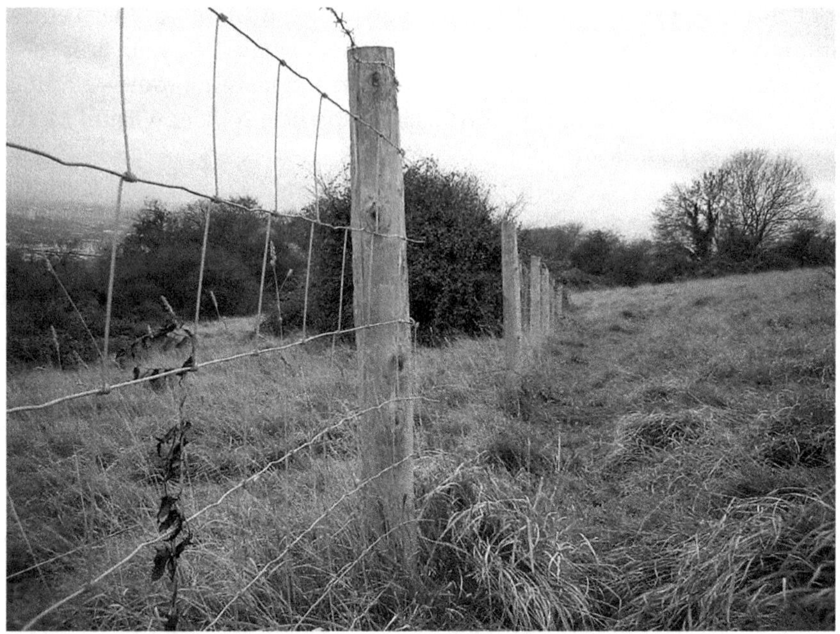

Figure 3.1
Heath Bunting and Kayle Brandon, *D'Fence Cuts*, 2001. Performance trace. Wire fence cut, Purdown, Bristol.

made their circular tour, stealthily, by night, it was "to cut some fences as research for the *Borderxing* project."[11] They called it *D'Fence Cuts* (figure 3.1). They thought of themselves as hackers in physical space, and crossing borders entailed cutting whatever impeded their passage. Some of the breaches they made have survived—"We went there the other day and this place where we'd cut the fence now has a path leading up to it because people have been using it"—and others became passageways for animals.[12]

Welsh writer Iain Sinclair has taken a number of shaped walks in London. *Skating on Thin Eyes*, the first of *9 Excursions in the Secret History of London* described in *Lights Out for the Territory,* aimed "to cut a crude V into the sprawl of the city, to vandalize dormant energies by an act of ambulant signmaking. To walk out from Hackney to Greenwich Hill and back along the River Lea to Chingford Mount, recording and retrieving the messages on walls, lampposts, doorjambs."[13] Armed with a cheap notebook and a camera, he and his companion planned to "transcribe all the pictograms of venom" that decorated their "near-arbitrary route." *Skating on Thin Eyes* uses language and page layout to deal with discontinuity. It is an essay on reading city surfaces. This theme is reflected in the spray-painted tags that Sinclair reproduces throughout his narrative in boldfaced capitals laid out like *caligrammes*:

LET THE
  DOGS BE
FREE
OR OTHERS WILL[14]

Although he sees them often as "a signature without a document," the equivalent of a brand name, as if to parody "the most visible aspect of high capitalist black magic," he concedes that they offer a means of catharsis for the otherwise powerless: "As newspapers have atrophied into the playthings of grotesque megalomaniacs, uselessly shrill exercises in mind-control, so disenfranchised authors have been forced to adapt the walls to playful collages of argument and invective."[15]

On the Beaten Path

The practice of deciding a walk's overall form in advance can give it a certain symbolic value. Religious or memorial processions, pilgrimages, and political demonstrations can take the form of shaped walks. One of the most improbable artist's walks was made in 2005 by Gianni Motti, who strolled through the Large Hadron Collider (figure 3.2). It is a circular tunnel 27 kilometers long, built 100 meters below ground to simulate the conditions in the universe just after the Big Bang occurred. Contrasting the speed of particles turning 11,000 times around the ring each second with the leisurely pace of a human being, Motti undertook another kind of experiment. He set out to walk around the entire ring. A cameraman followed him at a constant distance, filming him from the back, to record his progress in one traveling shot that is 350 minutes long: "In six hours," concludes the artist (referring to himself in the third person), "he accomplished what no scientist had ever thought of experimenting. In this 350-minute film (more than feature-length), time is abolished, as if it were no longer passing. The walker takes off like an atom lost in the cycles of the universe. A strange malaise seizes us, Einstein called it Relativity."[16]

Walking the Wall

When the walk involves a particularly long distance (4,000 kilometers) and a unique historical monument (the Great Wall of China), it conjures up a strong mental image. *The Lovers: The Great Wall Walk* builds resonance through its site, a series of fortifications built between the sixth century BC and the sixteenth century AD to protect the northern part of the Chinese empire from invasions (figure 3.3a). From March to June 1988, Ulay walked east from the southwestern edge of the Gobi Desert, while Marina Abramović moved west from the Gulf of Bohai on the Yellow Sea. They met halfway at Shenmu, in Shaanxi province.

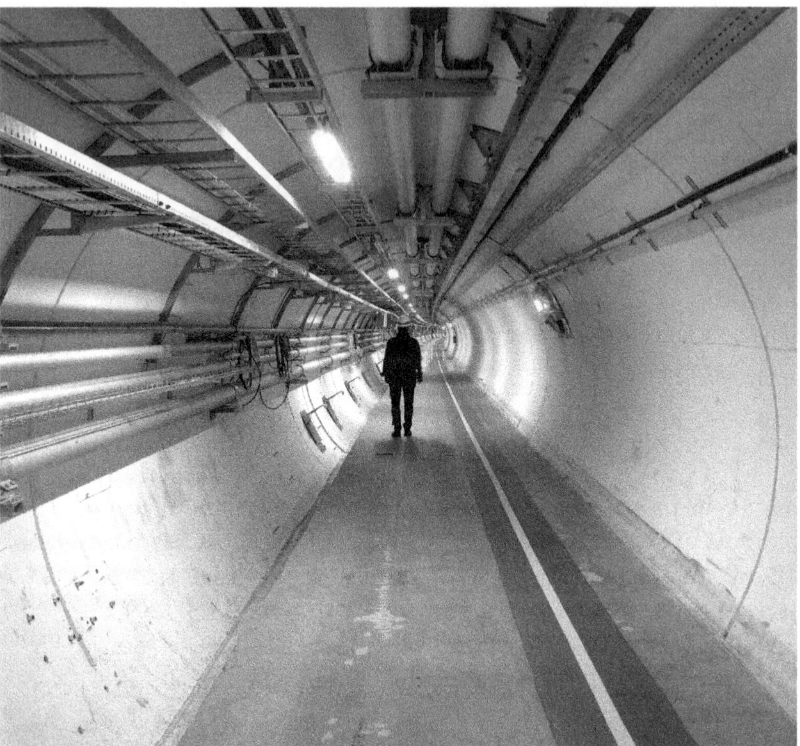

(a)

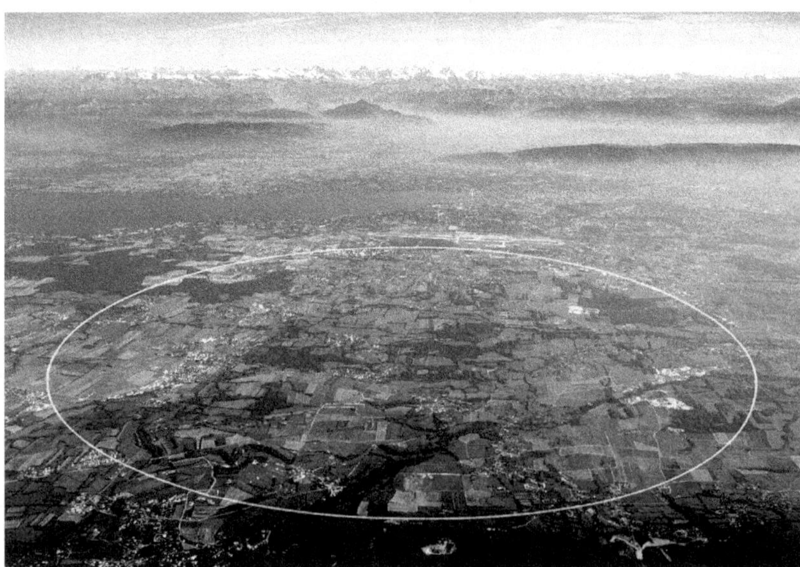

(b)

Figure 3.2
Gianni Motti, *HIGGS, In Search of Anti-Motti (HIGGS, à la recherche de l'anti-Motti)*, 2005, CERN, Geneva. Performance. Walk in the LHC (particle accelerator) 27 kilometers, 5:50 hours. © Gianni Motti. *a:* Motti descended 100 meters into the circular tunnel of the LHC (Large Hadron Collider) and walked the 27 kilometers at an average speed of 5 kilometers per hour (about 6 hours). The particles turn 11,000 times around the ring in one second. *b:* Aerial view of the LHC. Courtesy and copyright CERN.

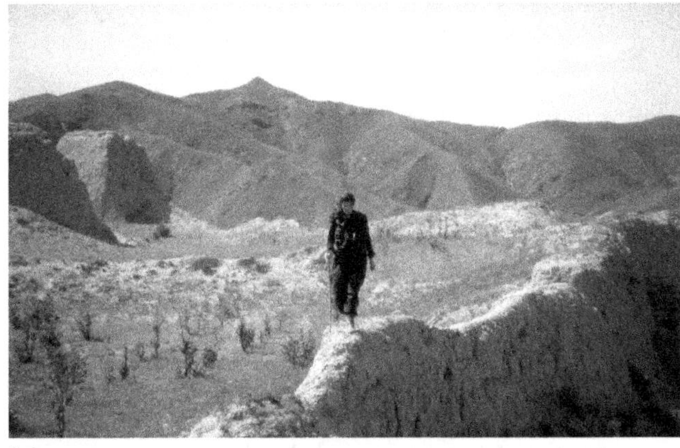

(a)

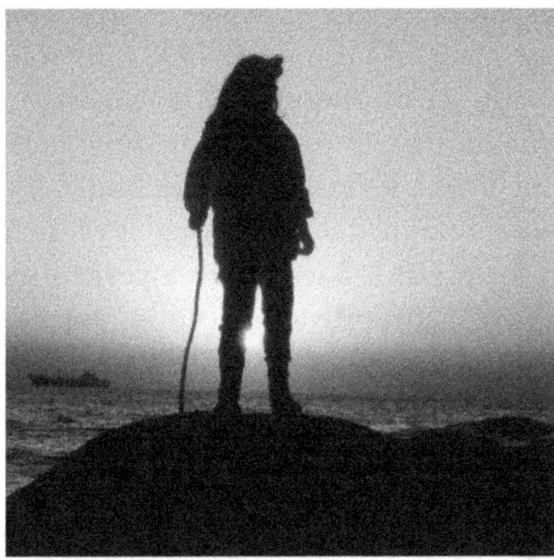

(b)

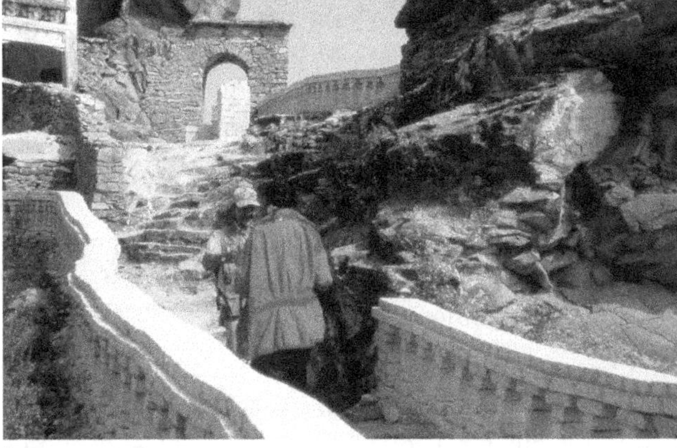

(c)

Figure 3.3

Marina Abramović and Ulay, *The Great Wall Walk*, March to June 1988. Performance, 90 days. © Marina Abramović. Courtesy: Sean Kelly Gallery, New York. *a* and *b:* Marina Abramović walking on the Great Wall of China. *c:* Marina Abramović and Ulay met halfway to say goodbye.

Using a precise protocol does not mean that everything is determined beforehand. *The Lovers: The Great Wall Walk* took six years to shape because the artists had to repeatedly modify their plans to obtain necessary permissions from the Chinese government. But it was also subject to change even as it was being carried out. The original plan called for them to walk for a year and meet midway for a traditional Chinese wedding ceremony. It was to be the culmination of their *Relations* projects, which had begun in 1976 with *Relation in Space,* in which the two naked artists repeatedly strode toward each other from opposite ends of a room, gathering speed before colliding in the middle.

When they were finally able to carry out the *Great Wall Walk*, it commemorated the dissolution of their relationship. "We each walked 2,000 kilometers to say goodbye," writes Abramović, "Duration: 90 days. Last meeting on June 3, 1988." By that time, the walk had reached a global scale involving artists, museums (the Stedlijk in Amsterdam), foundations (Amphis created to raise money for the project), diplomats, and government agencies. At one point when the project seemed almost doomed, the Dutch government stepped in to save it. The Chinese claimed it as an instance of their historic opening to the West. The time allotted for it was reduced from a year to six months and then three months, as the artists were transported between sections of the wall to bypass military installations, outbreaks of disease, and border skirmishes.

Autonauts and Passengers

A protocol can be followed strictly. Julio Cortâzar and Carol Dunlop prepared the protocol for *Autonauts of the Cosmoroute* in 1978, four years before they could make the trip. For their expedition on the A6 motorway in France, they felt that it was important to adhere closely to the four rules they assigned themselves:

1. Complete the journey from Paris to Marseilles without once leaving the autoroute.
2. Explore each one of the rest areas, at the rate of two a day, spending the night in the second one without exception.
3. Carry out scientific, topographical studies of each rest area, taking note of all pertinent observations.
4. Taking our inspiration from the travel tales of great explorers of the past, write a book of the expedition (methods to be determined).[17]

In other instances, a protocol offers a general framework on which a work is built. In 1989, as France was celebrating the two hundredth anniversary of its Revolution, François Maspero and Anaïk Frantz set out for a long journey on foot and by rail, following the path of the train they dubbed the *Roissy-Express*. They were not as militantly pedestrian as Sinclair was. They packed their bags, bid their loved ones goodbye, and embarked on the commuter train that runs from the Charles De Gaulle airport in Roissy, north of Paris, to the town of Saint-Rémy-les-Chevreuse in the southwest. Each day of their trip was devoted to exploring one of the thirty or so chunks of the train's path as it slashes through the suburban sprawl (their proposed itinerary excluded stops in Paris itself). Like Cortàzar and Dunlop, they were seeking to understand their surroundings by moving through them in an unusual way.

Maspero and Frantz had a master plan, but their trip involved an inordinate amount of negotiation. The rule seemed simple: every morning they would take the train to the next station, book a hotel for the following night, leave their bags, then venture out on foot for the day's visits. In practice, they found themselves occasionally backtracking or fast-forwarding to keep an appointment or find a hotel room (some towns had no hotel or no available room). They wore through quite a bit of shoe leather discovering that railway stations could be several kilometers from the towns they were named for.

Orbiting London

For *London Orbital*, the imposed figure was the circle. Iain Sinclair conceived his trip as a "pilgrimage" following the "124.5-mile, bumper-to-bumper procession" that unfolds every day around the city of London. Whereas the "autonauts" and the "passengers" made continuous journeys in the spirit of travelers on the Orient Express train, Sinclair and fellow pedestrian Renchi Bicknell broke up their expedition into manageable stretches of twelve day trips that were spread over a period of about a year. The road was to be their guide, and they would "snatch days" whenever they could, carrying on each time from where they had left off.[18] These walks were supplemented by a series of "secondary excursions" with various travel companions (including film director Chris Petit) during which Sinclair conducted interviews for the film *London Orbital*.

Sinclair and Bicknell did not actually walk on the expressway. They shadowed it: "the soft estates, the acoustic footprints will do nicely. . . . Noise and the rush of traffic, twenty-four hours a day, has pushed 'content' back. An elaborate scheme of planting (two million trees and shrubs, mostly in Surrey and Kent) would hide the nasty ditch with its Eddie Stobart lorries, its smoke belchers."[19]

The M25 beltway is more than just another road. Sinclair calls it a "grim necklace" that was inaugurated by Margaret Thatcher in October 1986—"a tourniquet, sponsored by the Department of Transport and Highways Agency, to choke the living breath from the metropolis." After being "the pet and pride of an autocratic government," it has "been rapidly downgraded to a rage-inducing asteroid belt, debris bumping and farting around a sealed-off city."[20]

Sinclair's walks were inspired by the annual circumnavigation of two friends whose aim was "to find out where the M25 leads."[21] In his own way, Sinclair asks the same question. Literally, the road leads nowhere. It goes round and round, 170,000 vehicles a day "wearing away the tarmac mantle" like a serpent biting its own tail. Figuratively, it has led to a situation that its proponents had not foreseen: "Built to solve the problems of flow and congestion," it "has now become the problem," a victim of its success. Burglars routinely use it for getaways; "the sexual service industries [take] advantage of the excellent parking facilities and discreet greenery"[22]; and commuters relish it as their "only contact with the changing seasons, the Surrey Hills," "the only respite from work stress, the on-line office, domestic responsibility."[23]

So why walk it? Driving it would only enforce "metaphors of madness": "The trick was to move back, step away, treat the road as a privileged entity, a metaphor of itself. Enlightenment came with distance, detachment," and what better way both to "come to terms with this beast" and achieve this enlightenment than walk where others drive "in the belief that this nowhere, this edge, is the place that will offer fresh narratives"?[24]

The calendar was chosen for its resonance. Just as Maspero celebrated in his own way the bicentennial of the French Revolution, Sinclair opted to finish his walk before the eve of the new millennium. One milestone was political, and the other carried religious or mystical connotations. Commemorating either one moved the artists to take stock of the world in which they lived.

Due East: Walking the Compass

Using a compass to chart a route, like following a walking algorithm, enables the artist to override subjective decision-making processes. Walking from Manhattan to Kennedy Airport on a sweltering day in August 1997, Laurent Malone and Dennis Adams trudged through graveyards and crossed highways. To record their journey, they had one 35mm camera between them. Each time one took a picture, he handed the camera to the other, who immediately framed the opposite point of view, whatever the subject, without changing either the focus or the aperture.

Following these arbitrary constraints forced them to enter areas they had no other reason to visit (and might have done well to avoid). Their journey undoubtedly linked adjoining streets that were separated by invisible barriers. In her 1961 book *The Death and Life of Great American Cities*, Jane Jacobs noted that pedestrians tend to avoid border areas, which become no man's lands. This is particularly true of "zones immediately adjoining massive simple uses," such as parks or housing projects: "Borders can thus tend to form vacuums of use adjoining them."[25] Although the crime rate in New York had dropped by 1997, many such areas were still deemed unsafe.

When Laurent Tixador and Abraham Poincheval set out to walk more than 750 kilometers from Nantes to Caen and from Caen to Metz in France, using a compass to ensure that their route followed as straight a line as possible, the danger came mostly from inclement weather. It is one thing to catch a few drops of rain while dashing from the subway stop to one's building and another to walk all day in driving rain and then settle for the bottom of a ditch as the most sheltered spot to pitch one's tent (figure 3.4). The often strong and glacial wind made them aware of the flimsiness of rain capes and the fragility of their fastenings. In his journal, Tixador describes the delicate maneuver of closing his companion's snaps while trying to prevent his own from coming undone. His conclusion: "Life under a poncho is as much a question of skill as it is an affair of judgment."[26]

The account closes with the diarist contemplating the lights of Metz in wonderment. It no longer mattered that they had no water and only two packets of leek soup; their goal was in sight.[27] It had taken them forty days of walking to make the journey. For the last, and coldest, leg of the trip they had had to step up their pace to arrive in time for the exhibition opening on December 17.

They had chosen to walk a straight line because they imagined that was what an explorer would do in uncharted territory. In fact, as historian Sylvain Venayre notes, real explorers tend to follow riverbeds. The straight line characterizes competitive sports, races, or record setting. In Jules Verne's *Around the World in Eighty Days*, Phileas Fogg hoped to win the contest by navigating in a straight line.[28] Unlike Christopher McCandless setting off in the Alaskan wilderness without even a compass, Tixador and Poincheval took a calculated risk. On the road, they knew they could count on people to help should an emergency arise. At stake here was survival, not in the wild but in the art world.

The Walk and the Artifact

Form, it has been said, is the shape of content. Without form, a thing is invisible. What form is involved in a walk?

"Space Unfolding in a Continuous Present"

Artists can constrain their trajectory to focus on walking. This limits the number of decisions that need to be made in the field and allows the performer to live the experience as it unfolds here and now.

Walking artists are in the real world without the mediation of a car window, a train schedule, or even bicycle wheels. Because the distances that they cover range from 20 kilometers to 2000 km, they develop different walking strategies. Abramović and Ulay hiked every day for three straight months, Malone and Adams made their trip in eleven and a half hours in one day, Tixador and Poincheval split their trek into two sections of sixteen and twenty-four days with a five-week break in between, and Sinclair and Bicknell walked a total of about 200 kilometers in twelve separate stretches.

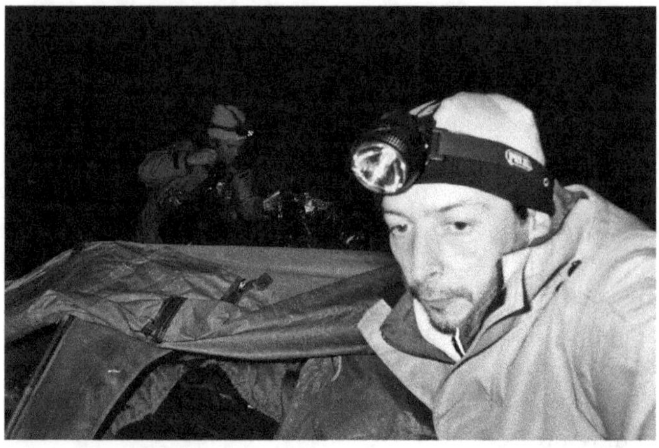

(a)

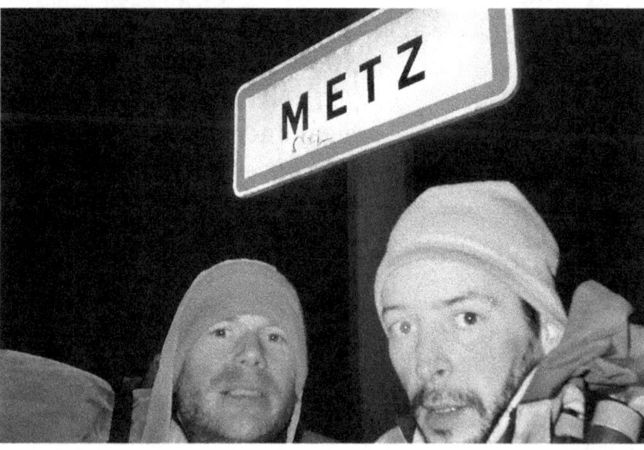

(b)

Figure 3.4

Laurent Tixador and Abraham Poincheval, *L'inconnu des grands horizons (The Unknown of the Great Horizons)*, December 2002. Performance, 16 + 24 days. Courtesy Galerie In Situ Fabienne Leclerc. *a:* The artists' hiking gear included headlamps useful for setting up camp at night. *b:* The goal is near.

The Shape of the Document

Most of these artists document their walks in ways that emphasize the shape of the itinerary. Stipulations concerning documentation (procedures for image gathering and shooting norms) are often included in the protocol. Presentation media include drawing on maps, photography, video, sculpture, and writing.

Richard Long's first piece of walking art, carried out while he was a student, was immortalized in a black and white photograph, *A Line Made by Walking* (1967). Long chose whatever he felt was the most appropriate form for his idea—a map, a photograph, a text, or a sculpture. His works owe their elegance to the fact that although they are ostensibly about the walks taken by the artist—during which he must have sweated, strained muscles, struggled against the wind, and got dust in his eye—the result gives no inkling of the physical process. *A Walk of Four Hours and Four Circles* shows only concentric circles neatly drawn on an Ordnance Survey map. Completing each of them is the indication *One Hour*. In the same way, *JFK* contains only the photographs that Malone and Adams took of their surroundings. The press photo showing the artists was not reproduced in the book.

Some of the writers walked with photographers—Maspero with Frantz, Sinclair with Atkins. Tixador and Poincheval made a video documentary using footage they shot of each other.

Abramović and Ulay's *Great Wall Walk* was recounted in a film, an exhibition, and a book. *The Lovers: The Great Wall Walk* (1988) is a feature-length film made for the BBC in which the artists describe their surroundings and the people they encountered as they made their way toward each other. The exhibition was held at the Stedelijk Museum in Amsterdam in 1989. The book, which also served as an exhibition catalog, presents each artist's perception of the experience in writing and photographs, with additional framing texts by Wim Beeren, Frank Lubbers, Thomas McEvilly, and Dorine Mignot.

Ulay's text bears the title "The Wall / The Walk / The Alien," summarizing his experience in three nouns—the place, the activity, the subject (the word *alien* figured on his visa). He counts his steps and measures his breath. He writes of "reading the earth's landscape with the soles of my feet. Yet finding myself a stranger. Who am I to establish contact?"[29]

Abramović titled her part of their joint project "Boat Emptying / Stream Entering." *Walking the Great Wall* taught her to cast off ballast to make way for a new stream of energy to flow in.

To transmit her experience to the public, she invented an art form that she called "transitory objects." The exhibition *The Lovers* featured an installation called *Green Dragon Lying*, a bed made of bronze with a crystal headrest that is meant to give form to the energy stream the artist encountered in China. By lying on the bed, the visitor could feel the energy it generated. Abramović made a series of stone pillows called

Dragons, on which viewers could rest their heads. Two *Black Dragons* from 1988 to 1989 allowed people press their foreheads against a concave, polished surface of hematite or obsidian, while *Green Dragon Lying* required visitors to lie on a copper plinth with their head cradled in green quartz. The contact with each mineral is meant to evoke a different level of primary consciousness. The artist has said that these transitory objects "have to function in my place in order to trigger the experience of others. I set up everything in such a way that my presence is not needed."[30]

The word *transitory* connotes the ephemeral, fleeting, short-lived, yet the objects were made from minerals that convey a sense of permanence. From a cosmological perspective, all matter changes over time, no matter how rigid it seems to us now. Walking the Great Wall helped Abramović to understand, as she puts it, "the relationship between landscape and different states of mind, and the importance of the magnetic energy lines."[31] Both symbol and ritual play an important part here. Symbolism makes things clearer, she says, while rituals "do a mental job in another state of reality. . . . In the West we are disconnected from the sense of time, the sense of ourselves, the sense of energy. It is like the head is not connected with the rest of the body."[32] Just as this walk was for her a way to reconnect them, so too do visitors connect with these objects.

Contemporary Travelogues

Most of the artists discussed in this chapter have produced books to document their walks. What does Sinclair's 577-page opus have in common with Brandon and Bunting's 40-page booklet? Can we compare Abramović and Ulay's lavishly illustrated catalog with Tixador's terse journal entries?

Like most travel writing, *Roissy Express* ostensibly describes "one place after another" and in doing so delves into the multilayered history of each one. It is organized geographically and chronologically, alternating descriptions, encounters, and portraits with historical asides that were garnered from Maspero's reading.

It is divided into three main parts—*Plaine de France* (Plain of France), *La Petite Couronne* (literally, "the small crown," a name given to the suburbs bordering on Paris), and *Hurepoix* (the plateau south of the city). With the exception of Arcueil (a working-class town) and Les Ulis (the projects), the southern suburbs tend to be wealthier than those in the north. That section of the B line took so many professors from homes in the southern suburbs to universities in the Latin Quarter that it was known as "the little train of the Sorbonne."

The greater part of *Roissy Express* is devoted to the working-class suburbs in the north. There, Maspero and Frantz visit local landmarks from the Air Museum in Le Bourget[33] to the Guy Môquet People's Center in La Courneuve.[34] From the beginning, he asserts their subjectivity. This was not an exhaustive study, so why force themselves to describe everything? "Following their interests, their curiosities, their pleasures and also the sun and the wind, they always wanted to remain free not to note, not to photograph, if their hearts weren't in it."[35] Moving through the Parc de Sceaux with its groomed lawns, ornamental lakes, and Puget statues, Frantz put away her camera: "I wasn't made for postcards." And Maspero adds, "she finds the people morose and colorless: life becomes monotonous."[36] "All in all," says Anaïk, "A country where they love dogs and detest foreigners is a country that is off-course."[37]

A Path Made in Words

Richard Long often uses toponyms in his texts to denote the specific qualities of the places that he traverses:

> it's literally the same stones and the same surfaces of the world that people have always walked over and used. All the place names are like layers of history and different cultures. My work is just another layer on the surface of the world that has been shared by all these different generations, so it's really about continuity.[38]

London Orbital is closer to the paradigm of the travelogue, since the M25 highway gives it its shape. Iain Sinclair and his companion begin by walking away from "the Teflon meteorite on Bugsby's Marshes"[39] and end up moving toward it: "Here at last was the grail. Up-ended on a swamp in East London. Glowing in the dark."[40] *It* was the extravagant and controversial Millennium Dome that was built on the Greenwich peninsula to house an exhibition celebrating the third millennium. Sinclair had denounced the dome in a 1999 pamphlet.[41]

Sinclair describes *London Orbital* as "a narrative with a proper conclusion, a story that folded back to its beginning: an afternoon drinking on the Isle of Dogs, watching the labored preparations for the big night, millennium eve, the opening of the dome."[42] After two introductory chapters, "Prejudices Declared" and "Soothing the Seething," in which he explains his fixation on the M25 and his reasons for walking it, the "walk proper" begins on page 125.

Each of the five middle sections recounts a stretch of the road. The walk begins and ends at Waltham Abbey, which is located on the Greenwich meridian: "the most tainted spot on the map of London"[43] because it is located at the heart of a controversial real-estate development scheme. Each part of the book bears a metaphoric title affixed to a topographic subtitle. The themes include "Paradise Gardens," "Diggers & Despots," "Salt to Source," and "Blood & Oil." The epilogue recounts the millennium eve, thereby closing the circle.

Despite these framing devices, *London Orbital* spills out in all directions like the postindustrial landscape it charts. Sinclair has described his writing as "baggy." He gravitates toward extravagant metaphor, accumulation, and hyperbole. Like Maspero, he aims to articulate a broader political vision by showing the physical traces of public policy on the countryside. Successive waves of gentrification have moved the insane asylums, chain-link fences, factory waste, drying out clinics, and dog kennels out of the center and dropped them just outside the city—out of sight (and earshot), out of mind.

JFK: A Road Movie in 486 photographs

Malone and Adams portray the outer boroughs of New York through images in their book *JFK* (2002). The 243 pairs of photographs they made are displayed on alternate pages in the order in which they were shot: on one page is the chosen picture, and opposite it, the photo created by chance.

The book opens vertically like a wall calendar, so the reader must turn the pages up. The walk protocol is printed on the spine in lowercase letters. Both front and back covers are made of a black rubbery material. On one, the date and publisher, nearly invisible, are printed in black on black. Just inside is a photograph showing an expressway sign: *Welcome to John F. Kennedy International Airport.*

Printed full bleed, one per page recto-verso, without captions or page numbers, the photos are all horizontal. When the bottom page is right-side up, the top one is upside down, facing opposite directions, like the photographers themselves standing back to back in the press photograph. Both pages have equal weight. Indeed, it is hard to tell which photo was intentional and which random. We do not know which photographer took the picture or even how often photos were taken. Malone and Adams chose not to adopt the precise timeframe that was popular in 1970s conceptual art (for example, "release the shutter every two minutes while driving along a road for 24 minutes," Douglas Huebler).

The direct path, "as the crow flies," and the picture-taking ritual allowed them to express their subjectivity within limits. The book, with its chosen shots and its blind ones, is an unedited photographic record of the walk: no image was omitted or even cropped.[44]

For Laurent Malone, walking is a "critical tool," a way of becoming "an integral part of the city."[45] *JFK* is one of a series that he calls "transects." In geography, a transect is a method for sampling populations and analyzing a territory by moving through it in a straight line while recording occurrences of the phenomenon under study. In this way, one can measure the changes between two or more areas.[46] In urban planning, it refers to a model created by Andrés Duany—a series of zones that move progressively "from sparse rural farmhouses to the dense urban core. Each zone is fractal in that it contains a similar transition from the edge to the center of the neighborhood."[47]

Turning the pages, we move slowly through a complex landscape that is devoid of human presence. Graffiti, signs of all shapes and colors, refuse, and abandoned vehicles. Is this the ruins of World War III? One pair of pictures offers a sharply drawn alternative. On one side are words stenciled in yellow paint on a solid brick wall:

T&T SCRAP METAL
ALUMINUM. COPPER. BRASS. ETC. . . .
$ TOP DOLLAR PAID $

Across the street, a chain-link fence protects a car in a lot. A rectangular red-and-white sign hangs behind the fence: *DANGER KEEP OUT*.

The point of view of the spectator/camera is an important structural element in *JFK*. Because the two photographers shoot the same location nearly simultaneously, they reveal a two-sided reality that could not have been seen from a single camera angle. Both protocol and book recall Michael Snow's 1975 *Cover to Cover*, in which two photographers follow the artist, one on either side. In *JFK*, too, the photographers and their opposing points of view alternate, cross-cutting from one page to the next, creating a kind of respiratory rhythm. Three-dimensional space is transposed onto the recto and verso of the pages, allowing the process to determine the work's final form.[48]

The only narrative structuring the work is the physical space in which we presume that the walk takes place. Could the photographers have focused on certain areas more than others? When I tried following their route using Google Street View, nothing matched. *JFK* undermines any attempt at making sense of this chaotic urban landscape. As long as we stay in our cars and stick to the road, we are offered at least a facade of order, as in Edward Ruscha's panoramic foldout *Every Building on the Sunset Strip*, photographed from a moving truck.[49] Ironically, the straight line followed by Malone and Adams reveals what the facade hides. As soon as we get out of the car to explore our surroundings from a point of view denied the driver, the facade dissolves. Things fall apart.

(De)Tour(n)ing Fences

Just as Xavier de Maîstre took his readers on an epic journey around his room and Robert Smithson turned the pumping derrick, wooden bridge, and sandbox from his New Jersey hometown into *Monuments of Passaic*, so Kayle Brandon and Heath Bunting invited their friends to join them in April 2002 for *Tour de Fence*, "a hands and feet on tour of Bristol's finest fences" (figure 3.5).[50]

As documentation, the Web site offers a bright red square rimmed with thumbnails of the climbers in action, set against a fluorescent green background. It is a psychedelic remake of the minimalist grid. The artists detail techniques and examples for would-be fence climbers, beginning with a typology of barriers and ways of scaling them. These include "wall climb with sign suspension," "stretched wire cling," and "tree to air" (here a silhouette figure leaps into the void like a latter-day Yves Klein). The fences themselves are identified by location and climber's first name. Photographs chronicle subsequent events in Berlin, Montreal, and Warsaw.

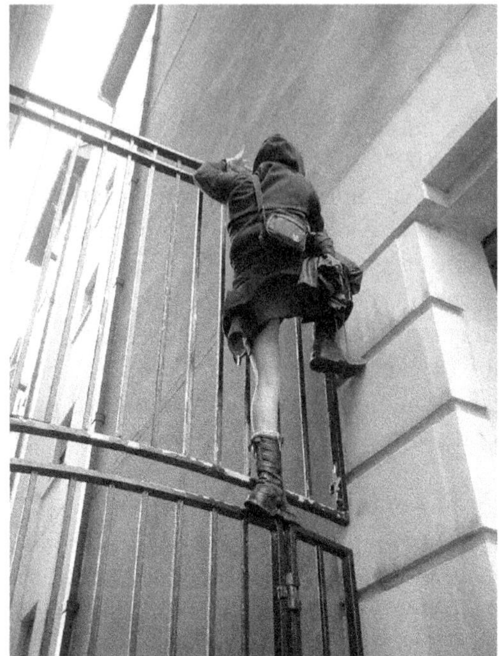

(a)

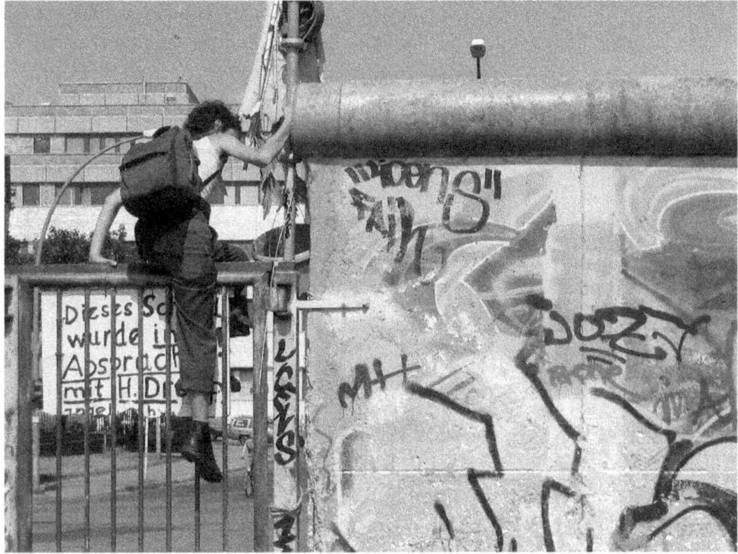

(b)

Figure 3.5

Heath Bunting, Kayle Brandon, and others. *Tour de Fence*. Performance. *a:* Bunting, Brandon, and members of Irational.org and Bureau of Inverse Technology, *Tour de Fence*, April 27–28, 2002, Bristol. *b:* Bunting, Brandon, and Transmediale workshop participants, *Tour de Fence,* 2003, Berlin.

In 2003, the duo organized a workshop at the Transmediale festival in Berlin. For this occasion, they published a booklet documenting the project in which they promote a situationist-inspired *Tour de Fence* attitude:

> tour de fence is the answer to your real needs. while the internet promised to level out all barriers, tour de fence enables you to surmount the fences out there that people erect to obstruct your way every day. from wire netting to rustic fence, from steel door to close security system, tour de fence offers you the necessary know-how for unhampered movement. tour de fence is the direct way.[51]

Events like this as well as *Tunnel Treasure Hunt* (2003) and *International Tree Climbing Day* (inaugurated in 2003) are "part of Irational's ongoing involvement with hacking the city's familiar physical surroundings in order to find more mentally enriching, physically challenging and socially exciting ways of using them."[52]

Irational's urban hacking conflates *bricolage* and *détournement*. Bricolage, from the French verb *bricoler* (to tinker), means to make use of materials that are on hand regardless of their original purpose. It characterizes any art form in which participants create works, texts, or scenes using available materials. It has also been used by biologists "to describe the apparently cobbled-together character of much biological structure," by researchers in other fields, and by the educator Seymour Papert, for whom it is "a way to learn and solve problems by trying, testing, playing around" rather than analyzing.[53] So even fences can be used to find out about the world and inhabit it differently.

Détournement (literally, "derailment" or "hijacking") is a term first used by the situationists to designate the reuse of materials from the "literary and artistic heritage of humanity" that are modified to create a new work with a different message, often negating the original.[54] Likewise, if we extend the meaning to other types of cultural signs, cutting or climbing fences (instead of being deterred by them) turns barriers into points of passage.

Climbing fences is a humorous but pointed way to reclaim public space from private encroachment. In Montreal, climbers sharpened their skills on a fence that separated "the rich of the Town of Mount Royal from the poor of Park Extension."[55] Are they only thumbing noses in the face of a few authoritarian fences? Heath Bunting, Kayle Brandon, and their friends dare (us) to play when they (we) ought to be working. The lighthearted tone suggests the absence of a real threat, but the remnants of the Berlin wall in several pictures remind us that climbing fences is not always as easy as it looks.

Unknown Horizons

For *L'inconnu des grands horizons*, Laurent Tixador and Abraham Poincheval produced a twenty-four-minute video. Tixador also published an illustrated travel diary (see figure 3.6a). It is divided in two parts—Nantes-Caen and Caen-Metz. He considers his account to be neither anthropology nor journalism. Unlike Maspero and Franz, he

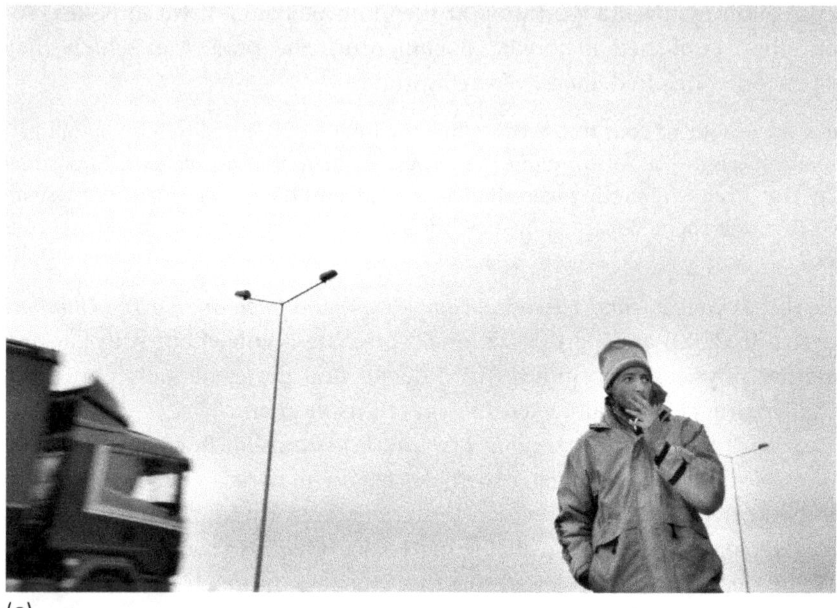

(a)

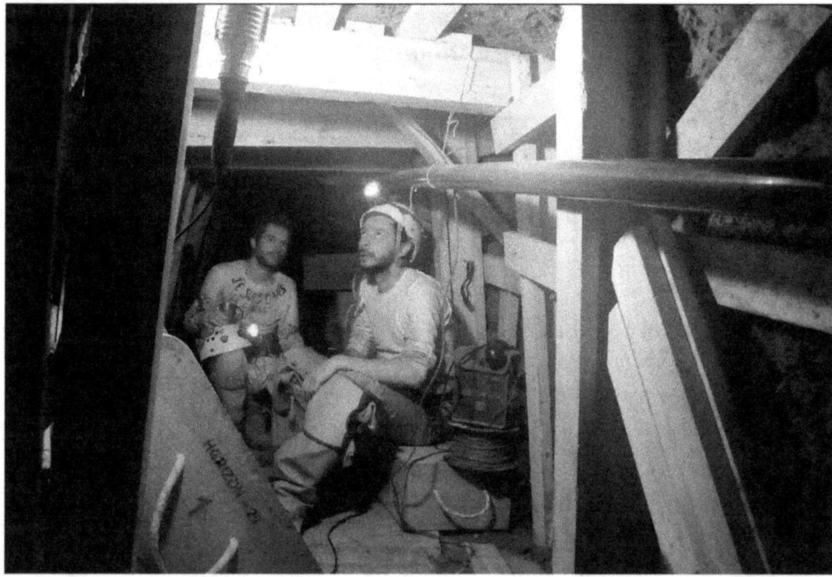

(b)

Figure 3.6

Laurent Tixador and Abraham Poincheval, *a: L'inconnu des grands horizons.* Cover photograph on Laurent Tixador's travel diary. *b: Horizon moins vingt,* March 2008, Performance. Courtesy Galerie In Situ Fabienne Leclerc.

was not interested in bringing back a picture of France today. The trip was about coping in an unfamiliar environment. The images show the two adventurers on the road in compositions that often parody "explorer portraits."

In contrast to the open-source model championed by Heath Bunting and Kayle Brandon, the "endurance art" of the French duo is anchored in the contemporary art paradigm. While Bunting claims rhetorically that his "self taught and authentically independent work . . . has never been awarded a prize or been bought or sold" and that most of his projects have been funded by "None, None, None,"[56] Tixador and Poincheval find backing for their expeditions from regional art centers, public commissions, or private sponsors. Before undertaking an expedition, they exhibit drawings and scale models of future projects alongside objects made during previous adventures in the entrepreneurial spirit that was made famous by Christo and Jeanne-Claude. The opening party can include a meeting of the "Adventurers' Club" to which they invite spelunkers, mountain climbers, soldiers of fortune, and art critics. The group sits around a table drinking whiskey and exchanging traveler's tales.

Sometimes the order of events is reversed, and the exhibition opening showcases the incongruous return of the artists from the wilderness—tired, sweaty, wearing three-day beards and dirty t-shirts. When they arrived in Metz at the gallery of the art school after their cross-country walk, they projected unedited video footage fresh from the camera.

During (or between) expeditions, they use materials gathered in the field to make objects in forms recalling folk art. They have sculpted cuttlefish bones and shovel handles, painted watercolors of food wrappers, gathered potsherds, and painstakingly filled "impossible" bottles with tokens of their adventures—tiny hammers, shovels, toilet paper cutouts (*La grande symbiose*, 2007), miniature flags fixed in plaster mixed with water from polar ice packs (*Pôle Nord*, 2005), and earth, bone, string, stone, snail shell, root, and color video (*Horizon moins vingt*, 2008). They often exhibit figurines that represent themselves in the field sleeping in mummy-style sleeping bags, digging underground clad in yellow jumpsuits and miner's helmets, or walking in their hiking gear.

In a period when high-profile artists have their works made by fabricators, this labor-intensive art seems to rehabilitate the notion of craft. At the same time, in fine art tradition, much of their elbow grease is channeled into Sisyphean endeavors, like spending twenty days digging a tunnel at the rate of one cubic meter a day, which they fill up just as soon as they have cleared the next cubic meter (figure 3.6b).[57]

Although at first sight, their handcrafted objects look like naive imitations or even tie-in products, they are part of a whole that the viewer cannot apprehend by just looking at it. Like the photographs, books, and videos cited earlier, what they document is not things so much as processes. And since we have passed from what Jacques Rancière calls a "regime of representation" to an "aesthetic regime of art," the visible form of an artwork is just one facet of the whole—the actualization of a concept, the result of a process.[58] The walk retains its primacy.

So Near, So Far

In most of these projects, the walk itself rearranges the landscape and shows us things that from force of habit we have forgotten how to see. Space travel revealed to us our own blue planet. Marina Abramović and Ulay implicitly claim this reading of their work when they describe their project with a pair of quotes spanning two millennia:

"The earth is small and blue. I am a small crevice in it."
—Huang Xiang, *Confessions of the Great Wall*, second century

"From up here, the earth looks small and blue."
—Yuri Gagarin, first cosmonaut, 1961

Zooming In

Artists zoom out by traveling to China or the Antarctic and zoom in to describe the path of a commuter train. Maspero is careful to note that he and Frantz made their trip not as professionals—journalists, historians, or sociologists—but as ordinary vacationers who were drifting with the current, toting maps, guidebooks and cameras: "They would contemplate the landscapes . . . look for traces of the past, visit museums and go to shows on occasion. They would try to grasp the geography of the places and the people: look at their faces. Who were the people that had lived there? How had they lived, loved, worked, suffered? Who was living there today?"[59]

Maspero got the idea for his book in China when he realized that he knew more about housing in Shanghai than in towns just half an hour from home.[60] He wanted to see beyond media clichés—"the suburban problem," "security," "immigration." "Why photograph *that*?" people would ask Anaïk Frantz. "*That* is the world we can't see even when it is right before our eyes: this world of borders that scares each of us a bit. . . . Sometimes we realize that it's our own world too."[61] Theirs is the tactic of social scientists who focus on phenomena that are close at hand, making unfamiliar again what appears all too familiar, whether it is the city sidewalk (Jane Jacobs), the urban square (Georges Perec) or the subway (Marc Augé). In the early 1990s, sociologist Pierre Bourdieu and his colleagues interviewed people in suburban housing projects like those described in *Roissy-Express* for their seminal study of the contemporary zeitgeist, *La misère du monde* (The Weight of the World).[62]

Surviving

The attraction of adventure comes partly from its dangers. To prepare for their trip along the Great Wall, Ulay visited camping stores to buy equipment that he never needed, and Marina Abramović, anticipating the physical ordeal, worked out at a gym on a treadmill. She said, "You have to be open to adventure and at the same time, prepare for life, take care of yourself."[63] Until recently, Laurent Tixador and Abraham Poincheval prided themselves on their complete lack of physical preparedness for what they too call "adventure." They focused on their own vulnerability as modern city dwellers who were no longer (or barely) capable of the physical skills that allowed their ancestors to survive in a competitive environment. This is why, for *L'inconnu des grands horizons*, they chose not to use a map or a guidebook. On the first day of their cross-country hike, Laurent Tixador wrote in his diary: "The adventure is beginning. We're carrying on our backs completely new equipment, wearing hiking boots that have never seen a pebble and clothes with visible creases. The smell we leave in our wake is that of shopping malls, and our walking experience, very theoretical, can be summarized in four words—we prefer the subway."[64]

They also tried living on figs and mussels for a week as paleolithic hunters and gatherers on the Mediterranean island of Frioul, which is opposite the city of Marseille. They spent a month in the middle of a cow pasture "like eskimos in earthenware igloos," using only the resources they found in their immediate environment. They are always looking for new situations, under unusual or extreme conditions that often border on the absurd and that require them to find ways to overcome obstacles. In this spirit, they undertook a bicycle trip in France from Nantes to Nantes, following the path of a circle drawn on a map (*Verdun*). Their protocol stipulated that they send photographs of their progress and that they keep a diary of the experience on toilet paper. After two weeks, they threw in the towel—the Tour de France was not for them—calling it a "successful failure."

Are their projects meant to reflect our relationship with nature? Should today's city dwellers prepare themselves to survive in the wilderness, like Boy or Girl Scouts? How will extreme conditions of climate transform our relationship with our environment? Tixador and Poincheval claim not to be interested in nature or ecology per se, but their sphere of action belies this posture. Perhaps it is more correct to say that they are concerned with evolving methods for survival. For them, the survival of the human species in extreme environments begins at home, with the cold wind of the eastern plain. Latter-day adventurers can up the ante by moving on to the North Pole (*North Pole*, 2005) or burrowing underground (*Horizon moins vingt*, 2008).

Their enterprises place them in situations of risk that we all may face as the climate becomes more unstable. In the future, we all may need to cultivate our skills at *bricolage*, taking advantage of what is available. No opportunity is too trivial. In his diary, Tixador noted that while walking he passed his time thinking out a rational organization of his pockets. Since it would be impossible to find an object that had not been put away in its proper place, he wrote that, out of sheer habit, he had become "a kitchen cupboard in which one can predict without thinking what is hidden behind each of its doors."[65]

They have prepared more recent expeditions in minute detail. For *Horizon moins vingt* (Twenty below Horizon) (2008), which required them to dig an underground tunnel at the pace of one cubic meter a day, they studied the feasibility of each aspect of the operation, which included devising a ventilating system to pump in fresh air and pump out depleted air.

It has been suggested that this art deals more with learning about the world than representing it.[66] This means that the artists explore an idea or a situation until it becomes familiar and then move on to something new (for them). Rather than perfecting their skills at painting, photography, or video, they bring to each project the passion and learning curve of amateurs.

Playing by the Rules

At the opposite end of the nature-culture scale, others reflect on the notion of rules. This question underlies all works that use protocols.

Anna Halprin tells her dancers what must be done but not how to do it. Otherwise, for her it would be "fascism." Telling people what to do gives them limits that encourage them to go a long way to conquer their material and carry out their tasks, she notes, but not explaining how to do so leaves them free to find their own language.[67] When composer Morton Subotnick collaborated with her to create *Parades and Changes* (1965), they explored choice within the confines of an aesthetic environment. For this work, Subotnick's compositional technique consisted of creating pieces called "cells" or "blocks" that could be assembled in different ways. Each section of the dance contained a set of tempo instructions that indicated what was to be done and, to a limited extent, which approach to adopt. This meant that for each performance, the participants had to invent new ways of moving from one dance segment to the next.[68]

Playing by the rules is a behavior that is instilled in children when they are young. Following (or breaking) arbitrary rules is a holdover from childhood games, as Brandon and Bunting's fence-climbing expeditions show. Julio Cortâzar and Carol Dunlop note that for children playing is obligatory and the rules of hopscotch or tag are part of that obligation:

> Entering into the game . . . was perhaps the least painful apprenticeship of that loss of liberty we associate (uselessly?) with growing up, "living in society" where the rules are no less arbitrary, at least for the most part . . . than those of hopscotch.[69]

What happens when the rule is infringed? Does it lose its force? One after the other, both Cortâzar and Dunlop are tempted to step off the *autoroute*, just for a minute. No one would be the wiser. At the edge of the rest area, down by the fragrant tree, Dunlop notes: "the little door was ajar; on the other side a narrow path, three tiny houses, a doghouse and a clothesline with a sheet and two or three shirts hanging from it." She responds by turning on her heels and hightailing it back to the van. Breaking their rule would have meant putting the whole enterprise in jeopardy, even if no one else knew: "This trip, without its rules, would be nothing more than stupidity (crossing the country from Paris to Marseilles, is of interest only for sight-seeing, while making the journey . . .)."[70]

Closing the Circuit: A Walk as a Gestalt

Shaped walks offer a clearly delineated image in which the parts are subordinated to the whole, a *gestalt* that appeals to the imagination. According to the law of *prägnanz* (conciseness), humans tend to order their experience in a manner that is regular and symmetric. A simple shape that contrasts with the background is more striking—and easier to remember—than one that is complex and irregular.

Some walks take the form of an archetypal figure. The line is an expression of oneness, "a potential of existing time,"[71] while the circle is a potent and archaic symbol, representing not only the cycle of life, death, and birth (the serpent biting its tail, the eternal return) or a self-contained milieu (enclosed cities, fortifications) but also equality (the round table). Maspero ironically describes the suburbs of Paris as a "circular purgatory"—although its center is not Satan, but "Paris-Paradise."[72] Iain Sinclair uses a similar analogy: the M25 expressway is the outer circle, "the point where London loses it, gives up its ghosts."[73] Walking it counterclockwise was for him "a way of winding the clock back."[74]

In each case, the figure is imaginary because this kind of walk is predicated on the existence of a map. The walker follows a line that he imagines seeing from a satellite circling over the earth.

Many of the artists discussed in this chapter have made walks that followed the path of a train, a road, or a wall to reflect on that object. Just as the Great Wall offered Abramović and Ulay the opportunity to span East and West and the M25 let Sinclair explore the boundary that separates London from England, the suburban train line gave Maspero and Frantz access to a cross-section of contemporary French society. As Maspero acknowledges in the postface, their protocol was inspired by *Autonauts of the Cosmoroute*. Here, too, the project involved exploring a place that we normally pass through on our way to somewhere else, but unlike Cortázar and Dunlop, whose object of study was the motorway itself, they used the train stations only as jumping-off points.

Executing these walks may not be as cut-and-dried a process as Sol LeWitt would lead us to believe. However much they are shaped by the preliminary idea, they are carried out by the artist, and in most cases, the act of walking is incorporated (although not always represented) in the final work. Richard Long explains that it is essential to his work that he make it himself: "The point of my work is my own physical engagement with the world in different ways, whether it's walking, or making fingerprints, or throwing stones."[75]

Most of these walks offer a kind of closure. They were performed and embodied by the artists at a particular time. They are finished, wrapped up and presented in some form or another. They are no longer just projects. They can be repeated by others, but then they would become something else, like Pierre Ménard's *Don Quixote* in the Borges story.

4 Directions but No Map

in all my recent music . . . there are parts but no score.
—John Cage, *Indeterminacy*

Some walking protocols can have simple premises, but the walks they offer are not easily identifiable. The paths are not readily memorized, nor do they produce recognizable forms. Like the open styles of architecture described by Robert Morris, "knowledge of their spaces is less visual and more temporal-kinesthetic than for [walks] that have clear gestalts. . . . Anything that is known behaviorally rather than imagistically is more time-bound."[1] If a circular walk is seen as a noun, then these works are more like verbs. Above all, they retain their potential as projects. Even though they have been carried out—often more than once—they remain unresolved and await new interpretations to bring them to life again.

Instructions and Scores

Today's conception of "art by instruction" has often been attributed to Marcel Duchamp.[2] At the beginning of the twentieth century, when artists were assumed to be both creator and craftsman, Duchamp sent instructions to his sister Suzanne and her husband, Jean Crotti, to make themselves a work of art as their wedding present. They were required to hang a geometry text on their balcony so that the wind could "go through the book [and] choose its own problems." The result was an *Unhappy Readymade*.[3]

At about that time, to "kill art," as André Breton put it,[4] Tristan Tzara proposed a tongue-in-cheek recipe for a poem:

Take a newspaper. Take a pair of scissors. Choose an article as long as you are planning to make your poem. Cut out the article. Then cut out each of the words that make up this article and put them in a bag. Shake it gently. Then take out the scraps one after the other in the order in which they left the bag. Copy conscientiously. The poem will be like you. And here you are a writer, infinitely original and endowed with a sensibility that is charming though beyond the understanding of ordinary people.[5]

Both sets of instructions are polemical. Aimed at undermining the myth of the creative genius, they are purposefully vague. There was no reason for Duchamp to explain how to attach the book, at what angle, with what materials. Tzara's aim was to demystify art and mock art-world elitism: look how easy it is for anybody to create an original work of art.[6] No more detail was necessary. Contrast their approach with László Moholy-Nagy's precision. When he ordered a series of three enamel paintings from an industrial sign painter in 1924, he specified their color, shape, and proportions, using standardized color charts and geometric forms reproduced on graph paper. There was to be no ambiguity here: "The result was not an industrial product, not even a model, but a perfectly composed and artistically constructed work of art: a Suprematist composition appearing not on canvas but on a slightly curved metal plate."[7]

Chance and Indeterminacy

Wilfried Hou Je Bek notes that he and his friends "wanted to stroll around in a way that resembled John Cage's dictum that he gave his musicians 'directions but no map.'"[8] Cage himself explored various methods for inviting chance and structuring randomness. A lecture from 1958 shows how indeterminacy is found even in Johann Sebastian Bach's *Art of the Fugue*. Although the composer noted structure, method, frequency, and duration, he did not specify timbre and amplitude: "This indeterminacy brings about the possibility of a unique overtone structure and decibel range for each performance of *The Art of the Fugue*." The performer is like someone who fills in color where only an outline is given. He can do it "in an organized way" that can be analyzed; "arbitrarily, by feeling his way, following the dictates of his ego" or "as in automatic writing, the dictates of his subconscious mind"; or even by using an operation exterior to his mind, like tables of random numbers or chance procedures.[9]

After discovering in Harvard's anechoic chamber that silence is not acoustic but "a change of mind, a turning around," Cage decided to devote his music to the "exploration of non-intention" for which he "developed a complicated composing means using *I Ching* chance operations."[10] His responsibility was to ask questions, not to make choices.

For a recording in which Cage read his stories and David Tudor played piano, each performer developed his sequence independently. Tudor played his part of the *Concert for Piano and Orchestra* (1957–1958), "using tracks from the *Fontana Mix* (1958–1959) as noise elements where these are notated in the *Concert*. [He] was free to make any continuity of his choice. There was no rehearsal beforehand involving both the reading and the music, for in all my recent music (since *Music for Piano*) there are parts but no score. Each one of us rehearsed alone and employed a stopwatch during the actual recording session. Each did what he had to do, bringing about a situation which neither had foreseen."[11]

Later, in *Indeterminacy: New Aspect of Form in Instrumental and Electronic Music,* he explains how he organized his one-minute stories:

> My intention in putting the stories together in an unplanned way was to suggest that all things—stories, incidental sounds from the environment, and, by extension, beings—are related, and that this complexity is more evident when it is not oversimplified by an idea of relationship in one person's mind.[12]

Many of the artists associated with Fluxus and happenings attended Cage's classes at the New School for Social Research in New York between 1956 and 1960. Cage's approach gave rise to several very different types of scores. Allan Kaprow's happenings were highly structured and included detailed scripts that were meant to be followed closely. During *18 Happenings in 16 Parts,* enacted in the fall of 1959 at the Reuben Gallery in New York, audience members performed on cue at the sound of a bell.[13] Unlike Cage, who encouraged audience participation as a way of relinquishing "authorial control," Kaprow used audience members as "props through which the artist's vision was executed."[14]

Score-Driven Dance

Various methods of written notation have been developed by choreographers, historians, and ethnologists to plan, document, analyze, and reconstruct choreography. Notation systems, especially those based on interfaces already used by many people (music notation) or that use mimesis (figurative drawing), allow the choreographer to document dance steps for future performances. Methods developed to notate movement include abstract symbols, figurative representation, track or path mapping, numerical systems, adaptations of music notation, and various forms of graphic notation. The two systems that are used most frequently in Western dance are Labanotation (based on Rudolf von Laban's 1928 publication) and Benesh movement notation (invented in the late 1940s by Rudolf and Joan Benesh).[15]

Labanotation, for instance, uses abstract symbols to set four parameters—direction of movement, body part that is involved, level of movement, and length of time that it takes to do the movement. The shape of the symbol indicates one of nine directions in space, and the shading specifies the level of the movement. The symbols are placed on a vertical staff, whose horizontal dimension represents the symmetry of the body and whose vertical dimension represents time.[16] Bar lines mark time measures. Other dimensions—spatial distance, spatial relationships, transference of weight, center of weight, jumps, turns, body parts, paths, and floor plans—can all be notated by specific symbols. The abstract symbols represent shapes, and the categories of effort appear in the notation as an effort graph.[17]

In the composition class that Robert Dunn gave at Merce Cunningham's studio in the early 1960s, he encouraged students to use scores to generate dances. He showed them scores by Cage and Karlheinz Stockhausen, viewing them "not as musical forms but as time-structures 'derived from and applicable to all the arts. . . .'"[18] For Dunn, writing choreography was important because it let choreographers objectify the composition process. They could see a range of possibilities for a particular dance and make decisions that no longer depended on personal taste or intuition: "By planning the dance in a written and drawn manner, you have a very clear view of the dance and its possibilities. . . . Graphic notation is a way of inventing the dance. It is part of the conception of the dance. . . . The human body and its doings are so full of meaning that most of what you have to do is release and channel this meaning."[19] Cage's graphic score for *Fontana Mix* (which comprises ten sheets of paper and twelve transparencies)[20] and the number structure of Erik Satie's *Trois Gymnopédies*, for instance, offer dancers multiple paths for further exploration. Some of Dunn's composition exercises evoke the "cut-up" in literature, as well as the rule-based experiments of the OuLiPo group.[21]

Fluxus Event Scores: Musicality

Fluxus artists carried Cage's (and Dunn's) approach one step further by blurring the borders between the arts and writing open-ended scores for all manner of events—actions, games, paintings, sculptures, and walks.[22] Some Fluxus scores were elaborate, and some consisted simply of verbal instructions. Writing scores was second nature to those who were composers, but others followed suit. Ken Friedman refers to this as the principle of "musicality," a key Fluxus idea. For him, this means that Fluxus scores could be realized by artists other than the creator—by anyone in fact:

> This means that you can own a George Brecht piece by carrying out one of Brecht's scores. If that sounds odd, you might ask if you can experience Mozart simply by listening to an orchestra play one of Mozart's scores. . . . Perhaps another orchestra or Mozart himself might have given a better rendition, but it is still Mozart's work.

He argues that musicality "is central to Fluxus because it embraces so many other issues and concepts: the social radicalism of Maciunas in which the individual artist takes a secondary role to the concept of artistic practice in society, the social activism of Beuys when he declared that we are all artists, the social creativity of Knizak in opening art into society, the radical intellectualism of Higgins and the experimentalism of Flynt."[23]

Map Pieces

Fluxus scores did not have to be realized at all. In one of the most deceptively simple of her *Map Pieces*, Yoko Ono exhorts us to "draw a map to get lost" (1964).[24] Like the situationist ambiance maps, this approach can provoke a fresh look at places that have become all too familiar. Another of her *Map Pieces* (1962) tells us to

> Draw an imaginary map.
> Put a goal mark on the map where you want to go.
> Go walking on an actual street according to your map.
> If there is no street where it should be according to the map, make one by putting the obstacles aside.
> When you reach your goal, ask the name of the city and give flowers to the first person you meet.
> The map must be followed exactly, or the event has to be dropped altogether.
> Ask your friends to write maps.
> Give your friends maps.[25]

Like this map, Ono's directions for "paintings to be constructed in your head" resemble philosophical thought experiments in which we visualize a situation and mentally carry out an operation for which we imagine the result. Since it is often physically impossible to set up a real experiment, a thought experiment helps us to gain some understanding of a phenomenon just by thinking it through.[26] Ono has said that her "painting method derives as far back as the time of the Second World War, when we had no food to eat, and my brother and I exchanged menus in the air."[27]

Her map pieces recall the "Psychogeographical Game of the Week" that appeared in the first issue of the lettrist journal *Potlatch* in 1954, though they lack its irony:

> Depending on what you are after, choose an area, a more or less populous city, a more or less lively street. Build a house. Furnish it. Make the most of its decoration and surroundings. Choose the season and the time. Gather together the right people, the best records and drinks. Lighting and conversation must of course be appropriate, along with the weather and your memories.If your calculations are correct, you should find the outcome satisfying. (Please inform the editors of the results.)[28]

Like Young's *Draw a Straight Line and Follow It, Map Pieces* could also be understood as tracing out a lifelong pursuit. "Take charge of your life," Ono seems to say: "Tread your own path. Streets can be made if one really wants them. Just move the obstacles aside." Unlike happenings, these pieces aim for "a dealing with oneself." They extricate the performer "from various sensory perceptions" to foster a sense of wonder. She has said that an instruction work "has no script as Happenings do, though it has something that starts it moving—the closest word for it may be a *wish* or *hope*. . . .After unblocking one's mind, by dispensing with visual, auditory and kinetic perception, what will come out of us? Would there be anything? And my events are mostly spent in wonderment. . . . We never experience things separately . . . but if that is so, it is all the more reason and challenge to create a sensory experience isolated from other sensory experiences, which is something rare in daily life. Art is not merely a duplication of life."[29]

Ideas as Machines

Rejecting the trite "Tenth Street touch" of late abstract expressionism,[30] other artists coming of age in the 1960s aimed for impersonal distance in their works, looking to mathematics and science for inspiration. They wanted to make art that no longer depended on the skill of the artist as a craftsman.[31] Sol LeWitt declared: "An architect doesn't go off with a shovel and dig his foundation and lay every brick. He's still an artist."[32] Some went so far as to exchange their paint-spattered jeans for three-piece suits. Yves Klein maintained that he used nude women as living paintbrushes to "stay clean" himself: "In this way . . . I no longer dirtied myself with color, not even the tips of my fingers. The work finished itself there in front of me, under my direction, in absolute collaboration with the model. And I could salute its birth into the tangible world in a dignified manner, dressed in a tuxedo."[33]

Giving instructions for their works to be built let artists delegate the execution to someone else, whether that someone was a foundry worker, an assistant, or a museum curator.[34] One of the first artists to do this was Robert Rauschenberg in 1962, when curator Pontus Hulten wanted to show his "white paintings" at Stockholm's Moderna Museet. Rauschenberg had painted them in 1951 while he was a student at Black Mountain College, using a roller to prove that there was no such thing as a blank canvas. In the meantime, they had been lost, so Rauschenberg sent Hulten the measurements of the panels together with samples of the white pigment and canvas, and Hulten had them re-created.[35] By the late 1960s, typewriters and cameras had begun to displace paintbrushes in downtown studios. For his first exhibition catalog in November 1968, Douglas Huebler typed up descriptions using maps and photos as illustrations. His dealer, Seth Siegelaub, had no gallery. The catalog became the exhibition.

In 1968, the Museum of Contemporary Art in Chicago planned an exhibition called *Art by Telephone*, which consisted of works in different media that were conceived by artists all over the United States and Europe and executed in Chicago on their behalf. According to curator Jan van der Marck, "The telephone was designated the most fitting means of communication in relaying instructions to those entrusted with fabrication of the artists' projects or enactment of their ideas. To heighten the challenge of a wholly verbal exchange, drawings, blueprints or written descriptions were avoided."[36] This choice echoed the situationists' use of walkie-talkies to organize their *dérives* and prefigures the use of mobile phones in contemporary walking projects. The exhibition was finally abandoned because of technical difficulties. All that remains is the catalog, a 33⅓ revolutions per minute vinyl recording on which the artists detail their projects.

By 1969, instruction art became ubiquitous. It let curators show avant-garde art without the overhead costs incurred by shipping works. Lucy Lippard incorporated this principle into the design of the exhibition *557,087* in Seattle: "I executed all the works, with friends' help, since there was no money to bring the artists."[37] Robert Smithson, writing from New York, put in an order for "400 square snapshots of Seattle Horizons—should be empty, plain, vacant, surd, common, ordinary, blank dull level beaches, unoccupied uninhabited, deserted fields scanty lots houseless typical average void roads sand bars remote lakes distant timeless sites—use Kodak instamatic 804."[38] Museum staff members were to present these photos of generic sites as a wall grid: "9 rows of 50." For a sister show in Vancouver, *955,000* (the numbers represent the population of each town), "Jan Dibbets sent directions for recording a tape of the sounds of a car trip of up to thirty miles, with the driver verbally counting out the miles driven, to be played continuously in the exhibition under a map of the route taken."[39]

Although Sol LeWitt's well-known formula[40] suggests that, for him, the problem of intentions and realizations had been resolved once and for all, he explored these issues for over forty years in a body of work that encompasses both plans that were derived from a logical system and instructions that defied logic.[41] In 1971, he wrote: "The artist conceives and plans the wall drawing. It is realized by draftsmen (the artist can act as his own draftsman); the plan (written, spoken, or drawn) is interpreted by the draftsman. . . . The draftsman may make errors in following the plan. All wall drawings contain errors, they are part of the work."[42] The use of natural language with its ambiguity gave his assistants a certain leeway in their interpretation (although he did furnish diagrams).

When the Precursors Are Followers

Other artists prepared scores they interpreted themselves. One way of courting chance is to set up a situation in which one's course of action depends on decisions made by total strangers. In October 1969, Vito Acconci devised *Following Piece*, a gamelike performance that injected art into real life as part of a program of street works organized by the New York Architectural League. Actions like this were conceived in terms of the particular city he was in: "a piece in New York had to be different from a piece in Los Angeles—had to be different from a piece in Milan—what would people do here? how could I pressure them? how might they fight back?"[43] One way to "key" or "tie" himself into that city was to have a mailbox there: "To be in a show at the Museum of Modern Art, my space in the Museum of Modern Art is my mailbox, my mail is delivered there. Whenever I want mail, I have to go through this city to get my mail."[44]

Another way was to select people in the city to follow. The rules here were simple. Every day for twenty-three days, the artist would randomly choose a passer-by and follow that person until he or she entered a private place that the follower could not legally enter without being invited. The pursuit could last a few minutes (if the person got into a car or disappeared into a building) or a few hours (if the prey continued walking in public space). Acconci related his actions in typewritten texts that he mailed to selected members of the art world.

Acconci has said that when he started following people, he had the desire to be nobody: "I'm using my own person in pieces, but I'm trying to turn my person into a nonperson in the sense of a person without will, without volition. I'm subjecting myself to a scheme."[45] He wanted to let someone else take over: "Any time you do something, you make decisions about time and space. I wanted those decisions to be out of my hands. I could be dragged, carried along by another person, I could be a receiver."[46] Later he did a two-channel video installation called *Remote Control* (1971) in which he played the opposite role, controlling the actions of a young woman from a distance via technology.

Here, like the narrator of Edgar Allan Poe's story "The Man of the Crowd" (1840), he subjected his own movements to those of the people he followed. Although he considered himself "the agent of the overall scheme," the form of his walk was not decided in advance. He would decide that his space was "going to change now" without any idea where it was going to take him.[47]

"In January 1980," recounts Sophie Calle, "I followed a man whom I lost sight of a few minutes later. That very evening quite by chance, he was introduced to me at an opening. I found out he was planning a trip to Venice. I decided to shadow him."[48] Calle's *Venetian Suite* (1980) lasted two weeks. It came to an end when the man realized she was following him.

Acconci was following people as a way of moving his concrete poetry out into the city space. He often combines autobiographical content with an impersonal, "behaviorist" account.[49] When he discusses sensations, his approach is analytical. Explaining how he came to make "Following Piece," he says: "I saw the page as a field over which I as a writer could move and you as the viewer could move too. I then figured that if I was so concerned with space, why was I limiting myself to a piece of paper when there is a floor or a street to work with."[50]

Sophie Calle relates her pursuit in terms of how she feels, in intimate detail. For instance, just as she is about to enter the hotel where her quarry is staying, she wonders whether an encounter is what she really wants: "I hardly dare lift my eyes to meet the closed door; I go past it without slowing down. *My investigation was unfolding without him. Discovering him may upset everything, hasten the end. I'm afraid.*"[51] We are a long way from Acconci's deliberately nonexpressive style. She explains: "When I wanted to publish *Venetian Suite,* I was told that Vito Acconci had also followed people. I wanted to make sure. I went to New York. I made an appointment with him. I showed him my photos and asked him: 'So, it's true, you've already done that?' He told me our motives were different, they had nothing in common, his work wasn't related to emotion, feeling. In short, he gave me his benediction."[52] If her statement is taken at face value, then a similar action that arises from a different intention will somehow be shaped differently, leading to a different artwork. If we examine only the artworks, Calle's defense of the originality of her following piece may not hold up to close examination: it was the same Acconci in his 1971 *Seedbed* performance who masturbated below a ramp installed in the Sonnabend gallery, while voicing his fantasies about unseen visitors walking above his head. Yet when we factor in the different social meaning of the two artists' very similar actions, the contrast becomes evident. Calle shadowed one particular man all the way across Europe, whereas Acconci followed a different, arbitrarily chosen, person every day.

A year later, Calle set up a more tangible reversal of Acconci's *Following Piece*. She had her mother hire a private detective to shadow her through Paris. The artist followed an itinerary prepared in advance to include places of personal significance to her (*The Shadow*, 1981). Unaware that Calle was "taking him for a walk" or that he also was being followed, the detective prepared an appropriately impersonal report of the day-long job. When Calle exhibits the piece, she juxtaposes three narratives: (1) the detective's photographs and typewritten report, which begins at 10 a.m. and ends at 8 p.m. when she comes home; (2) her own account, which finishes as she drifts off to sleep after a party, wondering if the detective found her attractive; and (3) the pictures of the detective that were taken by a third person. All three are incomplete, limited, as they are, by their particular point of view on the same sequence of events, all part of Calle's idiosyncratic orchestration.

Bottom-Up Walking

A preplanned shaped walk strikes the imagination through its overall form, highlighted by an unusual setting or approach. Other kinds of walks, by contrast, provide a set of instructions, and the execution of the instructions creates the shape. Instead of a blueprint, projects of this type begin with a set of simple rules that are usually open-ended. Theoretically, this type of protocol could be followed indefinitely for hours, days, or weeks. Sometimes the artist fixes arbitrary limits, either temporal or spatial.

With most shaped walks, the artist does the walking and brings back news of it to the rest of us. Bottom-up walks are planned by artists but are carried out by others. Instead of merely reading about it, we are out in the streets "doing it." As performers, we share with the artist at least a token responsibility for the outcome.

"If-Then" Procedural Walking

One art lover ambles through Central Park in New York City while listening to a portable CD player, another strolls around the Lower East Side with a cell phone pressed to her ear, and a third pauses in the middle of the Rivington Street pavement to read aloud to her companions. Although they may seem indistinguishable from passers-by, many of whom are tapping numbers on cell phones or paging through guidebooks, all three are involved in different experiments.

Janet Cardiff prepares the equivalent of a radio theater broadcast that is played back as the visitor follows a preset route through the park. Lee Walton's *City System* (2002) and Kate Armstrong's *Ping!* (2003), however, offer rules for walking set out in the form of modular "if-then" procedures presented as menu lists. Each "if" leads to a different "then" that offers a new set of choices. These are primitive examples of what has become known as generative art,[53] an emergent artistic practice in which the artist sets up rules for the artwork to be performed. Like Fluxus event scores, these rules can be carried out by one or more performers.

You the pedestrian are the hero(ine) of Walton's 120-page *City System*, "a device created for navigating step-by-step through a city. Resulting from simple observations and chance occurrences, the '*City System*' will determine each action in a sequence meant to frame one's experience in that city. Originally created in 2002 for San Francisco, the *City System* has been adapted to guide people through New York, Paris, Amsterdam, Indianapolis and Portland"[54] (figure 4.1).

To experience the *City System: NYC*, the author recommends having "about $4–$12 in dollar bills and at least one hour of unhurried, purposeless time to amble through the City." In a world that is defined by dried-up bubble gum (you will check for gum on the ground between your feet) and dumpsters (you will determine how full they are), you may feel that you are being subjected to a mild form of hazing. You dash after a passer-by who wears red shoes, note an employee who is smoking in front of her workplace, and enter a coffee shop where you examine the person taking your order to see if he has a pierced nose or eyebrow. You follow rather arbitrary instructions: "Begin walking EAST"! "Get on the bus"! "Stop! Do not move your feet."

Walton often requires walkers to interpret visual clues: "Keep your eye out for a vehicle parked in a spot with an expired parking meter"; "Look for the nearest building without a visible fire escape"; "Pay close attention to the mouths of every oncoming person that you pass. If you see somebody smiling or laughing, follow him/her to the nearest corner"; "Stand with your back against the buildings so that you can observe pedestrians passing by. Wait for 10 men to pass by. Note the 11th man. If the 11th man has . . . Glasses—go to p. 33. Hat—go to p. 40. Mustache or goatee—go to p. 66. A dog—follow for 2 blocks—then go to p. 30."

Occasionally, other senses are solicited: Listen for "a horn honk, the hydraulic braking of a very large vehicle (or) a police siren"; "Close your eyes and count to 10, when you reach the number 10 note the direction of the wind. Walk against the wind."

City System revels in mundane details that locate individual experience in a world that we share. Walton's approach is intuitive: "I wanted it to feel personal, so that your own history determined direction as well. Things like height and shoe size, but

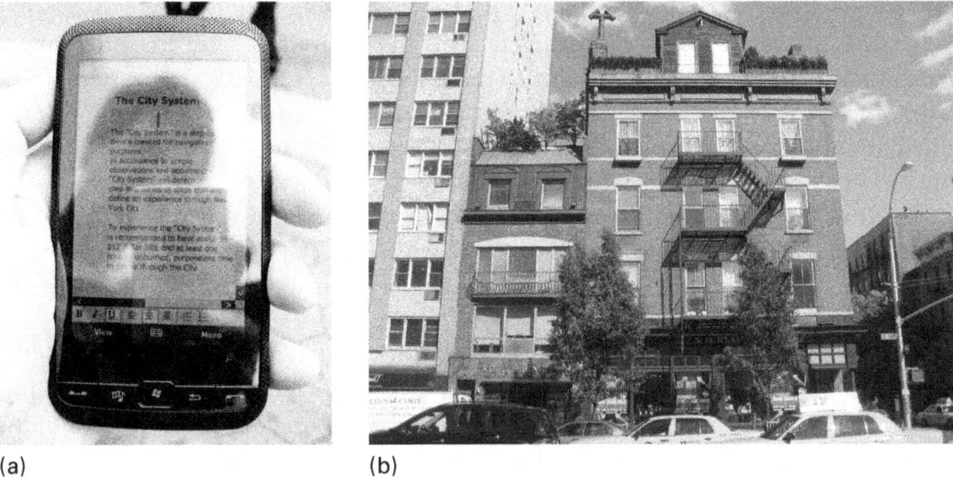

(a) (b)

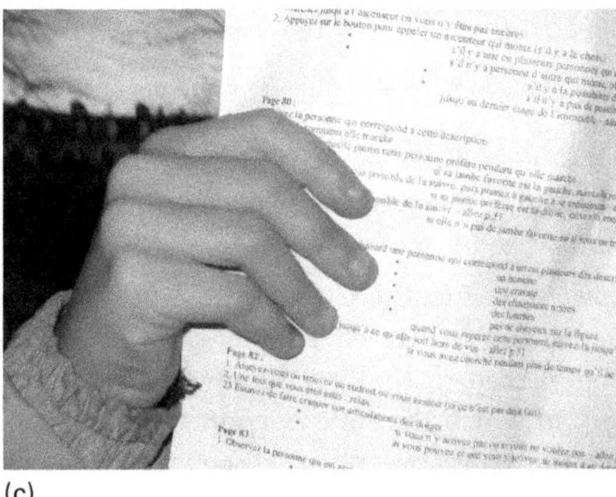

(c)

Figure 4.1

Lee Walton, *City System*, 2002. A device created for navigating step-by-step through a city. Resulting from simple observations and chance occurrences, *City System* determines each action in a sequence that is meant to frame the participant's' experience in that city. *a:* A PDF version for cell phones, June 7, 2010. *b:* The place of the greatest life-altering decision, June 7, 2010. *c:* Consulting the French translation in the rain, Paris, January 14, 2004.
Photograph: Karen O'Rourke.

also some subjective things like 'home' or 'the length you could throw a baseball.'" What does it mean to "walk in the direction of your birthplace"? In Paris, one student heads for the northern suburb of Saint-Denis, while another takes a southeasterly route with Srinagar (Kashmir) in her mind's eye. Kevin Lynch notes that according to the orientation systems in parts of Africa, the key direction may not be abstract or constant but rather the direction toward the speaker's home territory.[55]

To write the texts, Walton immersed himself in the life of the street, alternately "sitting around observing things" and "walking around taking notes": "I wanted to work from almost any point in the city. I was sort of never looking further than the next step."[56]

Actions often involve mental gymnastics: "When parking meter is found, note the current amount of minutes until meter will expire."[57] Walton says that he wants "the player to have to speculate a bit and know that the final decision will determine the outcome of the experience" and that he likes "asking people to find the exact midpoint." Sometimes the instructions involve transgressing taboos, like putting money on the sidewalk, or are so complicated that they invite rebellion:

> Get dollar out and ready. Examine the dollar bill's serial number. Note the numbers furthest to the outside of the serial numbers. If the left number is greater than the right number—walk the difference (L minus R) that many blocks to the left. Then go to p. 11. If the right number is higher than left number—get on next bus and get off the number of stops equal to the difference (R–L) Go to p. 34. If numbers are equal—put dollar on sidewalk. Go to p 68.[58]

This may be a way of bringing people fully into the *City System*, emptying the mind of the chaff of everyday worries to be able to reach another level of understanding, a self-induced trance. It can be likened to the Zen Buddhist koân or the use of paradox in therapeutic technique,[59] in which the state of confusion produced by an overload of information occupies the conscious mind, discourages rational discursive thinking, and allows access to holistic processes in the right hemisphere of the brain.

Walton asked people to help him adapt the basic script to each new city in which it was played. Sometimes the modifications are minimal: in Paris, for example, a New York Mets baseball cap became a t-shirt with the colors of the local soccer team, and a hot-dog vendor was replaced by a kebab stand. But others alert us to different cultural mores. In France, higher education is state-funded to ensure equal opportunity. Public institutions charge only token tuition, and costs to students are kept to a minimum. When a student translated the booklet into French for her classmates, she wanted to omit all the instructions calling for money to be spent. Had she done that, she would have amputated a significant part of *City System*. Whether or not we are aware of it, economic exchanges, even the nickel and dime variety, account for many of our interactions and, to a certain extent, guide us through the city.

As it was, the students using the *City System* in Paris found themselves continually navigating between Scylla and Charybdis. They found it difficult to strike a balance between the demands made by their surroundings and Walton's instructions urging them to disrupt the normal flow of things. Apparently trivial problems arose and had to be dealt with: How to toss a coin while holding an unwieldy umbrella? How to inspect a bicycle seat without leading passers-by to think that you are preparing to steal it? What to say to the delivery man arriving at his van just as you are leaning across the hood to examine the note fixed under the windshield wipers? How to catch up with the person in red shoes after losing her in the crowd as you thumb frantically through the booklet looking for page 108? As one student put it, "Lee Walton placed us in a situation of uncertainty."

Later with a different group, I tried out Kate Armstrong's mobile phone project *Ping!* (figure 4.2) in the Parisian suburb of Fontenay-aux-Roses. This work, which premiered at Psy-Geo-Conflux in New York in 2003, uses a telephone menu system to distribute commands to participants in the street. The choices made by the caller produce directions for physical movement through the city.

At my request, Armstrong sent us the schematic diagram and the menu choices that she had drawn up when programming the piece. We planned to use it without

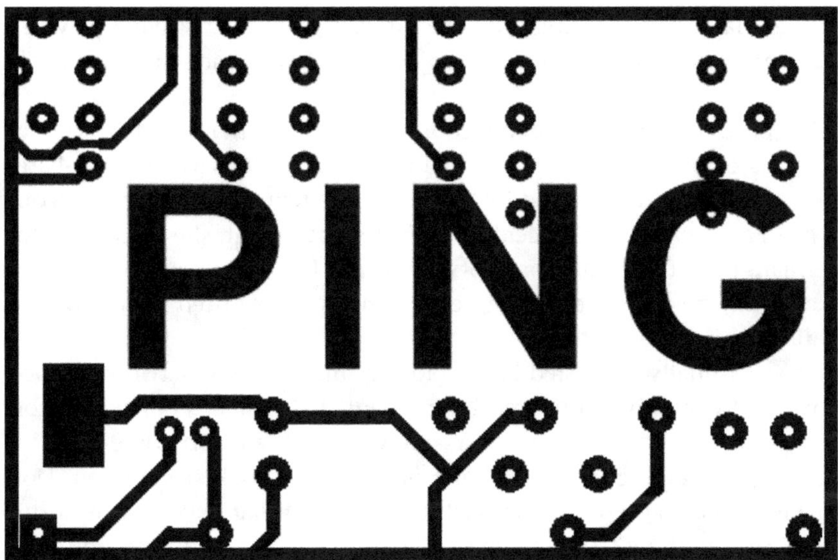

Figure 4.2
Kate Armstrong, *Ping*, 2003. Mobile phone application. This work uses a telephone menu system to distribute commands to participants in the street. The choices made by the caller produce directions for physical movement through the city.

the phone system, which we could not afford.[60] It allowed us a behind-the-scenes look at her project, much like reading a play or a musical score. The students faced choices such as these:

Press 1 for castles.
Press 2 for endless walls.
Press 3 for little forgotten bars or mammoth caverns.
Press 4 for casino mirrors.

How could they relate this allusion to Ivan Chtcheglov's *Formulary for Unitary Urbanism* to the suburban park they were walking through? In the passage quoted here, Chtcheglov suggested that the density of occupation may be a problem in modern European cities: "All cities are geological. You can't take three steps without encountering ghosts bearing all the prestige of their legends. We move within a *closed* landscape whose landmarks constantly draw us toward the past." For him the way through was almost a way out: "Certain *shifting* angles, certain *receding* perspectives, allow us to glimpse original conceptions of space, but this vision remains fragmentary. It must be sought in the magical locales of fairy tales and surrealist writings: castles, endless walls, little forgotten bars, mammoth caverns, casino mirrors."[61]

The students finally decided to make arbitrary associations, such as we will take that grove of trees over there to be "endless walls." Spending money was hard to imagine, but even harder, in academia, was the instruction to play. Playing may be a good way of learning, but one wonders if it can be at the same time spontaneous and obligatory.[62]

To set up her project, Armstrong used a commercial service that builds voice mail systems for businesses, allowing her to construct these connections using a Web-based interface. When *Ping!* was first enacted in New York, the text was read by the "computery voice of an automated text reader."[63] For a later enactment, she asked an actor, Jennifer Silverman, to read the voice prompts. Hearing a human voice rather than an automat undoubtedly modifies the listener's expectations. Our written version was yet another variation.

She says she was initially interested in the "idea of instantiating network protocol in physical space, of exploring an existential moment that happens on the network all the time when one machine asks another—are you out there? Do you exist?"[64]

The script begins by asking just that: "First off, stop and look around you. Note existing ambient zones. You must ask yourself a question. What is your relationship to your current surroundings? Do you exist?" The player has only one option to press—1, which indicates "Yes, I exist," and the voice responds: "Thank you. Your existence has been confirmed. Locate the nearest intersection. Quickly, without engaging in analysis, decide on a direction in which you would like to travel and begin to travel in that direction. As you are walking, heroically resist incorporation into the milieu through which you move."[65]

From then on, the player is presented with many choices. As in any automatic phone answering service, the menu items can be repeated. The lists, sometimes extensive, juxtapose options of a completely different nature: some "ifs" relate to where we are (near a French *tabac,* within view of a deep pit), inquire about our surroundings (is the neighborhood sad or pleasant?), and others ask us to define our mood ("unexpectedly joyful," "fearless, disoriented, and infused with the spirit of playful constructive behavior") or our perception of the ambiance ("a noticeable shift between two ambient zones" or "generalized angst"). People must qualify the degree to which they feel like a flâneur and the effect on their "mental state" of "the dominating action of a center of attraction."[66] The structure and tone recall the *BIT Phone* from 1996, a voice-mail system that was built as "a hopelessly complex hyper-architecture of menu choices" with options like "Press Pound to Resolve Ambiguity" and "Press Star to Regret Your Choice."[67]

Armstrong too interweaves questions concerning "the order of things"[68] into the perception of our surroundings. Traditional categories like playground, street, private property, and public space are called into question by ubiquitous technologies. "*Ping* is about the overlay of network space and physical space," says Armstrong. "It can be any street, it can be any person, any time, and to some extent the pattern of the text fragments possess a kind of infinity as well."[69] She considers it site specific "because it is a system that isn't activated until the moment when a person uses it to navigate through a cityspace, and in that moment it becomes specific to that place."[70]

Her approach offers up a model or a blueprint for site specificity, much like Tzara's prototypical dada poem. In so doing, it questions the current art-world paradigm in which the same group of artists travels from Venice to São Paulo, Gwangju, and Istanbul, from biennial to art fair, seeding site-specific works in their wake.

Both Walton's and Armstrong's projects involve implicit parody of "interactivity" in the form of multiple-choice questionnaires. In this, they bring to mind experiments from the 1960s like OuLiPo founder Raymond Queneau's "Un conte à votre façon" (A Tale in Your Style),[71] a postmodern fairytale proceeding from choices made by the reader.

Negotiated Walking

Up to this point, viewers/walkers have negotiated their paths individually via instructions contained in some form of guide. For individual pedestrians to become mappers, however, they must enter the fabric of the city and participate in a larger movement. They need not form an organized group with someone calling the shots. They can begin on the street by influencing one another in relatively simple ways. Then through their interactions, they might begin to form a higher-level structure, a collective body.

Ici-Même (Right Here)

The Grenoble-based group Ici-Même [Gr] (Right Here [Gr]) uses constraints as a basis for negotiation. Since its founding in 1993, Ici-Même [Gr] has carried out a variety of experiences in dance, performance, architecture, video, and sound art. They use objects as props and ask, What is the place of art in our fragmented society, and can we slow down long enough to elicit new perception? Thirty-foot PVC pipes serve as conversation starters. Carrying them in restricted, crowded places causes passers-by to react—generally helpfully by opening doors for the pipe carriers to ease their passage. A pipe is an unusual prop: it does not cause passers-by on their way to work to bristle with hostility as cameras and bicycles sometimes do. It can sometimes be bought in a nearby hardware store at the beginning of an urban walk and turned back in for reimbursement at the end.[72]

Ici-Même's scenarios are prepared in advance and continually modified to deal with situations they have brought on. I participated in a transect walk through the 15th arrondissement of Paris (figure 4.3).[73] The first rule was to follow a straight line on a map (drawn by the artists) as closely as possible. The second rule was: "join the two ends."

This resembled a top-down event score, like Laurent Malone's transects. As our path did not correspond to any existing street, we found ourselves entering buildings to see if there was a path leading to the next block. We tramped through tiny courtyards that were crowded with discarded objects and dumpsters, new buildings with spacious gardens that were off limits to strangers, and a grocery store whose employees welcomed any out-of-the-ordinary event. Once we scrambled over a wall to get a look at the other side. We were, as Corinne Pontier put it, investigating the porosity of the city. Some cities offer multiple routes parallel to public streets—they have more than their share of empty lots, unused and open spaces, chinks in the urban fabric—while others, like downtown Paris, are more densely occupied.

Was our quest the contemporary equivalent of Thomas de Quincey's search for the Northwest Passage within London, the hidden city within the city? In *Confessions of an English Opium-Eater*, he describes navigating the labyrinth of London by ducking and diving through the puzzle of alleys and courtyards: "Seeking ambitiously for a northwest passage, instead of circumnavigating all the capes and headlands I had doubled in my outward voyage, I came suddenly upon such knotty problems of alleys, such enigmatical entries, and such sphynx's riddles of streets without thoroughfares. . . . I could almost have believed, at times, that I must be the first discoverer of some of these terrae incognitae, and doubted whether they had yet been laid down in the modern charts of London."[74] This search for channels, as Simon Sadler notes, "in the capitalistic land mass to permit the drift a clean sweep across the city" characterized situationist psychogeography.[75] In today's Paris, most of these channels have disappeared, leaving only "unrepresentable"

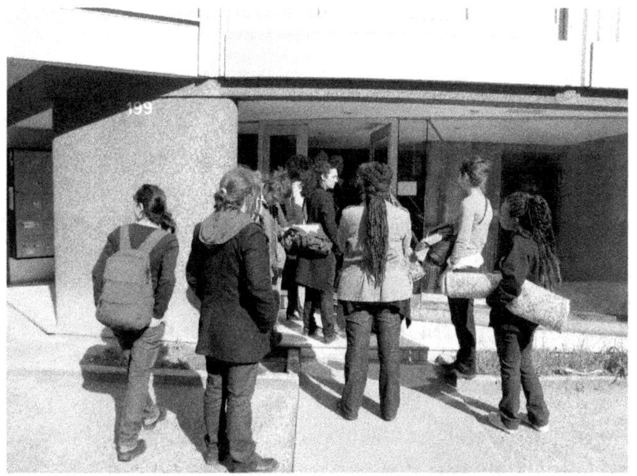

(a)

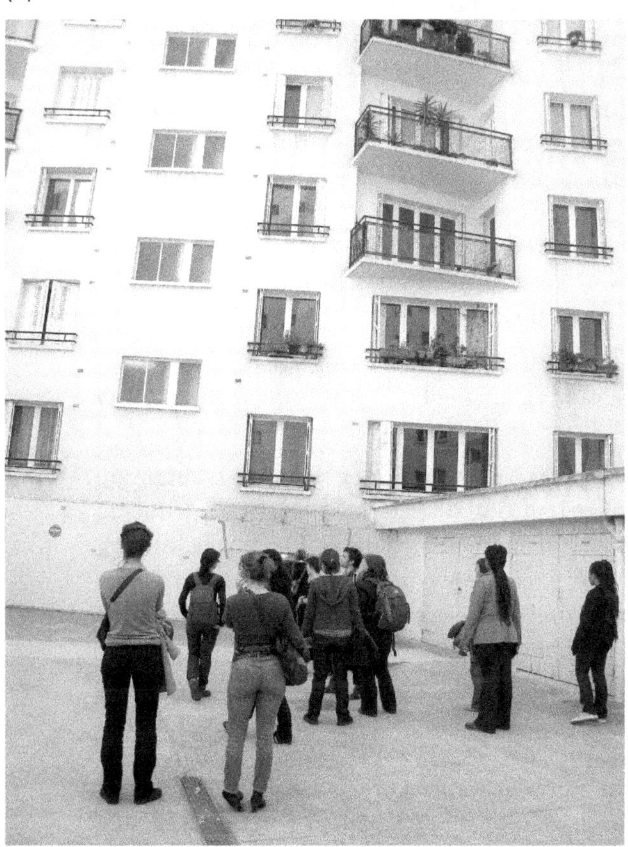
(b)

Figure 4.3
Ici-Même [Gr], *Workshop "En marche,"* Paris, 2009. Transect walk through the 15th arrondissement of Paris. On the map, the artists drew a straight line that we followed as closely as possible. Photographs: Karen O'Rourke. *a:* As our path did not correspond to any existing street, we found ourselves entering buildings to see if there was a path leading to the next block. *b:* We tramped through courtyards trying to find a direct way through to the next block.

blank spots on the map, located, as Philippe Vasset discovered, at the city's outer edges.[76]

The Universal Psychogeographic Computer

After several algorithmic drifts, Wilfried Hou Je Bek decided that walking should be used for more than just transportation. Why not harness the combined power of several walkers who followed their algorithms to form a foot-powered supercomputer? The Universal Psychogeographic Computer (UPC) was born. Invited to lead walks in Toronto and New York, Hou Je Bek attempted to show that "you can solve quite complex computations by stripping them down to their smallest factor & have a interesting walk at the same time." These experiments became the project *.Walk*.

In an online tutorial, *Programming .Walk for Dummies*, he set out "fundamental concepts that might be used to program a non-electric computer."[77] It comprises examples of pseudocode and comments. What happens, for instance, when two psychogeographers meet and exchange their "export code"?

.Walk (dotwalk) is pedestrian software used to build a "psychogeographical computer that will use the city as hardware." Here individual agents are connected through this exchange of code that enables them to coordinate their movements locally. Working together, the participants, like small programs (applets), function as a computer: "an interconnected bunch of small applets, called *.walk* software . . . that runs (or rather walks) on top of the hardware, the street grid."[78]

The definitions are slippery. If the body is wetware, then *.Walk* must be "walkware" (it is not clear what difference there is, if any, between an algorithm and a pair of shoes). The key to understanding may be its floating syntax:

> Applets can be written in any way, can mimic any known computer language. . . . .walk is not merely an offshoot of something that is already existing but . . . it is a whole new field of research.[79]

Walton and Armstrong played with concepts borrowed from networked computing, but here Hou Je Bek attempts to generalize and systematize the metaphor, producing in the process some excellent examples of the ambiguity of natural language. Among several variations on this theme, *Forkbomb .Walk* transposes to walking the principle of the forkbomb. Computer programmers use this term to designate a piece of code that, when it is executed, creates a process that reproduces itself twice before terminating. Each one of the two processes that it has created does the same. Recursively, the bomb spreads quickly until it paralyzes the system. No one can stop a forkbomb, not even its initiator, since the process at its root no longer exists.

In a psychogeographical forkbomb, a group of walkers breaks off into two groups at each intersection, "making the city a garden of forking paths." After a while, the processing units are all divided, and the computer stops in its tracks. To be effective, the metaphor does not have to go very far. He adds, with a note of irony, that "in other circumstances the 'fork' command can be useful when a group of psychogeographers need to be placed so that a territory is completely covered; for instance during a collaborative mapping project or during a rescue operation."[80] It would take a rather large psychogeographical rescue team to cover even a small number of streets because the combinations are exponential. Trying it out with a group of students, we split into smaller and smaller groups until each of us was alone: collectively, as a computer, we had shut down long before that. The same effect can be seen in the wild at the end of every workday when employees leave their office and head home. The workplace computer breaks up into individual processing units, just as the rush-hour traffic machine powers up.

For Wilfried Hou Je Bek, code illustrates the performative aspects of language: "I am interested in code as an invented language to express instructions, because that is what they are, a computer comes only after the fact. .walk which turns a group of pedestrians into a computer was done when I hadn't learned to code."[81] New tools and languages have made programming easier for nonspecialists, thus offering possibilities that were unknown even just a few years ago. The fact that software plays such a big part in our everyday experience incited him to reflect on "the way it looks and functions as well as it being vulnerable to attacks and crashing at the wrong moments." Computers and artificial intelligence have given us "so much new information about humans, about what makes up intelligence, and about how little we understand of ourselves."[82]

Street Games: Teleguided Theater

Other artists explore the potential for coordinated collective movement, combining theater, dance, and live art with mobile technology. The situationists used walkie-talkies to link up different parts of the city in the early 1960s, but the twenty-first century has given rise to hybrid games played using cell phones, global positioning system (GPS) coordinates, and wireless connections.

Catch Me If You Can

In *Can You See Me Now?*, the streets of the city, beginning with Sheffield in 2001, became the setting for an action game in which members of the group Blast Theory (Matt Adams, Ju Row Farr, and Nick Tandavanitj) chased the avatars of online players. The online players, who could be anywhere in the world, tried to escape from their pursuers by using mice and joysticks. These fast-paced games ran about fifteen minutes each. On both the moving and the fixed screens, the players seemed to run side by side, almost touching as they strained to catch or elude the other. Which one is virtual? Each of the three players in the streets of Sheffield was equipped with a pocket personal computer that was connected to a GPS receiver, which transmitted his geographical position to the online players. He could view on his screen the position of each virtual player. The online players could exchange instant messages and listen to conversation, breathing, and background noise that was captured by the runners' walkie-talkies as they moved through the city space.

Only a dozen years previously, this kind of feat would have required the help of the National Air and Space Administration (NASA), like Kit Galloway and Sherrie Rabinowitz's *Satellite Arts Project* (1988), one of the first performances to unite dancers 2,000 miles apart on a single screen. Now the numbers of screens and potential players have multiplied exponentially, and in the process, they have both become mobile.

Blast Theory explored the "emotional tenor" of these hybrid spaces, drawing attention to the complex nature of online relationships. Can intimacy exist on the Internet despite its lurkers, pedophiles, spambots, and flame wars? The interactions within a game range from "insults, teasing, goading and humor" to moments of empathy or "mute tenderness."[83]

Since 2000, the group has been working with the Mixed Reality Lab at the University of Nottingham on a series of multiplayer street games. Unlike the "if-then" works discussed earlier, these pieces give players an explicit goal and a precise timeframe. In 2003, the group developed *Uncle Roy All around You*, an "interactive espionage movie" that was a cross between a treasure hunt and a detective story (imagine a live game of *Where in the World Is Carmen San Diego?*). This game associated players online and on the streets of London, who were given sixty minutes to find Uncle Roy's office. Other gamelike projects using mobile technology include *I Like Frank* (2004), touted as "the world's first 3G mixed reality game," which took place online and in the streets of Adelaide (Australia), and *Rider Spoke* (2007), where participants rode bikes around London, making recordings when prompted ("Describe yourself. What are you like? And how do you feel?" or "Find a place that your father would like and record a message about it").[84] These were electronically "planted" in various locations for other players to find.

In 2008, the group staged another online chase game, *You Get Me*. To connect two neighboring sites, the group had to bridge a social and cultural divide. Blast Theory worked with eight teenagers from the Mile End area of London to map participants' personal geographies. Wearing track suits and carrying walkie-talkies, the young people were linked to audiences in the Royal Opera House for three days in August. Audience members chose a player whose question they had to answer while the other players tried to knock them out. The more the audience learned about the partner's personal geography, the better the answers and, presumably, the tighter the teamwork. In fact, it sounded like there was no other game to play, just a heart-to-heart conversation with a stranger in which the teen agent, grappling with the problem of, say, leaving home, asked "you" "how it was for you": "does it get easier over time? Are all parents so obstructive and uncomprehending?"[85]

Instruction-Based Theater

The collective Rimini Protokoll (Helgard Haug, Daniel Wetzel, and Stefan Kaegi) has been exploring similar territory. Their "theater of experts" involves nonprofessional actors playing themselves—Bulgarian truck drivers, European third-culture kids, Egyptian muezzin, or Indian call center operators.

In *Call Cutta,* theatergoers walked through a neighborhood, guided by the telephone voice of a call center employee. This one-on-one experience mixing theater and real life, was staged by the group in Kolkata (Calcutta) in February and March 2005 and then in Berlin for three months. A new version, *Call Cutta in a Box,* brought the project to several European cities in 2008.

Like Blast Theory, Rimini Protokoll's work arises out of a theatrical tradition. "We are exploring theater as a model for experience instead of representation. But what you represent and what the other represents—this is what we can play with and make experiences with, in the framework of what theater can make happen," says Daniel Wetzel.[86]

In India, the artists observed call center operators who were taking orders for a pizzeria in Manhattan. The operators had undergone specific training so that they would give customers the impression that they were just around the corner instead of 20,000 miles away. The first performances of *Call Cutta* took place in Hatibagan, North Kolkata. After buying a ticket at the Star Theater, theatergoers were handed a cell phone. When it rang, the voice at the other end proceeded to guide them through the city streets. This kind of wayfinding is particularly adapted to Kolkata, a city for which there is no accurate, up-to-date map. As Rimini Protokoll discovered, "the available maps mention only the streets built and named by the British. Most of the people live in the areas in the maps which show no streets and where one would least expect habitation. There the city has expanded without any plan."[87]

In the next step, for a period of three months, the Indian call center employees guided theatergoers, via mobile phone, through Berlin, a city in which none had ever set foot. Props (including photographs and newspaper articles concerning Jagadish Chandra Bose, a Bengali inventor who had lived in Berlin) were planted in various parts of Kreuzberg, making the walk into a treasure hunt in which each participant's experience was different. While guiding their correspondents, the Indians asked questions that many Westerners deem too personal: "Have you ever fallen in love on the phone?" or "How much do you earn?"

The authors have compared their project to a computer game, "a sort of user interface for theatergoers," a blind date, or "a movie you shoot with your own eyes." At the beginning, the group had trouble getting theatergoers out of their seats and into the streets. Stefan Kaegi thinks this is because "Indians are just not used to having flaneur-walks through the city. The city is seen as something loud and polluted and definitely not a place to have personal phone calls. Even in Berlin it took the audience a while to appear. But in Berlin you have these people who want to see things that sound mysterious or a personal experience, a place you come back from and have something to tell."[88]

Although the first *Call Cutta* had the spectator follow walking directions through the streets of Berlin given by someone on the other side of the world, *Call Cutta in a Box* focuses on the conversation itself (figure 4.4). Here the voice on the phone guides the theatergoer indoors around a small office, and in the process, they chat. In the original version, conversation was limited because the long-distance connection was fragile and noisy, and both parties were concentrating on finding the way. Here, the logistics were simplified to let people "really talk."[89] *Call Cutta* was limited to two specific cities, but *Call Cutta in a Box* has played all over Europe and beyond (from Auckland to Abu Dhabi). In Paris, two one-hour performances were scheduled at a time with two "operators": one spoke English, the other French.

Journey around a Globalized Office

It was opening day for the new Parisian arts center Cent Quatre. The building that I entered was freshly remodeled, and when I reached the top floor office, I sat on a small white sofa to wait for my call. The waiting room was tastefully decorated: a reddish oriental rug on the floor and a black coat rack contrasted with the white walls and furniture. Facing me was a desk with a computer, a webcam clipped to its screen, a telephone, a potted plant: all the trappings of a receptionist's office. A printer sat on a side table. The wall behind it was decorated with a photo of Descon Limited headquarters in Salt Lake (Kolkata). It lacked only the receptionist.

When the phone rang, it was Madhusree Mukherjee ("please call me Madhu"). At her suggestion, I went over to the window and served myself some apple cinnamon tea by pouring hot water over a teabag: any resemblance to the spiced milk tea boiled for hours I remembered drinking in India was purely fortuitous. Madhu told me to open the top drawer in the desk, where I found a small packet of sweet "pan," a mixture of betel leaf, coconut, and menthol she chews when she is at work. In South Asia, pan, a breath freshener, is offered to guests as a sign of hospitality and as an "ice breaker" to start a conversation.

Later, the printer on a side table produced a picture of a woman standing in front of a stove. This was the family's cook, explained Madhu. When I activated the webcam, I saw my correspondent seated in her cubicle, surrounded by her colleagues at the call center. We continued to chat a bit nervously. At one point, she sang me a Bengali song and abruptly asked me to sing something. I thought of an old Irish ditty that I had learned as a child: "In Dublin's fair city, where girls are so pretty, I first set my

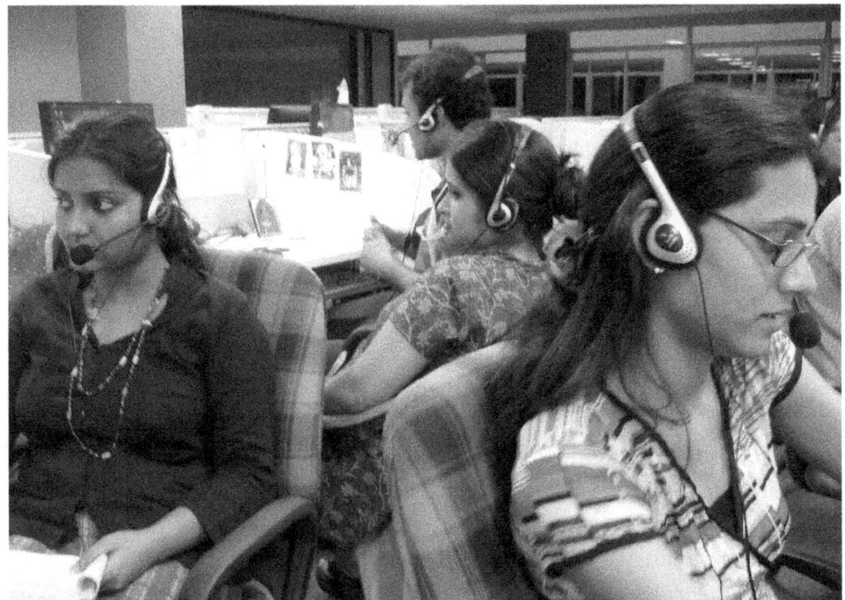

(a)

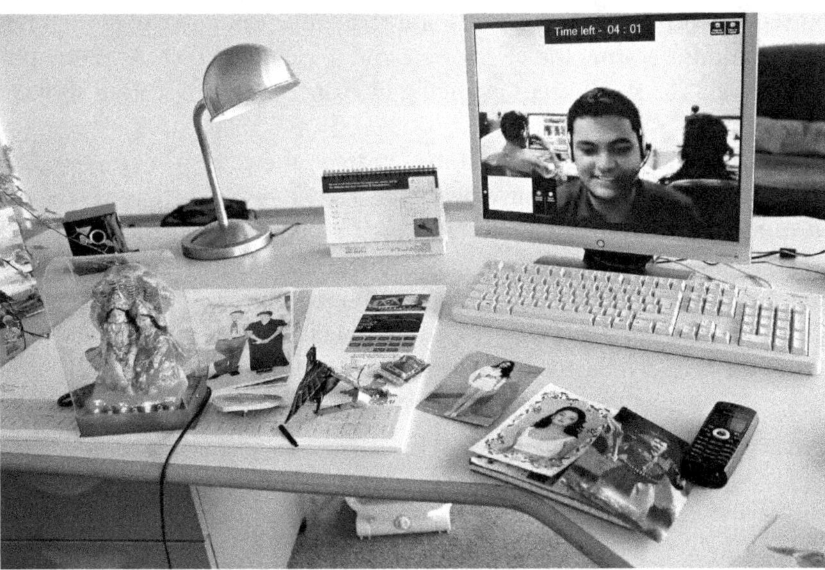

(b)

Figure 4.4
Rimini Protokoll, *Call Cutta in a Box*, 2008. In this play, the voice on the phone guides the theatergoer around a small office, and in the process, the two players chat. Rimini Protokoll, in cooperation with the Hebbel am Ufer, HAU 2, directed by Helgard Haug, Stefan Kaegi, and Daniel Wetzel, simultaneous premiere on April 2, 2008, at the Willy-Brandt-Haus in Berlin, the Schauspielhaus Zurich, and the National Theater in Mannheim. *a:* Operators at the Descon Limited call center in Salt Lake (Kolkata). *b:* Props used in the performances at the Willy-Brandt-Haus in Berlin.

eyes on sweet Molly Malone." The words and melody came back: "She wheeled her wheelbarrow, through streets broad and narrow, crying cockles and mussels, alive, alive-o." My cheeks flush at the memory of my off-key rendition, all the way through to the refrain.

"There are about 20 to 50 percent of scripted materials in each conversation," says Stefan Kaegi. "The amount of this depends on how much you as an audience are more a listener, a singer or a walker."[90] I assumed that my correspondent was a call center operator, but this may not have been true. Because some operators were reluctant to participate in an art project, the collective also hired a few students and actors.[91]

For *Call Cutta in a Box*, the members of Rimini Protokoll developed the script with performers over the phone. They originally planned to develop a more extensive story line, but after experimenting, they realized that the situation they had created—bringing together an Indian performer and a Western European theatergoer for an hour—was rich enough in itself. As Kaegi wrote in 2008, "People wanted to explore this like a game rather than watch it passively like a play. So in the rehearsal process, we quite soon started with tryouts on friends and test audiences, and the more interesting the conversations became, the closer we came to our final text. Actually, this process is not over yet. The script keeps changing in *Call Cutta in a Box* from show to show."[92]

When I asked him if this play could be created elsewhere—in Tunisia, for example, where call centers have developed for French-speaking customers—he replied: "*Call Cutta* is a very Indian project because a lot of the Indian society was built on this idea of service industry and postcolonial strike-backs from your back office. Bengalis are not only great singers over the phone but also very good listeners."[93] Instead of stereotypes (where is Kolkata's fabled poverty?), *Call Cutta* asks viewers to reflect on relations based on power and trust. Who wields the real power here—the customer who has paid for her ticket or the guide, without whom she would be lost?

"Pawns Are the Soul of Chess"

First orchestrated by Sharilyn Neidhardt in New York in 2003, *Human Scale Chess* transformed participants into pawns who were manipulated via cell phone on an eight-block square chessboard. The idea of a life-size chess game played in the streets of a city is not new. The town of Marostica in northern Italy has been staging a human-scale chess game every two years since 1923. The event commemorates a legendary chess game played in 1454 by two young men to win the hand of a noblewoman. In the United States, such games are highly choreographed events staged with costumed actors at commercial Renaissance fairs. Their resemblance to an actual game is only visual.

Neidhardt's games are actually played. She may have been the first to incorporate chess into the locative-media trope of the early twenty-first century.[94] She drew up a plan of her urban chessboard to encompass an area on the Lower East Side of New York. Chess pieces were recruited online and among the artist's friends. Each person who was playing a piece was required to have a mobile phone in working order "to be excruciatingly on time" and ready to spend about three hours awaiting orders. In the middle of the street grid at the ABC No Rio gallery, the main game was played by two expert players on an ordinary chessboard. Each time a piece was moved, its correspondent in the street received a call or a text message—"go to F7"—and on foot, by bike, or on roller skates, depending on the distance, the piece travels to F7. After a piece was captured, the person became an ordinary citizen again.

To date, eight games have been played, beginning in Manhattan in May 2003 and moving to San Francisco, Vancouver, and Austin. Their organization involves two master players, thirty-two pieces (sixteen for each side), volunteers to man the phones and transmit orders to the players in the street, others to track game play on a map by using adhesive notes bearing each piece's name and phone number, and still others to document the process.

As they make each move, experienced chess players try to keep track of the relationship of pieces on the entire board. To win the game, they must see patterns and dynamics of the whole, keeping in mind the ways in which individual moves can maintain or perturb the balance at a higher level. As they play, they project sequences of movements: if I do this, what next move will my opponent be likely to make, and what might be the consequences?

This project focuses on the individual chess pieces. To get the best view, participation at street level is highly recommended. A longtime chess player, Sharilyn Niedhardt has distilled some advice for newbies: center pawns should prepare for early capture, bishops and knights can expect to cover a lot of territory, and kings are likely to have a low-key opening game and an energetic endgame.[95]

The costumed players cycle through as wide a range of emotions as sports fans. After the first game in New York, a black knight called Zach recounted his two hours in the street. Moving from boredom to lust at the sight of an attractive passer-by ("both Bishops express regret that they are men of the cloth"), he experiences a burst of adrenaline ("We appear to be on the attack! I eagerly await my own orders to move") and slumps back into boredom again as the action passes them up (the entry for 1:51 p.m. states simply "Wind picks up. I put on sweater"). Later, a retreating bishop reports setbacks: "he seems depressed and says that things appear to be going badly for us."[96]

The "Humanchess fotolog" used to bear the title "pawns are the soul of chess." When chess pieces are out in the street, they cannot see the whole board. If they are "only a pawn in their game" (or a rook or a knight), it is a game that the pieces can only imagine. Neighboring pieces may be in view, but they can easily disappear into a side street.[97]

Armies are composed of individual human beings who are instruments, yes, but endowed with goals, whatever their rank. Flank pawns have a small degree of social mobility. If one reaches the opposite end of the board, it can be promoted, just as Alice was changed from pawn into queen in *Through the Looking Glass*. Here, the piece's ultimate fate still depends on the moves of the far-away expert players—not quite the American dream. If a piece's destiny is out of its hands, it can at least spend its time on the board or ground as it wishes, whether for ten minutes or three hours—a lifetime of sorts.

Live and Mobile

At one end of the game spectrum, there is *Human Scale Chess*. The individual chess pieces in the streets must be available to receive their orders and carry them out. Although individual motives cannot be completely dispensed with (this is why war brings with it not only disciplined soldiers but resisters, deserters, defectors, profiteers), the glitches come mainly from faulty communications.

During the game, the chess pieces are discouraged from pursuing goals of their own, at least for a few hours. There is little room here for personal expression, unless it invests secondary avenues like costuming, acting ("camping it up," says the artist), or reporting.

At the other end, there is *Call Cutta* and *You Get Me*. Their instructions become a loosely structured script guiding the actor/expert/runner, who in turn shapes the conversation with the audience. Their relationship is built on trust, much like a tutor and a pupil.

Delving into the Black Box

Daniel Wetzel has compared Rimini Protokoll's theater to a black box: you put something in, and something else comes out, but you don't know what happened inside. Rimini develop its plays with experts according to rules defined by both parties, but "it is not important to define the output; we care only about the protocol. . . . In this sense, the black box is a state that makes the theater constellation of audience space and stage productive. . . . These people come with their own texts, after all."[98]

This willingness to let the output or outcome be, to a certain extent, indeterminate is perhaps the most important distinction between shaped and open-ended walks. No hard and fast line separates them. Most artists use a combination of the two. Richard Long says, "In some of the road walks, I'm simply following an idea. In other kinds of works, the walking can reveal the idea."[99] Janet Cardiff develops her audio tours using bottom-up methods but presents them engraved on a CD.[100] Here the walker's experience in the park brings it back into the realm of the open-ended.

All the projects discussed here involved some kind of protocol that was set out in advance, giving the operation its cover and title and gluing together the different parts—the idea and its execution, the author and the participant. The differences can be better appreciated on a continuous scale from entirely preconceived to entirely self-organized (both extremes are theoretical), with each specific work falling somewhere in between. In the next chapters, we break into the black box.

5 When Walking Becomes Mapping: Labyrinths, Songlines

Strasbourg, June 2004. One end of the Syndicat Potentiel gallery space has been transformed into a makeshift stage. The audience is seated on folding chairs. What are they waiting for—the monthly meeting of the local geographic society? The lecturer begins to speak, moving back and forth between blackboard, screen, and podium (figure 5.1). It is not exactly a lecture. Till Roeskens is giving directions: *How to Get to Krimhilde's*—on foot, one step at a time, from the Strasbourg railway station.

Krimhilde's is a snack bar south of Kehl where motorists can scarf down an order of french fries while their car's gas tank is being filled. The name Krimhilde evokes the myth that Richard Wagner adapted for his opera *Das Rheingold*. The story of a medieval heroine who avenges her husband's murder was later retooled by Nazi propagandists. But our motives are never questioned. To get to her place, we must follow the railroad tracks, cross loading zones, and walk across the Rhine River into Germany. On our way, we pass the Gold Washer's Fountain, "where a sign gives details of the extraction of gold from the sand carried by the Rhine and deposited in its meanders . . . until the rectification of the Rhine in 1875, a significant change in the landscape that happened just after what the nearby war memorial calls 'the glorious war of 1870.'"[1]

Till Roeskens moves continually—pacing, gesturing, drawing maps on the blackboard, manipulating slides in the projector, and approaching the screen to point out a detail we might have overlooked. His disjointed pantomime undermines the authoritative directions of the spoken map, amplifying the confusion brought on by an overload of pointless information (how many of us will actually make the trip?). By the end of the performance, we are irremediably lost.

Cognitive Mapping

Mapping is rooted in wayfinding. We begin by making sense of our surroundings so that we can go somewhere. Some of the earliest European maps, like the Peutinger Table, a fourth-century Roman map, take the form of itineraries. Many of these maps were made for pilgrims headed for Jerusalem, Rome, or Santiago de Compostela.[2]

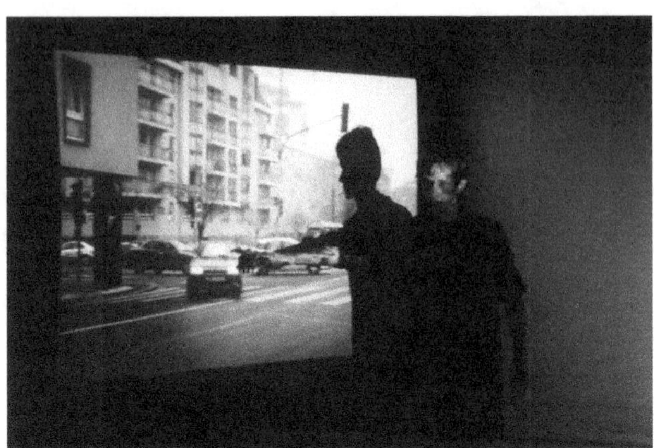
(a)

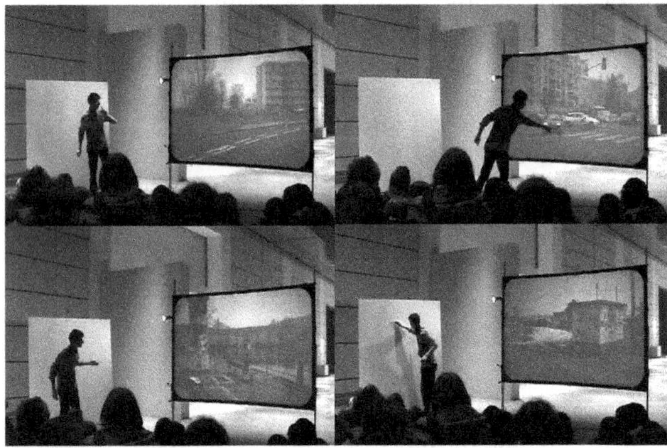
(b)

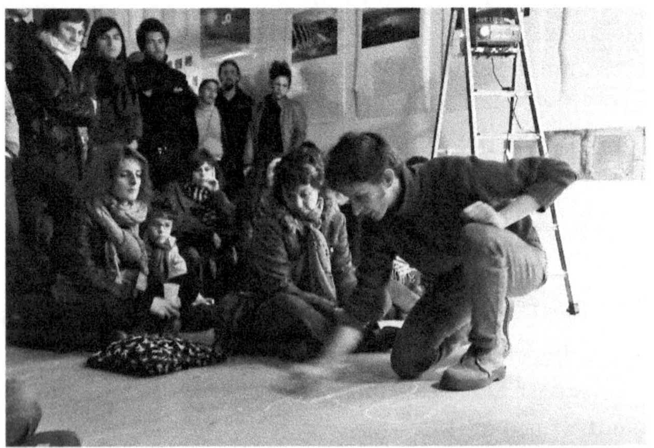
(c)

Figure 5.1
Till Roeskens, *How to Get to Krimhilde's (Comment aller chez Krimhilde)*, 2003. Performance lecture. The speaker is giving directions on how to get to a snack bar south of Kehl in Germany on foot, one step at a time. *a:* At the Syndicat Potentiel, Strasbourg, 2004. *b:* At the Musée d'Art Moderne et Contemporain de Strasbourg, 2006. *c:* At Vol de Nuits, Marseille, 2010.

Kevin Lynch was one of the first to apply the notion of mental map to urban wayfinding. Wayfinding implies "a consistent use and organization of definite sensory cues from the external environment."[3] Lynch stressed the importance of wayfinding skills in everyday experience. The ability to structure and identify one's environment is vital for mobile animals, who use sensory clues, visual sensations (color, shape, movement, light, and shadow), smell, hearing, touch, and kinaesthesia to locate food and shelter. Most of them feel the pull of gravity, electric, or magnetic fields.

In humans, the sense of sight is predominant. We use the environmental image to orient us both in the immediate physical sense but also as a general frame of reference. A highly differentiated landscape can structure activity and order knowledge. The symbolic organization of the landscape reassures people, even (especially) when surroundings are rapidly changing. People who lose the ability to organize their surroundings recognize objects but cannot structure them into any connected system.

Lynch maintained that certain visual qualities of a city contribute to its legibility. The components of our urban environment need to have a recognizable identity and a perceptible structure in which the limits, transitions, and passageways are clearly indicated, and equally important, they must have meaning for the users of the space. In *The Image of the City* (1960), Lynch made recommendations for city planners to help them organize the urban environment in a way that facilitates spatial orientation.

Why, then, do many artists go out of their way to disorient their public? Till Roeskens, for example, states that his goal was "to explain in the clearest and most scrupulously accurate way how to get completely and utterly lost."[4] The profusion of details creates a verbal labyrinth in which listeners become entangled. The challenge for them is to find their way out.

No Playing in the Labyrinth

The Labyrinth of Knossos was a complex structure built by the artisan Daedalus to hold the Minotaur that was designed so cleverly that the builder himself had trouble escaping from it. Today, a labyrinth can denote a confusing series of pathways, a complex branching system that has many paths and directions and is "designed to baffle or deceive those who attempt to find the goal to which it leads," or a structure that has only one through-path or no goal. Some consist of a winding path between two walls or hedges, others have neither walls nor hedges. Any vast and complicated series of rooms and columns is said to be labyrinthine.[5]

In short, a labyrinth is a spatial structure that is apprehended progressively by moving through it. Labyrinths on church floors are meant be experienced on one's knees to replicate the spiritual journey they represent. Both designing a labyrinth and finding one's way through one require mapping skills. For some, it can be a constrained, tomblike trap or an apotropaic sign designed to avert or ward off evil, while others focus on its playful qualities. Hedge mazes have long been a place where lovers dally and children play hide and seek.

The situationists designed labyrinths to further their revolutionary agenda. Aiming to bring down the Cartesian civilization that was responsible for a sign at the Jardin des Plantes (Botanical Gardens) in Paris that said "No Playing in the Labyrinth," Guy Debord proposed a project for an *Educative Labyrinth*.[6] Conceived for the first exhibition of psychogeography in Brussels, it called for a series of identical corridors that were arranged to make it impossible to find one's way. Debord's goal was to confuse the visitor to bring about a change in perspective. This could be accomplished visually by writing slogans on the walls; creating lighting contrasts, ambient sounds, useless numbers, false windows, and conflicting maps; and encouraging certain kinds of behaviors. "Comrade psychogeographers" wandered through the corridors speaking to passers-by, trying to borrow money from them, or giving them sealed letters with upsetting contents, and assigning future rendezvous. Wine and alcohol were available. The only way out brought people through an oddly furnished room where Abdelhafid Khatib and Guy Debord were playing a parlor game they had invented for the occasion—Kriegspiel, the game of war.[7]

Debord finally withdrew from the exhibition, and his labyrinth never materialized. After the foundation of the Situationist International, Constant began conceiving plans for *New Babylon*. The original project was a design made for a permanent gypsy camp in the Piedmontese town of Alba, Italy. Conceived for "an uneven, muddy, desolate terrain," "that project is the origin of the series of maquettes of *New Babylon*. Of a *New Babylon* where, under one roof, with the aid of moveable elements, a shared residence is built; a temporary, constantly remodeled living area; a camp for nomads on a planetary scale."[8]

The architectural structures of this planetary town would be made for and by a society of creative people, whom automation had freed from stultifying routine work. *Homo ludens* (playing man) now had time to wander and get lost, make discoveries, experience new sensations, and meet fellow drifters. Like Günther Feuerstein's proposals for "impractical flats" with tortuous routes, noisy doors, and useless locks,[9] the dynamic labyrinth was designed to reduce the "temporal efficiency and economy" of "utilitarian society" to promote "the disorientation that furthers adventure, play, and creative change": the "labyrinthine form of New Babylonian social space is the direct expression of social independence."[10]

As the number of inhabitants increases, the group takes on complexity while individual control of space decreases:

> The collective use of space entails qualitative change since it tends to reduce passivity. The activity of the occupants of a space is an integral part of the ambiance. . . . In a social space where the number of individuals is ceaselessly changing, along with the relations between them, each

and every person is prompted to change his personal ambiance. . . . One arrives, then, at the image of an immense social space that is forever other: a dynamic labyrinth in the widest sense of the term.[11]

At the same time, other artists built immersive spaces through which the visitor walks, like *Dylaby* (Dynamic Labyrinth), made for an exhibition at the Stedelijk Museum in Amsterdam in 1962.[12] *Dylaby* offered a succession of interactive environments, from Niki de Saint Phalle's "shooting galleries" (where visitors could aim at "bags full of paint that hang above white sculptures suggesting phantasmagorical animals, dinosaur skeletons, and plaster heads") to Jean Tinguely's colored balloons blown about by fans.[13] Daniel Spoerri created two room-sized environments: in the first, viewers made their way in the dark by touching "surfaces of various textures, sometimes warm, or wet, assailed by diverse sounds and smells," and in the second, paintings and sculptures were presented at a 90 degree angle so that visitors felt as if they were walking on the wall. The artists conceived their works as experiences rather than collectible objects: when the show ended, most of them were discarded.[14]

Corridors: Itineraries of Oppression

Not all makers of labyrinths adhere to Constant's vision of *Homo ludens* drifting through the city. In 1961, Robert Morris created an oppressive environment called *Passageway* in Yoko Ono's Chambers Street loft in Manhattan. Morris built a curved, fifty-foot cul-de-sac out of plywood that seemed to squeeze visitors as they advanced through the narrowing corridor and in the end were trapped in a claustrophobic vise.[15] Morris said he wanted to create a self-sufficient space, "a kind of tomb," as he put it, "a totalizing, enclosing space within which I exist with the object. . . . Others who visit *Passageway* leave messages written on the walls such as 'Fuck you too.' I repaint the gray walls once a week."[16]

For him at the time, art was "a closed space, a refusal of communication, a secure refuge and defense against the outside world, a dead zone and buffer against others who would intrude."[17] Later, after reading Michel Foucault's *Discipline and Punish* in the late 1970s, he invoked the oppression of the body by normative forces.[18]

The forces in Ilya and Emilia Kabakov's *Labyrinth (My Mother's Album)* (1990) are those of a totalitarian society. For this installation, the Kabakovs created a narrow corridor that the visitor enters and follows to the end. Dimly lit, spiral-shaped, it was meant to evoke the corridor of a community apartment from the Soviet era, with its dangling light bulbs and cracks in the walls (figure 5.2). As visitors move along it, they encounter a series of doors—some boarded up, others half open.

Like Morris's *Passageway*, this installation proceeds from the artist's personal memories: "Numerous corridors have persecuted me all my life," wrote Ilya Kabakov, "straight ones, long ones, short ones, narrow ones, twisted ones, but in my imagination, they

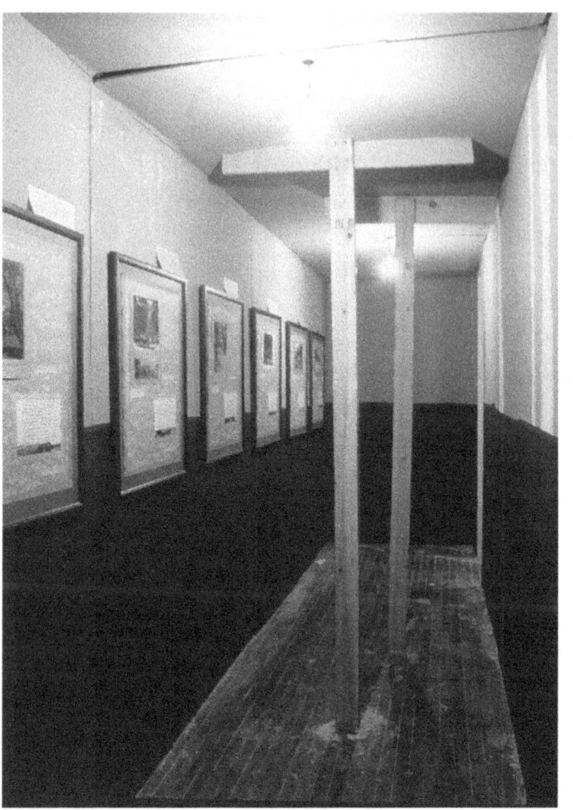

(a)

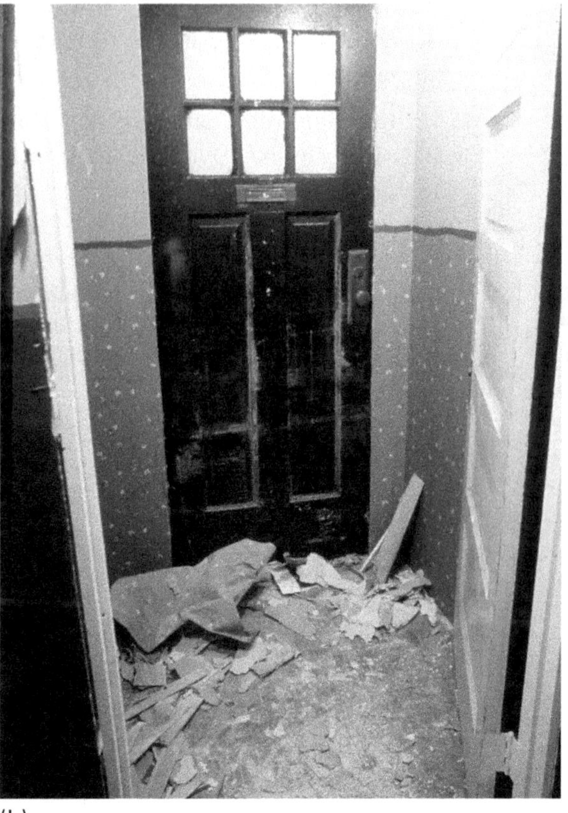

(b)

Figure 5.2

Ilya and Emilia Kabakov, *Labyrinth (My Mother's Album)*, 1990. Installation views, Ronald Feldman Fine Arts, New York. Photography: D. James Dee © Ilya and Emilia Kabakov. Courtesy: Sean Kelly Gallery, New York. *a:* Dimly lit, spiral-shaped, the corridor was meant to evoke that of a community apartment from the Soviet era. *b:* At the heart of the labyrinth is a tiny room cluttered with debris.

are all poorly lit and always without windows, with closed or semi-closed doors along both sides. . . . All the corridors of my life, from earliest childhood on, have been connected with [the] torture of endless anticipation."[19]

On shoddy gray and reddish brown walls, seventy-five framed panels assemble photos, typewritten texts, and postcards that show fragments of city views. At the heart of the labyrinth is a one-meter-square room cluttered with debris. Visitors can hear a voice humming softly off-key, a melancholy song that grows louder at the center and then fades away when they move on. At the top of each panel are color photos from the 1950s, the period of triumphant socialism, that show the construction of the country of beauty and justice.[20] The text in Russian, purportedly written by Kabakov's mother, aligns events from an ordinary life in a provincial town, evoking Chekov and Gogol. Although the account is laced with irony (witness the letter addressed to Comrade Leonid Breznev requesting help in obtaining a more comfortable apartment),[21] the discrepancy between two world views, alternating despair and hope, however fragile, lends the itinerary the power of archetype. The labyrinth follows the path of life as a purgatory of sorts.

Lost in the Funhouse: Mirror and Media Mazes

Other labyrinths tantalize visitors with false paths, hallucinations, and mirages, luring them to move through the looking glass. An early work of this type was a collective *Labyrinth of Light* made by the Groupe de Recherche d'Art Visuel (GRAV) for the Eindhoven exhibition *Kunst-Licht-Kunst* in 1966. After building several didactic labyrinths in 1962 and 1963, the artists[22] aimed to create "a varied and abundant succession of situations to provoke the viewer's perceptual saturation, and enable him to feel the totality of the experience."[23] The components of the labyrinth were meant to accumulate as viewers progressed through the maze, gradually overwhelming them and "producing a shock, an enchantment, a surprise, a reaction" that would eventually spur them to revolutionary action. Here, as with the situationists, art was conceived as therapeutic shock that was predicated on revolutionary ideas of abolishing the individual artwork and fostering collective creation. GRAV members saw this work as a fusion of art and life, with the viewer at the center; art critics at the time saw only the hallucinatory effects of an amusement park attraction.

Bruce Nauman's *Corridors* are often claustrophobic spaces that offer an experience of disorientation. The first one appeared in a 1968 video, *Walk with Contrapposto*, where it restricted Nauman's movement as he walked. The next year, it was exhibited on its own so visitors could experience it firsthand. In works such as *Performance Corridor* (1969), viewers walk through a narrow space mediated by closed-circuit television. In *Live Taped Video Corridor* (1969–1970), viewers see themselves walking down a corridor, filmed from behind. As they move toward the screen, they watch themselves walk away: the closer they get, the farther away they appear on the monitor. This nightmarish effect is compounded when the installation combines time-delay imagery as in *Going around the Corner Piece* (1970), where four monitors are connected to four video cameras and confront viewers with a time-delay view of themselves that was filmed a few seconds earlier from behind. *Stairway*, a recent work built for a collector in northern California, clarifies viewers' paths but requires them to take their time climbing the three hundred steps. The experience of walking on it is, says Nauman, "a lot of work."[24] That "work" is recreational, recalling Constant's labyrinthine city (which was impossible to cross quickly) and also experiments like *City System* (described in chapter 4). The effort required here induces a trancelike state in which learning and change are most likely to occur.

Inspired by Nauman's experiments and music by Terry Riley and Steve Reich, Dan Graham began using feedback loops to develop the idea of an extended present time. An early work, the time-delay video installation *Present Continuous Past(s)* (1978), uses mirrors to reflect an infinite number of "present-times." The camera registers everything in front of it, including both viewers and their reflections on the mirrored wall opposite. A tape delay causes the images recorded by the camera to appear eight seconds later in the video monitor connected to a second, playback machine. When viewers look at the monitor, they see images of themselves from eight seconds earlier and reflections on the mirror from the monitor eight seconds prior to that, creating both a *mise en abyme* and a recursive sequence of delays, an infinite series of images nested within images like Russian dolls, each separated from the one containing it by an interval of eight seconds. In contrast to the bodily experience of the viewer within the room, another mirror placed above at a 90 degree angle, shows the whole process from the viewpoint of an outside observer.[25]

Graham had read James Gibson, who claims that we "discover things visually by moving our body in a particular location." In Renaissance perspective, a scene is viewed from one fixed vantage point, but kinaesthetic perception implies apprehending different aspects of our environment sequentially as we walk along. The visual experience "happens in an extended time period as we move around in space. There is a feedback between the part of body that we see, which is part of the body below the eye, not just the eye, and the actual environment that we are in."[26]

Graham's ongoing investigations into the way architectural spaces affect human behavior led him to design hedge labyrinths using mirrors. In the *Two-Way Mirror Hedge Labyrinth* (1989–1993), which was built for a collector's home in San Diego, he combined the hedges of Baroque garden labyrinths with the mirrored glass of corporate buildings. His labyrinths for gardens in Minneapolis and Nantes and rooftops in New York and San Francisco have combined the two-way mirrors that characterize much corporate architecture since the 1970s and the living hedges[27] that evoke the seventeenth-century garden mazes of Chantilly and Versailles. Both are representations of power. The shaped French garden hedges that require daily trimming are emblematic of aristocratic hegemony: their rigorous symmetry demonstrates the order that humans impose on nature. In suburban America, hedges separate public and private spaces. Corporations favor two-way mirror glass for its apparent transparency: it is reflective from the exterior (like a pond, it reflects the sky, which helps the company project an "ecologically correct" image) and transparent inside (so that the executives within can observe what is going on outside without being seen).

Graham plays with this implicit order by making walls that are both transparent and reflective to varying degrees. His outdoor works are meant to be walked through and around, so their walls are seen both from the inside and the outside. In them, we can observe the surrounding environment: the mirrored surfaces reflect the changing sky. The clouds and sun alternate as they interact with our own reflections in an extended present time such as that experienced when we see ourselves in a feedback loop. He is interested in how viewers perceive themselves in the different mirrors, evoking the mirror stage that takes place when the young child becomes aware that his reflection is an emanation of himself and not another child. These structures combine seduction and hallucination: in one work, Graham uses both convex and concave mirrors so that a child on one side sees himself as bigger than life, while an older woman on the other sees a slimmer form of herself.

Here the labyrinth triggers not so much a path as a state of contemplation. Every turn proposes a new view of one's relation to the surroundings. Graham has likened it to the experience of taking drugs, situating his work "in that area of the cinematic, hallucinatory, kaleidoscopic which virtual reality will now fill—a cinema/amusement park sensibility."[28] It has its roots in the halls of mirrors that filmmakers have used to evoke the elusive nature of appearances, allowing Charlie Chaplin to escape from his pursuers in *The Circus* (1929). In *The Lady from Shanghai* (Orson Welles, 1947), the optical illusions in the magic mirror maze emphasize the main character's deceitfulness.

Confirming Dan Graham's intuition, this sensibility has played an important role in works of virtual reality and telepresence. *Labylogue* (2000) by Maurice Benayoun, Jean-Pierre Balpe, and Jean-Baptiste Barrière was a "conversation space" in which the visitors navigated among the words. In three French-speaking cities—Brussels, Lyons, and Dakar—that were linked via Internet, visitors equipped with a joystick and a microphone wandered through a virtual labyrinth looking for each other (figure 5.3). Although they were unable to see one another, they could start conversations. The computer interpreted what they said using speech recognition software and, on a bluish background ("the memory of the exchanges"), projected its own interpretation of the dialogs that it captured. This procedure invites distortions and misunderstandings, shaking up the stereotypes of what are often purely phatic exchanges. The interpretations were generated automatically to ensure that each visitor's itinerary was unique.[29] Although two visitors in different places could see their images on screen

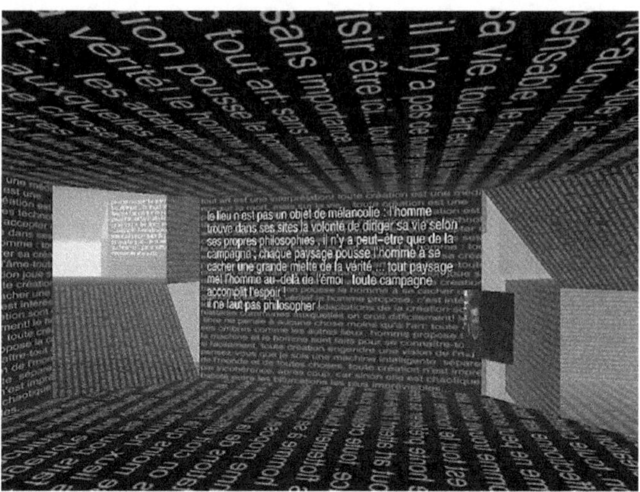

Figure 5.3
Maurice Benayoun, Jean-Pierre Balpe, and Jean-Baptiste Barrière, *Labylogue,* 2000. Interactive installation, a "conversation space" for visitors navigating among the words. In three French-speaking cities—Brussels, Lyons, and Dakar—that are linked via Internet, visitors equipped with a joystick and a microphone wandered through a virtual labyrinth looking for each other.

when they were in the same part of the labyrinth, the ongoing interference between sound and text gave the labyrinth its particular polyphony by allowing words to become sounds again and move beyond the conscious intentions of their speakers.

Following the labyrinths of GRAV, virtual-reality installations such as this have often been attacked by art critics as pandering to the public's desire for sensation, when in fact they have rendered this desire problematic. This is evident in Maurice Benayoun's immersive *World Skin* (1998) installation, in which viewers become camera-toting tourists walking through the land of war. Every time that they press the shutter release, they literally take a photo. As each succeeding visitor removes one or more images from the surrounding warscape, printing them out and taking them away, the environment is gradually whited out, like the media landscape during the first Gulf War, even as television news channels were ostensibly offering around-the-clock live coverage.

Labyrinths and Maps

The labyrinth is an archetypal theme that artists have used to different ends. It can be a device to entrap unwitting viewers, clasping them in a deathlike vise. Some works evoke the mazes leading to the burial chambers in the Egyptian pyramids, which were meant to confuse and ensnare potential tomb robbers. Today, customers are ensnared when the principle is transferred to the design of stores that optimize browsing and transform it into buying. Updating the grand tradition of nineteenth-century department stores described by Emile Zola in the novel *Au bonheur des dames*, the furniture manufacturer IKEA has hired "crowd physicists and spatial hackers" to model "a switching IKEA labyrinth" that "can snare cool hunters into a continuous delirium of consumption, only releasing them when bankruptcy is just one shelving unit purchase away."[30]

For others, like Constant, the labyrinth is closer to the game end of the spectrum. Like the *jeu de l'oie* (Snakes and Ladders), the game echoes life itself with its ups and downs. When Yoko Ono created *Amaze* (1971), a labyrinth with plexiglass walls, she aimed to build "a house whose walls would become visible only because of the particular prismatic effect of sunset."[31] A photographer asked the artist to pose in her "dematerialized" maze; she walked to the center but got lost trying to return by the same path. She said, "In life you think you can do whatever you please, because the obstacles are invisible. Eventually you always stumble into something and realize that the direction was forbidden or not possible."[32] Her maze plays with visitors' expectations. When they enter, they wonder what is at its heart—forbidden treasure, the holy grail, the philosopher's stone? When they finally arrive there, they find only a toilet.

The labyrinth is a figure of initiation: unlike the straight line, it is never the shortest path. Adolescents go through it only once and undergo a complete change. When they emerge, they have become their adult selves. Life is a journey between the starting point and the exit, the point of no return, the central point or the place of the ultimate trial. The labyrinth can also represent the joining of the spiral (a symbol of infinity and destiny) and the braid (a symbol of the eternal return).[33]

The labyrinth is a way for contemporary artists to reactivate these traditions. An archetypal figure, the labyrinth reappears every time we make a decision for which we have trouble predicting the consequences. Whether it is to obtain the reward at the center or to find our way out, navigating a labyrinth encourages us to create a mental map. Sometimes, as in Yoko Ono's *Amaze*, we learn to mistrust our senses. When we see the end in sight, we may be in reality farthest from our goal. Inversely, when we turn our backs on the goal, we may be closer than we realize.

Ultimately, we adapt, using these experiences of confusion to make sense of our surroundings and find our way in or out. Kevin Lynch evokes the experiments of Brown and Warner's "spatial integration in a Human Maze."[34] A maze through which subjects were asked to move blindfolded seemed to them at first to be one unbroken problem. On repetition, part of the pattern, especially at the beginning and end, became familiar and assumed the character of localities. Finally, when they could tread the maze without error, the whole system seemed to have become one locality.

Wayfinding as Learning as Remembering

Sigmund Freud conceived his *Interpretation of Dreams* (1899) as "an imaginary walk [*Spaziergansphantasie*]. At the beginning, the dark forest of authors (who do not see the trees), hopelessly lost on wrong tracks. Then a concealed pass through which I lead the reader my specimen dream with its peculiarities, details, indiscretions, bad jokes and then suddenly the high ground and the view and the question: which way do you wish to go now?"[35] Like Freud's imaginary walk, a mental map is a symbolic diagram of how the components of a perceived intellectual environment fit together.

Orators in antiquity used the spatial organization of places and objects to memorize long speeches. The main treatises on the arts of memory[36] recommended that an orator build in his mind a spacious and diversified edifice with an antechamber, living room, bedrooms, and salons where he can place figures and "active images" (to stimulate the memory, these *imagines agentes* needed to be striking—obscene, odd, grotesque, and so on) capable of evoking the arguments he wants to remember. As he delivers his speech, in his mind's eye he walks through the different rooms to pick up the images he left there.[37]

Cognitive mapping refers to the process of structuring and storing spatial information. We visualize our physical environment in terms of shapes and relationships, thus reducing cognitive load and enhancing learning.[38] This expression has also been defined as "an internal awareness of a familiar environment" that is used by humans and animals for orientation.[39] In mammals, this process takes place in the hypothalamus area of the brain.

Cognitive maps are embodied maps. As Maurice Merleau-Ponty asked, "Is not to see to see from somewhere?"[40] We map our environment as we move through it, aiming to reach our goal while avoiding, as Georges Perec noted facetiously, bumping into things. "In dance," writes dancer Mélodie Gonzales, "we work from mental scores or maps. I know the entire dance: spatially, dynamically, musically, physically, and even emotionally sometimes. The dance exists somewhere in my memory (mental and physical). The movement pathways within the body are also mapped, in detail actually! But notation can't record all of this information. It records only general information about the dance like spacing, dynamic, shapes of the body, and body parts. But the map within the body is created and recorded only by the dancer himself as he learns or creates the dance."[41]

The expression *cognitive map* was first used by Edward C. Tolman in his 1948 article "Cognitive Maps in Rats and Men." He postulated that "in the course of learning, something like a field map of the environment gets established in the rat's brain. . . . Although we admit that the rat is bombarded by stimuli, we hold that his nervous system is surprisingly selective as to which of these stimuli it will let in at any given time." He compared the rat's brain to a map control room: "The stimuli, which are allowed in, are not connected by just simple one-to-one switches to the outgoing responses. Rather, the incoming impulses are usually worked over and elaborated in the central control room into a tentative, cognitive-like map of the environment. And it is this tentative map, indicating routes and paths and environmental relationships, which finally determines what responses, if any, the animal will finally release."[42] The notion has been much debated in recent years, and the image of the central control room has been called into question.

Kevin Lynch spent five years interviewing people in Los Angeles, Boston, and Jersey City. Proceeding empirically, he asked his respondents to draw maps showing the way from one place in the city to another. Examining these representations, he could better understand how people perceive and find their way in urban space. From these interviews, he distilled five elements that compose their mental maps. Since "people observe the city by moving through it," potential paths are a key feature: "streets, walkways, transit lines, canals, railroads."[43] Unlike paths, edges ("linear elements not used as paths") are perceived boundaries between two places, such as walls, buildings and shorelines. As we zoom out, we become aware of districts—shopping areas, residential zones and historical city centers. Important focal points (such as busy intersections where several path lines meet) clarify things, as do prominent landmarks, which are easily identifiable objects that serve as reference points.[44]

Mapping Edges and Boundaries

Kevin Lynch saw boundaries and edges as important components of people's mental maps. "Edges," he wrote, ". . are usually, but not quite always, the boundaries between two kinds of areas. They act as lateral references."[45] Lynch was concerned with the built environment. Mental maps can also register ephemeral boundaries traced by people who occupy a certain space momentarily.

The term *territoriality* designates the ways that humans communicate ownership, however temporary, of particular spaces. For example, individuals sitting in public places often place objects to mark the limits of the area surrounding them that they regard as theirs. Others reclaim space by speaking loudly or wearing particular clothing, insignia, or perfumes. Invasion of personal space can cause the victim to feel discomfort, anger, or anxiety.

The anthropological concept of territoriality is rooted in the observation of similar animal behaviors. In ethology, the term *territory* refers to an area that an animal consistently defends against members of its own species (and sometimes other species). Zoologist Heini Hediger described a number of standard interaction distances that are visible in animal behavior. Flight distance (the distance at which an animal will run away) and critical distance (when it will attack) come into play when animals of different species meet, whereas personal distance and social distance are observed during

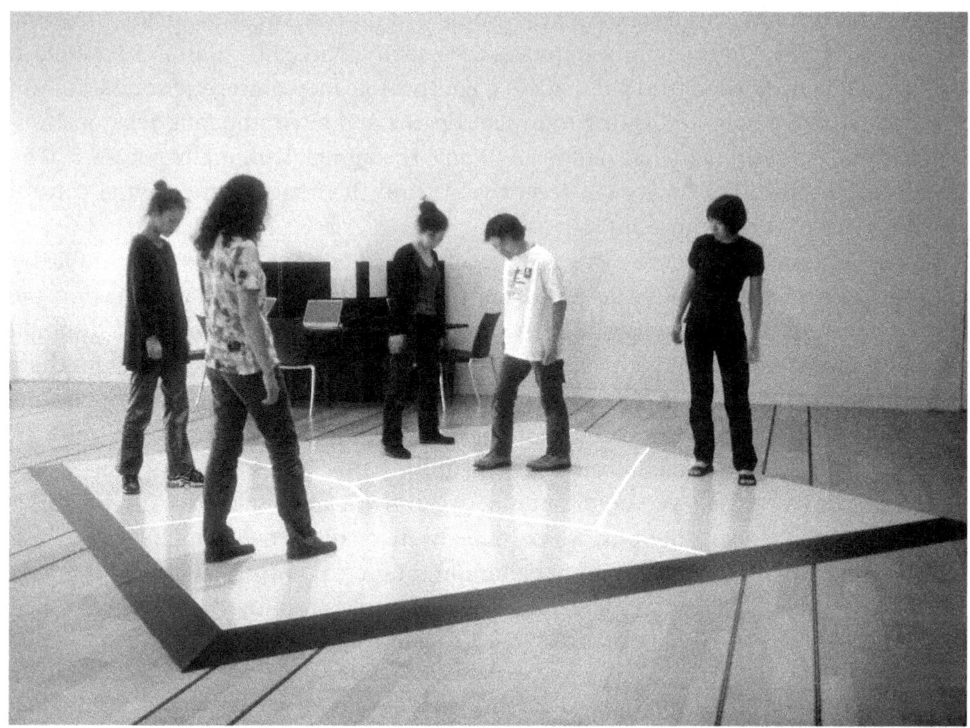

Figure 5.4
Scott Snibbe, *Boundary Functions,* 1998. Installation view. Credit: Photo courtesy Tokyo Intercommunications Center, 1998.

interactions between members of the same species. Adapting Hediger's findings to the study of humans, anthropologist Edward T. Hall studied the physical distances that people unconsciously maintain from each other and found that they obey unspoken cultural rules.

Scott Snibbe's installation *Boundary Functions* (1998) makes these boundaries between people visible (figure 5.4). It projects a set of lines onto the gallery floor that separate visitors from each other. If there are at least two people present, a single line cuts between them, dynamically changing as one or both of them move, always bisecting the space. With more than two visitors, the floor divides into cells: everything within each cell is closer to the person inside than to anyone else.

Snibbe's software calculates the areas surrounding each person according to Voronoi diagrams. Used in many fields, from biology to marketing, these diagrams describe patterns of human settlement, animal dominance, and plant competition: "The diagrams represent as strong a connection between mathematics and nature as the constants *e* or *pi*. By projecting the diagram, the invisible relationships between individuals and the space between them become visible and dynamic. . . . here is a virtual space that can only exist with more than one person, and in physical space."[46]

Snibbe's title comes from Theodore Kaczynski's 1967 Ph.D. thesis in mathematics. Kaczynski, the Unabomber, built a cabin in the mountains of Montana where he lived as a hermit. When developers started building roads and cutting down trees in *his* wilderness, he felt driven to defend it by mailing bombs to the institutions he thought responsible. Snibbe sees Kaczynski as "a pathological example of the conflict between the individual and society. . . . The thesis itself is an example of the implicit antisocial quality of some scientific discourse, mired in language and symbols that are impenetrable to the vast majority of society." His own installation uses dynamic visual representation to make a mathematical abstraction "instantly knowable."[47]

In everyday situations, boundaries become visible when they are violated. Our perception of otherwise invisible limits is highlighted in the *Invisible Labyrinth* (figure 5.5), created by Jeppe Hein for the Pompidou Center in September 2005 and later shown in other venues. Spotlights line the ceiling on either side of the Espace 315. Their beams are directed at the white walls of the boxlike exhibition space. About twenty people are walking on the freshly waxed hardwood floor. As more and more visitors arrive, they begin forming conversation clusters. A well-known creator of happenings is talking with a young woman, and both are wearing headphones. His looks like a pair of sunglasses perched on a helmet of thick white hair. Other headset-clad viewers move cautiously, stop abruptly, change direction, veer to one side, and back up again as they navigate. Do they see something that we don't?

If participants put on a pair of headphones and walk around, it takes a few minutes to understand that the headphones vibrate to indicate the presence of "walls." Viewers keep moving and let themselves be guided by relying not on eyes but on the whole body. Thanks to proprioceptive feedback, the action of walking segues into mapping, and participants begin to recognize sections of the invisible labyrinth, gliding up and down its passages with a newfound freedom built on constraint. At this point, participants can even warn fellow pedestrians of imminent barriers and dead ends.

When Hein was invited to conceive a work for the Pompidou Center, he toyed with the idea of using water, smoke, or flames, but those materials would have violated the building's safety regulations, so he decided to exhibit nothing. The acoustic structure of this nothing is modified regularly, so that returning visitors must rediscover it, play the game again, and find the way through the labyrinth. Unlike *New Babylon*, however, here the artist, not the player, changes the layout.

In March 2009, *Invisible Labyrinth* was reactivated in the hall of the Théâtre National de Chaillot. This time it included seven contemporary artworks chosen by the artist.[48] The labyrinth here becomes a stage set. Like some of the walking protocols examined in the previous chapter, the actual experience depends on the viewer. A few people

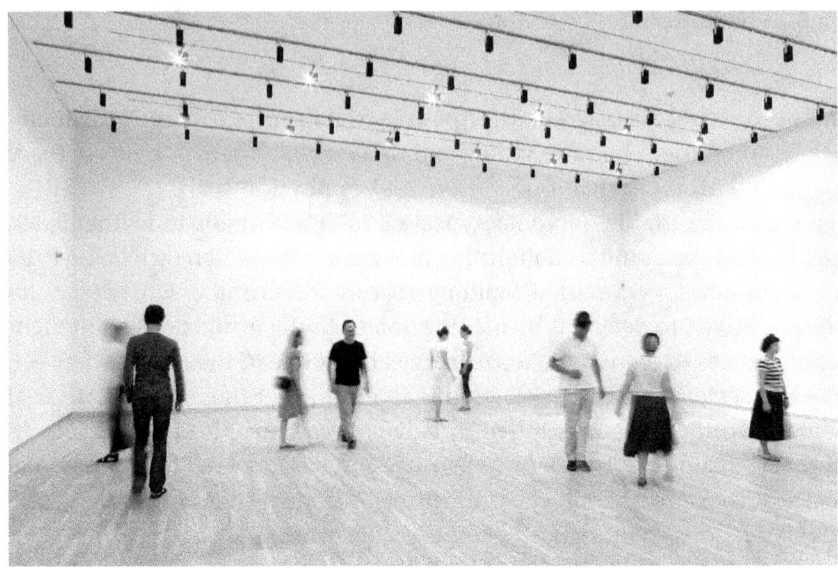

(a)

(b)

Figure 5.5

Jeppe Hein, *Invisible Labyrinth,* 2005. Headsets, infrared lights, infrared sensors, format variable, edition of 3 + 2 AP. In everyday situations, boundaries become visible when they are violated. Participants' perception of otherwise invisible limits is highlighted in this installation. Photos: Anders Sune Berg. Exhibition: *Invisible Maze,* Statens Museum for Kunst, Copenhagen, Denmark, 2006. Courtesy of the artist and Johann König, Berlin. *a:* View of the exhibition. *b:* The headphones vibrate to indicate the presence of "walls."

were walking through the exhibition space without headphones, either though ignorance or because they refused Hein's terms. But ignoring the constraints was like wearing ear plugs at the movies.

For those who chose to negotiate the labyrinth, the addition of visual elements made them feel more acutely the restraining influence of the "walls." Visitors were not allowed to move freely around the artworks to see them from different angles as they usually do. They had to follow an itinerary set out for them. This was clear in front of Florence Dorléac's liquified flower pot on the floor. Because the piece was fragile, a staff member was on hand nearby to prevent visitors from stumbling over it. Here the emphasis on the labyrinth played down the importance of the visible. Barnett Newman once facetiously described sculpture as something you bump into when you back up to look at a painting. Here the art objects were mere props. Hein chose their images from digital files for their form and color or their playful humor (for example, Bruno Peinado's motorcycle equipped with bicycle pedals).

The viewer modifies this work simply by moving through it. This was obvious to the visitors who took pictures of each other as they negotiated the unseen barriers. In this sense, Hein has accomplished his goal to create "an incongruous dialogue between the art and the viewer and to use humor to broaden the limits of conceptual art" and "to show that the work isn't anything on its own, it is only what the public informs it with."[49]

In his seminal article "Notes on Sculpture," Robert Morris claimed that "The object is but one of the terms in the newer aesthetic . . . because one's awareness of oneself existing in the same space as the work is stronger than in previous work. . . . One is more aware than before that he himself is establishing relationships as he apprehends the object from various positions."[50] This is true when the viewer experiences Morris's own labyrinths. *Untitled Labyrinth* (1974), for example, was based on the spiral design of the labyrinth in Chartres cathedral, which the faithful can follow on their knees as they retrace the pilgrimage to Jerusalem. Jeppe Hein's *Invisible Labyrinth* reiterates but alters the Chartres design. Like the members of GRAV, he sees the "labyrinth as a place of experience [that] is deliberately directed toward eliminating the distance between the viewer and the work."[51] Like Constant's labyrinthine *New Babylon*, it can also create contact zones—social spaces where people literally bump into each other.

Tracking and Pathfinding

Kevin Lynch also stressed the importance of potential paths in defining our image of the city. Moving outward from our immediate surroundings to places unknown to us, we depend on external clues to guide us.

Researchers recently tested the ability of humans to walk on a straight course through unfamiliar terrain in two different environments—a large forest area and the Sahara desert. By capturing their walking trajectories via GPS, they found "that participants repeatedly walked in circles when they could not see the sun. Conversely, when the sun was visible, participants sometimes veered from a straight course but did not walk in circles." People were also unable to maintain a fixed course while blindfolded; instead, they walked in circles, although rarely in a systematic direction: "These results . . . suggest that veering from a straight course is the result of accumulating noise in the sensorimotor system, which, without an external directional reference to recalibrate the subjective straight ahead, may cause people to walk in circles."[52]

To find their way, Aboriginal Australian peoples have long used environmental clues that are nearly imperceptible to others.[53] To survive in the outback, they need to move quickly and efficiently, so mapping has been a matter of life or death. Kevin Lynch cites the example the Luritja of central Australia, who were driven from their territory by four years of drought and yet survived thanks to the precise topographic memory of their elders. From experience gained years before and the instructions of their grandfathers, they were able to find the chain of tiny water holes that led them out of the desert to safety.[54]

For Australian Aborigines, territory is not a piece of land enclosed within borders but "an interlocking network of 'lines' or 'ways through.'"[55] Each clan is responsible for its own totemic ancestor's "footprints" (one part of the songlines), but through exchange, negotiation, singing, and storytelling, the paths of the different families are linked. A knowledgeable person finds his way by singing the song that identifies waterholes and landmarks.[56]

When they describe a place, they evoke both its mythical and physical attributes. In a bark painting made in 1974 by Luritja artist Big Peter Tjupurrula, the image that shows the Muranji escarpment and Dreaming is both story and map.[57] The map depends on the story to make sense. It shows the relative location of the places described in the myth where an old woman pursues a small boy. Instead of a series of places being used to remember a story, the story leads the listener through the landscape.[58]

There is a direct correlation between storytelling, verbal evocation, tracking, and wayfinding.[59] David Lewis notes that when the people that he traveled with were in less familiar country, they used a variety of guidelines: "Animated discussion of every conceivable aspect of places visited or known by repute makes up a good part of camp and wayside conversation. This is an important factor in extending a person's range—and it solves the water problem."[60]

Even today, Aborigines' acute sense of direction is legendary. Curator Arnaud Morvan tells how Warlpiri artists Steven Jampijinpa and Lance Sullivan determined landmarks to guide their wayfinding in Lyons, France, a town that is located at the confluence of two rivers. In French, le Rhône river is masculine, and la Saône is feminine. Using clues like this to deal with unfamiliar surroundings, the Australian guests were able to guide their hosts.

Many explanations have been proposed for Aborigines' unerring sense of direction. One applies to speakers of geographical languages like Guugu Yimithirr, an aboriginal tongue from north Queensland. Instead of using egocentric coordinates (such as left, right, or behind) to describe position, speakers of Guugu Yimithirr use only cardinal directions. To speak a geographic language, "you need to know where the cardinal directions are at each and every moment of your waking life. You need to have a compass in your mind that operates all the time, day and night, . . . since otherwise you would not be able to impart the most basic information or understand what people around you are saying. Indeed, speakers of geographic languages seem to have an almost-superhuman sense of orientation. Regardless of visibility conditions, regardless of whether they are in thick forest or on an open plain, whether outside or indoors or even in caves, whether stationary or moving, they have a spot-on sense of direction."[61]

Although Kevin Lynch emphasized the visual components involved in wayfinding, aural signals play an important role, too. In Warlpiri, another Australian language, notes Barbara Glowczewski, the word for *talking* (*wangka*) is also used for *birds*, *thunder*, and any number of natural phenomena expressed by sound: "from the Warlpiri perspective, everything speaks because its sounds can be interpreted by those who know how to 'track' them."[62] Rhythm too plays an important role. The same journey can be made in one day or three, depending on the number of waterholes that can be found on the way. Desert dwellers must move faster in the dry season.

The concept of tracking provides a clue to the flexibility of the Aboriginal system. For the compact disk that Glowczewski made with the Warlpiri, she chose the title *Dream Trackers* (figure 5.6) "because tracking is really the core of most Aboriginal philosophy. A place marked by a track . . . is an access to the whole, a key to investigate past, present and future actions. A track is like the imprint for a prototype, from that track you can reconstitute the performance."[63]

She stresses the "essential dynamism in Aboriginal culture" where the track is "the trace left by something that is moving, dancing, or walking." Glowczewski designed *Dream Trackers* as "a multimedia tool linking images of rituals and landscape, photos of acrylic paintings, sound recordings of myths and songs." It is based on a "mind map" that shows "how elements of knowledge connect with each other in the learning process of the Warlpiri themselves."[64] To enable users to understand this process, Glowczewski chose a small sample of fifty places and fourteen dreaming tracks that can be visualized interactively. Users are invited to link different kinds of data the way the Warlpiri do: each image, dance, and song is related to a specific place (a sacred site), a story line (myth), and a geographical trail that connects sites and story elements. Hyperlinks appear as users navigate, and they suggest ways to criss-cross story lines and layers of meaning in appropriate ways.

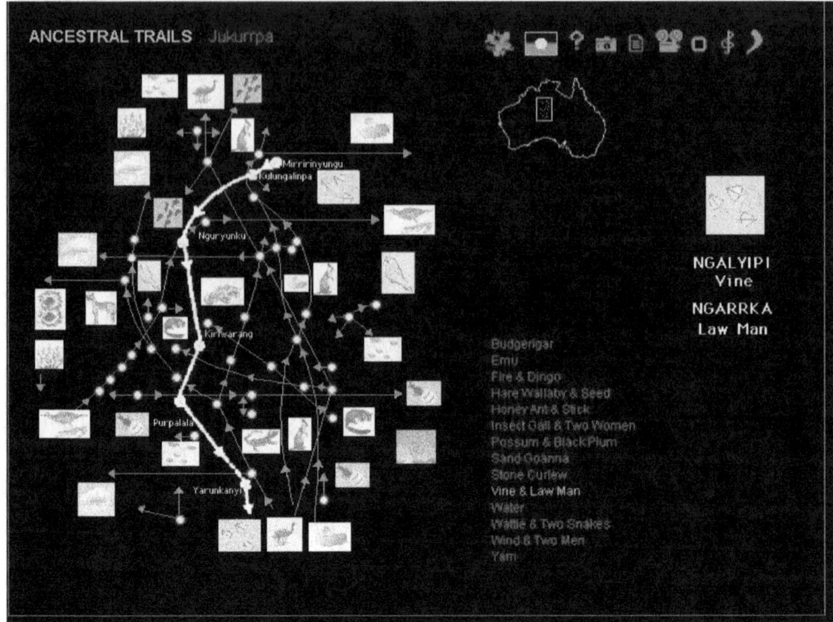

(a)

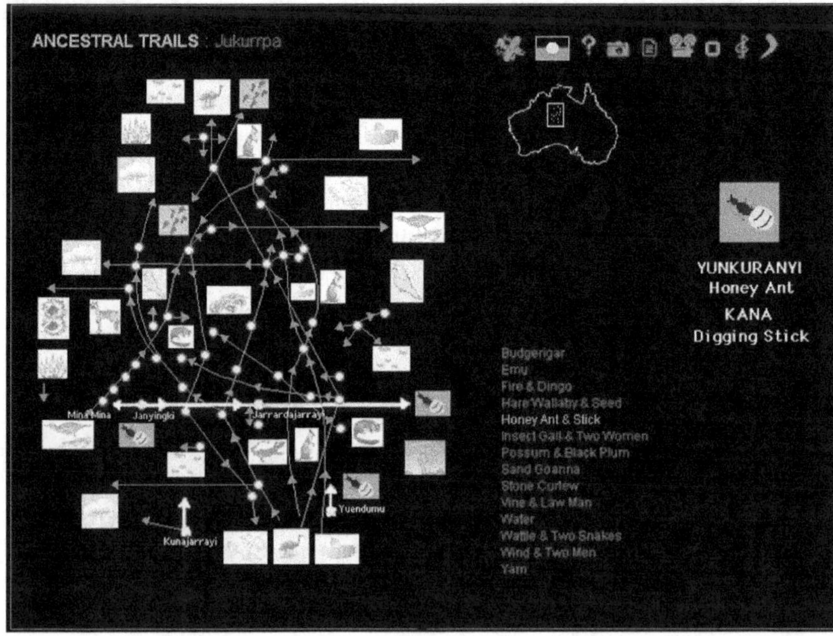

(b)

Figure 5.6

Barbara Glowczewski, Ancestral Trails: *Jukurrpa* (Dreaming). Interactive map showing four different totemic pathways on the Warlpiri land. *a:* Vine and Law Man (top left). *b:* Honey Ant and Stick (bottom left).

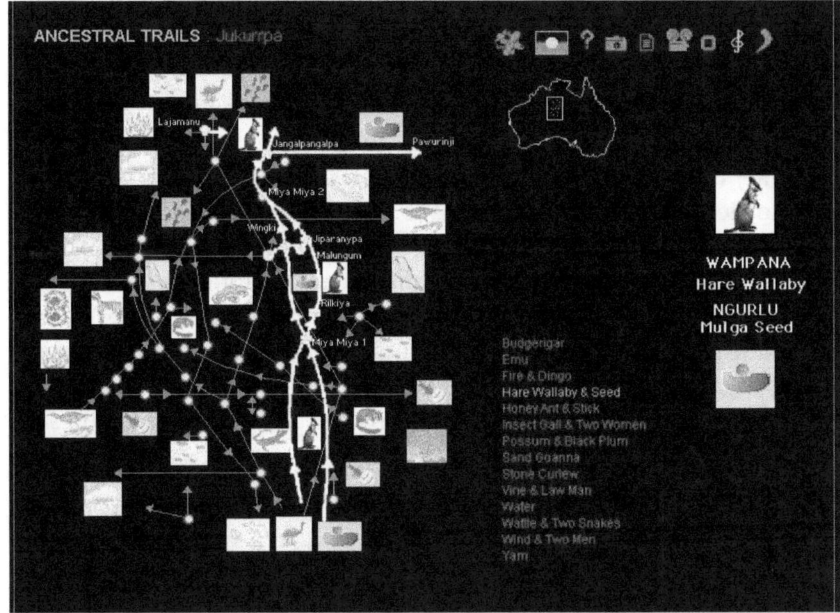

(c)

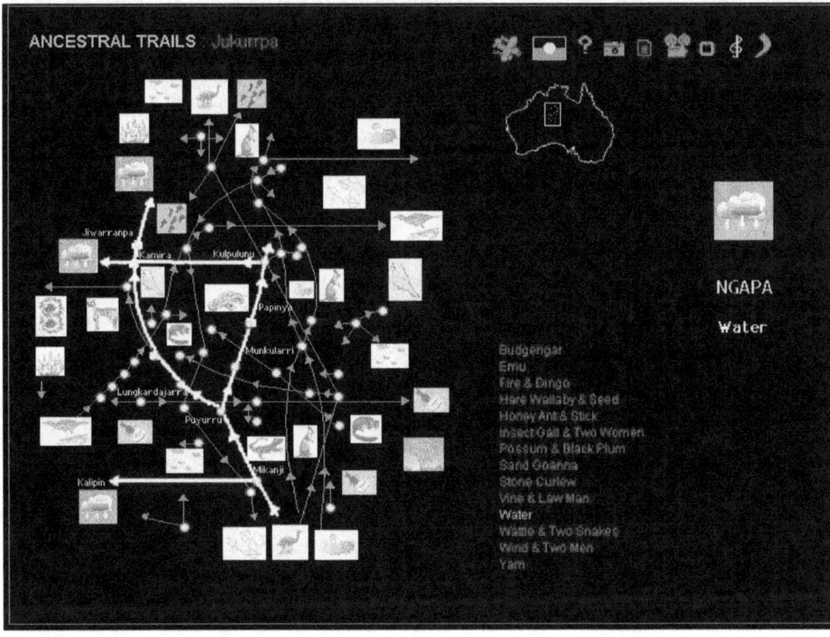

(d)

Figure 5.6 (continued)

c: Hare Wallaby and Seed (top right). *d:* Water (bottom right). Images from the English, French, and Warlpiri compact disk, Barbara Glowczewski, *Dream Trackers: Yapa Art and Knowledge from the Australian Desert* (Paris: UNESCO, 2000).

Unlike the songlines it portrays, the disk itself is finite and embedded in a particular form that depends on proprietary software. Although the project was originally conceived as a Web site, the council of elders at Lajamanu in the mid-1990s objected to making secret knowledge available over the Web. To give the elders more control, Glowczewski adapted the project to the compact disk medium. Today, the Warlpiri have become more technologically aware, so to transmit this information to the next generation, she is readapting the CD as a networked database to which the Warlpiri can contribute and which can be used to enable children to "get a map in their heads" (as bark paintings do). The arts are interlinked, with physical places leading to stories and ceremonies involving song, dance, manipulation of ritual objects, body and sand painting.

Making One's Way: An Aesthetics of Cognitive Mapping

Henri Lefebvre enjoined his contemporaries to produce a space for revolutionary society: "Change life! Change society! These ideas completely lose their meaning without producing an appropriate space. A lesson to be learned from Soviet constructivists from the 1920s and 1930s and from their failure is that new social relations demand a new space and vice-versa."[65] Fredric Jameson sees a "convergence between the empirical problems studied by Lynch in terms of city space" and Althusser's reformulation of ideology as "the representation of the subject's *Imaginary* relationship to his or her *Real* conditions of existence."[66] If urban alienation can be attributed, at least partly, to the impossibility of mentally mapping one's local cityscape, then disalienation "involves the practical reconquest of a sense of place and the construction or reconstruction of an articulated ensemble which can be retained in memory and which the individual subject can map and remap along the moments of mobile, alternative trajectories."[67]

Can we regain our sense of place as we move through the world by practicing alternative mapping strategies? If so, what are these strategies? Chapters 6 and 7 develop some approaches that have been devised by artists.

6 Lines Made by Walking

Urban Trails

Space does not just exist; it has been produced from a primary matter, nature, argues Henri Lefebvre. It is the result of activity—political products and strategic spaces—that implies economics and technique but goes beyond them. There is not one social space but many.[1]

For the past twenty years, Belgian artist Francis Alÿs has used walking as a way of producing space. In his first series of walks, *The Collector* (1990–1992), he pulled a magnetized toy dog on wheels through the streets of Mexico City, collecting bits and pieces of cast-off metals as he walked. Like Pistoletto's *Scultura da passeggio* (1967) and Gabriel Orozco's plasticine sphere *Piedra que Cede* (1992), this project evokes the Baudelairean image of the poet as ragpicker.[2] The project is documented in a video showing a cross-section of Mexican night life: people gather in squares, cars shine their headlights, and dogs in kennels or strays in the streets eye the artist's toy.

Beginning in São Paulo in 1995, Alÿs made a series of urban walks with a pierced paint can, tracing his path with dribbling paint. On October 17, 2003, the Musée d'Art Moderne de la Ville de Paris relocated temporarily to a former convent in the Latin Quarter while its building was being renovated. To make the move official, Alÿs decided to walk from one space to the other. He pierced a can of blue paint with a knife and dripped his way from the museum on the right bank of the Seine to its temporary headquarters on the left bank. A fourteen-minute video shows the highlights of Alÿs's performance *The Leak: Version Colonial Blue*. Two cameras follow the sneaker-clad artist, who has a travel bag slung casually over one shoulder and the dribbling paint can in the other hand, as he descends staircases, crosses bridges, and jaywalks through the early morning traffic, stopping only once to add water to his can to dilute the paint before arriving at his destination, where he sticks the can to a wall. This seemingly casual mise en scène abounds in allusions, including Ariadne's thread, Tom Thumb's breadcrumb trail, Jackson Pollock's paint traceries as filmed by Hans Namuth, and the passing of the Olympic flame. Along the way, Alÿs offers viewers a tour of the streets at ground level. He deftly skirts patches of dog excrement and tramps on fallen leaves. Several times, he glides out of the camera frame as the videographer moves on, swinging his weight from one leg to the other.[3]

The winding streets of Paris may not be the deep canyons of New York, but they do allow us a view of the territory claimed by practitioners of walking. In Israel, Alÿs revisited *Leak* once again and called it *The Green Line: Sometimes Doing Something Poetic Can Become Political, and Sometimes Doing Something Political Can Become Poetic*. In June 2004, he used his dripping can to mark with green paint the armistice boundary that Moshe Dayan had traced on a map with green pencil at the end of Israel's War of Independence in 1948. The next year, he asked prominent Israelis and Palestinians (such as Dayan's daughter Yael) what they thought the role of the green line was today. Does it still function as a social and spiritual division in the city of Jerusalem? Alÿs asks:

> Can an artistic intervention truly bring about an unforeseen way of thinking, or it is more a matter of creating a sensation of "meaninglessness" that shows the absurdity of the situation? Can an artistic intervention translate social tensions into narratives that in turn intervene in the imaginary landscape of a place? Can an absurd act provoke a transgression that makes you abandon the standard assumptions on the sources of conflict? Can those kinds of artistic acts bring about the possibility of change? In any case, how can art remain politically significant without assuming a doctrinal standpoint or aspiring to become social activism?[4]

Alÿs may be walking outside the museum, but ironically, his influence in the art world allows his actions to be relayed to the world outside. I return to these questions in chapters 8 and 9.

Drawing Lines with Locative Media

Locative and mobile media overlay geographical space with an invisible layer of radio waves that connect it to data space. They include global positioning systems (GPS), wireless Internet, sensor networks, and automatic identification technologies that use radio signals to transmit information from one computing device to another. The expression *locative media* served as a title and locus for a 2003 workshop at RIXC, an electronic art and media center in Riga, Latvia.[5] For Jo Walsh, it is the equivalent in media arts of what she calls "the 'geo' hype in free software circles," and both resulted from the "descrambling of the GPS signal [in 2000] so that for the first time 'civilians' could enjoy something like the geopositioning accuracy that the military had enjoyed for so long."[6] In 1999, Ben Russell proposed a definition that conveys both the promise of these media and the dangers that they carry:

> *Locative media* is a term that ties together a set of questions, critical perspectives, and practices. Its catalytic premise was civilian awareness and engagement with a particular "operational con-

struct" with military origins. A combination of GPS, mobile data communications and mobile computing would allow the annotation of space. . . . Locative media is many things: A new site for old discussions about the relationship of consciousness to place and other people. A framework within which to actively engage with, critique, and shape a rapid set of technological developments. A context within which to explore new and old models of communication, community and exchange. A name for the ambiguous shape of a rapidly deploying surveillance and control infrastructure.[7]

Related and overlapping terms used in technology circles include *augmented reality* (enhancing reality with computer-generated sensory input), *pervasive computing* (computers embedded everywhere), *ambient intelligence* (electronic environments that respond to the presence of people), and *the Internet of things* (the networked interconnection of everyday objects).

The term *locative media* is often used to refer to art that is enabled by this technological infrastructure. Writing in 2005, Tuters and Varnellis assign it an origin in the new media art community, where it was a real-world answer to "the decorporealized, screen-based experience of net art."[8] It was also a way for artists to renew with the tradition of site-specific art that left the rarefied air of museum and gallery to investigate the world outside.

Others point to the new paradigm in computer science that was imagined by researchers at Xerox Palo Alto Research Center (PARC) in the late 1980s—ubiquitous computing.[9] As Mark Weiser's groundbreaking article notes, "The most profound technologies are those that disappear. 'They weave themselves into the fabric of everyday life until they are indistinguishable from it." He thought it was time to shift the focus from personal computers to computing that "takes into account the natural human environment and allows the computers themselves to vanish into the background."[10]

Weiser opposed it to virtual reality, which "is only a map, not a territory." Instead of simulating the world using the "enormous apparatus" of virtual reality, he proposed to invisibly enhance the existing world, bringing the "'virtuality' of computer-readable data—all the different ways in which it can be altered, processed and analyzed—. . . into the physical world."[11] In this way, he thought, "embodied virtuality will make individuals more aware of the people on the other ends of their computer links."[12]

Early Work with Mobile Technologies

The artistic use of ubiquitous and location-aware technology goes back to the 1980s and early 1990s. Sometimes the location awareness of the technology itself was minimal. Diverting it from its original purpose, artists gave us a glimpse of new possibilities. In 1986, Gwek Bure-Soh used radio transmission to communicate instructions for a performance to a group of artists traveling by car. During that decade, several artists used analog fax transmissions to materialize invisible lines tracing their passage through space. In 1989, Stephan Barron and Sylvia Hansmann drove due south from Villers-sur-Mer on the English Channel to Castillon de la Plana on the Mediterranean Sea, following the path of the Greenwich meridian. Along the way, they gathered traces of their trip, which they faxed to eight European locations. The imaginary line they drew with their bodies was materialized by the fax transmissions in the exhibition spaces.[13] At the time, fax machines were equipped with rolls of paper, which made it possible for the images to be printed out of the machine in a continuous line. Gilbertto Prado organized a simultaneous event in three cities (*Connect*, 1991) in which participants in each place drew on the thermal paper as it spewed out of one machine and before it was fed to another and the results transmitted to the next city. The thousands of miles separating Paris from Pittsburgh or São Paulo were compressed, "embodied" in the six feet that separated the two machines, thus drawing what Prado called "a loop in telematic space." Here location was marked by the time code and machine name and was automatically recorded by the fax receiver.

Others explored what artist-engineer Steve Mann calls "existential technology." Beginning in the early 1980s, Mann built a backpack-based computer controller for photography and a system for real-time transmission of photography, video, and text. His best-known inventions include the WearComp, an eyepiece that transformed the wearer into a cyborg, and the EyeTap, an example of "Electronic news gathering wear." I discuss his work later in chapter 9.[14]

Among the pioneers of art using GPS, we can cite Masaki Fujihata, Laura Kurgan, Stephen Wilson, Andrea Wollensak, and Teri Rueb, who all made works in the 1990s. Many early experimenters took data obtained in the field and processed it to create gallery-based exhibitions. Wollensak showed inkjet prints and computer animations of her walks in the Canadian Rockies, whereas Fujihata made several representations of data he created while climbing Mount Fuji: "a topographical layer model made of laminated wood, a computer graphic, a video database" (figure 6.1). Neither of these works used GPS to allow people to access information on site in the "real world," although Fujihata did invite visitors to his 1994 show at the ICC Gallery in Tokyo to borrow data rucksacks and add their own contributions to what he called the "videographically acceleratory surveillance of the urban space."[15]

Laura Kurgan made it her business to reveal the opacity and limits of this technology developed by the U.S. military (which, in the 1990s, reduced the precision of the GPS signal available to civilians). This scrambling, known as *selective availability*, could generate inaccuracies of up to 100 meters. From November 1995 to February 1996, Kurgan set up a GPS antenna on the roof of the Museu d'Art Contemporani de Barcelona. Measurements were taken at regular intervals, but deliberate errors introduced in the civilian signal caused the location of the stationary receiver to vary from one reading to the next, giving the impression that the building was moving.[16]

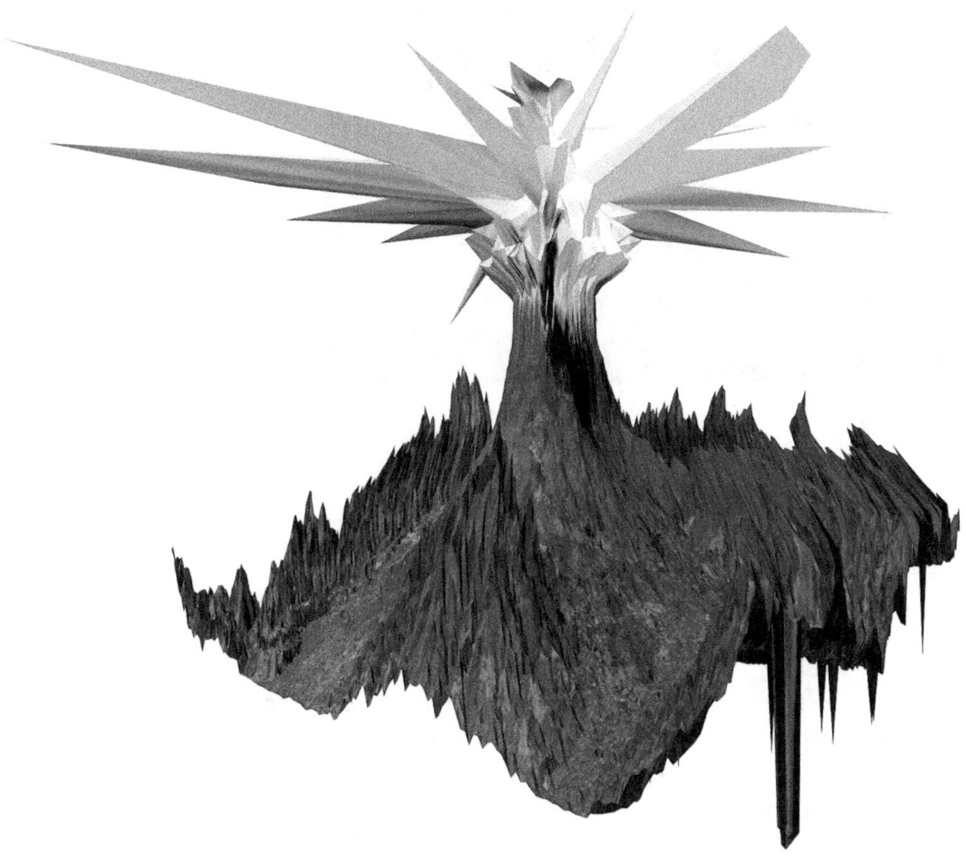

Figure 6.1
Masaki Fujihata, *Impressing Velocity (Mount Fuji)*, 1992–1994. Detail. The artist climbed Mount Fuji equipped with a head-mounted video camera, a GPS receiver, and a laptop computer in a backpack. As he and his companions approached the summit, their pace slowed, and the recorded velocity followed suit. When he mapped the data to a 3D model of the volcano, Fujihata distorted the representation to reflect the climbers' pace: as they approached the peak, the geometrical spikes became more jagged. © Masaki Fujihata.

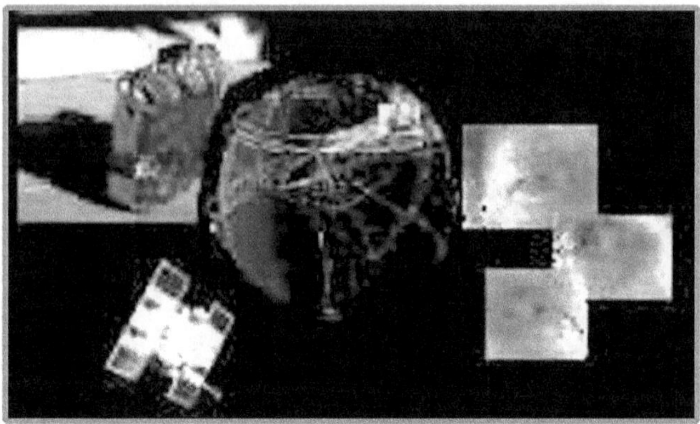

Figure 6.2
Stephen Wilson, *The Telepresent*, 1997. A gift-wrapped magic box containing a laptop computer, a wireless modem, a GPS receiver, and a digital camera that automatically uploaded images to a Web site. *The Telepresent* was designed to wander the world through networks of friendships and gift giving.

High-Tech Potlatch

Stephen Wilson's *Telepresent* was among the first projects that let people other than the artist gather GPS data by walking (figure 6.2). It consisted of a "magic box" that contained a small computer, a GPS receiver, and a digital camera that automatically sent images from wherever it was to a Web site, chronicling its travels as it goes, "showing whatever each recipient thinks is important or interesting—providing a small window on the world's diversity of personal lives and cultural niches."[17]

The artist built a prototype that was tested by his students in San Francisco. Each person given the *Telepresent* had to decide what to do with it. There was debate about how best to live with it: Should its bearer take it to out-of-the-way places to give Web viewers a stimulating experience? Or was the audience better served by a glimpse of someone's everyday life? People fought over who should get it the next day. Friendships were tested. One participant suggested that it should be thrown off the Golden Gate Bridge to give Web viewers a vicarious experience of suicide. The artist's response was less than enthusiastic: "I wasn't going to let her do it with my $3000 worth of equipment!"[18]

The *Telepresent* raised questions about the nature of gift giving and the responsibilities that people accept when they receive a gift. In his classic anthropological essay "The Gift: The Form and Reason for Exchanges in Archaic Societies" (1923), Marcel Mauss argued that the exchange of objects builds relationships between people. Giving an object creates an obligation for the receiver to accept the gift and to reciprocate. Both receiver and giver are entangled in a web of obligation. Mauss wrote, "The gift not yet repaid debases the man who accepts it."[19] At the same time, it procures respect, standing and power for the giver, who has shown himself to be generous.

The *Telepresent* proved to be something of a *cadeau empoisonné*, in keeping with the ambivalence of the word *gift*. In a short essay entitled "Gift-Gift" (1924), Mauss notes that in German, the word *gift* means *poison*. The gift-giving and exchange practices that Mauss described were at once self-interested and beneficial to the group. Analogous practices exist in modern societies, such as what has been called the gift economy of art or scientific research. When scientists read papers at conferences or publish articles in professional journals, they could be said to give away the results of their research.[20] The same is true of hackers who write code within the free-software, open-source movement.[21]

When Wilson built the *Telepresent* in 1997, he imagined it "traveling the world through networks of friendship and gift-giving." The artist wrote custom software that allowed it to upload images and download comments from the Web.[22] Online viewers would see whatever the *Telepresent* saw and respond with comments that would be spoken by a speech synthesizer. But the reality did not scale: "wireless Internet was available in only a few cities in the world. There was no good method for keeping all the batteries charged. People were supposed to send/give it to the next person each day. Airlines were not about to allow GPS devices in their baggage. It probably would work if it stayed in one city, but that was not as interesting. It was visionary but fraught with technical problems. The prototype was only activated for a few days in San Francisco."[23] He notes ruefully that to realize the project today, a simple cell phone would do.

Time Capsule: Radio-Frequency Tracking

Another prescient work from 1997, Eduardo Kac's *Time Capsule*, is a microchip that was incorporated into the artist's ankle. Radio-frequency identification (RFID) tags, or transponders, can be embedded into almost any object, allowing automatic data capture and transfer. Unlike bar-code technology, RFID systems do not require contact or line of sight for communication, which means that data can be read through the human body, clothing, and nonmetallic materials. Examples of RFID use in everyday life are individually programmed ID tags for pets and livestock and automatic passes used in subways and toll booths.[24]

In an event staged at the Casa das Rosas Cultural Center in São Paulo, Kac used a special needle to insert the transponder under his skin, which was then scanned. A low-energy radio signal allowed the microchip to transmit its unique and unalterable numerical code to the scanner's liquid crystal display (LCD) screen. The identification number was then registered with a database in the United States that is used for tracking lost animals. Kac listed himself as both owner and animal.

The performance took place on a hospital bed against a backdrop of sepia-toned photographs and involved an online computer, a telerobotic finger, and broadcasting equipment (figure 6.3). Although a "medical professional" was present, Kac performed the operation, like Napoleon in David's painting crowning himself emperor under the watchful gaze of the pope.

Theoretically, Kac's implant can be scanned remotely from anywhere in the world. Within the body, computer circuits vie with electrical impulses from the brain, while connecting it to the global digital network. We are no longer confined within our skin. Kac's project might suggest the prospect of a corporate Big Brother that is able to monitor even our vital organs, where "I've got you under my skin" is no longer a stale metaphor and employees can be monitored like household pets, but it also evokes more positive developments in medical research. Microchips can also simulate bodily functions from a distance, via protheses like artificial retinas.

Kac's description emphasizes the symbolic gesture of incorporating the transponder into his own body. We are left to imagine the results. This work anticipates bioart with its wet interfaces and hybrid databodies and alludes to the ethics of surveillance. This sort of tracking has become more plausible in the post-9/11 world, since our portable devices have begun communicating with each other behind our backs.

Who has access to these databases now? Had we registered a pet in 1997, could we locate the animal today? With technology evolving rapidly, even ten years can seem like a long time: how quickly does such a device become outdated? In 2010, I asked Kac if he still had the transponder in his ankle: "Yes, I do, and for my retrospective at the Instituto Valenciano de Arte Moderno (IVAM) in 2007, we celebrated the tenth anniversary of *Time Capsule* by allowing local and internet participants to scan me again."[25] Kac's work points to recent developments in ubiquitous computing, such as the rapidly developing Internet of things. I return to these issues later in chapter 9.

Playing the City: Riffs on Real Time

Real-time projects deal with actions, although the traces are often ephemeral. Combining the theatrical tradition of live art with computer real time, *Can You See Me Now?* set the tone for the whole genre of mobile games. Unlike artists who create GPS drawings for posterity, the members of Blast Theory use the technique to locate players and show their current location to online participants without preserving the track data. When they do record it, the tracks are not made public: they serve only to improve game play.[26]

Another type of project pursues Max Neuhaus's injunction to *listen* while allowing people to perform a combination of music and dance as they walk in the city. Ambient sounds become raw material to be captured, transformed, and played back through wireless interfaces.

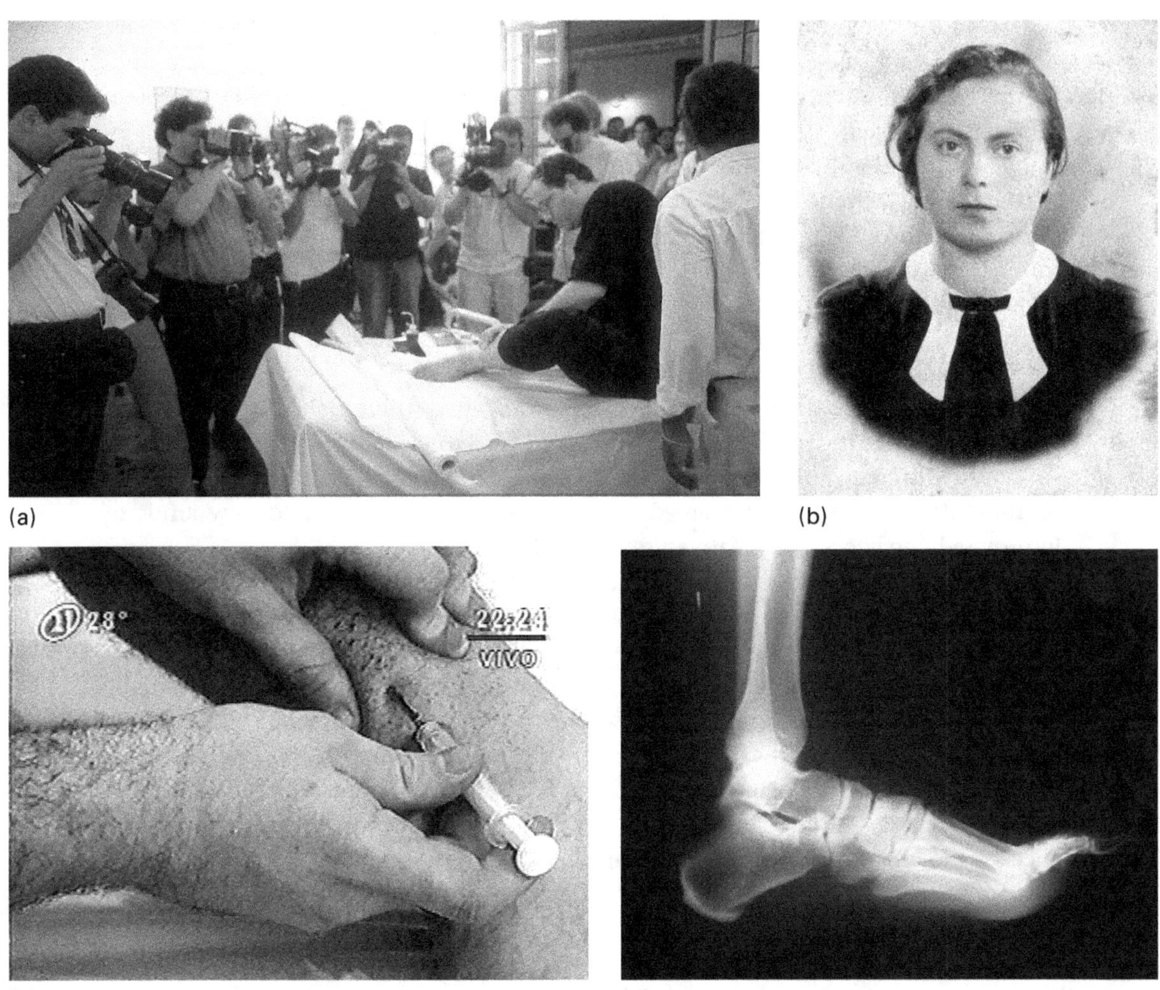

Figure 6.3
Eduardo Kac, *Time Capsule* 1997 (details). Microchip implant, seven sepia-toned photographs, live television broadcast, Webcast, interactive telerobotic Web scanning of the implant, remote database intervention, X-ray of the implant, dimensions variable. Collection BEEP, Spain. *a:* Microchip implant. *b:* One of seven sepia-toned photographs. *c:* Live television broadcast. *d:* An X-ray of the implant.

Developed conjointly by designers and engineers in Göteborg, Sweden,[27] *Sonic City* (2002–2004) used real-time interactions between the wearer and his surroundings to create music (figure 6.4). It encouraged people to explore city sounds through improvised movements. Here, paths became musical compositions as the listener wandered through the shifting environment of a city. The system retrieved information about his actions and his whereabouts and mapped it to real-time processing of urban sounds. The result was music heard through headphones. When wearing this system, urban atmospheres, random encounters, and everyday activities all participated in creating music for walking.[28] The irony is that although he was made aware of what was going on around him, the resulting musical creation did not reach anyone else.

Lalya Gaye notes that when the prototype was tested, users "felt that the city was more in control of the music than they were and tried to regain this control by actively seeking appropriate urban contexts or by modulating city input with their body posture." In this way, what seemed at first to be frustrating led "to new kinds of improvised behaviors and creative use of physical space."[29]

Picking up where *Sonic City* left off, a recent project in development, *Interac Wearing* by the group Experientae Electricae,[30] allows users who are wearing special suits to make sounds that others can hear and respond to. The collective call them "functional interactive textiles" since they were built to foster group interaction. When I tried one out in June 2009 during a prototyping session at the Paris festival Futur en Seine, the interaction was still at an early stage. Each of the beige jumpsuits had loudspeakers that were sewn into the collar and sensors in the hem of the pants. Instead of groping for switches and squinting at tiny screen menus, the wearer could focus on the experience of moving through space. I glimpsed other users strolling around in similar outfits but was not able to determine if or how our actions affected each other.

Drawing by Walking

In their article "Beyond Locative Media," Marc Tuters and Kazys Varnellis divide locative media projects into two groups: "annotative—virtually tagging the world—or phenomenological—tracing the action of the subject in the world."[31] Following in Richard Long's footsteps, a number of artists have taken to locating themselves as they move around the world, but now they use GPS as a drawing medium. GPS devices can be made to produce sketches on paper, on screen, or on other surfaces. The artists use their own and others' bodies to make trails that often are intended to last. Jeremy Wood describes his own approach: "The work is located in the actions and methodologies of drawing. GPS drawings are exhibited as printed editions and sculptures as part of ongoing research into writing over the earth and drawing with ourselves as we move."[32]

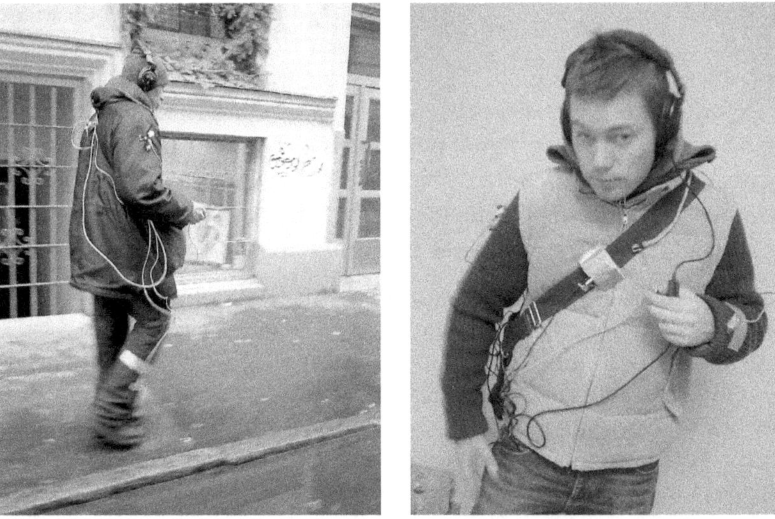

(a)

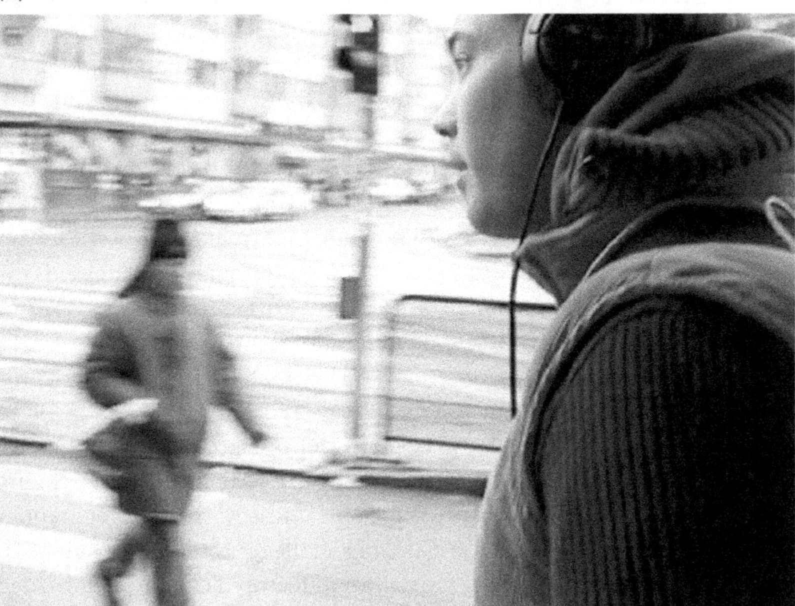

(b)

Figure 6.4

Lalya Gaye, Ramia Mazé, Daniel Skoglund, and Margot Jacobs, *Sonic City*, 2002–2004. This system, developed by a team of designers and engineers, created music from the real-time interactions between the wearer and his surroundings. Future Applications Lab (Viktoria Institute) and PLAY Studio (Interactive Institute) (Göteborg, Sweden). *a:* Components of the Sonic City system. *b:* Testing the prototype in the streets of Göteborg. The system retrieved information about wearer's actions and whereabouts and mapped it to real-time processing of urban sounds. The result was music heard through headphones.

Since his first experience using a GPS unit to record an airline holding pattern in October 2000, Wood has been making digital trails of his travels. He calls them "visual journals that document a personal cartography."[33] Like Teri Rueb and Andrea Wollensak, he is interested in the aesthetic quality of GPS traces that are made by the body as it moves through space and compares them to marks made on paper:

> Seeing the rhythms and patterns of one's tracks can have the effect of seeing your own ghost. The qualities of line in GPS drawings can reveal a great deal about movement and process. Just like a pencil drawing where smooth lines have a different speed to jagged edges, GPS drawings can detail the elegant lines of a railway and a squiggly walk to the local shops. As a pencil . . . momentarily pauses in its progression, we might hesitate or wait before crossing a road. The speed of travel can also be colored to indicate the cold blues of slow dithering to red hot top speeds, and the altitude of tracks can add pressure and depth of line.[34]

Although most GPS receivers provide information on the user's current position, GPS drawing requires the device to keep a record of where the user has been by automatically recording trackpoint data, saving it, and sending it to a computer via a cable or a wireless device. The GPS information can then be rendered, sculpted, and animated. Jeremy Wood uses custom software for 3D representation and animation of the GPS tracks. Thus, travel itself becomes "a geodetic pencil or a cartographic crayon."[35] Recent prints combine drawings of one subject, such as his journeys through London. *My Ghost* (2009) (figure 6.5) writes up nine years of Wood's movements in one simultaneous image, recalling Gjon Mili's photographic "light drawings" in which the shutter remains open in an attempt to capture the passage of time. In 2010, Wood walked for seventeen days, accumulating 238 miles of GPS tracks to make a campus map of the University of Warwick at 1:1 scale (*Traverse Me*, 2010) (figure 6.6).

Observing that "our everyday movement is highly choreographed, whether we realize it or not,"[36] Teri Rueb created *The Choreography of Everyday Life* in 2001 (figure 6.7). When she was invited to collaborate with Denise Tassin and choreographer Amanda Thom Woodson for a show at the Goucher College Rosenberg Gallery in Baltimore, each artist proposed a work. Rueb's installation featured closed-circuit video cameras and monitors, maps, and GPS tracings that were archived in sculptural stacks. The cameras captured the movement of dancers when they performed in the space and visitors as they walked through the exhibition.

The real-time component allowed one or two dancers to be tracked as they moved around the city. Their movements were translated into animations that were presented as an applet on a Web site. There was no choreographer. Rueb asked the dancers to carry GPS units with them on their daily trips on campus and throughout the city—recording their movement both manually and automatically: "Working with dancers allowed me to juxtapose the notions of formal choreography and dance and the highly scripted nature of our everyday movement in the built environment."[37] She thinks

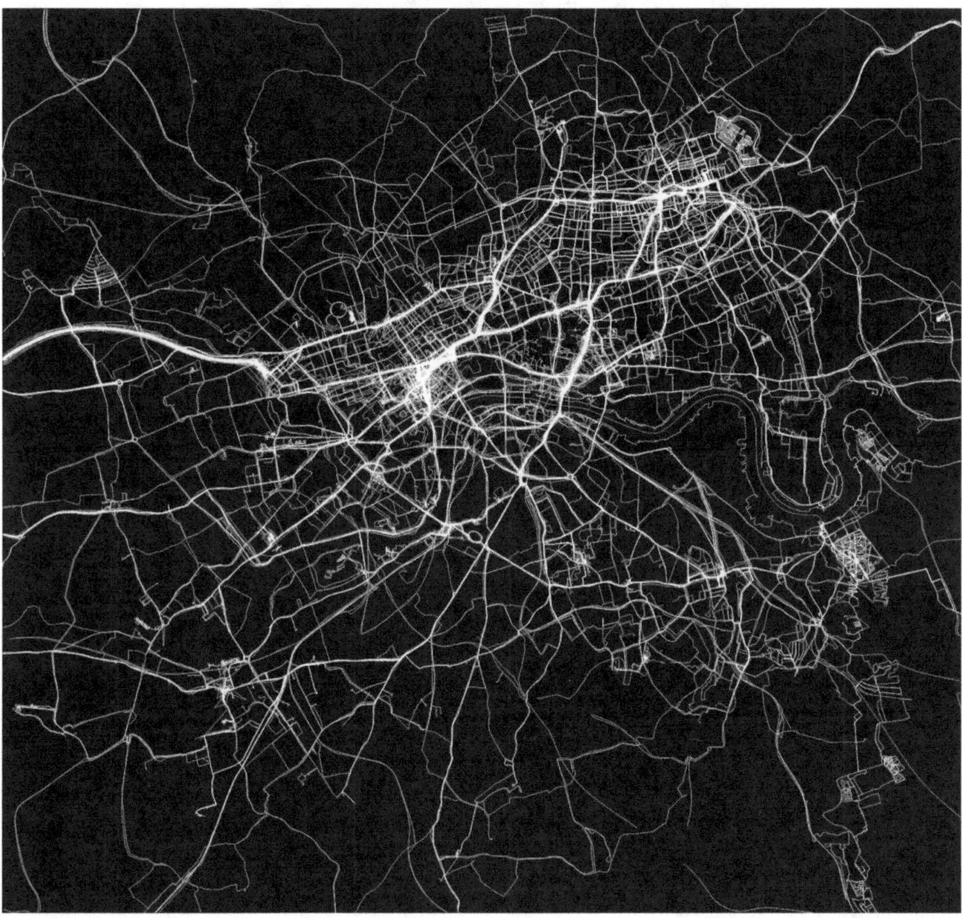

Figure 6.5

Jeremy Wood, *My Ghost,* 2009. GPS drawing. In the drawing, travel itself becomes "a geodetic pencil or a cartographic crayon." Jeremy Wood has made maps combining drawings of one subject, such as his journeys through London (*My Ghost,* 2009). Courtesy of the artist.

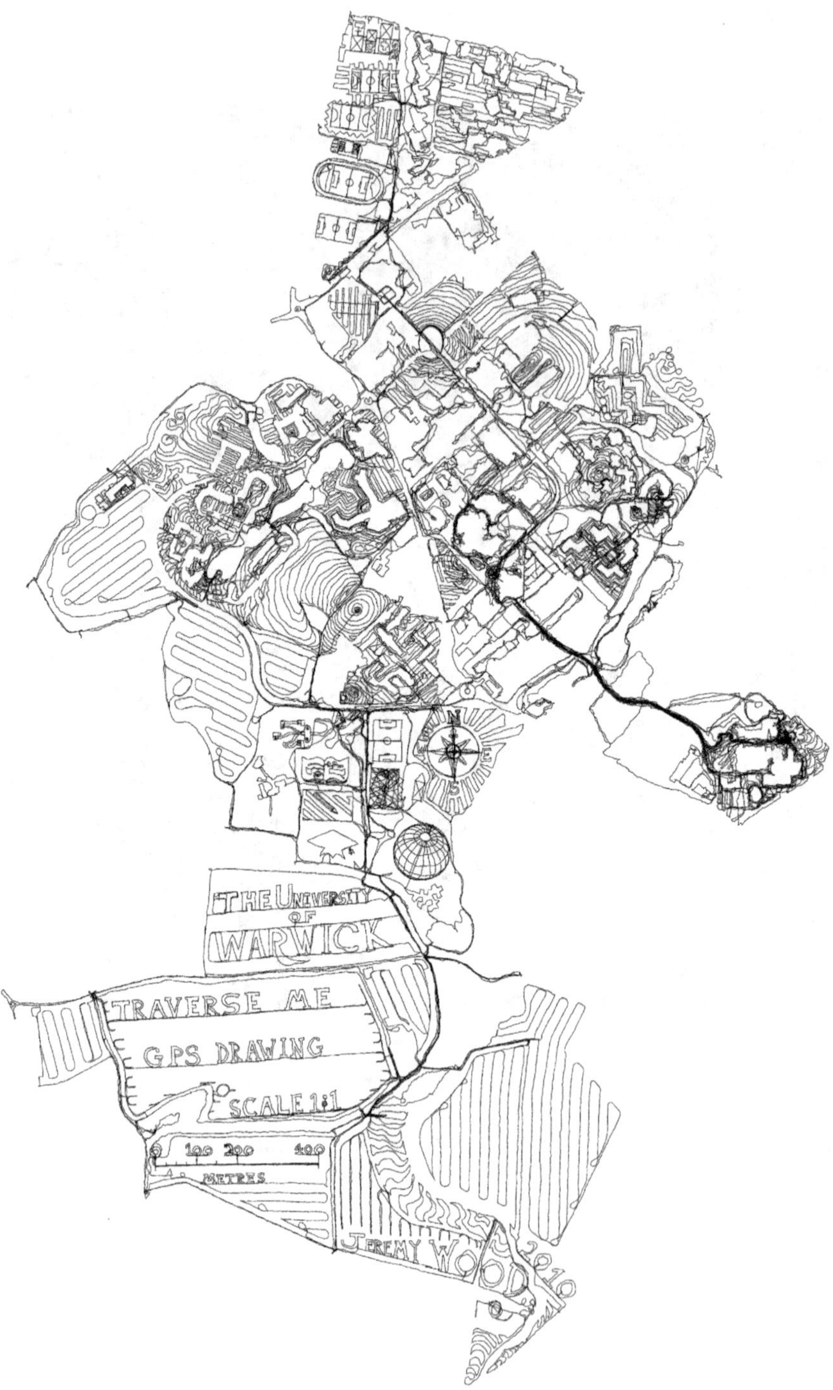

Figure 6.6
Jeremy Wood, *Traverse Me,* 2010. GPS drawing. The artist walked for 17 days accumulating 238 miles of GPS tracks to "draw" a campus map of the University of Warwick at 1:1 scale. Courtesy of the artist.

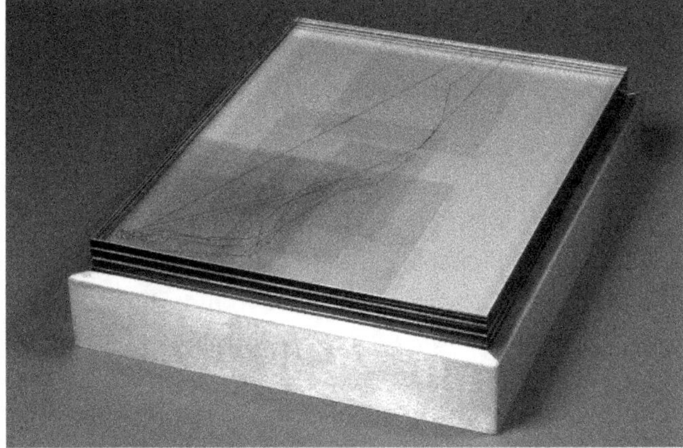

(a)

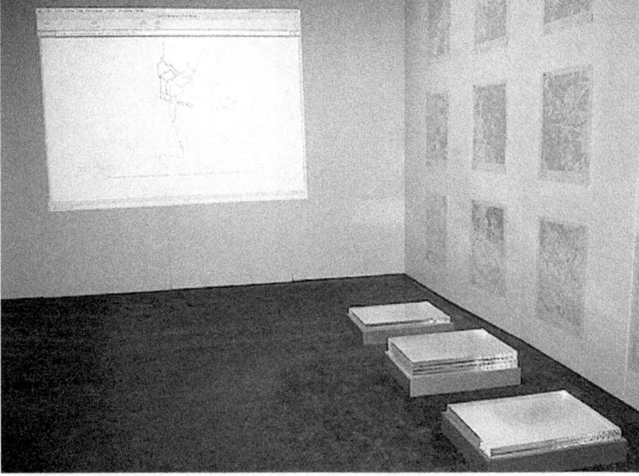

(b)

Figure 6.7

Teri Rueb, *The Choreography of Everyday Life*, 2001. Installation. This installation featured closed-circuit video cameras and monitors, maps, and GPS tracings that were archived in sculptural stacks. The cameras captured the movements of dancers and gallery visitors, while the real-time online animation tracked two dancers at a time as they moved around the city. *a:* A stack of GPS tracings. *b:* Installation view. Courtesy of the artist.

that our behavior reflects the cultural, social, and political forces embodied therein and reveals an increasing awareness of the ubiquity of video surveillance.

Real-Time Tracing

Another real-time approach combines GPS tracking with narrative. One of its foremost practitioners, Esther Polak, combines an eye for detail and characterization with an infectious enthusiasm. *Amsterdam RealTime* (2002) (figure 6.8) was her first locative media project. Supported by government and telecommunications funding, it was realized at a much larger scale than Rueb's *Choreography*.[38] For two months in the fall of 2002, visitors to the exhibition *Maps of Amsterdam 1866–2000* at the Amsterdam City Archive could watch a wall-sized video projection that showed colored lines as they were drawn on a black background by ordinary people from different professions

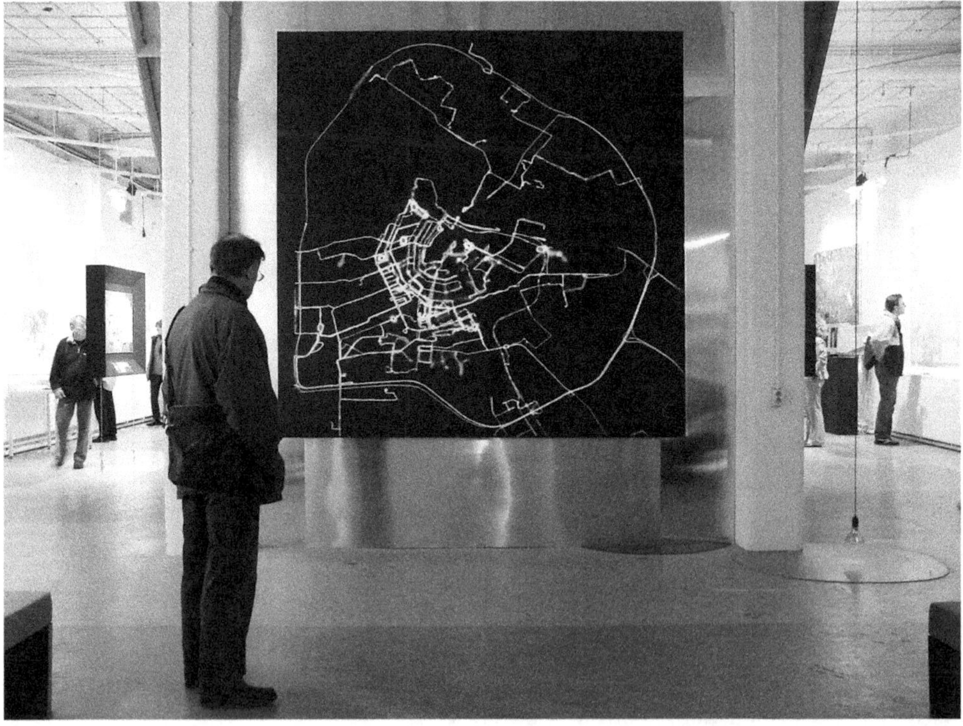

(a)

Figure 6.8

Esther Polak, Jeroen Kee, and Waag Society, *Amsterdam RealTime,* 2002. Installation. Ordinary people moving around Amsterdam leave GPS trails on a map that is updated in real time. http://realtime.waag.org. Courtesy: The artist. *a:* Exhibition view.

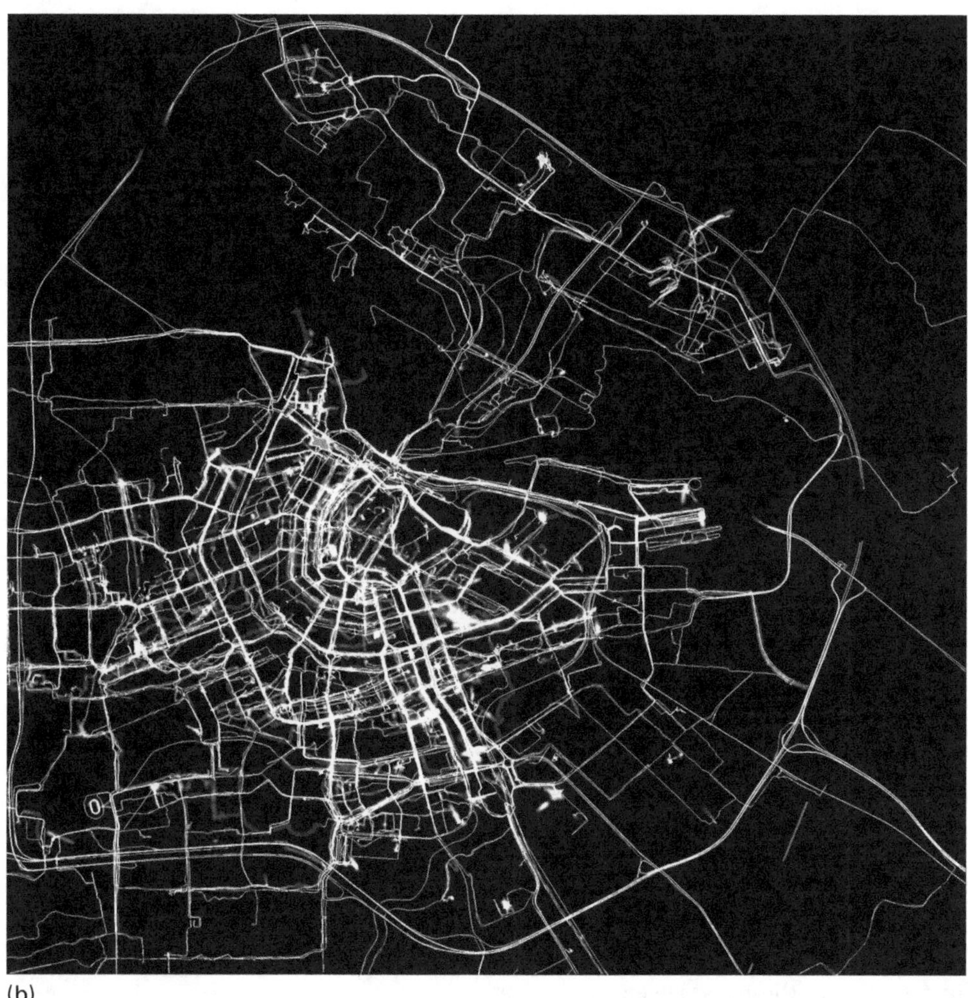

(b)

Figure 6.8 (continued)
b: Screenshot.

and age groups as they moved through the city.[39] These people had two things in common: their daily routines took them to the city center, and they were willing to give up some privacy in exchange for seeing what Esther Polak calls their "diary in traces." Each week, ten people carried a GPS tracer unit that they could switch on every time they went outside on their daily business. As their different paths stretched across the city, crisscrossing, they gradually built up an intriguing map of Amsterdam without streets, blocks, houses, or landmarks—an interlocking tracery of lines.

In themselves, GPS units are not tracking devices. They have receivers but no transmitters.[40] For *Amsterdam RealTime*, the Waag Society built ten portable but cumbersome devices that they equipped with GPS sensors and linked to a networked hand-held computer. The tracer used information transmitted by satellites to calculate its geographical position. The latitude and longitude coordinates collected by each participant were sent in real time[41] to the Waag Society server. The computer compiled images based on the accumulation of a participant's points over specified periods of time, and the data were visualized against a black background in the form of lines. From the paths of people moving through space, a map of Amsterdam gradually "drew itself." Frequently traveled points became brighter over time and turned yellow, with the most densely traveled spots accumulating red "burn marks." Pale gray showed the participants' pseudonyms (annemarie, ruby's papa), marking their current activities as they continued to form the map.[42]

What can we infer from our ordinary paths through the city? In the late 1970s, Jean-François Augoyard asked inhabitants of the Arlequin housing project in Grenoble to recount their daily walks, particular walks, and how and where they walked. He was interested in their spoken descriptions. As he says, "oral expression seems to mimic the act of strolling: it is fluid, prone to digressions, capable of forgetting what is essential and of lingering over details."[43] He conducted a series of interviews with their attendant social constraints: the memorable and the narrate-able often emerged in response to the interviewer's questions.

Conversely, the *Amsterdam RealTime* map showed where people actually went on a particular occasion, not necessarily where they said or remembered they had gone, and in this way, it produced a story in actions. Esther Polak notes that after receiving a printout of their personal routes through the city, many participants reacted emotionally. As they examined their paths on the map, confronting their memories and their mental maps with the printed projection, they told her why they had taken a particular route and what had happened on the way.

Although the visualizations could have been shown on a Web site in real time during the exhibition, Polak chose not to do so. To see them, the audience had to visit the show and watch the traces unfolding. She thinks that it made them identify with the participants instead of just looking on from a distance.[44]

Esther Polak situates her work within the phenomenological tradition, although, as she explains, "my focus is to create new visualizations of these tracks and see what new kinds of experiences of space these visualizations bring about."[45] *Amsterdam Real Time* occupies an intermediate area between Blast Theory's ephemeral games and projects that create a more permanent trace. Here walking literally becomes mapping.[46]

Actualizing "Paths Taken"

GPS tracks are qualitatively different from physical traces like paint. The lines that materialize on the computer screen as participants move through the city are just one way of visualizing the information. They were calculated in real time by a computer program set up to show relevant data (the criteria of relevancy were determined in advance).

The past decade has seen much research using real-time GPS data. *Real Time Rome* (2006), created by Carlo Ratti and the MIT SENSEable City Lab, collected the movement patterns of people and transportation systems, using data trails left by cell phones and GPS devices to study real-time urban dynamics. The result is a single interface that combines several datasets: real-time data, GIS data, and bitmap images. The group then devised an open-source real-time control system called *WikiCity* (2008). Here the goal was to use bottom-up methods to improve the efficiency of urban systems. When the prototype was tested in Rome, participants could monitor nearby events in real time. How does access to the dynamics of real-time data alter the decision-making process? If people can see how a traffic jam emerges as it happens, will they avoid behavior that contributes to gridlock?[47] We are a long way from the situationist drift.

Cabspotting was an online system that anonymously tracked the movements of taxis in and around San Francisco and visualized these data. Its core engine, the online *Cab Path Tracker* created by Scott Snibbe and Stamen Design, produced an alternative base map showing the travel patterns of yellow cabs in the Bay Area. Rather than mapping the urban street grid with all the possible routes, it displayed the paths that actually were traveled, much like *Amsterdam RealTime*, generating a series of time-lapse videos. The *Tracker* calculated an average of the last four hours of cab routes into a ghostly image and then drew in real time the routes of ten "live" taxi rides over it. As the viewer watched, these cabs were taking people to destinations all over the city, creating, as they moved, a dynamic map. Two artworks explore the cab-path database. Tomas Apodaca's *Fly Cab* is an interactive three-dimensional fly-through animation of one cab's travels through the city over the course of five days: "As soon as a point on the cab's trail is drawn, it starts to sink down, so that each new point on the trail is slightly higher than the point preceding it. As the trail gets longer, it builds a 3-dimensional structure of the cab's travels through the city over time."[48] *In Transit* by Amy Balkin attempts to make sense of the GPS data trails that are drawn by the cabs. Yellow arrows, dotted lines, and tiny squares or crosses appear on top of the

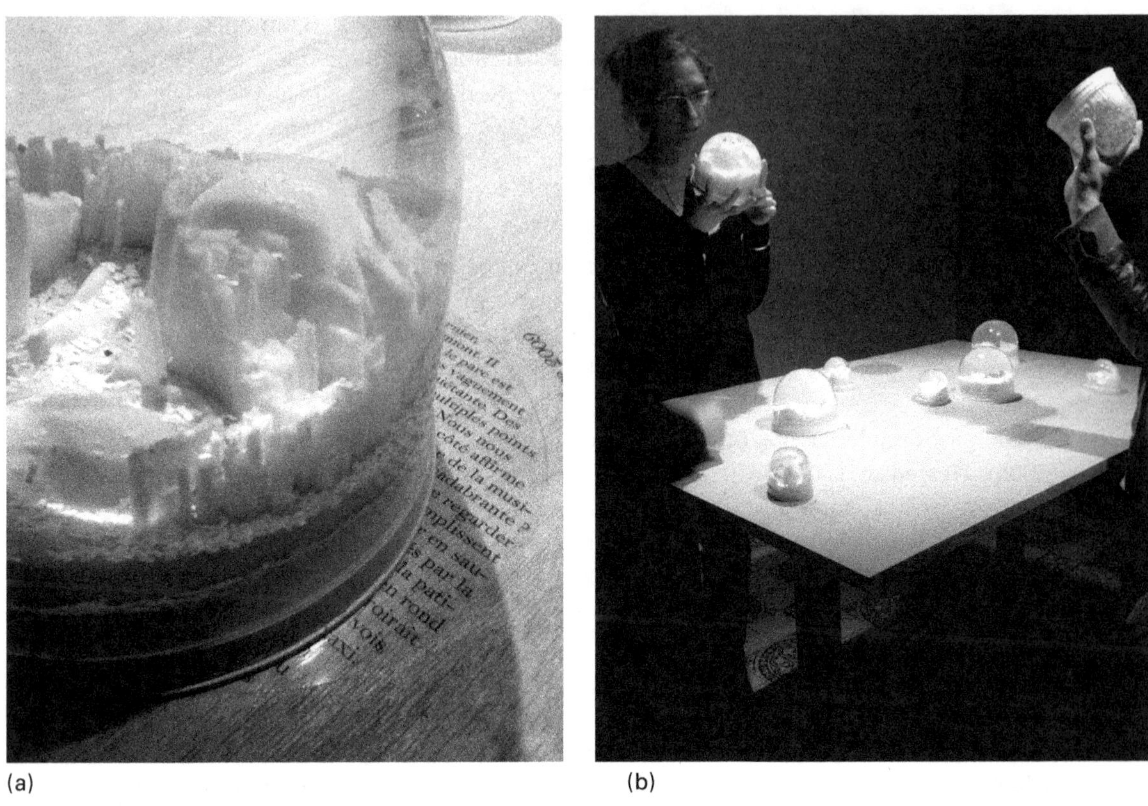

(a) (b)

Figure 6.9

Mayumi Okura and Dominique Cunin (concept and realization), *Paris Souvenirs*, 2009–2010. Installation. *Paris Souvenirs* attempts to represent the precision with which people remember the streets that they took. Small sculptures represent the time a person spends in a particular place. A short time produces small abstract blocks, and a longer time increases the size of the blocks. Produced by the Citu as part of the research project Terra Numerica, with support from the l'Ecole Nationale Supérieure d'Art de Nancy. *a:* Each itinerary is printed in 3D and enclosed in a small snowstorm paperweight. *b:* Visitors can pick up the paperweight and shake it.

white cab trails, forming a new semantic layer. At each of ten sites in greater San Francisco, a speech bubble points out some aspect of the visualization: tiny squares mark sites where cab drivers were murdered on the job (a photo shows a turbaned Sikh man who died after a post-9/11 attack), crosses show locations of hospitals (taxis are often used as cheap ambulances), and arrows indicate directional patterns.

Mayumi Okura and Dominique Cunin, with their *Paris Souvenirs* (2010) (figure 6.9), propose another form of subjective map that is based on an individual's perception of places. They note that when we move around the city following our everyday paths, we tend to walk quickly along paths that we know well without being aware of the form of the buildings around us. When we visit a new city, we move more slowly and pay more attention to our surroundings. The variable nature of our attention creates different types of memories. *Paris Souvenirs* attempts to represent the degree of precision with which we remember the streets that we walked along. In a series of small sculptures, the artists shape 3D maps showing only the buildings along the person's path. The representation of places is distorted to show the time a person spends in a particular place: a short time is shown by small abstract blocks, and a longer time increases the proportions of the building by using the sculptural equivalent of a magnifying glass. Each itinerary is printed in 3D and enclosed in a small snowstorm paperweight that visitors can pick up and shake.

Annotating Space: Site-Specific Documentary

Michel de Certeau developed Merleau-Ponty's contrast between geometrical and anthropological space by distinguishing place (*lieu*), founded by "inert bodies," and space (*espace*), determined through operations that "specify spaces by the actions of historical subjects.": for him, space is "a practiced place. Thus the street geometrically defined by urban planners is transformed into a space by walkers."[49] Stories have the power to transform places into spaces by awakening inert objects and to transform spaces into places by putting to death heroes who transgress laws of place. His own research dealt above all with "the uses of space . . . the ways of frequenting or dwelling in a place."[50] In the last decade, this dialectic of space and place has been mined by a number of artists.

Augmented Walking

Inspired by Bruce Chatwin's book *The Songlines*, a meme swept through contemporary media arts in the early years of the twenty-first century. Imagining the city (and the world) as a set of crisscrossing paths, embedding stories and sounds directly in the landscape, practitioners of locative media tried to emulate aboriginal "bush erudition."[51]

Instead of "colonizing space" as maps have often done by eliminating the traces of the practices that produced them,[52] spatial annotation projects aimed to reintroduce layers of stratification into maps, allowing us to collectively haunt one another. In these forms of augmented reality, the outside world is enhanced with additional layers of digital information and made accessible to passers-by via wireless technologies. This involves assigning geographical coordinates and other spatial metadata to media files, allowing them to be accessed by people who are equipped with appropriate devices in specific real-world locations. In a sense, as Drew Hemment notes, spatial annotation projects aim to "make the world 'programmable' and readable through a transparent interface between an object and the spatial metadata assigned to it."[53]

The city of Los Angeles may be a strange place for a flâneur walk. In the project *34 North 118 West* (2003) by Jeff Knowlton, Naomi Spellman, and Jeremy Hight, users can listen to bits of Los Angeles's "hidden history" as they wander through the downtown area (figure 6.10). It resembles the audio guides discussed in chapter 2 with two notable differences. First, there is a visual component—a map showing visitors' current location in real time. Second, the fictional narratives can be heard only in the locations for which they were conceived. The narrative is embedded in the place itself through juxtaposition and overlap, with layers appearing and falling away.[54]

Marking Space

Rather than producing and distributing their own texts, the authors of several geoannotation projects prefer to curate other peoples' stories. Whereas *34 North 118 West* allowed people only to comment on an existing narrative, these works function as a platform dedicated to archiving and presenting users' contributions, thereby multiplying the perspectives on each particular place.[55] Produced in Yoho Park in the Canadian Rockies in 1999, an early curatorial project, *Trace* (1999) by Teri Rueb, was a site-specific sound installation that transformed trails near the Burgess Shale fossil beds into a landscape commemorating personal loss. Wearing a backpack equipped with a laptop computer, headphones, and a GPS receiver, visitors could wind their way through poems, songs, and stories that played in response to her movement along the trails (figure 6.11). The artist likened it to a memorial sculpture garden in which the monuments are acoustic rather than visual.[56] Based on a digital database of recordings submitted by artists, it anchored their commemoration in the listener's own body.

Many curatorial projects have been staged in urban settings by artists exploring the way multiple data layers affect people as they move around in cities. How is collective memory modified by mobile communications and social networking systems? As wireless electronic devices replace pen and paper, what does it mean to "write the city"?[57] Two seminal projects that were active between 2002 and 2004—*Urban Tapestries* in the guise of research and *PDPal* as public art—addressed these questions.

Initiated by the art and design studio Proboscis in collaboration with academic and corporate partners, *Urban Tapestries* was "a research project and experimental software platform for knowledge mapping and sharing."[58] It was developed to investigate ways in which people could use mobile and Internet technologies combined

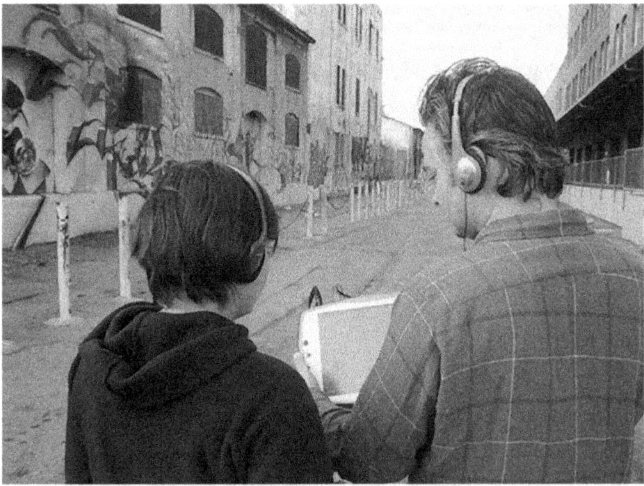

(a)

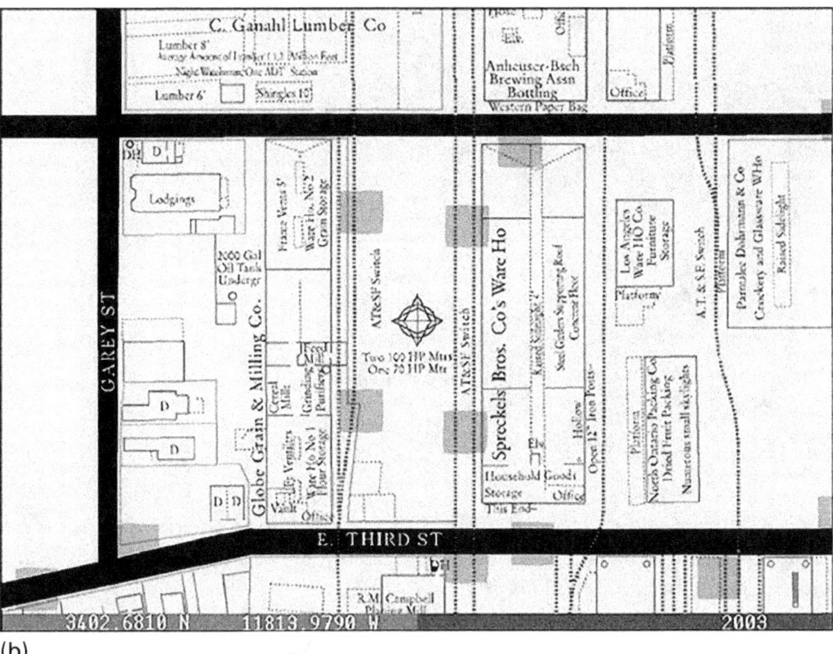

(b)

Figure 6.10

Jeff Knowlton, Naomi Spellman, and Jeremy Hight, *34 North 118 West*, 2003. Participants wearing headphones walk along with a GPS unit that is mounted on a laptop computer. *a:* The laptop displays a map with a marker that tracks the participants' location as they move through the city grid. Data triggers are set along points in the physical city by latitude and longitude. *b:* As the users walk through each of these areas, they hear narratives read by actors superposed over the ordinary city sounds. Images: Jeremy Hight.

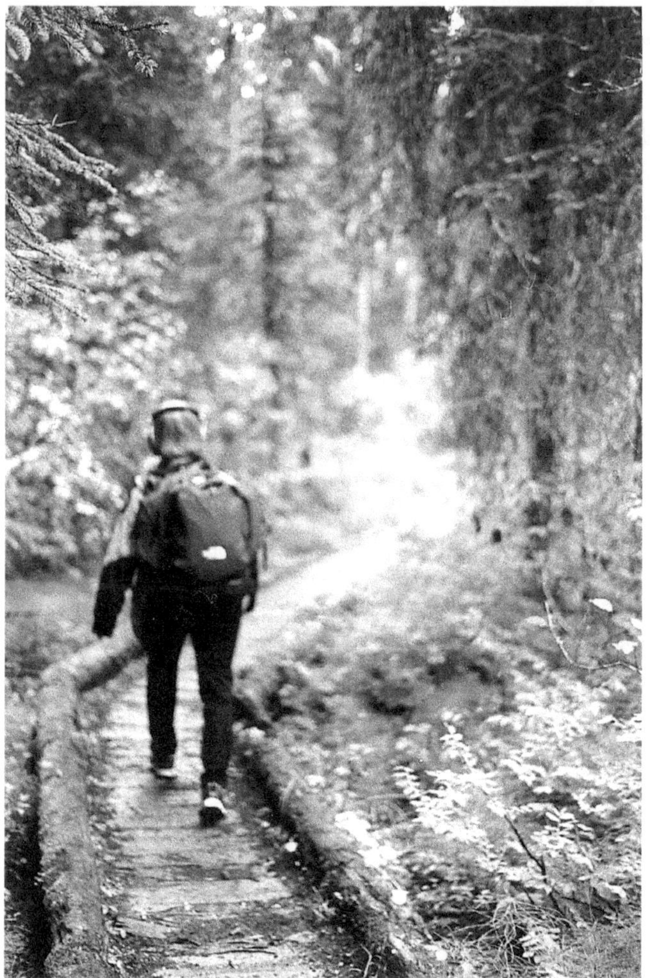

Figure 6.11
Teri Rueb, *Trace*, 1999. Installation. Produced in Yoho Park in the Canadian Rockies. *Trace* was a site-specific sound installation that transformed trails near the Burgess Shale fossil beds into a landscape commemorating personal loss. Photo: Eric Conrad.

with geographic information systems to "author" their environment. Like the founders of Mass Observation, a social research organization that was devoted to everyday life in Britain in the 1930s and 1940s, Proboscis adopted new technologies with a view to "sharing everyday knowledge and experience."[59]

PDPal was a public art project for personal digital assistants (PDAs), mobile phones, and the Web that was created by Marina Zurkow, Scott Paterson, and Julian Bleecker. The artists called it a tool for the collaborative mapping of emotions ("emotional GPS"). It differs from *Urban Tapestries* by its eccentric interface design and its impertinent tone. It featured a cartoon character, the Urban Park Ranger, who urged viewers to write their city.[60] Kiosks were set up in places like Times Square in New York, and they exhorted passers-by to "create a playful log of their daily encounters while traveling through the frenetic urban environment—transforming everyday routine into a realm of imagination and possibility."[61] The application would then create a "map of personal-digital experience based on a set of emotive coordinates—Social, Preposition, Texture, Speed and Weather," explains Julian Bleecker: "The 'map' was a kind of pictogram of the intersection of these coordinates."[62]

The *Urban Tapestries* software ran only on portable devices. It allowed people to create place-based content (text, audio, photos, and video) and consult information that had been added by other participants. Users could add new locations, location content, and the threads that link individual locations to local contexts. They could follow a selected thread by receiving a map of the locations that were associated with it or individual alerts when they were close to a location. They could also create and customize their own threads.

Urban Tapestries' collaborative map-making system was more flexible and user-friendly than that of *PDPal*, whose Urban Park Ranger was, in spite of his cuteness, highly directive (like a parody of Microsoft's cheerful assistant Bob). Although users may have balked at the rigidity of the Ranger's multiple-choice questions, these restrictions made it easier to visualize the responses: the aggregate information that people entered could then be plotted on a shared map, unlike responses to open-ended questions.[63]

At the time of this writing, both projects have gone offline, but the artists' Web sites offer a wealth of documentation. *PDPal* went through several iterations—the bus shelter with a two-sided durable transparency, shown in New York; the kiosk at the Minneapolis Sculpture Park; and finally *Mobile Scout* at Banff Center for the Arts in the Canadian Rockies.[64]

During *Urban Tapestries*' four-year existence, Proboscis ran several tests of the software. The first was held in December 2003 in London, where one hundred participants used pocket-size personal computers and a wireless network in Bloomsbury. Another took place six months later and covered a 3 kilometer square area of Central London. About fifteen participants tested the system for four weeks to give the developers "a sense of why, what for and how people will use it over time."[65]

Although both projects addressed the way people appropriate city space and mobile technology, only *Urban Tapestries* used the global positioning system.[66] By actively refusing GPS, *PDPal* tapped into the "anti-cartesian" mystique of the situationists. The project was engaging in part because of the way it used a variety of objects (kiosks, stickers, printed maps, animation) to embed meaning. It communicated itself by proposing colorful, animated images and short, pithy texts, the kind of public project that could appeal to audiences outside the art world. *PDPal*'s graphic persona and cheeky questions conveyed a veneer of New York chutzpah, capitalizing on the art world's enthusiasm for playful, situationist-inspired provocation. The artists intentionally *détourn*-ed (diverted) PDAs that, at the time, Bleecker says, "were gadgets for people with jobs and a sense of urgency about managing the minutiae of their lives. The idea of geographically uncoordinated maps, and maps coordinated by these five peculiar categories was antithetical to the sensibilities of PDA owners."[67]

What is disruptive in the gardens of an art museum may not have the same effect in Times Square. There, the animated Urban Park Ranger on the Panavision screen seemed to blend in with the many blinking signs.

It is difficult to know how many people actually used *PDPal* and what they did with it. Unlike projects that are identified as research, the artists' documentation does not foreground user testing. Curator Steve Dietz notes that

> Open systems need to take on a life of their own—to emerge—if they are to be truly successful. During the launch and promotion of *PDPal*, it received significant use, but it is unclear whether the narratives being told are enough to keep the communicity growing. However, each iteration of the project has made enormous conceptual leaps and adjustments, and particularly as the ability to add any base geographic map into the system is enabled, *PDPal* has the potential to be a virtual locus for homuncular storytelling.[68]

As it turned out, this did not happen, at least not in the sense Dietz evokes here, the kind of continuous online presence required to build up the "user-base" necessary for emergence. Today, the interactive Web site is offline. When the work was exhibited in 2011 at *Talk to Me* at the Museum of Modern Art in New York, it was in the form of an object. As an installation work, a project of this kind relies heavily on its physical presence. The kiosks can presumably be taken out of storage and reassembled, but anything digital must also be reprogrammed to run on current computer operating systems. This may be one reason why few public media art projects have staying power. The exception confirming the rule is the *[murmur]* project begun in 2003 and, at the time of this writing, still developing.

Oral Histories: Other Voices

Oral history is history from the ground up and involves recording both eyewitness accounts of historical events and individual recollections of everyday existence at a particular place and time, often weaving the two into a common thread. Oral history can be a messy form for historians because speakers' accounts are often recorded many years after the fact and can be notoriously inaccurate. Even so, they do reflect the diversity of individual viewpoints. Listening to the voices of students, professors, and townspeople as they recount their experiences brought back the 1970 shootings at Kent State University far more effectively than just reading their words.

Tapping into the power that voices carry in defining places, *[murmur]* is a series of oral histories launched in 2003 by a trio of Canadians—Shawn Micallef, James Roussel, and Gabe Sawhney. The artists record people's personal histories about significant places in their neighborhoods. At each location, they post an ear-shaped sign bearing a telephone number that passers-by can dial to listen to a story while standing on the spot where it happened.

The artists began by mapping Toronto's Kensington Market neighborhood, where Victorian buildings house a multiethnic population. In recent years, *[murmur]* has mapped other parts of Toronto, and offshoots have sprung up as far away as Edinburgh's Leith district and Eastern Beach in Geelong, Australia.[69] In each city, the focus is on a limited area.

Invoking the dialectic of space and place developed by Michel de Certeau (yet unwittingly reversing the terms), Micallef notes that "Living and interacting in the city is as much about places as it is about people . . . so what intangible things can turn a space (a word so loved by architects) into a place?"[70]

Like *Trace* and *34 North 118 West*, *[murmur]* plants sounds electronically in places that listeners visit, allowing them to listen as they move around. Although the first two projects use satellite positioning, *[murmur]* relies on a computer-based telephone answering system and interactive voice response (IVR) software. Unlike Teri Rueb's sound repository—which gathers songs, dirges, requiems, acoustic, and experimental works by invited artists that deal with a single theme, commemoration—*[mumur]* focuses instead on a specific genre, the personal story.

The *[mumur]* artists chose to filter material that was submitted by the public, screening out unsuitable contributions and optimizing the experience for their audiences. After a story has been selected, a group member meets the author to record it *in situ*. The artists cultivate marks of authenticity—a speaker's hesitation, a recognizable accent—that reflect the community in which they are embedded.[71] This is counterbalanced by an attention to form to make the stories compelling for listeners as well. The narratives must be short—from one to three minutes long.[72] The artists incite novice storytellers to draw out universal elements in their accounts to which others can relate.

For the moment, the project functions in a distributed manner, like a franchise. Its different iterations have been funded by arts and culture grants, local community organizations, and even private sponsors.[73] In Geelong, Australia, for instance, it was developed by a team of Australian artists as part of a three-year arts project, Connecting Identities, with a view to "celebrating links between people and places across

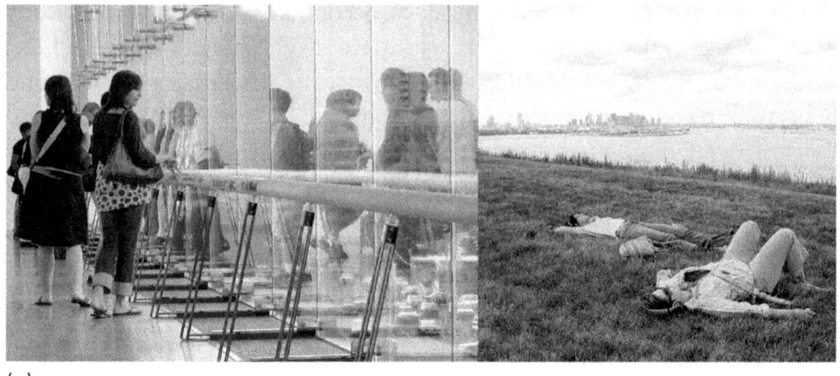

(a)

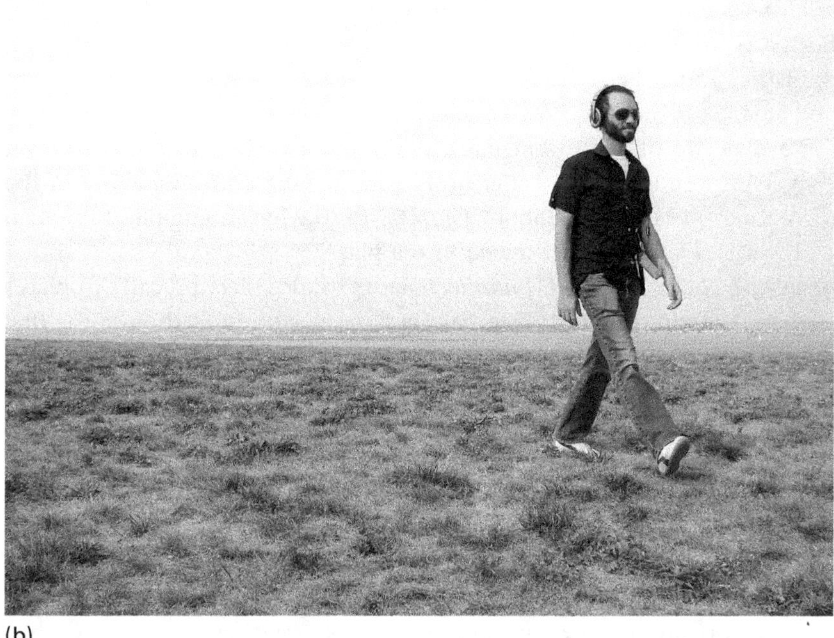

(b)

Figure 6.12

Teri Rueb, *Core Sample*, 2007. Installation. *a:* Rueb's site-specific sound walk and indoor sound sculpture link a public landfill park in the Boston Harbor Islands to the Institute of Contemporary Art on the downtown waterfront. *b:* The GPS-based interactive installation allows hikers equipped with headphones to explore the topography of Spectacle Island. Layered sounds evoke the material, geological, and cultural histories of the island as visitors explore the grassy terrain, pick up stones on the beach, and climb hills. Courtesy of the artist.

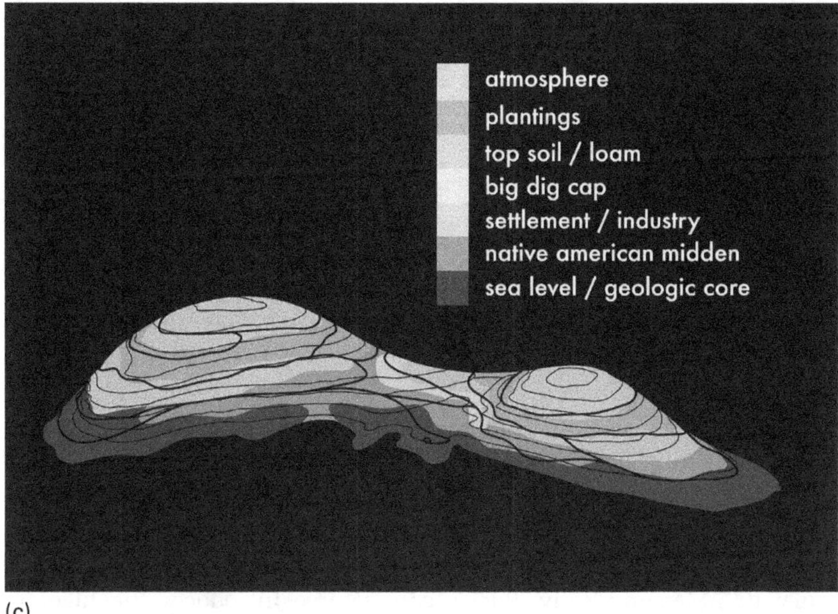

(c)

Figure 6.12 (continued)
c: Plan of core sample sound mapping with thematic content of sounds organized according to elevations. Courtesy of the artist.

Geelong."[74] When there are volunteers to record the stories and maintain the platform, a cell-phone-accessible sound archive is a cost-effective form of public art. And giving local residents a place to be heard can reinforce governments' efforts to foster cohesion among their various constituencies.[75]

Détournements?

Marc Tuters and Kazys Varnellis see spatial annotation projects as the contemporary heirs to the situationist practice of *détournement*,[76] yet none of these works really diverts or hijacks anything. They use technological tools to tell what at the time were unfamiliar stories. Since then, the combination of social media and mobile applications has brought ordinary people's stories into the mainstream. And although the term might characterize *[murmur]*, it is difficult to see how it could apply to research projects like *Urban Tapestries*, which was conceived and developed in partnership with collaborators such as Orange, HP Research labs, France Telecom R&D UK and Ordnance Survey. In the arts community, projects like this were criticized for their lack of autonomy, since the base map they used was restricted by copyright conditions imposed by Ordnance Survey. In exchange for backing, pioneers of spatial annotation were finding themselves in an uncomfortable position, either doing the legwork for military-industrial interests or supplying content to corporations that offered locative services.[77] Today, these debates have subsided as users of social networks eagerly supply whatever content is needed and locative media artists move into territories abandoned by industry.

Robert Smithson famously contrasted the brownfield sites where he made his earthworks with the "nonsites"—"abstract maps made into three dimensions"[78]—he exhibited in museums and galleries. Using GPS triangulation and sound layering, Teri Rueb has found a way to reconcile the two. Her site-specific sound walk, *Core Sample* (2007) (figure 6.12), links a public landfill park in the Boston Harbor Islands and the Institute of Contemporary Art on the downtown waterfront. The GPS-based interactive installation lets hikers equipped with headphones explore the cultural topography of Spectacle Island, while on the other side of the harbor, the indoor sound sculpture offers samples of it to visitors in ICA's Founders Gallery. A core sample is a cylindrical piece of material (such as rock) that is removed by a special drill and brought to the surface for examination. Such a sample can be used to determine the rock's porosity, to investigate the features of a particular zone of strata, or to show the order in which different strata accumulated.[79] Metaphorically, Rueb's core sample introduces the hiker to the different material, geological, and cultural layers underpinning the five-mile long footpath. As visitors climb uphill and down and walk along the beach, layered sounds evoke specific people and events in the island's history. The ambulatory sampling is completed at the ICA in Boston by a sound sculpture, a core sample that is presented horizontally in the form of a rail in front of the museum's glass wall overlooking the harbor. When visitors lean on this physical rail, they discover that it emits sounds from Spectacle Island.[80]

7 Hybrid Datascapes: Envisioning Space and Time

In 1945, Gjon Mili used strobe lights and long exposures to photograph figure skaters with small lamps attached to their skates. In a sense, the skaters were drawing lines on Mili's film as they jumped in the dark. When he traveled to Vallauris to photograph Pablo Picasso in January 1949, he showed the artist these shots, and Picasso took a flashlight with which he began drawing in the air. Mili captured his performance on film in a series of photographic prints by combining long-shutter openings with strobe flash to freeze the artist's position at different points during the execution.[1] With these "light drawings," Mili and his subjects created a hybrid medium, combining in one image the methods of two art media.

A hybrid in genetics is created by combining different species. So too the combination—hybridization—of index and icon here. In Charles Sanders Peirce's theory of signs, the index has a direct physical connection to its referent, unlike the icon: "There may be a mere relation of reason between the sign and the thing signified; in that case the sign is an *icon*. Or there may be a direct physical connection; in that case, the sign is an *index*."[2] Examples of indices include weathervanes, pointing fingers, footprints, and photographs: "an index . . . is a real thing or fact which is a sign of its object by virtue of being connected with it as a matter of fact. . . . A photograph, for example, not only excites an image, has an appearance, but, owing to its optical connection with the object, is evidence that that appearance corresponds to a reality."[3]

Half a century later, Bertolt Brecht questioned whether "the mere 'reproduction of reality'" in a photograph could say anything about that reality: "A photograph of the Krupp works or the AEG reveals next to nothing about these institutions. Actual reality has slipped into the functional. The reification of human relations—the factory, say—means that they are no longer explicit. So in fact 'something must be built up,' something 'artificial,' 'posed.'"[4]

Responding to Brecht's challenge, artists have attempted to construct artificial means to represent those realities that elude photography. In the 1920s and 1930s, this gave rise to an aesthetics of collage and photomontage. Since the development of personal computers, artists have included media hybridization among these means. Going beyond the mere juxtaposition of media, they have developed an aesthetics of the hybrid that now encompasses the global positioning system (GPS), radio-frequency identification (RFID) tagging, photography, video, sound, text, drawing, and animation.

What are the main components of hybrid mapping media? How have they been combined?

Drawing with Time and Space

At first sight, psychogeographical filmmakers seem to turn their backs on the twenty-first century. Their films are characterized by immobility. They are projected to a seated audience in darkened theaters or galleries. Rather than the rapid-fire cutting, zooming, and panning we have become used to, many eschew or severely limit camera movement.

Variations on the Long Focus Stare

Perhaps the quintessential psychogeographical film essay based on long takes and off-camera narration is Patrick Keiller's *London* (1994). The camera ostensibly follows the unseen protagonist Robinson, a part-time art lecturer who is doing research into "the problem of London" and whose thoughts are spoken by the narrator (Paul Scofield). The camera films fragments of space-time as the two characters move around London, visiting psychogeographical landmarks from Horace Walpole's Gothic villa Strawberry Hill to the docklands where Arthur Rimbaud used to wander. When the duo search for the school in Stoke Newington where young Edgar Allan Poe was once a pupil, they find no trace of it but instead find the house in which Daniel Defoe wrote Robinson Crusoe. Searching for the man of the crowd, they find shipwreck.

Keiller's experimental film essay counters our predilection for motion. In a series of long takes, the unmoving camera films tableaux of mostly outdoor public spaces. There are no close-ups or dolly shots, no visible characters, no dialog, and little ambient sound. As Keiller films the sequences, passers-by climb into buses, mill about on the railway platform, and move past the camera in the marketplace. The soundtrack alternates narration and fragments of mostly classical music—the slow movements of Beethoven's last string quartets, for instance. The shots are framed as symmetrical compositions with many "all over" fields, flattened perspectives, and facades that are parallel to the picture plane: circles and ripples in the Thames, flowers in a field, ivy on a wall. Billboards fill the frame, heralding the publication of "Diana: Her True Story. Part 2" in the *Sunday Times*, or Richard Long's 39-hour, 120-mile walk from River Avon to River Thames.

London offers an idiosyncratic portrait of the city in 1992, "a city under siege from a suburban government which uses homelessness, pollution, crime, and the most expensive and run-down public transport system of any metropolitan city in Europe as weapons against Londoners' lingering desire for the freedoms of city life." After many years abroad, the narrator has come home to "Dirty old Blighty, undereducated, economically backward, bizarre. A catalogue of modern miseries with its fake traditions, its Irish war, its militarism and secrecy, its silly old judges, its hatred of intellectuals, its ill health and bad food, its sexual repression, its hypocrisy and racism and its intolerance. It's so exotic . . . so home-made."[5]

1992 was the year that saw the reelection of John Major. In front of 10 Downing Street, we observe the arrival of the prime minister, while the narrator describes what this Tory victory will mean for the film's protagonist, Robinson:

> His flat would continue to deteriorate and its rent increase. He would be intimidated by vandalism and petty crime. The bus service would get worse. There would be more traffic and noise pollution, and an increased risk of getting knocked down crossing the road. There would be more drunks pissing in the street when he looked out of the window, and more children taking drugs on the stairs when he came home at night. His job would be at risk and subjected to interference. His income would decrease. He would drink more, and less well. He would be ill more often. He would die sooner.[6]

Later, the film shows the wreckage after bombings by the paramilitary Irish Republican Army (IRA). Among other things, the film critiques the conservative government's economic policies, its "love of pomp and circumstance," and its neglect of the city's infrastructure: "Robinson's first reaction [to the election] was one of spleen. There were, he said, no mitigating circumstances. The press, the voting system, the impropriety of Tory party funding—none of these could explain away the fact that the middle classes in England had continued to vote Conservative because in their miserable hearts they still believed that it was in their interests to do so."[7]

The accompanying narration is dense. Like a tour guide's spiel, it offers names, dates, and statistics. In one shot, people going to work in the City walk toward the camera while the narrator explains that the City with its 6,000 residents and 300,000 commuters has its own police force and 16 million square feet of empty office space.[8]

Despite the problematic relation of images to reality, the narrator expresses faith in the power of perception: "Robinson believed that if he looked at it hard enough, he could cause the surface of the city to reveal to him the molecular basis of historical events, and in this way he hoped to see into the future."[9] As applied to his films, the term *psychogeography* doesn't sit well with Keiller: "It's always seemed to me that whatever psychogeography was, it belonged to its initial lettrist and situationist protagonists and, probably, to their period, so I've tried to avoid the word. The difference, as I understand it, between what they were doing then and what we do now is that for Debord and his contemporaries, psychogeography, the dérive and so on were preliminary to the creation of some revolutionary, new space, something like that envisaged as New Babylon. I don't detect anything like this in the more recent activity."[10]

I think Keiller is wrong about this. His film-essays excel at revealing the "distinctive psychic atmosphere" of the places they portray, in keeping with the goals of the "science of relations and ambiances" that was psychogeography. In "Introduction to a Critique of Urban Geography," Debord insists on the "pleasing vagueness" of the term he and his friends adopted to identify the phenomena they began investigating in the summer of 1953: "Psychogeography could set for itself the study of the precise laws and specific effects of the geographical environment, whether consciously organized or not, on the emotions and behavior of individuals. The charmingly vague adjective *psychogeographical* can be applied to the findings arrived at by this type of investigation, to their influence on human feelings, and more generally to any situation or conduct that seems to reflect the same spirit of discovery."[11]

Three years later, Keiller made a sequel, *Robinson in Space* (1997), in which Robinson and the narrator explore the whole of England in a similar way. After another thirteen years, a third movie was released, *Robinson in Ruins* (2010).

Keiller was inspired by Chris Marker's *La jetée* (1962), a movie that was made with still photographs and narrated by an off-camera voice. Stylistically, his long shots evoke non-narrative experimental films by Michael Snow, Andy Warhol, and Chantal Akerman. In *News from Home* (1976), Akerman films New York in a series of long shots of ordinary places, while on the soundtrack, in a voiceover, the filmmaker reads from letters her mother sent to her from Brussels.

Keiller's fixed camera and dense narrative style have inspired many younger artists, including Nick Relph and Oliver Payne whose *Driftwood* (1999), is both a dérive and a guide through the city of London as seen by a skateboarder and Marie Preston whose *Un pointillé sur une carte* (A Dotted Line on a Map) (2007) recounts a walk from Paris to Saint-Denis. *Driftwood* opens with a pale and shaky image of what looks like skateboarders, while a voice declares emphatically: "Nobody knows London. There is no knowledge which can understand it, no scientific measure to gauge its spell. The London map is a meaningless set of lines, long since distorted—a handbook for the blind. You have to succumb. Become a tourist in your own city and get lost." The film begins at London's South Bank Centre, where skateboarders defy the authorities. The now stable camera focuses on the spikes and fences set up to discourage skateboarding, while in the background skaters glide back and forth. The narrator, Ben Keyworth, speaks quickly with a very pronounced accent (nothing like Paul Scofield's BBC English which he delivers in a practiced, somewhat amused tone). The commentary is by turns peremptory and scornful ("Put up barriers and watch skateboarders scale (skate) them. Carve grooves in the pavement before high sets of steps and watch high-heeled pigeon women trip and break their ankles. . . . Send down a security guard and watch 'im get smacked in th' fuckin' mouth"), ironic ("Youth culture has been stolen—taken away and repackaged. But that's OK; you can buy it back. . . . It's over the counter culture") and vehement ("Don't bother thinking because the new softback edition will be out soon at a new low price, your ideals reduced to slogans . . . watered down and sold back at a price"), lashing out against digital fog and mobile phone users, branding and gentrification. The only users of public space who find grace in their eyes are punks, graffers, and the skaters, who navigate the winding streets of London "a pack-donkey city" (Le Corbusier) as if it were "a man's city" with straight roads. After relating skaters' behavior to situationist ambiance maps with their "vortexes and strong currents," the narrator quotes at length from Ivan Chtcheglov's "Formulary for a New Urbanism." Moving from the South Bank to Canary Wharf and Hyde Park, they describe the public executions held at Marble Arch and the origins of Soho as a place for exiles and outcasts. Regent Street was, the voice tells us, "designed by John Nash in the early nineteenth century as a 'cordon sanitaire' between the scruffs of Soho and the toffs of Mayfair." There is no mistaking on which side of the street their sympathies lean. The video closes with a call to "smash the symbols of the empire in the name of nothing but the heart's longing for grace", and after a succession of images recapitulating its main themes, shows a trash can on which someone had written in white letters "I love you."[12] Like Keiller, Relph and Payne have expanded the idea geographically. *Driftwood* is the first film in a spatial trilogy that moves gradually outward from the city center. *House and Garage* (1999) gives the suburbs the same disenchanted tone, while *Jungle* (2001) deals with the country.

French artist Marie Preston has made two films based on walks in La Plaine Saint-Denis that link the medieval martyr Saint Denis to the present-day town north of Paris that bears his name (figure 7.1). After being beheaded by third-century Romans in a place often identified as Montmartre,[13] Denis, "bishop of the Parisii," picked up his head and walked over the plain to Catullacia, the location of the present-day Basilica of Saint Denis, where he gave his head to a pious woman, Catulla, who buried it there.

Preston's first walks took her from Montmartre to the Basilica of Saint Denis along the route the saint was said to have taken in the third century. On one trip, she was accompanied by an architect who discussed urban building projects in progress and on another by a member of the French federation of hiking who pointed out places of touristic interest. She went back with a professional video camera that she placed on a tripod to record the places they described using tilting and panning to slowly reveal each spot. The sixteen-minute video *Un pointillé sur une carte* (A Dotted Line on a Map) shows these places, one by one, beginning with the statue of the saint in a Montmartre park and ending with a busy pedestrian thoroughfare in the center of Saint-Denis, facing the cathedral, while the soundtrack plays her companions' walking commentaries.

In the nineteenth century, La Plaine Saint-Denis was the site of industrial development. The towns of Saint-Denis, Saint-Ouen, and Aubervilliers attracted successive

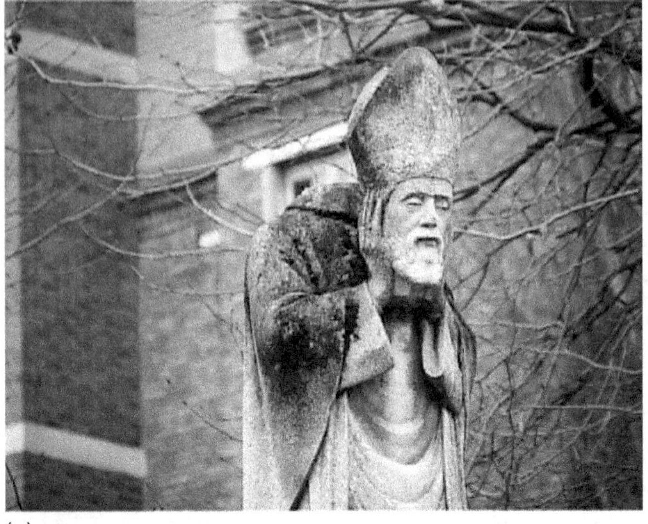

(a)

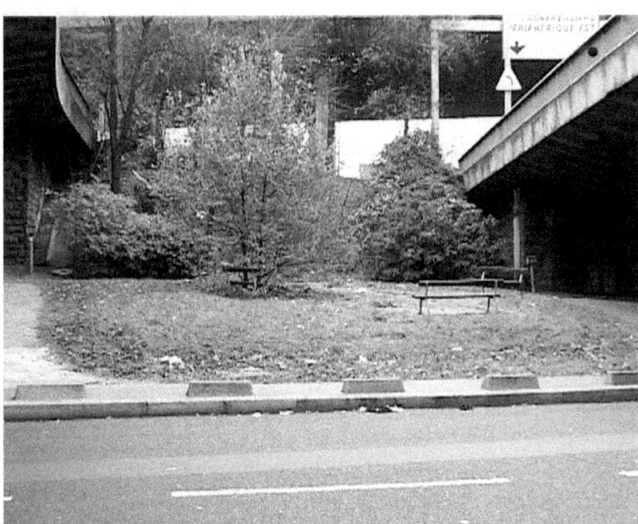

(b)

Figure 7.1

Marie Preston, *Un pointillé sur une carte* (*A Dotted Line on a Map*), 2007. Video, 16 minutes. Accompanied by an architect and a member of the French federation of hiking, Marie Preston walked from Montmartre to the Basilica of Saint Denis along the route that Saint Denis was said to have taken in the third century. *a:* Statue of Saint Denis holding his severed head in a Montmartre park. *b:* Part of Saint Denis's route.

waves of immigrants who found work in the machine tool factories. After most of the factories closed in the 1960s and 1970s, leaving many residents unemployed, La Plaine Saint-Denis became the locus of a vast urban renewal project that began with the construction of a national sports stadium. As the architect notes, it is an "emergent city."[14] Cities used to have limits—fortifications, gates—separating them from the surrounding countryside. Little by little the country between the cities has vanished, as the conurbation has continued to spread. The town of Saint-Denis was formerly an independent city. Now it is experienced as an extension of Paris, simply a dotted line on a map, cutting arbitrarily through the shapeless sprawl.

When the Camera Goes for a Walk

An early film attraction was the phantom ride, in which a camera recorded continuously from the front of a train. Visitors at fairs in the late nineteenth and early twentieth centuries were thrilled at being projected through space by an invisible force. A variation on the phantom ride is the psychogeographical walking tour in which the camera follows the movement of the filmmaker's body. Jonas Mekas was among the first experimental filmmakers to abandon the tripod for a hand-held movie camera to film the short sequences of his *Walden: Diaries, Notes and Sketches* (1969). Shigeko Kubota videotaped a tour of SoHo led by Fluxus founder George Maciunas with friends who each describe a building in his or her own language—*George Maciunas with Two Eyes 1972 George Maciunas with One Eye 1976* (1994).[15] In the 1980s, Nelson Sullivan documented his own life in the downtown New York art world. By carrying the video camera at arm's length and using a wide-angle lens, he was able to film himself in his environment as he walked across town, in *Nelson Sullivan's Trip to the East Village in 1989* (1989), and *A Walk to the Pier, the Last Day* (1989) while improvising a stream-of-consciousness monologue.

Marie Preston's video *Plaine* (Plain) is built around four walks that were filmed in La Plaine Saint-Denis. Preston carried the camera pointed straight ahead at waist level to approximate the height of the saint's gaze when he was carrying his head (the way he appears on the facade of Notre Dame Cathedral in Paris). For each of the walks, she is guided through a different neighborhood by people who live there—including an 80-year-old Spanish woman who points out community gardens, a group of women who take her to see the planted esplanade over the expressway and two Sri Lankan children who appear at regular intervals between sections of the video.[16] The children lead the filmmaker around the block to show her where individual homes were torn down to make way for the high rise apartment buildings under construction.

Here, the artist is no longer the guide but the one guided. She organizes the tour but, like an ethnographer doing fieldwork, lets local "informants" choose which places to show her, creating situations as well as objects. To include passers-by in the ritual of art making, the artist set up a table with a supply of modeling clay in front of the cathedral. When people stopped at her table, she asked them to sculpt a head for her. This video was presented in an exhibition, together with a hundred fist-sized clay heads that had been modeled by inhabitants of Saint-Denis, (*Plaine—Sans Tête*, 2008).[17] In her work, Preston argues for a "poetics of relationships." Because these sculptures result from activities carried out collaboratively, they give the relationship a visible form. As the artist puts it, "The sculpture takes on symbolic effectiveness during the collaborative activity insofar as the symbolic is born of shared imagination. . . . Creating the relation [by walking with people or asking them to sculpt] generates the symbolic dimension."[18]

Another subjective point of view is offered by Canadian artist Jana Sterbak in two video installations. In *From Here to There* (2003), viewers accompany the artist's Jack Russell terrier, Stanley, who wears a head-mounted camera as he trots along the snowy banks of the St. Lawrence River. In *Waiting for High Water* (2005), they are taken for a dizzying run through the flooded streets of Venice at *acqua alta* (high tide). For this three-channel video installation, Stanley was equipped with three miniature video cameras—one in front and the other two on each side simulating what his eyes see.[19] The footage was edited to form a hallucinatory triptych that was nine meters by two and a half, showing Venice at ground level from the perspective of an animal whose presence we feel rather than see. Synched to the dog's gait, Alex Weimann's harpsichord music adds to the otherworldly effects of the images.

A final example of camera walking comes from mainstream cinema. To show the events leading up to a mass school shooting that was inspired by the 1999 killings at Columbine High School in Colorado, the camera in Gus Van Sant's film *Elephant* (2003) follows individual students as they move through the school hallways—a blond boy whose father is too drunk to drive him to school, a photographer, a solitary girl on her way to the library to shelve books, two boys who have been pelted with spitballs in class. The tracking shots draw on the tradition of adventure games to create a nonlinear space-time that closely associates walking and mapping, backtracking in time to show events that take place in the same ten-minute period. Scenes in which characters cross paths are shown from the viewpoints of each participant, one after the other. The DVD of the film proposes a scene breakdown in the form of an interactive map of the high school.

Van Sant has explained that the title was borrowed from Alan Clarke's 1989 film about Northern Ireland, which he took to be an allusion to a famous Buddhist parable. In it, a group of blind men touch an elephant, each forming his own idea of the animal according to the part that he has touched—the trunk, the tusk, the ear, the leg, the side.[20] The subjective point of view shows the film's characters groping in the dark, each one expressing his or her impression of the beast.

Hybrid Datascapes

In a prescient article published in 1982, Bill Viola developed the idea that contemporary art, when seen as a diagram structuring "data space," renews a lost tradition in European art. He showed that this loss was part of a "progressive distancing of the arts away from the sacred and towards the profane" and that this structural aspect of the image "was preserved through the Renaissance . . . in the continued relation between the image and architecture. Painting became an architectural, spatial form, which the viewer experienced by physically walking through it. The older concept of an idea and an image architecture, a memory 'place' like the mnemonic temples of the Greeks, is carried through in the great European cathedrals and palaces, as is the relation between memory, spatial movement, and the storage (recording) of ideas."[21]

GPS tracks are mathematical visualizations of a chronological sequence of track points. In this sense, they too are diagrams. Many recent projects explore the potential of media hybridization by combining GPS tracks or motion-capture data with sound sampling and photo or video imagery. Each of the component media objects is indexical in that it was produced by objects in real space, but often it is digital as well, which means that whatever we see or hear is just one of the ways the same information can be presented. Texts, images, sounds, and videos are all made of and can be visualized as algorithmic code.

Three-Dimensional Experiences

Hybrid maps bring a new dimension to landscape. Begun in 1992, Masaki Fujihata's *Field-Works* series develops datascapes from GPS position data combined with moving images captured by video.[22] These projects "reconstruct collective memories in cyberspace as a kind of video archive":

> *Field-Works* stretches and pulls at the coordinate system—in the same way that dancers play with shifting the center of gravity of the body to create a kind of distortion in the fabric of space-time—by introducing multiple view points, using a camera mounted gyroscope to translate even the intimate movements of the physical gaze as a part of the resulting work, and, in earlier versions of the project, representing the physical terrain as a function of the speed at which it is encountered.[23]

In 2005, Fujihata made two projects based on interviews. For *Talking Tree,* a series of GPS-video interviews with residents of Graz, Austria, one of the town's oldest women put him in touch with her friends, who in turn recommended other friends, and as the number of connections grew, the project blossomed like a tree (figure 7.2). *Landing Home in Geneva* focused on the "border between country and language." For this project, the artist interviewed seven professional interpreters who left their native

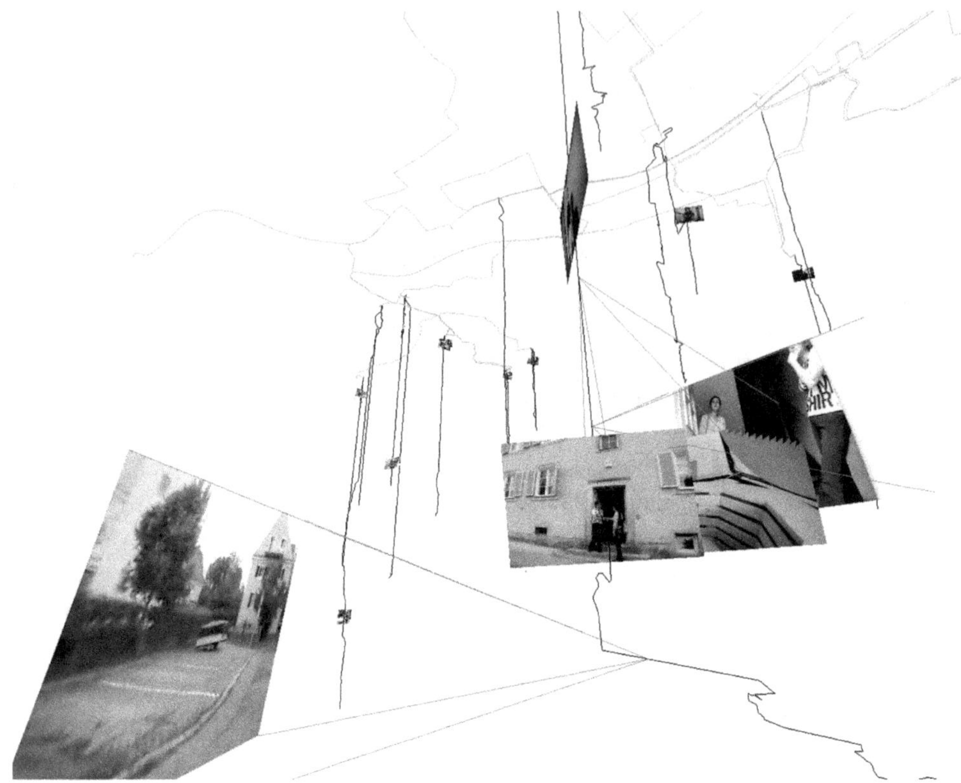

Figure 7.2
Masaki Fujihata, *Talking Tree*, 2005. Video and GPS. Fujihata made a series of GPS video interviews with residents of Graz, Austria. In this photo, the lines correspond to the GPS trails, along which the videos are placed at the exact spot and angle from which they were shot. © Masaki Fujihata.

countries and lived in Geneva, Switzerland (figure 7.3). Each interview started at the interviewee's home or apartment and ended in a place in which she was comfortable enough to invite Fujihata. As in the other *Field Works*, the spaceline and the timeline coincided.

This was the first time he had used a panoramic lens for video recording and projecting a cylinder shape in cyberspace: "the cylinder shakes, moves, travels along the movement of the cameraman, and he cannot escape from being recorded."[24] In a sense, he is actualizing Nelson Sullivan's subjective camera by combining it with objective GPS position data and posing philosophical problems of gaze, vanishing point, and projection.

Fujihata's technique of connecting video recording and data capture and using an unusual camera orientation "could become a new standard in film-making," writes

Jean-Louis Boissier: the artist has discovered "a way of relating to people and to their space, which is at once poetic and documentary, subjective and objective. If the image is a panorama, the cameraman is rejected from his privileged place 'behind the camera' to join the others in the space being filmed."[25]

Fujihata considers technical invention as part of art making: "I see media art not so much as 'using' new kinds of media as the creativity to 'make' those media. If you take the view that using new media constitutes media art, you end up talking about 'new media art' and 'digital media art' in the same way people refer to 'oil painting art' or 'art sculpture.' The essence of media art, however, lies not here but in creating new media. I believe therefore that a new medium should be formed with each individual work."[26]

Following Masaki Fujihata's example, Liliane Terrier and Daniel Sciboz have created specific modes of presentation for each of their *GPS Movies*. Both works were based on walks through La Plaine Saint-Denis north of Paris with a synchronized video camera and GPS. Sciboz wrote custom software in Director and Processing to model 3D representations of the experiences.[27] Presented as a diptych on a computer screen, *GPS Movies 1* (2004) shows side by side a video that was shot by a webcam fixed to a laptop computer and its cartographic trace (the 3D trajectory built from the GPS coordinates). In *GPS Movies 2* (2005), the GPS automatically sets off or stops the video recording, creating a hybrid object that includes both landscape and map.[28]

Both works combined collective performance and exploratory walking. *GPS Movies 1* took the form of a four-day workshop with a group of students and artists in October 2004, followed by a two-day exhibition at the Fratellini Academy of Circus Arts.[29] The walks took participants to places ranging from Thomas Hirschhorn's art studio in Aubervilliers to a community garden in Paris (ECObox). Several walks explored local "non-places"—a highway bridge, slaughterhouse, a vacant lot, an industrial wasteland. One of the most memorable meandered through the halls of the university as part of a performance led by Ben Patterson. A computer was carried in front of the operator in a baby sling and recorded both video and time/position data from the GPS unit. On a split screen, parallel video and spatiotemporal data (on a dynamic 3D map) were shown from the same place at exactly the same time.

More tightly orchestrated, *GPS Movies 2* was an hour and a half walk that took place on June 25, 2005, in an area north of Paris. It was led by Liliane Terrier and Daniel Sciboz, together with a group of artists and students (figure 7.4). Two teams set out from opposite ends of La Plaine Saint-Denis, one moving east from Saint-Ouen and the other moving west from Aubervilliers. Following a precisely timed protocol, they each took the same route from opposite directions, crossing paths midway. Each computer-controlled camera was set to film alternatively, so that when one team was filming, the other was not.[30] The final result braided the two interlocking 3D videos

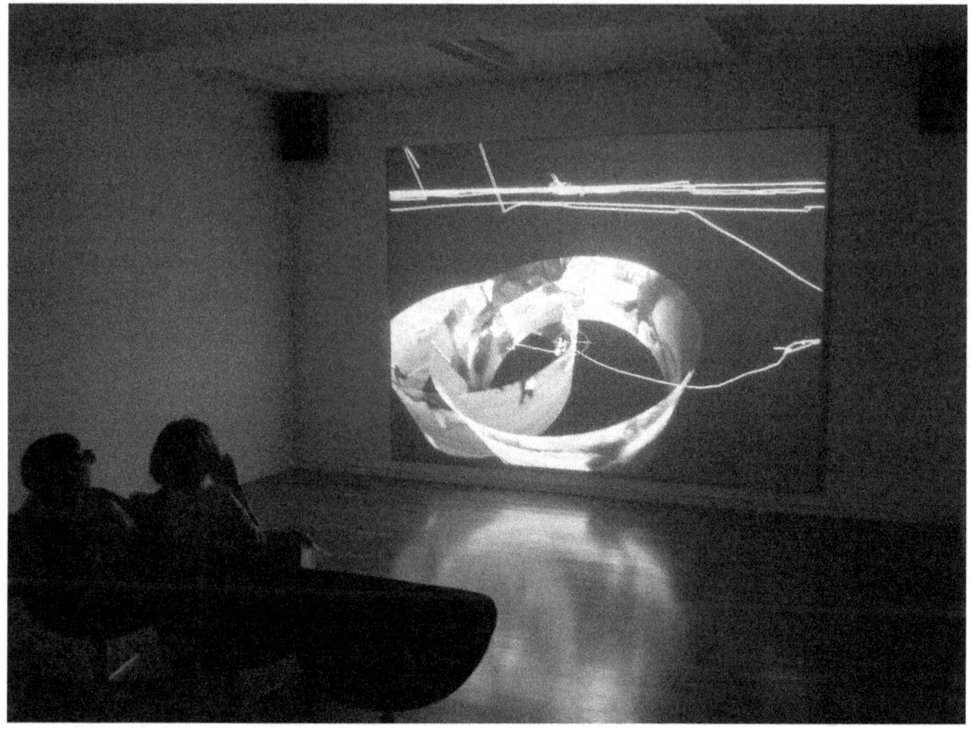

(a)

Figure 7.3
Masaki Fujihata, *Landing Home in* Geneva, 2005. Panoramic video and GPS. © Masaki Fujihata. *a:* Installation view.

to show staggered views of their combined path. The path unfolds in real time like an accordion, prompting Sciboz to compare it to Edward Ruscha's book *Every Building on the Sunset Strip*.

Mapping as a Storytelling Tool

Esther Polak has continued to combine the graphic and narrative possibilities of GPS to create what she calls a new kind of documentary that uses GPS traces to explore human landscapes. After spending time with bird watchers, she said her familiar landscape had become populated with birds that she had never seen before: "The question struck me: what do I not see now?"[31] Before 2003, she did not see milk routes: how does milk find its way from the cow to our coffee cups? This blind spot was partially corrected by realizing *Milk* in collaboration with Ieva Auzina. *Milk* featured GPS traces and filmed interviews with participants all along the milk chain, from dairy farmers in Latvia to cheese eaters in the Netherlands. Imagining Europe as one might

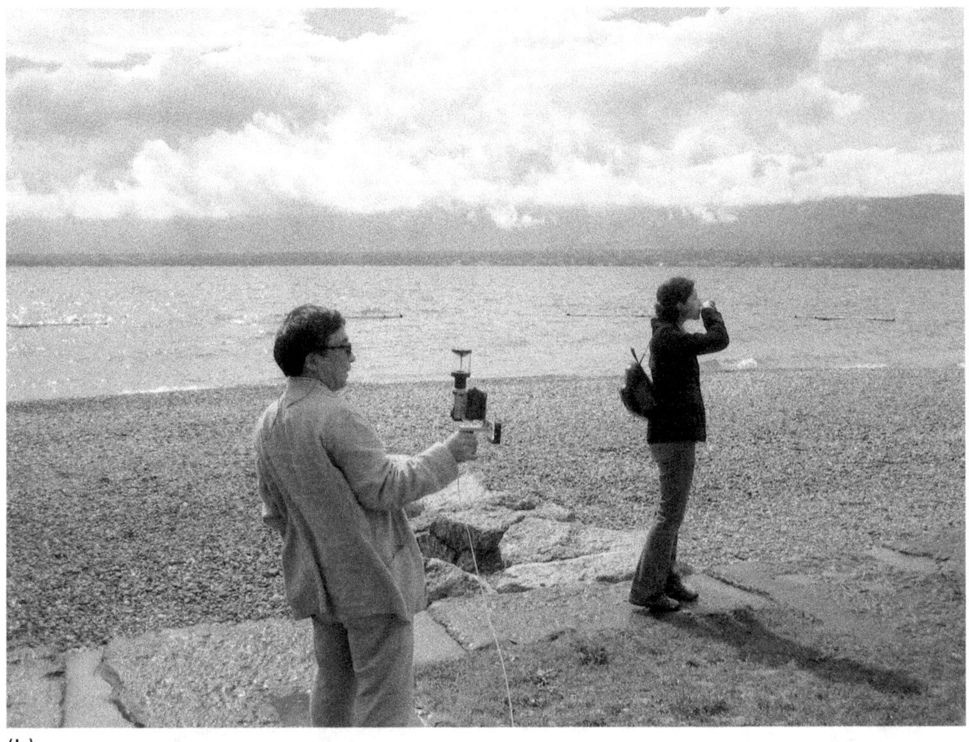

(b)

Figure 7.3 (continued)
b: The artist used a panoramic video camera that included his own image in the shots. © Masaki Fujihata.

see it from space ("No borders, just land with people and things. People and things that move"), they created a map that "follows the milk from the udder of the cow to the plate of the consumer, by means of the people involved."[32]

Participants were given a GPS device that they carried during the course of an ordinary working day. The artists visited them to show their paths and gather their reactions. The final work is a documentary hybridization of GPS tracks, video and audio. Polak and Auzina portray various people, from the "master of inventive stable-building" in Vidrizi, Latvia, to a couple of "gourmet connoisseurs" who buy their food every week at the Utrecht open-air market. Along the way, we meet two sisters who "manage to make their twenty-four cows laugh," a milk collector who starts his 136-kilometer route at 4 a.m. and thereby links all the farms, an Italian cheese maker, a Dutch cheese trader and the director of the local milk factory

This was an opportunity to explore the human aspect of globalization and bring the existence of Latvian farmers to the awareness of western Europeans whose lives

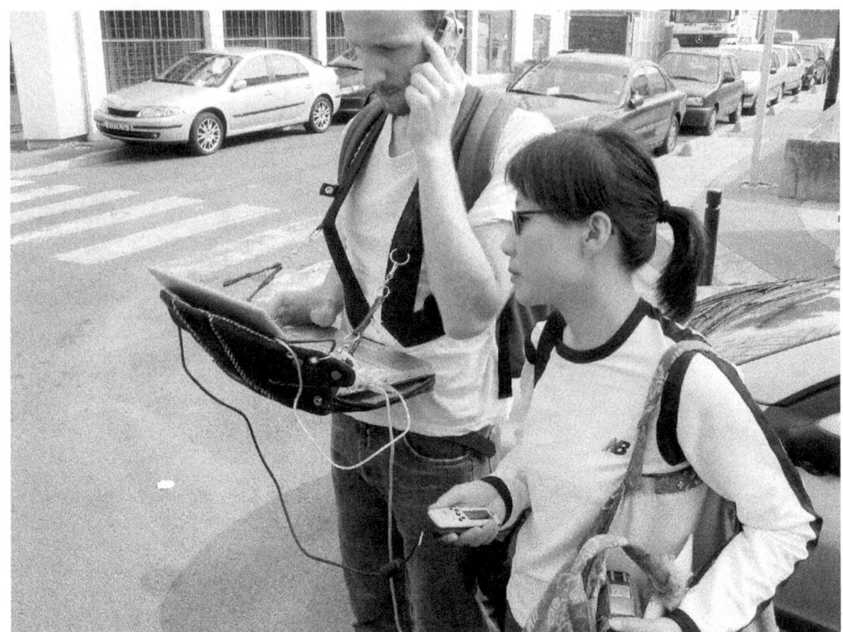

(a)

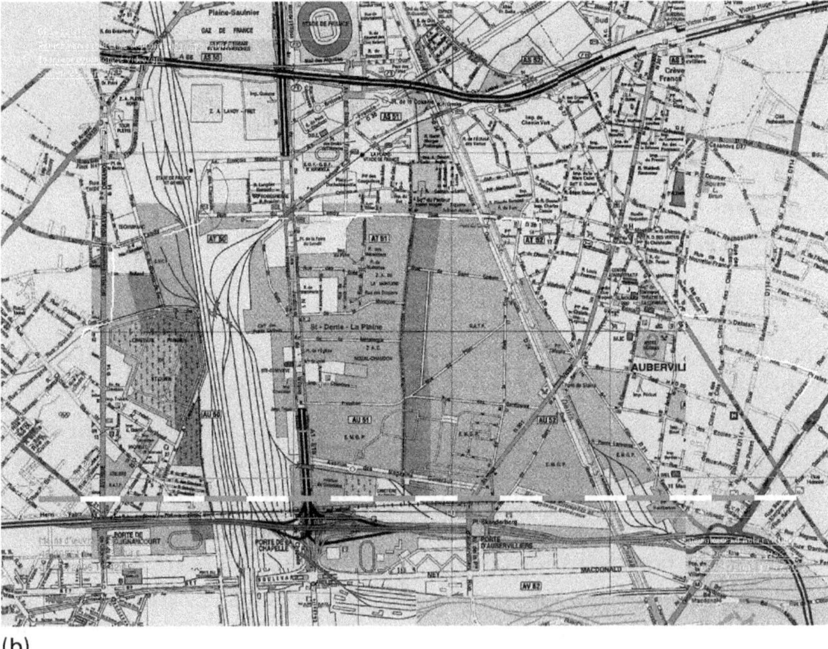

(b)

Figure 7.4

Liliane Terrier and Daniel Sciboz, *GPS Movies 2*, 2005. Video and GPS. Two teams equipped with a computer and a webcam set out from opposite ends of La Plaine Saint-Denis. Images: © Jean-Louis Boissier, 2005. *a:* The making of GPS movies. Team 1, Loïc Horellou et Yi Hua Wu. Starting point, Mains d'Œuvres in Saint-Ouen. *b:* A map of the walk showing the two braided paths.

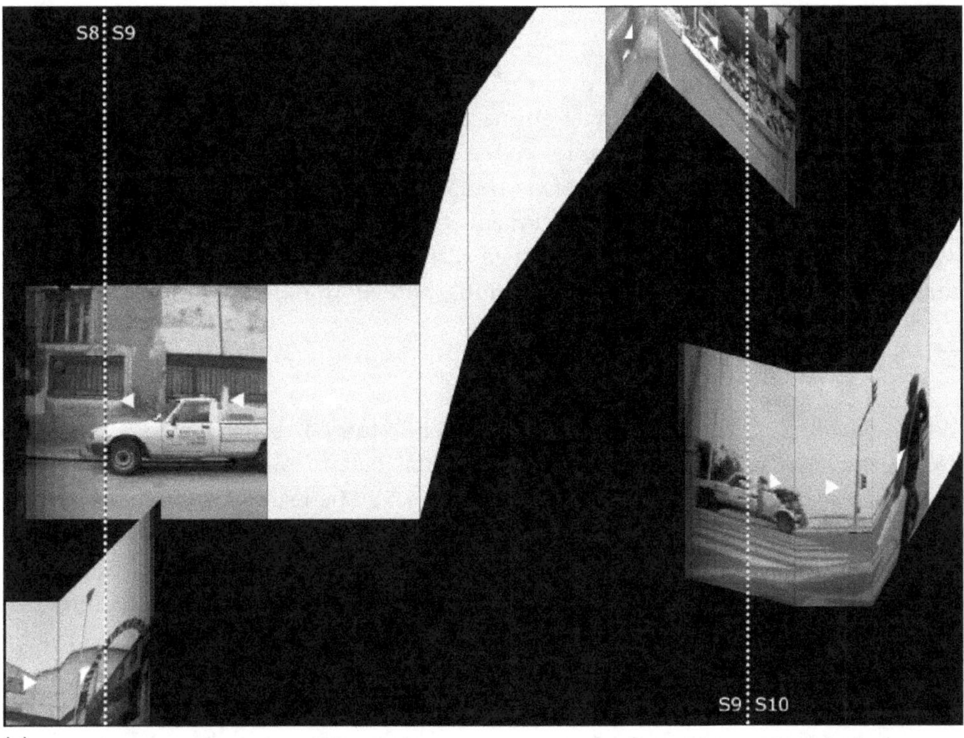

(c)

Figure 7.4 (continued)
c: Diagram showing the work's structure. © Jean-Louis Boissier.

they impact. *Milk* was immensely popular and won a prize at the Ars Electronica festival. Locative media practitioners cite it to vindicate their art form, which is often stigmatized for its proximity to the military-industrial complex.

This betrays more than just nostalgia for the fast-disappearing mom-and-pop food chain. In a globalized world that is dominated by the factory farms of an opaque agribusiness, the provenance of our food is largely unknown. Since the mad cow scare of the 1990s, butchers in France display a poster showing a cow behind a barbed wire fence, proffering its identity card. The tag-line reads "to get into this butcher's shop our beef had to show its papers," reflecting a populist parallel between illegal immigrants (*sans papiers*) and imported meat. Customers' desire for information about where an animal was raised (and when it was slaughtered) reveals how widespread the desire is for more transparency, to assure people that complex economic processes can be known. This desire is not new. One of Dziga Vertov's *Kino Glaz* films from 1924 rewinds the film reel to go back in time: meat comes back to life as a bull, and loaves of bread return to being wheat harvested in the field.

Evidence that these questions matter today can be found in the growing number of documentary projects that are devoted to commodity chains:[33] "Where does our food come from? How did it get to our table?" For a class on food politics, Tracy Ore's students research and publish fact sheets on items found on supermarket shelves, including aspartame, baby formula, coffee, mushrooms, and olive oil. The online visual encyclopedia *How Stuff Is Made* (*HSIM*), researched by Natalie Jeremijenko's engineering and design students, documents the production of consumer goods such as fortune cookies, neon signs, and bottled spring water. Their photo essays chronicle manufacturing processes, working conditions, and environmental effects.[34]

Shifting Perspective

With *NomadicMilk*, begun in 2006, Esther Polak returned to the "milkscape" motif: "Milk, she says, has always been a fundamental part of our diet and as such has sculpted our lives and our landscapes"[35] (figure 7.5). She teamed up with an anthropologist and a robotics engineer to explore one aspect of the globalized economy—milk distribution systems in western Africa. The word *our* now includes inhabitants of the global south and denotes a shift in point of view. The first installment of *NomadicMilk* showed, via GPS tracks, the migration of nomads and their herds of cattle during the dry season in northern Cameroon. Later, Polak and her team traveled to Nigeria, where they used satellite technology to track the paths of both Fulani herders and truckers transporting imported Peak brand milk from the harbor in Lagos to the capital, Abuja. In both cases, GPS data was fed to a custom-built robot, which used sand to draw the recorded routes, allowing the participants to see and comment on their own tracks. This kind of output device, which did not need the usual paraphernalia of projection (screen, projector, darkened room, and electrical power source), was conducive to having large groups of people gather around the sand map and discuss it. Like the participants in *Amsterdam RealTime*, the nomads, she says, "immediately recognized themselves in the sand routes as the robot carried them out. . . . It let people look at the patterns they made based purely on memory, based on their own route. It is not about how people read or use maps. For me it's all about revisiting spatial experience—as a way of bringing about a new perception."[36]

The results are generally shown (in Europe) as an installation. In an early configuration, Polak displayed a GPS drawing representing one day of cow herding with the Amadu Idiris family in Plateau State, Nigeria, in December 2006. The film footage was projected on one wall while the robot moved around the room, spitting out sand as it went. Waypoints (such as river crossings) were indicated on the floor by photos planted on sticks. In later shows, individual routes were pictured in a set of twelve 70- by 100-centimeter sand-colored prints made using the robot. The set of monoprints on canvas form a grid, either on the wall or the floor. They are accompanied by two video projections.[37]

Renewing the Documentary Form?

Polak aims at renewing the documentary genre with the techniques of media hybridization she foregrounds in her practice. One influence she drew on for the *Milk* projects is *Let Us Now Praise Famous Men*, a 1941 book that documented the lives of tenant farmers who worked the Alabama cotton fields during the Great Depression. Writer James Agee and photographer Walker Evans carried out a "technological experiment" she compares to her own: they "lived for months among three tenant families, won their trust, took pictures, made notes, did their documentation. In the final book, this resulted in the photography and the text being equally important. . . . In *Milk*, we also based the project on the equal use of several documenting techniques: visualized GPS-tracking, sound recording and photography. . . . Although recording the subject as realistically as possible, each technique gives a different point of view, showing that there is never such a thing as total truth, and clearly demonstrating that the medium influences the message."[38]

As an outsider, she had misgivings about her own role, as did Agee and Evans before her: "I almost felt like I was stealing something. Something totally private, the exact locations and times of their activities." However, "the special combination of comments, photography and GPS-imaging . . . transform the people into active 'pencils,' drawing in their own landscape, instead of passive objects whose ways were being documented." When the artists accompanied them in the field to record their activities and showed participants their tracks, the result could be realistic, while clearly showing "the limitations of every one of the media we had used." They also subtitled the soundtrack (few viewers would have understood all the languages spoken), which adds another layer to the mix. For her, this combination undermines the realism of each technology yet paradoxically "makes the whole experience even more realistic." Here she revives the modernist convention of medium specificity that was shunned by the postmoderns: "this tool shows the story of landscape, space and people, in a way that would not have [been] possible with another means."[39]

In the presentation system devised for *NomadicMilk*, the GPS tracks are replotted to a reduced spatiotemporal scale: proportions are distorted for the sake of legibility. The robot contains a bottle full of sand with a hole in the lid, moves along the ground, and draws the shape of the GPS tracks by leaving a trail of sand behind it. Sand drawings are made both on site (to present the tracks to the participants) and afterward when the project is exhibited, so "the robot functions as a performative tool, making the GPS tracks tangible and physically present." The artist found it difficult to represent the tracks in a way that is understandable to the audiences. Like the dream work

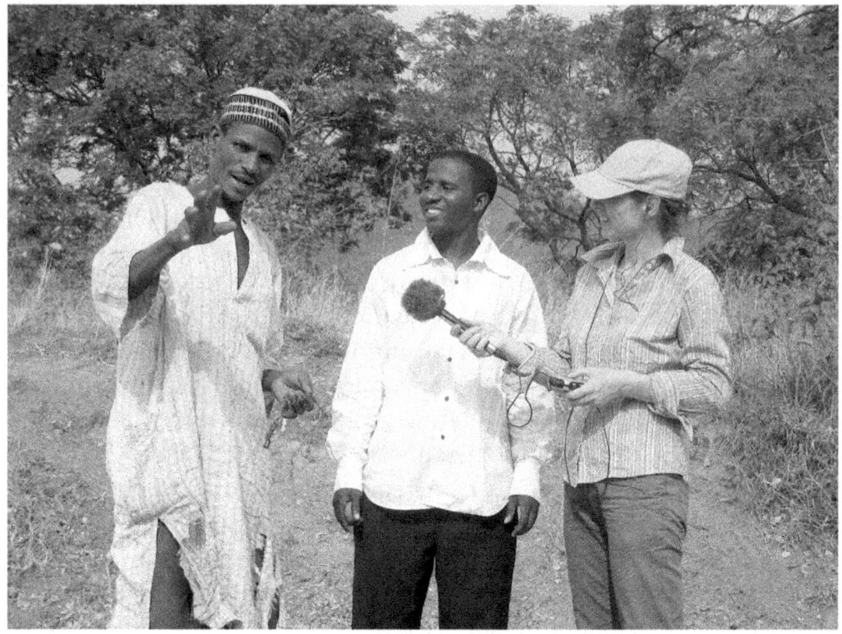

(a)

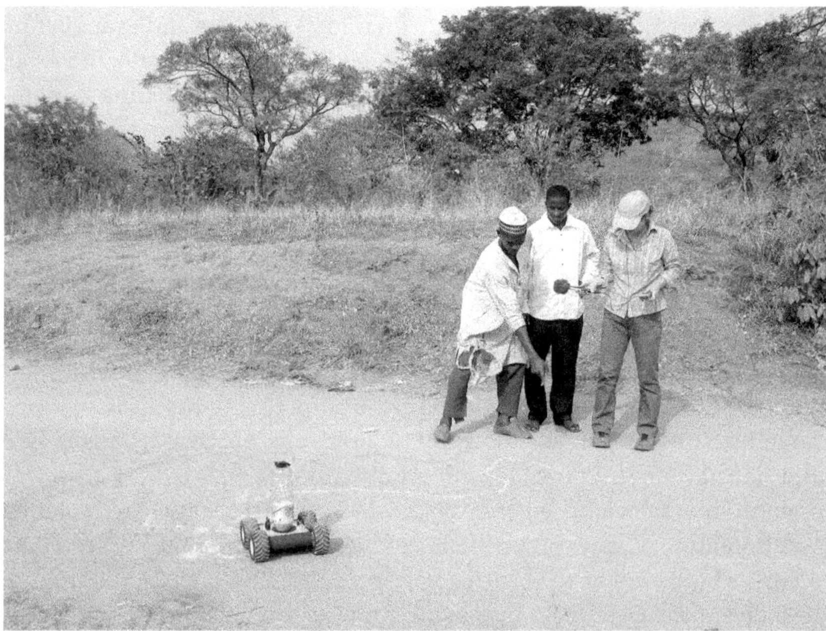

(b)

Figure 7.5

Esther Polak and team, *NomadicMilk*, Nigerian version 2006. GPS technology is used to draw the paths of nomadic Fulani herders and truckers transporting imported milk from the harbor in Lagos to the capital, Abuja. *a* and *b:* A robot used sand to draw the recorded routes, allowing the participants (here Fulani herder Mr. Idiris) to comment on their own tracks.

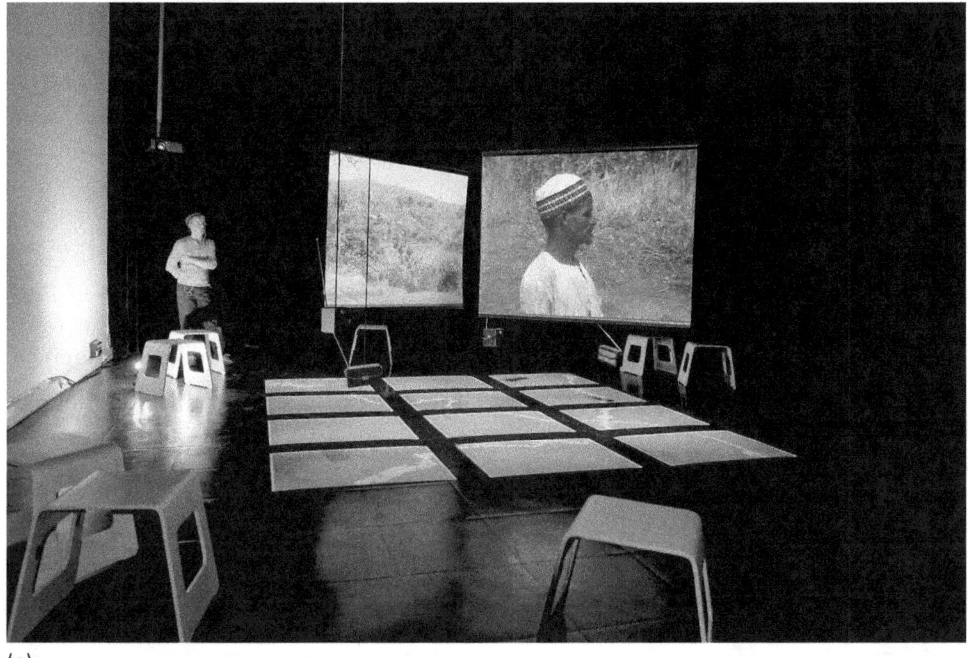

(c)

Figure 7.5 (continued)
c: A view of the installation exhibited at Zaal 5 in Den Haag, The Netherlands, in February 2010.

in Freud's analysis, with its emphasis on condensation and displacement, "The representation of both time and space had to be compressed, scaled, and deformed in order to make the robot draw a sand line that is a representation to which the participants and audiences can relate in a direct manner."[40]

The trickiest part was to combine "the vastly different spatial and temporal scales of the two dairy economies . . . into one intersecting drawing." To do this, she built a basic editing tool for GPS data. The manipulated tracks can be situated somewhere between the traditional sketch map drawn from memory and "hardcore GPS route registration," but she was surprised to discover that "when GPS tracks become elastic, open for flexible plotting, radical editing even," the "manipulated tracks became even more 'real' in the experience of the participants . . . if being recognizable as belonging to the self is a criterion for realism."[41]

Although *realism* is often used to designate any illusionist style of art that depicts phenomena the eye can see, the term also refers to an artistic movement that arose in France in the 1850s. In reaction to the emotional effusion of romanticism, the realists aimed to render what they considered to be objective reality in works that were undistorted by personal bias. They valued truth and accuracy, mimesis rather than idealization—no matter how sordid. In the same spirit, Polak's GPS works depict ordinary people at work in everyday settings.

For the presentation to European audiences with no direct personal relation to the GPS data, "another layer of editing needed to be added even to communicate the realism of the tracks. This seemingly contradictory approach between elastically manipulating data and aiming for realism raises questions for future artistic and theoretical developments in mapping and locative media projects."[42]

The GPS tracks are not seen by the eye, so how can they be called realistic? The lines are made mathematically, and viewers visualize them by linking a series of positions on a map, unlike tracks that are made by a foot hitting the ground or a tire moving on a soft surface. Relating the lines to a shared knowledge of mapmaking conventions, we can evaluate only their *vraisemblance* (whether they appear to be true). Are they believable? And our evaluation depends on our point of view.

Smooth Hybridization

Whereas Esther Polak calls attention to the artifice involved in realistic rendering, other artists have blurred the lines in ostensibly two-dimensional cinematic works that incorporate hybridization. Lev Manovich has coined the term *deep remixability* to distinguish the kind of hybridization that involves "not only content from different media but also their fundamental techniques, working methods, and ways of representation and expression."[43] This was facilitated, as he notes, by software manufacturers in the 1990s who began to develop tools (such as import and export functions) to make their programs compatible with each other[44]—what I will call *smooth hybridization*.

Compositing is one of the most common hybridization techniques that digital media have made available to the amateur photographer. The image of another place can be pasted in the background of a picture. To place something, say, behind a pair of living room windows, requires masking the part of the image that is to be shown in the foreground, in this case the window frame and the wall between them, while rendering the glass panes transparent. A photograph of a distant place can be spooled "behind" the glass and revealed progressively, thus transforming panes mirroring the room at night into windows looking out onto the world.

This technique is the principle behind Tania Ruiz Gutiérrez's *Annorstädes* (Elsewhere) (2010) (figure 7.6). Whereas most amateurs make images that are shown on computer screens, Ruiz Gutiérrez created a monumental video installation, the largest of its kind in Europe. Commissioned by the National Public Art Council of Sweden and Trafikverket, *Annorstädes* is a panorama made up of forty-six parallel video projections that are deployed over 360 meters at the main subway station in Malmö.

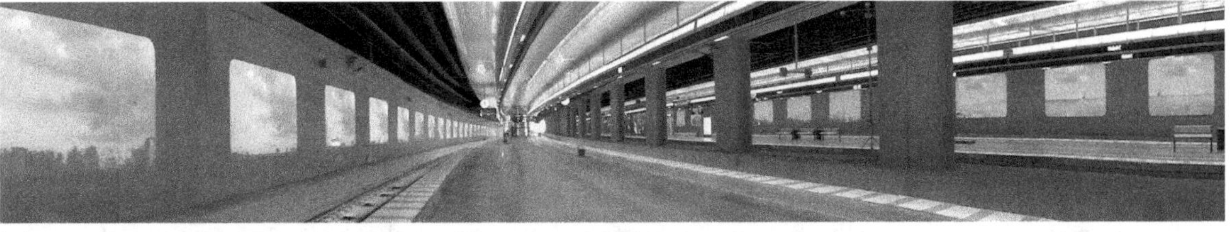

(a)

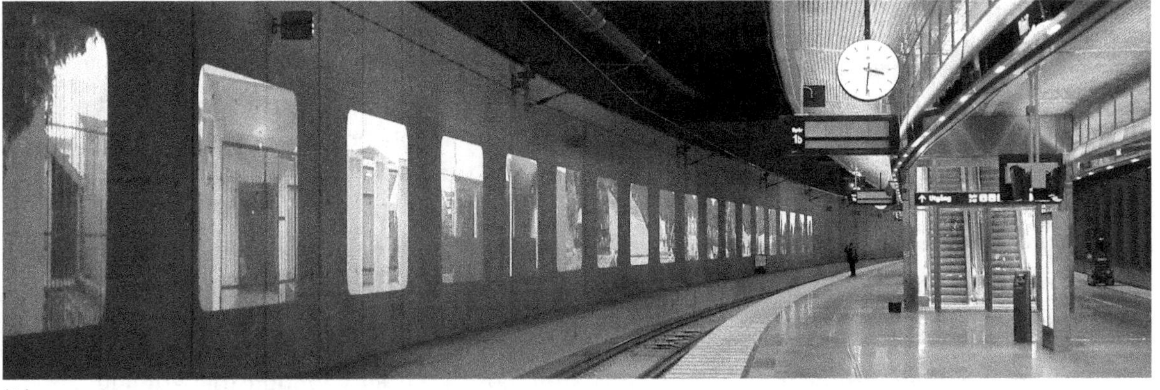

(b)

Figure 7.6
Tania Ruiz Gutiérrez, *Annorstädes/Elsewhere/Ailleurs*, 2010. Video installation. Video projections in the main subway station in Malmö, Sweden. Photograph: Martine Castoriano, 2010. *a:* A mockup by Tania Ruiz Gutiérrez. *b:* The completed installation.

Located on the southern tip of Sweden, Malmö is an industrial city that is converting to a postindustrial economy. Since the 2000 construction of the Öresund bridge that links Sweden and Denmark, it has begun to attract new businesses. A railway connection opened in 2010 now runs from the bridge to Malmö Central Station and has transformed the former terminus into a transit station. Subway cars press through the tunnel on their way to Copenhagen and the rest of Europe.

The architect's original design called for daylight wells, but these were omitted in the final plan, turning the station into "a huge concrete box, slightly curved," notes the artist: "I found that it definitely needed some windows, but of course this was not possible in an underground position, unless we project the windows. The idea of transforming the entire station into a train appeared to me simple and elegant."[45]

The main concourse in the new Citytunneln station has four parallel sets of tracks. Ruiz Guttiérrez's projections turn the two end platforms into rides through distant landscapes seen from a slow-moving train. Through the windows of the projected train, harassed travelers can wind down as they watch the whole world unfold at the steady, unhurried pace of a person walking: "From the salt flats of Uyuni to the roads of Saigon, from the plains of Siberia to those of Patagonia. . . . *Annorstädes*, like a lost river, flows continually into an underground passage."[46]

Ruiz Gutiérrez backpacked in forty countries on five continents to shoot hundreds of hours of video using a palm-sized video camera ("a small brush for a large canvas," she says). She recorded panoramas from trains, boats, and occasionally cars. The picture plane is generally shallow. She preferred moving parallel to it, shooting out of the side windows of vehicles to give the impression of riding a train.

In a prose piece called "Windows," Baudelaire wrote: "He who looks from outside through an open window never sees as many things as he who looks at a closed window."[47] Tania Ruiz Gutiérrez stimulates our reverie with views that we might want to project on that closed window. She chose to film "mainly borders, limits, frontiers. . . . The spaces in between the tentacular cities and the countryside, political borders, geographical borders. . . . Mainly human landscapes in fact. But people are only present in about half of the shots." Through her installation, she says, passengers arriving in Central station are linked to the rest of the world. Advertising has accustomed us to this kind of perception. In many cities, the subway walls are given entirely over to posters enjoining passengers to buy: Internet service, airline tickets, cars, perfume. Here, although the scenes range from postcard beauty to industrial grit and shantytown squalor, all recognizable advertising, even street signs, were removed from the footage. Viewers can guess the name of the place that they are contemplating but have no certainty.

From the train on the middle tracks, travelers might feel that they are moving past another train. In this way, the projection inadvertently references Claude Lévi-Strauss's famous comparison of cultures with moving trains:

> To show that the size and speed of a moving body are not absolute values but depend on the position of the observer, we recall that for a passenger who is sitting at the window of a train, the speed and the length of other trains vary depending on whether they move in the same direction or in the opposite direction. Now every member of a culture is as much a part of it as the ideal traveler is to his train.[48]

Ruiz Gutiérrez's installation contradicts this image of human beings as prisoners of their trains who are riveted to the culture in which they grew up. There may be no fixed point that is completely outside culture from which we can judge others, but much can be gained from moving around. Not only can passengers get off the train at Malmö C station, but they can choose the direction they take and the speed at which they walk. They can also sit still for a while and immerse themselves in the river of images.

For Ruiz Gutiérrez, "The structure of each side is not random. A huge video database is reedited by a generative software based on a simple grammar of oppositions and analogies." Yet each projection is autonomous. The projectors are located overhead so that the presence of passengers on the platform will not interfere: "The projection beam hits the top of the train when it enters the side tracks, . . . [and] the trains cut (and edit) the film." The database program ensures that the sequences are not the same twice.

Here, the database gathers hundreds of hours of video footage shot by one individual artist. What happens when a map is drawn by more than one person? The next chapter looks at the paradigm of distributed and collaborative cartography using networked databases.

8 Walking the Network

Database Cartography

Many mobile media projects involve creating maps, if only to picture the traces and locate the annotated spots. The maps, in turn, are predicated on the database form.

Like maps, databases are tools for organizing, elaborating, or preserving knowledge; they play an important part in modeling our perceptual world. Geographic mapping usually means representing a three-dimensional, continuous space in two dimensions, assigning correspondences between abstract symbols and physical points of reference. The database undermines the authority of any one map. It does this partly by its inclusiveness. Although the map selects, the database can incorporate more than one selection. It allows users to rearrange information in patterns that no longer bear any relation to a particular geographical space. When toponyms are sorted alphabetically, a small town in Florida can sit next to the Iraqi capital some seven thousand miles away. Here, geographical location is just one of the ways of ordering information. Instead of merely representing the territory, the map becomes a territory to explore in and of itself, allowing us to gather and search greater amounts of information; to sort, visualize, and scale it to fit particular needs; and to make new correlations.[1]

Image Maps: Maps as Interfaces

Nearly all the projects discussed in this chapter use maps as graphic interfaces to databases of geographically linked information. Some present static items that were gathered at one time, while others are regularly updated. Some are mere displays, while others can receive user input. How does the structure affect the type of information that is shown?

Maps can be used as interfaces to information compiled by the cartographer. One of the simplest, Jim Naurekas's *New York Songlines* Web site,[2] does not use a database. It is a linear street map that is spread over a series of HTML pages. The viewer clicks on direction arrows to travel along a street, turn onto another, discover texts and photos compiled by the author, and find features that were eventually developed by online mapping services. This type of map can range from in-depth studies of particular geographical areas to vast information panoramas.

Mapping the Infraordinary

One Block Radius (*OBR*) (2004) by Glowlab was typical of the genre of artists' projects that map archived images, sounds, texts, and videos to a particular location. *OBR* was for the authors a "psychogeographic documentary" of the block on the Bowery in New York City where the New Museum of Contemporary Art was getting ready to build its new facility in late 2004. It employs the now-familiar conceptual art strategy of inventory to call attention to aspects of our environment that are so ordinary they have become invisible. Glowlab members photographed, annotated, and classified hundreds of thrown-away objects and chance encounters with bureaucratic zeal: *Observations* included "Frozen shoe with chopstick," "Traffic control box—open, but no repair person in sight," and "Demolition inside 199 Chrystie"; *Interactions* were portraits and interviews (such as "Block resident Jimmy Wright describes the building at 4 Rivington Street"); and *Responses* were artworks (for example, a short video showing Lee Walton climbing fire escapes).

Their work involves sampling and collecting what Perec called "the infraordinary" in order to "question what seems to have forever ceased to surprise us."[3] This is similar to artist-botanist herman de vries's 950-page artist's book that showed the 473 plant specimens he identified in a sixteen-square decimeter area of prairie (*16 dm²: An Essay*, 1979) and to artist-sociologist Georges Perec's descriptions of the comings and goings of buses and passers-by during three days at the place Saint-Sulpice in Paris (*Tentative d'épuisement d'un lieu parisien*, 1975). Taken to an extreme, projects like Perec's are left unfinished: he had planned to describe two places each month for twelve years, charting the ways in which the places, his memory of them, and his writing about them gradually age.

Glowlab's goal seems reasonable—to work with just one city block. But this is not just any city block. It is the Bowery, the former haven of the down-and-out, home to innumerable flophouses and artists' lofts, New York's first community garden, the CBGB club, and the Ramones, that is currently undergoing gentrification. In gathering traces of a world slated to disappear, *OBR* draws on the chord of nostalgia. The building at 199 Chrystie, the shoe and the person who lost it, the delivery man and his cart have gone; the photographs may be all that is left.[4]

An ongoing art and science project that involves what could be called thick mapping, *Hidden Ecologies* focuses on recording "aspects of our immediate environment that normally lie beyond our usual perception."[5] To investigate transitional geographies of the San Francisco Bay area, architect Cris Benton attaches cameras to kites, creating panoramic photographs of specific ecosystems like the South Bay salt ponds, and microbiologist Wayne Lanier captures short movies through the field microscope with a compact digital camera placed above the eyepiece.

Kite aerial photography offers a unique vantage point a few meters above human eye level.[6] Because aerial images reduce sky reflection in the salt pond surfaces, this technique exposes colors, textures, and information from historic layers that are otherwise invisible to us from the ground. Writes Benton: "To this day the landscape holds remnants of wind-driven Archimedes screws, narrow-gauge railroads, entrepreneurial produce landings, industrial works, and abandoned towns. When researched, these remnants yield entertaining tales involving ingenious invention, Chinese laborers, camels, oyster wars, and bawdy houses."[7] In the same area, Lanier focuses on creatures invisible to the naked eye, like cyanobacteria, which are among the most ancient forms of life on earth.

The team confronts imagery that is collected in the field with out-of-copyright maps and aerial views from the past. Mapping here consists of devising ways to show the project artifacts—including geotagged photographs, field sampling procedures, and microscope movies—by juxtaposing scales and points of view. *One Block Radius* had a limited time frame, but *Hidden Ecologies* is a work in progress.

Routes and Roots: Elsewhere Begins at Home

Like their paper counterparts, database-powered maps tend to emphasize either places, their classification and structure (thematic maps, for instance, show hydrographic, climate, or demographic information) or paths linking those places (road maps).[8]

The two-sided, two-pronged exhibition *Native Land: Stop Eject* (2008–2009) that was held at the Cartier Foundation in Paris in 2008 and 2009 used the form of the chiasma to explore "the notions of the homeland, of taking root, of uprootedness, and the identity questions that are attached to these notions."[9]

Filmmaker Raymond Depardon portrayed members of isolated groups in Chile, Ethiopia, Bolivia, France, and Brazil who want to stay on their own land but, for various reasons, are faced with extinction or exile. Philosopher Paul Virilio asked if it is possible for anyone to stay put. According to some estimates, roughly 200 million people may be forced to flee their homelands by the year 2050, so migration might be an important part of what it means to be human today.

Native Land: Stop Eject dealt with the global acceleration of movement, what curator Virilio calls "the great migratory mobilization."[10] People are driven to migrate by war, famine, and global warming, which, with its attendant ills, such as the flooding of coastal cities, is likely to bring with it millions of climatic refugees.

It began with a room-sized installation that comprised fifty screens suspended from the ceiling and presented a continuous visual choreography of news clips. Musical comedy, modern tragedy. Busby Berkeley meets Nam June Paik. On one side, there was a video interview with Virilio: "The nature of being sedentary and nomadic has changed. Sedentary people are at home wherever they go. With their cell phones or laptops, [they are] as comfortable in an elevator or on a plane as in a high-speed train. . . . The nomad, on the other hand, is someone who is never at home, anywhere."[11] The migration of hundreds of millions of people (which is unprecedented in human history) plus an end of geographical space (or "the disappearance of the world's vastness") brought about by transportation and telecommunications revolutions announce the emergence of the "ultracity," the city of urban exile.

The last projection room showed a series of visualizations of human migratory data from the last few decades. Europeans imagine that people fleeing places beset by war, famine, and endemic poverty migrate in great numbers to the prosperous nations of northern Europe and America. But far more of the world's migrants move down the road to neighboring provinces and adjacent countries that are often poor themselves and unable to handle the influx of refugees. Although the media tend to focus on wars, more people are driven to emigrate by natural disasters. Developing countries receive three times as much money from their own expatriates than from all manner of foreign aid.[12]

Sitting in the middle of a circular projection that moves around the room, the audience is surrounded by bar graphs, animated maps, and explanatory texts that show who migrated to what place, from where, and when. The maps advanced so quickly that they could not be fully assimilated. It was like trying to make sense of a foreign city while moving through it on a roller-coaster. Were these constraints meant to represent the urgency that drives uprooted populations to move quickly or an attempt to shake up and remix the contents of viewers' world view?

Tourism by Proxy

Humans tends to focus on matters close at hand, while places farther away remain an indistinct blur. In the early 1990s, some observers noted that Americans needed a war to discover the existence of Iraq. In the intervening years, globalization has made us more aware of how events in one place can affect people who live in another many thousands of miles away.

Paula Levine was in San Francisco when the second Iraq war was declared. She conceived *Shadows from Another Place: San Francisco <–> Baghdad* (2004) as a series of "transposed maps" using GPS coordinates, urban sites, and the Web to show how political traumas in one location affect another place (figure 8.1). *Shadows from Another Place: San Francisco ↔ Baghdad* was conceived after the U.S. invasion of Iraq in March 2003. Locations that were struck by missiles and bombs in the Iraqi capital are mapped to places in San Francisco. Each mirrored site of impact in San Francisco ("Baghdad by the Bay") is documented with photographs, maps, and GPS coordinates.[13] Each site also holds a geocache, a small canister containing the names of all the American soldiers killed in the first year after the official end of the war. Placing these sites in areas where ordinary San Franciscans walk underscores the fact that

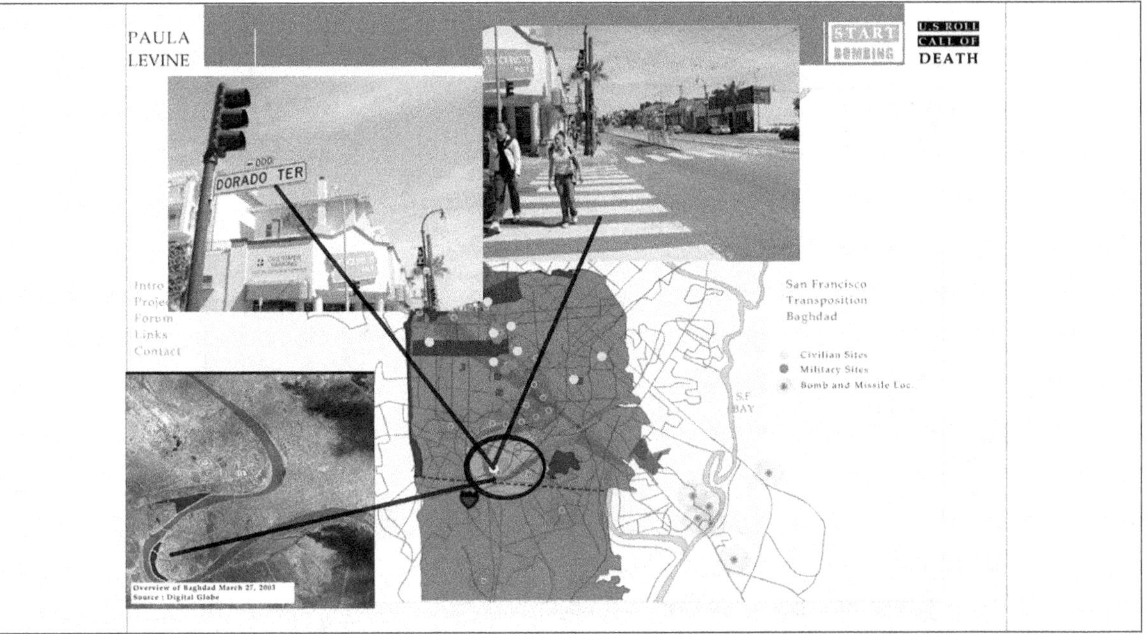

Figure 8.1
Paula Levine, *Shadows from Another Place: San Francisco ↔ Baghdad*, 2004. Web site, maps, GPS devices, site locations throughout San Francisco. These transposed maps use GPS coordinates, urban sites, and the Web to link political traumas in one location with another.

most victims of the attacks were civilians. It could have been you or me, if we had been in Baghdad that day.

In *Shadows from Another Place: TheWall.name* (2008), the path of a fifteen-mile section of the Israeli separation wall is traced on a map of San Francisco (figure 8.2).[14] After visiting Palestinian areas that are affected by the rapidly progressing wall in 2006, she realized "how easy it was to travel to Israel and never see Palestine," so she decided to explore the porosity of this boundary and document these areas east of Jerusalem.[15]

Other artists adopt a lighter tone. Playing the tourist at home is a favorite French sport, as can be seen in *Species of Spaces* (1974), *Autonauts of the Cosmoroute* (1983), and *Roissy Express* (1990). Stéphane Degoutin and Gwenola Wagon's *Attractions for the Suburbs of Paris* (2009) exploits this vein by transforming nondescript urban sprawl into utopian experiments through storytelling using text, video, image, fantasy architecture, and on-site intervention (figure 8.3). In October 2009, their projects were related to travelers by actress Nathalie Matter on a train journey from Noisy-le-Sec to Pontault-Combault.[16] The tour begins by evoking the paranormal state of tourism. The dim lights, relaxing atmosphere, and muffled sounds of the first attraction,

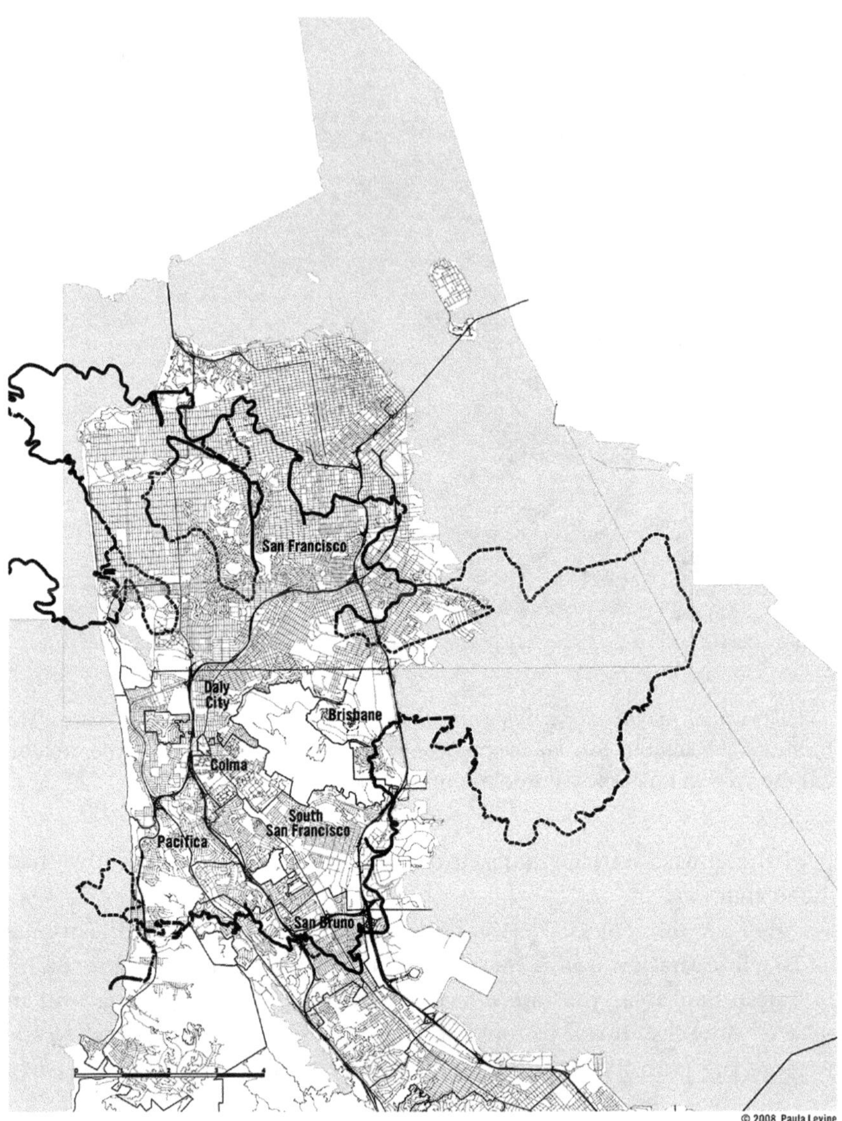

The Wall in San Francisco
From: TheWall.name 2008

Paula Levine,
paula-levine@sbcglobal.net

(a)

Figure 8.2

Paula Levine, *The Wall in San Francisco* (From: *TheWall.name*), 2008–current. Web site http://thewall.name. *a:* A fifteen-mile section of the Israeli separation wall is overlaid on San Francisco.

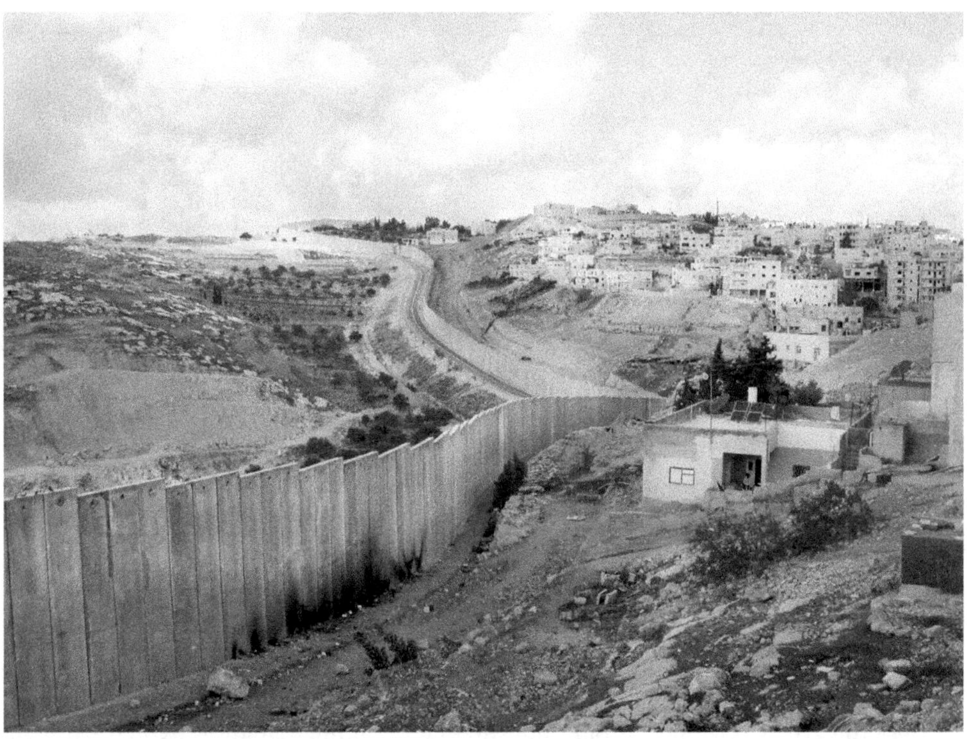

(b)

Figure 8.2 (continued)
b: The Wall in Abu Dis, 2006. The West Bank wall between Abu Dis in the south and Qalandiya in the north. *TheWall-TheWorld,* 2011 (Thewalltheworld.net), overlays that same part of the Israeli separation wall on any city a viewer chooses.

Hypnorama, lull train passengers into an optimal hypnotic state so they can be both present in and absent from the lands through which they travel.[17] Thus prepared, they can visit *Utopia Factory Abraxas,* a site for testing new utopias. A Gnostic deity embodying both good and evil, Abraxas was the original name of Thomas More's famous island. Today, The Spaces of Abraxas is a large postmodern housing complex by Ricardo Bofill in Noisy-le-Grand. Unlike these structures with their extravagant Greek columns and "prefabricated concrete perspectives," the utopias tested in Degoutin and Wagon's research center assume their limits: they "are perishable and not guaranteed. They are not perfect, far from it, but a way of setting society in motion."[18]

After visiting several sites like the *Museum of the Ideal Suburb* with its maze of roundabouts, the last stretch of the road brings them to *WikiForest.*[19] Here, Utopians try out John Zerzan's pre-Neolithic way of life in harmony with the environment in

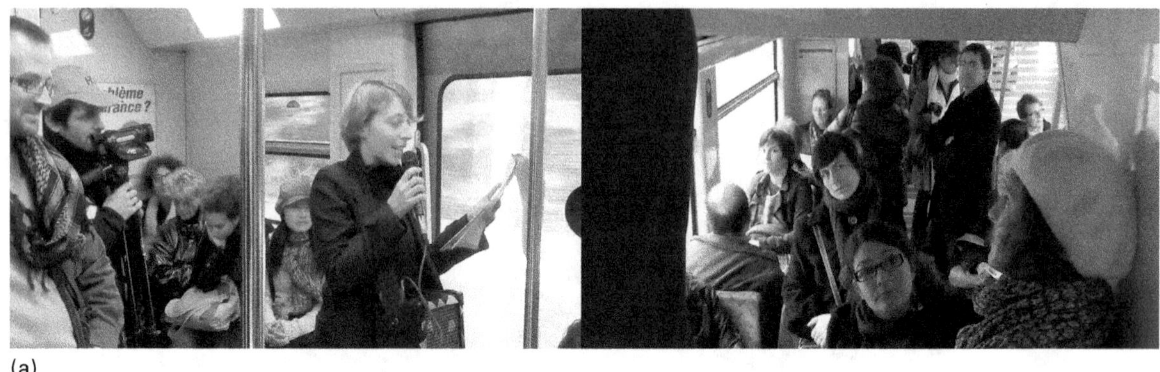

(a)

Figure 8.3
Stéphane Degoutin and Gwenola Wagon, *Attractions for the Suburbs of Paris* 2009. Performance. *a:* The performance on a train journey from Noisy-le-Sec to Pontault-Combault. Reader: Nathalie Matter, October 2009. © Stéphane Degoutin and Gwenola Wagon.

the Célie forest, far from civilization. Why go to the trouble of packing clothes, tools, food, and water when all they need are solar-powered laptops running Linux, and a wireless Internet connection? By consulting *Wikipedia,* they will teach themselves to build temporary shelters, hunt animals, light a fire, and feed on plants and berries.[20]

Here the artists poke fun at our cherished technophilic paradises, which led us to imagine that equipping schoolchildren with laptops would magically erase social injustice and bring about equality of opportunity. Inspired by the passengers of the Roissy-Express, Degoutin and Wagon inject humor and fantasy into a landscape that usually is portrayed in melancholic documentaries. They plan to build a genuine *Hypnorama* in the near future. If they follow the reasoning of hypnotherapist Milton Erickson, trance is the state in which change is most likely to occur.

Data Hijacking

The situationists altered existing maps to create their ambiance maps. They advocated giving up art in favor of *détournement* (diversion or hijacking). This kind of partisan propaganda reuses elements of previous images to create a new entity with a message that is opposed to the original. Scandal is old hat. Although they prefer Bertolt Brecht to Marcel Duchamp, they criticize Brecht for respecting the classics as they were defined by the ruling class:

> Any elements, no matter where they are taken from, can serve in making new combinations. The discoveries of modern poetry regarding the analogical structure of images demonstrate that when two objects are brought together, no matter how far apart their original contexts may be, a relationship is always formed. . . . The mutual interference of two worlds of feeling, or the

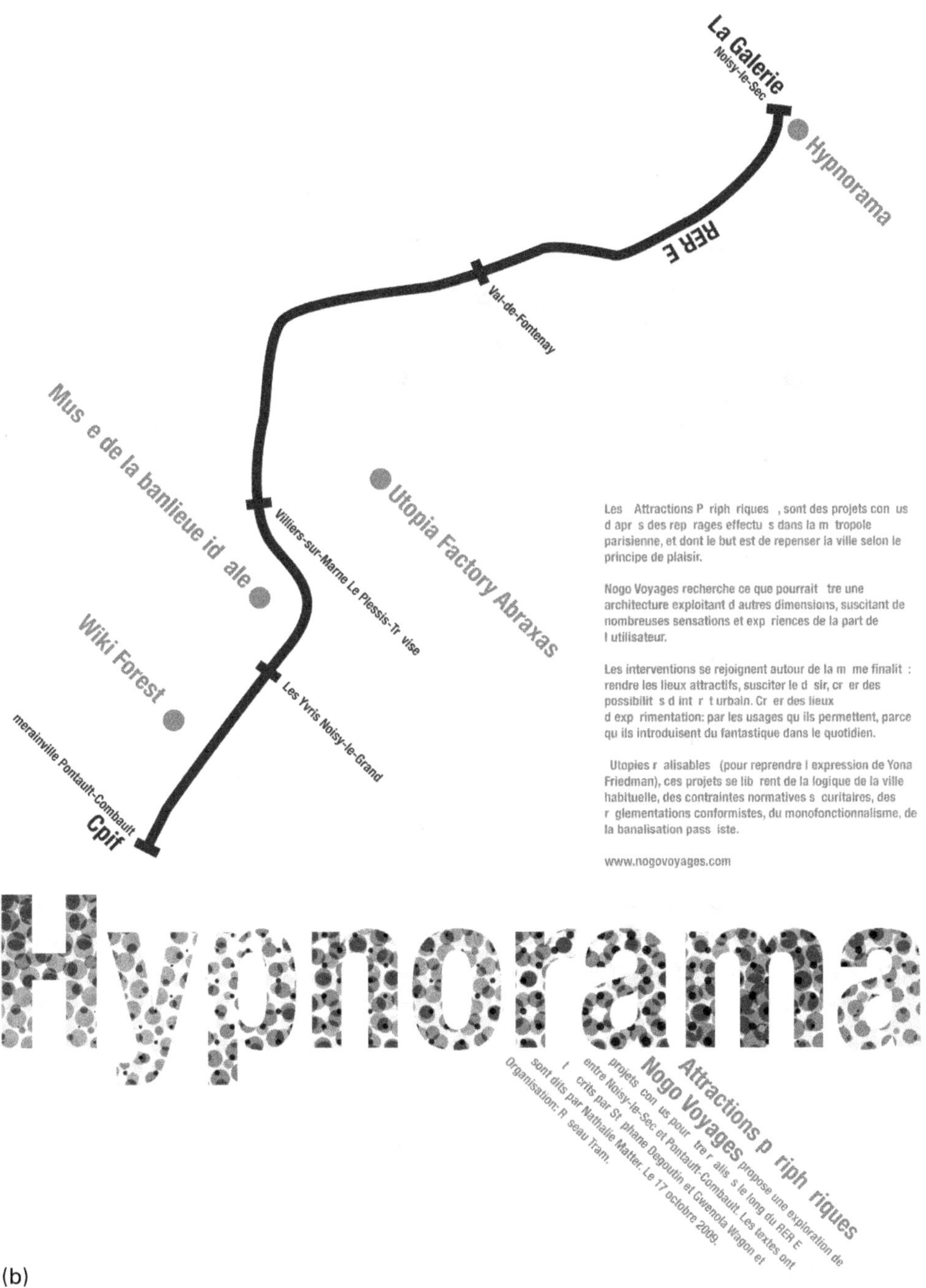

(b)

Figure 8.3 (continued)
b: A map of the *Attractions*.

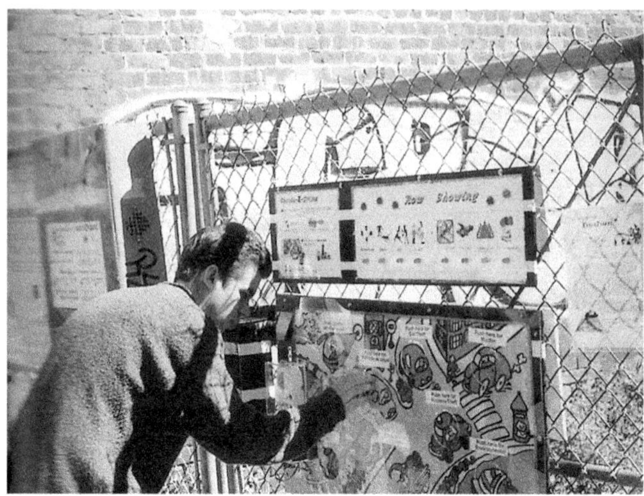

Figure 8.4
Stephen Wilson, *CrimeZyland*, 1998. Public art installation. *CrimeZyland* used San Francisco Police Department crime statistics to let visitors map crime locations in real time.

bringing together of two independent expressions, supersedes the original elements and produces a synthetic organization of greater efficacy.[21]

Today, as advertising has taken over the business of hijacking images from all periods and styles, mere *détournement* has lost its subversive edge. Even culture jammers have found that their techniques are incorporated into publicity campaigns, with Flashmobs becoming just another marketing tool.

One way out of this conundrum is to hijack information fluxes, inserting data obtained from bona fide sources into a fictive structure. In the outdoor installation *CrimeZyland* (1998), Stephen Wilson *détourned* San Francisco Police Department crime statistics to let visitors map crime locations in real time (figure 8.4). On this computer-controlled living map, light, motion, and sound marked the minute-by-minute statistical level of crimes committed in city districts.

For four months, Wilson's interactive theme park offered a festival of attractions just across from City Hall. On a map of San Francisco defined by California poppies and crime tape markers, "Map-Z-Crime" allowed the ten top crime spots to spring to life with toy police cars moving in, lights flashing, and devices whirling whenever the statistics from previous years predicted that a crime *could be* happening at that location.[22] "Choose-Z-Crime" let people determine the focus. Available were murder, rape, assault, robbery, car theft, air pollution, destruction of species, corruption, fraud, and negligence. Visitors could choose which statistics were shown. "Scan-Z-Crime" let them listen to live police transmissions to hear crime as it was happening via special scanner radios (publicly available police broadcasts).

As Wilson points out, crime is portrayed in the media as a kind of entertainment. Are street crimes worthy of more attention than those committed in corporate boardrooms or clandestine military prisons? What about people who make products that kill and maim or who ship oil in decrepit tankers that could destroy human lives and whole ecosystems? The media circus created around urban crime encourages city dwellers to stay home, abandoning the streets to drug dealers and rival gangs, and may also banish poverty and homelessness from public view. What is not seen does not have to be changed.[23]

Dynamic Maps

Other artists have sought to involve the public by building dynamic, self-organizing maps. In their projects, the focus is on the map as a means of making visible things that had been invisible. During the spring and summer of 2001, visitors to the Centre Pompidou in Paris were invited to digitize an object that they were carrying and add its image to George Legrady's database, *Pockets Full of Memories* (2001–2007) (figure 8.5).

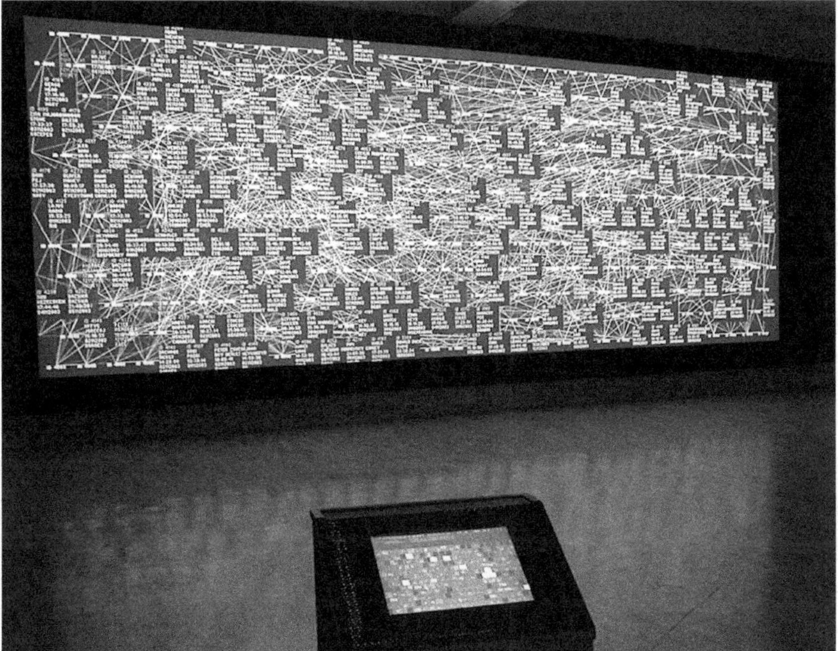

Figure 8.5
George Legrady, *Pockets Full of Memories*, 2001–2007. Interactive installation. Aura exhibition, C3 Cultural Center, Budapest, 2003. Visitors scan a personal object, provide information about it, and a self-organizing map algorithm positions it on the screen near similarly described objects.

The object had to be small enough to fit on the scanner. People scanned thousands of cell phones, keys, toys, watches, pressed hands and faces to the screen. They described the object by assigning it properties in response to a questionnaire, a mixture of closed and open-ended questions ("What is it? Keywords? Where does it come from?"). Then they positioned the object on a scale between old/new, soft/hard, natural/synthetic, disposable/long use, personal/not personal, fashionable/not fashion, useful/useless, functional/symbolic.

Pockets Full of Memories dealt with the dynamics of aggregating and visualizing large amounts of information using a self-organizing map.[24] Here the map is neither geographically nor visually organized: it charts relations between these objects according to their semantic value as each of them was defined by the person who contributed it. The archive was presented as a two-dimensional grid made from 280 scanned objects projected on the gallery wall.

Contributors could influence the way their objects were perceived through their choice of attributes. This is why, for example, a cell phone described as "old," "personal," and "symbolic" might be placed next to a stuffed animal rather than another phone. The program was set to process the data every minute, scanning the map line by line, repositioning objects to reflect changes in the order as people added new objects. The database arrived at its final state at the end of the exhibition.[25]

The self-organizing map made these familiar objects behave strangely, like automats, inert objects come to life. Freud called this the *Unheimliche* (uncanny). Watching cellular automata is similarly mesmerizing.[26] *Cell Tango* (2006–2010), created by George Legrady and Angus Forbes, is an interactive installation in which a dynamic collection of cell phone images submitted by the public are visually sequenced according to contributors' tags (figure 8.6). For each photo that was sent to the database, the par-

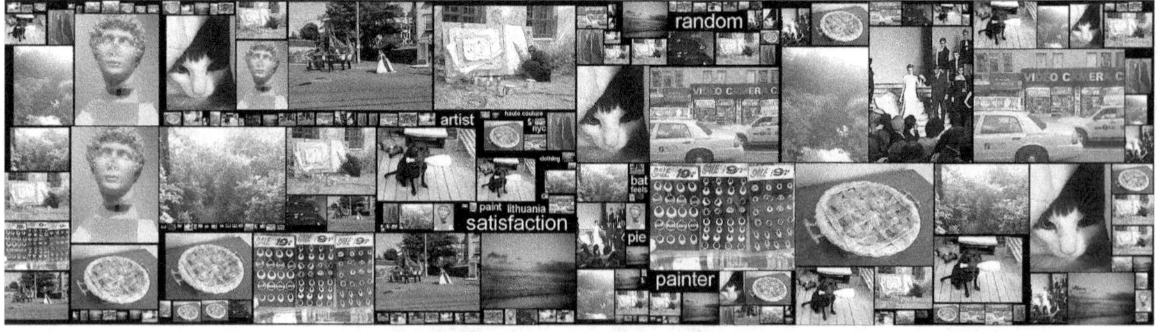

Figure 8.6
George Legrady, and Angus Forbes, *Cell Tango,* 2006–2010. Interactive installation, Wellesley College, 2009. Four animations feature different organization of cell phone images submitted by the public. The Binpacking algorithm shown here places large images randomly and then systematically fills in the blank spaces with smaller ones.

ticipant adds two to four tags in the subject heading, which is used to retrieve other images from the Flickr database and create clusters of images. Having visitors upload their own pictures directly from their phones simplifies the whole process. The project creates an automatic *cadavre exquis,* exploring the potential of chance juxtapositions in which common semantic labels lead to surprising visual rhythms. The images are presented in four animations recalling fireworks displays, each emphasizing a different method of organization.[27] Legrady sees this work as both "a conversation, a meeting place"[28] for the public and an object of study: the exhibition allows him to gather data for later analysis.[29]

Another kind of dynamic map appropriates Google's search results to create a world map of emotions. Maurice Benayoun's *Still Moving* (2008) is an interactive sound sculpture that is coupled with a real-time video projection (figure 8.7). The three-and-a half-meter sculpture takes the shape of a deflated globe that is deformed by the relief of the planet's emotions. The primary experience comes when visitors interact with the object. By touching it or lying down on it, they can feel the vibrations of the world's "emotional state" as it is filtered by Internet. The barely audible sound is composed of infrabasses and translates information coming via search engine from the analysis of news in 3,200 cities. A projection onto the sculpture translates in words and colors this dialog of bodies and global emotions.

It is the "14th act" of a corpus of works called *Mechanics of Emotions* (2005–2011) that Benayoun describes as "a desperate attempt to translate into something perceptible, accessible to the senses, the world filtered by its medias" (figure 8.8). He sees today's communication networks as an extensive virtual nervous system: "From anywhere in the world one can feel what's happening anywhere else in real time as long as it is connected to the Net and is English speaking."[30]

For *Still Moving,* the sum of all human emotions is synthesized in three key words—*ecstatic, nervous, anxious*—that were chosen to evoke feelings, contacts, and caresses.[31] The search engine reduces them to something that is quantifiable and capable of automatic treatment. Using the statistical frequency of these words in online searches, the algorithm portrays the earth (Google's earth) as a body where events in any one place have repercussions for the whole organism. Benayoun notes that, using the criteria he has defined (those in use on the Internet), Africa shows hardly any response and therefore becomes nearly invisible, like an amputated limb that does not even trigger ghost pains. To rectify the balance, other kinds of interventions may be necessary.

Participative Mapping

In the projects outlined above, the information gathered and modeled by the artists is accessed by viewers interactively. Another group of mapping projects integrates user information into a collectively written map.[32] Unlike route-finding systems,[33]

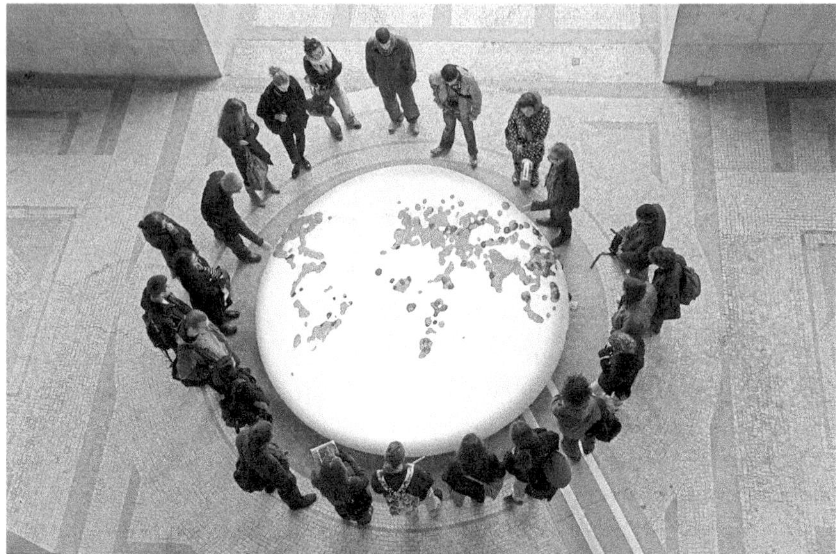

(a)

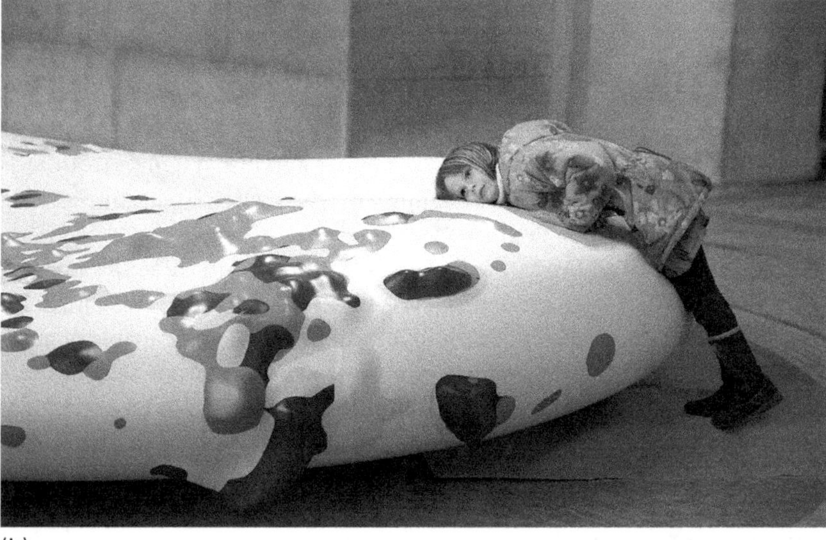

(b)

Figure 8.7

Maurice Benayoun, *Still Moving, Grand Palais,* 2008. Interactive sound sculpture coupled with a real-time video projection. Images: Maurice Benayoun. *a:* The three-and-a half-meter sculpture, which is shaped like a deflated globe deformed by the relief of the planet's emotions. *b:* Visitors can feel the vibrations of the world's "emotional state" as it is filtered by the Internet.

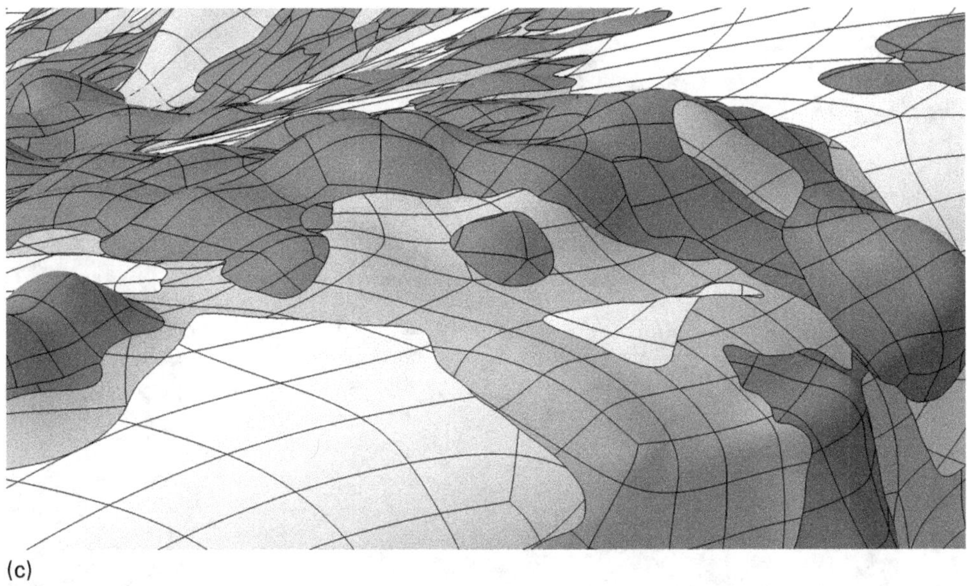

(c)

Figure 8.7 (continued)
c: *Still Moving Study* (coll. Fonds National d'Art Contemporain), 2008.

modifiable maps let online participants add their own information to the database, either directly or indirectly via a submission process.

Launched by Thomas Beller in the spring of 2000, *Mr. Beller's Neighborhood* is an online publication that is composed of short narrative texts. The map is used as an organizing device to link each piece of writing to a particular spot in New York, but the content is the stories themselves. Here the familiar New York streetscape is plotted to "the wildly internal, often unfamiliar emotional landscapes of the city dweller."[34] Situating a story in a real, physical location—for instance, the Brooklyn Bridge subway stop or 113 MacDougal Street—helps writers to focus. Much like the oral histories that were collected by the *[murmur]* project, they depict the city at street level from the viewpoint of a pedestrian.

In the tradition of small literary magazines, works are selected for publication by the site's editors. A link at the top of the page "Tell Mr. Beller a story" allows readers to submit their own works via a questionnaire. The criteria for inclusion are explicit: "A story should be reasonably short, vivid, specific, and true. It can recall a person or a place, or it can recall an experience that moved you. . . . Authorial tone, point of view, the personality of an author, writing style, these are immutable things," notes Thomas Beller.[35]

This makes for a robust, clearly delineated project that over the years has generated a community of writers. "The longevity of the site is the result of a continuing interest

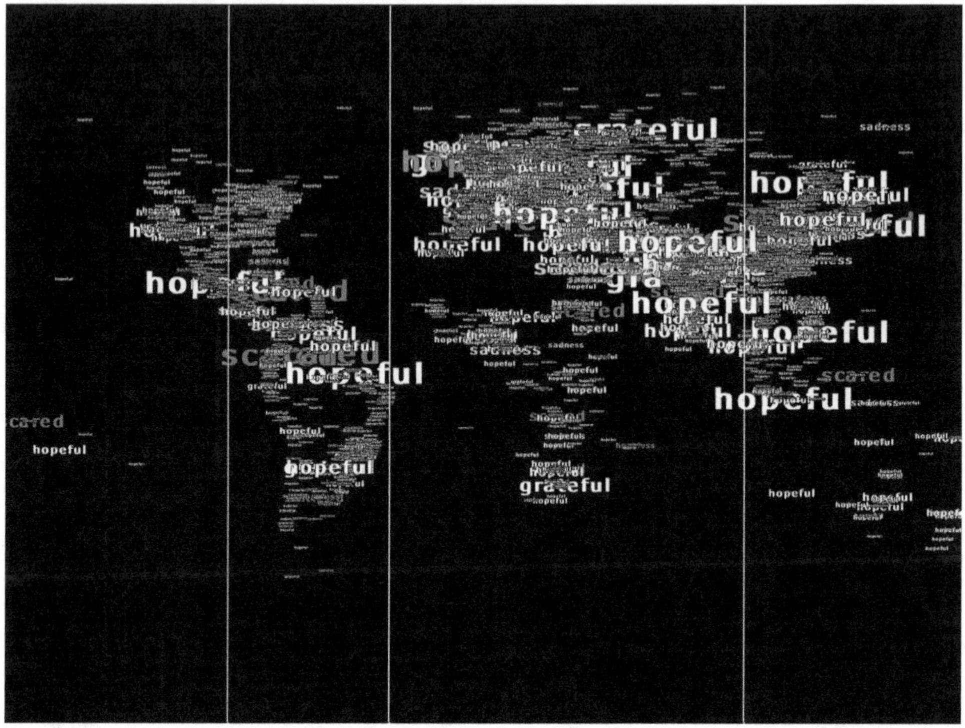

Figure 8.8
Maurice Benayoun, *World Emotional Map,* 2005. Internet, search engine, cartography. Belongs to *Mechanics of Emotions*, 2005–2011, an art opera in more than fifteen parts that the artist calls "a desperate attempt to translate into something perceptible, accessible to the senses, the world filtered by its medias."

among writers and readers," says Beller, "but especially writers, who feel the site is a congenial home for their work."[36] The presence of a Mr. Beller to listen to the stories may be a key factor in this success. Concessions to recent trends have meant occasional facelifts, like adopting a Google Maps mashup to replace its original map interface. In its latest makeover, the front page evokes a tabloid with photographs, multiple columns, and sections of top stories—music, drugs, sex, money. The map has lost its former status and is collapsed into a thumbnail link in the right-hand column. The Web site is updated regularly, with about three stories added each week. In 2009, it listed over a thousand original works.[37] Beller has likened the project to serial narratives of the nineteenth century that can be entered at any point and remain unresolved.[38] The steady rhythm of publication brings readers back regularly: many join the "Story of the Week" email list.

The site's title evokes the children's television program *Mister Rogers' Neighborhood* (1968–2001) that was hosted by Fred Rogers. Ambling through the online streets, readers at *Mr. Beller's Neighborhood* can join a community that holds periodic readings in real-world New York venues. Beller explains: "The method has been to mix writers I know or have sought out, my own work, and edited over-the-transom work. Many of the contributors become regulars." He notes that "all along there was a community—not the Internet sense of the word, but the community of sensibility, a shared vision of the experience of life and its literary manifestation, and I suppose the community . . . of people for whom New York is for some reason important, which has kept up a steady flow of submissions, many of which are good."[39]

Beller has no interest in hypertext as such or collaborative forms of writing, and his *Neighborhood* reflects this view. "Fiction readers are the most resistant to new technology," he argues. "That is a strength and speaks to something positive, even as it creates odd friction between the modern world and the literary community--friction that is perhaps intrinsic to the literary community." Part of the problem is that hypertext forms tend to expand one's view whereas writing requires sharp focus: "the act of writing starts with the whole world swimming in the writer's head. In many ways writing is an act of omission: you force out the whole world minus that one thing you want to evoke, and that turns into a sentence."[40]

The Internet serves here as a frictionless way of publishing work that might not have seen publication elsewhere. The Web site allows the individual pieces to riff off each other, while gathering them under a collective banner gives them more visibility. Its existence as a container may also make some of its writers more productive, although Beller says that is not true for himself.[41]

Like *Mr. Beller's Neighborhood, City of Memory* is an ongoing Web project offering stories located on a dynamic map of New York. Readers can submit works for publication. The difference lies in the use of visual and sound media (users can upload text, video, image, and sound files) and in the project's real-world component. *City of Memory* has also been presented as a kiosk in museums and outdoor public spaces.

It came about after the design studio Local Projects was commissioned to make *Memory Maps* by City Lore, an urban folk culture center, for the Smithsonian Folklife Festival in 2001. They created a twenty-foot styrofoam map of Manhattan and smaller ones for the other boroughs, onto which visitors thumbtacked three-inch squares of acetate with personal stories they had written.[42] *City of Memory* is the successor to that project.

In its latest configuration, the site distinguishes between stories that were curated by City Lore and those uploaded by users, which are filtered before publication. Some of the stories are excerpted from documentary films or books. Titles include "The Death of Black Benjie," "Delivery on the C-Train," and "The Empire State Building Run-up." Designer Jake Barton says that "visitors link stories together by theme, creating new 'neighborhoods' of narrative that can be walked by others. Stories can be recommended, giving new visitors a sense of the narrative created by the populace."[43] The site also offers a number of thematic "tours," like "K's New York: Going Going Gone," one of several "ghost maps" that chart places that have disappeared—a corner grocery, a luncheonette transformed into an Italian *trattoria*.

Like *Mr. Beller's Neighborhood*, *City of Memory* has the defects of its qualities. Curating stories guarantees they will all have a certain level of quality—no inappropriate content, no run-on sentences. At the same time, it levels that quality, lending the stories an identity that runs the risk of becoming ingrown.

Pulsing through both projects is nostalgia for the raw and raunchy New York that gentrification has all but banished. Eccentric characters, like flamboyant lit student Cybill Shepherd, seem to be one of the city's defining traits.[44] After recounting her run-ins with an oddball neighbor, Christine Nieland finishes her story ruefully: "And so she was gone. Replaced by a parade of attractive, fit, cheerful young career women, Katies and Jennifers and Stephanies. The change reminded me of Times Square. The seamy, dangerous and forbidden giving way to the corporate, bland and clean."[45]

Maps in Which You Are the Cartographer

Projects like *City of Memory*, *Urban Tapestries*, and *PDPal* allowed users to annotate existing maps, adding content but not form. The map structure itself was not open to change.[46] Other participative projects offer contributors a greater variety of roles. Impelled by an individual or a core group, some communities have begun making their own maps online. Jo Walsh, Schuyler Erle, and Steve Coast created the *London Free Map* project in 2003 to build free-access street maps of the British capital in collaboration with artists, geographers, and programmers.[47]

Why did they go to the trouble of mapping places that have already been extensively mapped? As the collection of data by specialists takes time and is costly, the work of national cartographic agencies like the Ordnance Survey in Great Britain or IGN in France is underwritten by taxpayers' money. In Europe, those taxpayers have limited access to the mapping data collected by their national agencies, and the access they have is expensive. This is why amateur cartographers began offering open-source alternatives.

Artists' projects can offer a fresh point of view on mapping. Heath Bunting has created a number of idiosyncratic maps using GPS data. One of them allowed cyclists and skateboarders to annotate a map and add details about the roads using a simple Web interface.[48] On his Web site, a static *Free Map of North Bristol* shows the areas covered, while the interactive *Downhill Map of Bristol*[49] allows the Web viewer to indicate a starting point and a destination, which leads the map to show the uphill (in red) and downhill (in green) parts of the route. As it stands, this map looks unfinished, more of an idea than a functional tool.

Many collective mapping projects like Bunting's just disappear once their initiators/instigators have moved on. *OpenStreetMap* may provide a workable alternative. Founded by Steve Coast at the University College of London in July 2004, it is "a knowledge collective that provides user-generated street maps. OSM follows the peer production model that created *Wikipedia*; its aim is to create a set of map data that's free to use, editable, and licensed under new copyright schemes."[50]

Many collaborative mapping projects are devoted to particular regions, but *OpenStreetMap* may be the only one to take on the whole world. It has subsumed local efforts like the *London Free Map*. The maps are created by participants who use data collected from portable GPS devices, aerial photographs, out-of-copyright maps, or local knowledge. Users can upload GPS track logs and edit the vector data using the editing tools. Both rendered images and the vector graphics can be downloaded in compliance with a Creative Commons license: "What makes such projects stand out is their knowledge production and ownership ethos. Under such open-source models, the rights of authorship are decentralized, and the knowledge gathered is seen as a common resource that can be distributed and reused without restriction or license. This approach has real potential to empower people to create their own knowledge and encourages reuse of cartographic resources in novel and creative ways."[51]

The wiki offers advice to amateur cartographers who wish to map their own neighborhoods. Mappers with a hand-held GPS device can set it to record tracks while they walk. At home, they upload the tracks to the *OpenStreetMap* Web site. Once the tracks are published, the person can use the online map editing tools to create a new map and add descriptive information.

Even without a GPS device, people can improve existing maps by correcting mistakes or adding street names and points of interest. In the United States, where *OpenStreetMap* has imported the U.S. Census TIGER/Line dataset, a rough map of the road network already exists. A recent tool called "Walking Papers" allows mappers to print out maps to add on-street detail. The drawings are then scanned and uploaded to *OpenStreetMap*.[52]

The database contains all the information that *OpenStreetMap* has collected up to present. The geographical data are presented on an interface called *Slippy Map*, which uses the open-source library OpenLayers to update the map display. Like Google maps, the display updates automatically as users drag it, filling in the new map tiles without reloading the whole page. There is a search function and an export tag. Although *OpenStreetMap* is not an art project, its ranks include artists. What seemed like a quixotic enterprise at its inception in 2004 has taken on a respectable critical mass.[53]

Collaborative mapping at *OpenStreetMap* works somewhat like its model *Wikipedia*, although at a more modest scale, given its specialized nature. It has a clear goal and fairly objective standards for assessing work submitted. It is made from small pieces, each of which is useful on its own.[54] People can map specific places that they care about as long as there are enough contributors with different skills in every place to ensure overall coverage. In theory, this kind of networked collaboration worldwide allows many new ideas to be tried out at a low cost. Trial and error on a large scale helps sort the good ideas from the chaff.[55]

Yet creating a context for people to collaborate is time-consuming. Projects like this can be maintained only through the continuing implication of both professional and amateur users. *OpenStreetMap*'s model depends on both the 80 percent who make modest contributions and the 20 percent who participate regularly and substantially.

Although many contributors edit the world map, the operation depends on a highly active group of about forty volunteers who create and improve the infrastructure, maintain the server, write and update the core software that handles the transactions with the server, and create the maps. A growing community of programmers develop software tools to make *OpenStreetMap* data available for other applications, software platforms, and hardware devices.[56] Steve Coast notes: "The dark secret of many open-source projects is that it isn't 1,000 people spending one minute working on things; it's one person spending 800 minutes, one spending 100, one spending 50 . . . and so on, and the majority reaping those rewards. So it isn't so much about large-scale people skills; it's about connecting and engaging those few who will take the project forward."[57]

OpenStreetMap coverage remains uneven. Even in London, where the project started, some areas are not completely mapped, and others have too few cartographers to ensure quality. *OpenStreetMap* operates on the principle that the more people who map an area, the more likely they are to correct errors, but this depends on mappers' interest and ability. Some are more skilled (or conscientious) than others when it comes to "ground-truthing" (gathering information on site).

Whereas the British national mapping agency, Ordnance Survey, is required to give universal service to all areas, with *OpenStreetMap* maps, some places are more equal than others. Leaving coverage up to participants cultivates a bias in favor of mappers' preferred territory—their own. Participants tend to be upper-middle-class, educated, technically savvy young men. Is it any wonder they choose to map affluent neighborhoods, highly populated city centers and tourist attractions?[58] To counter this bias, the London-based project *Mapping for Change* aims to engage populations from other areas and social groups to create maps that transform their locality: "Maps can show you where you are. But a good map can also show you where you want to go and show you what needs to happen so that you can get there."[59]

Mapping Performatively

A number of artists' mapmaking projects have overtly political goals. Some aim to reveal "the presence, behind a given situation, of forces that were hidden until then."[60] This is true of Mark Lombardi's pencil drawings on rolls of paper up to ten-feet long that visualize crime and conspiracy networks. After researching covert dealings such as money laundering and the abuses of power that led to political and financial frauds such as Whitewater, Iran-Contra, and the savings and loan scandals, he pictured them in the form of diagrams. The artist-archivist described these charts "as 'narrative structures,' ordering the complex facts of a scandal into a coherent whole and given logic by visual presentation in a manner reminiscent of corporate flow charts and systems diagrams." Lombardi gathered and assembled information on index cards "describing disturbing connections between a white-collar criminal class and various governments around the world." After accumulating many cards, "he began stringing out the various actions and relationships among the 'players' in graphic, linear structures that resembled sentence diagrams. He developed a vocabulary and a sort of grammar in an attempt to allow the viewer to apprehend the total picture."[61]

Among the many projects that use data visualization to map power relations, the best-known are *They Rule* (2002–2004) and the maps of Bureau d'Études. *They Rule* by Josh On and FutureFarmers is an interactive Web graphic showing interlocking networks of members of boards of directors of top five hundred companies in the United States using data collected from their Web sites and Security and Exchange Commission filings in early 2004. The French cartographic collective Bureau d'Études has created a number of handmade mind maps—*Governing by Networks, Infowar Psychicwar, Refuse the Biopolice*. "The great alternative project of the last decade," writes Brian Holmes, "has been mapping the transnational space invested primarily by the corporations, and distributing that knowledge for free." Working in a similar spirit, 16 Beaver Group is an artistic and political collective that is based in New York. The scrapbook-like map that it made for the New Museum's *Get Lost: Artists Map Downtown New York* "theorizes an instant connectivity between New York and London, Tokyo, Baghdad, Singapore, and Thailand, among others, marking Manhattan at the crossroads of international trafficking and global politics."[62]

Others aim to modify these structures. In keeping with Bertolt Brecht's injunction that art be not "a mirror to reflect reality, but a hammer with which to shape it," their maps aim not so much to reveal the state of the world as to remake it. They aim to move beyond merely furnishing content to the media, which belong to the dominant culture: "The bourgeois production and publication apparatus," wrote Walter Benjamin, is capable of assimilating "astonishing quantities of revolutionary themes . . . without calling its own existence . . . seriously into question."[63] He urged readers to change the apparatus itself by intervening directly in the process of production and distribution. To designate the transformation of the forms and instruments of production, Brecht coined the term *Umfunktionierung* (functional transformation).

Brecht imagined a radio that would listen to its audience: "So here is a positive suggestion: change this apparatus over from distribution to communication. The radio would be the finest possible communication apparatus in public life, a vast network of pipes. That is to say, it would be if it knew how to receive as well as to transmit, how to let the listener speak as well as hear, how to bring him into a relationship instead of isolating him. On this principle the radio should step out of the supply business and organize its listeners as suppliers. Any attempt by the radio to give a truly public character to public occasions is a step in the right direction."[64]

"The difference between author and public, maintained artificially by the bourgeois press, is beginning to disappear," noted Benjamin: "The reader indeed is always ready to become a writer, that is to say someone who prescribes or describes."[65] He cited constructivist writer, playwright, and journalist Sergei Tretiakov as an example of an "operative" artist who could be both reader and writer, mediator, and creator.

"A political tendency is a necessary but never sufficient condition for the organizing function of a work," wrote Benjamin: "This further requires a directing, instructing stance on the part of the writer. And today this must be demanded more than ever before. *An author who teaches writers nothing teaches no one.* What matters, therefore, is the exemplary character of production, which is able, first, to induce other producers to produce, and, second, to put an improved apparatus at their disposal. And this apparatus is better, the more consumers it is able to turn into producers—that is readers or spectators into collaborators."[66] Benjamin's program has been adopted by contemporary artists who instead of creating works themselves, set up platforms for others to make art.

In a sense, this was already true of Alighiero e Boetti's *Mappa* series of large-scale tapestry maps begun in 1971. The Italian artist commissioned Afghan families to embroider these world maps in which each country was represented by the colors and patterns of its flag. At the outset, the uneducated women who embroidered these maps had no understanding of what they represented. The process (each map took four embroiderers about one year to make)[67] helped them to acquire the cultural codes necessary to interpret the lines and colors. It is estimated that 150 maps were made over a twenty-year period (from 1971 to Boetti's death in 1994) employing about 500 people, first in Kabul and then in Peshawar, Pakistan. One of the families who had worked on Boetti's maps later produced carpets of their own depicting local and world geography for the first time in Afghan history.[68]

Mapping as Context Creation

In Boetti's wake, other artists today explore the aesthetic dimensions of the database by reimagining classification itself as an emergent system—-where names, categories, and associated data structures arise from the bottom up through collective usage. Projects like *Subtract the Sky* by Sharon Daniel use cartographic methodology to design dynamic, evolving systems that allow participants to create and archive their own maps online.[69] Begun in 1999, *Subtract the Sky* was a kind of metamap, a map of other maps.

Daniel later built on that experience to develop cartographic projects with specific user groups. *Palabras* (2006–2007) was a set of software tools and interfaces that enabled people from marginalized and technologically disenfranchised communities to acquire social and symbolic capital and represent themselves in the knowledge economy (figure 8.9).[70]

Daniel held workshops at local cultural centers in Buenos Aires, Kiel, San Francisco, San Jose, and Darfur (Sudan). The project began with a six-week residency at the Villa Tranquila in the Avellaneda district of greater Buenos Aires.[71] There, she taught participants to use inexpensive digital video cameras to document their daily lives, and custom-built Web applications to edit, organize, and publish their videos online. The software allowed them to draw connections between their stories and those of their neighbors, even across cultures. The interface was designed to allow even neophytes to conduct their own projects from beginning to end, filming stories, uploading, and tagging them thus contributing to an emergent, social taxonomy—or a "folksonomy."

This kind of project requires maintenance and frequent updating to improve the software tools and take advantage of current developments. Ideally, the communities themselves should take over the day-to-day operation. In the absence of spectacular, media-friendly events, sources of funding dry up, organizations are downsized, student assistants graduate and move on. Artists themselves must continually launch new projects if they want to keep their heads above water in the competitive market where symbolic capital circulates. The exponential development of the social networking industry may also give them the impression that their smaller-scale, localized efforts have become redundant. However much it expands, social networking always generates a population of outsiders and have-nots.

In this respect, Sharon Daniel's experience is representative. *Palabras* was anchored in specific communities, and the Web site serves to bring their concerns into the public eye.[72] Although it still proclaims that "Palabras is also an expanding network of ongoing collaborations with nonprofit organizations that serve socially marginalized and technologically disenfranchised communities,"[73] the project has lost its momentum. In 2010, Daniel noted that the platform had received sporadic use in cross-cultural school projects. She and four graduate students at the University of

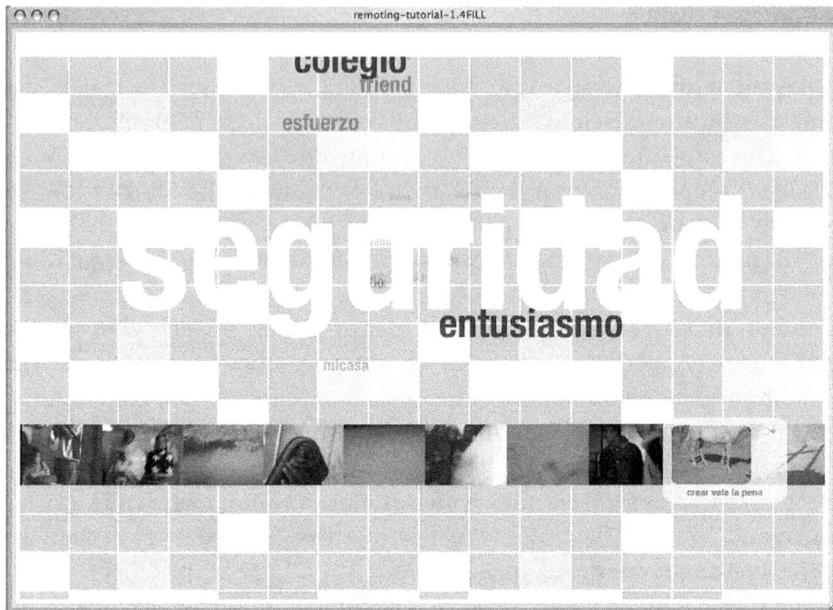

(a)

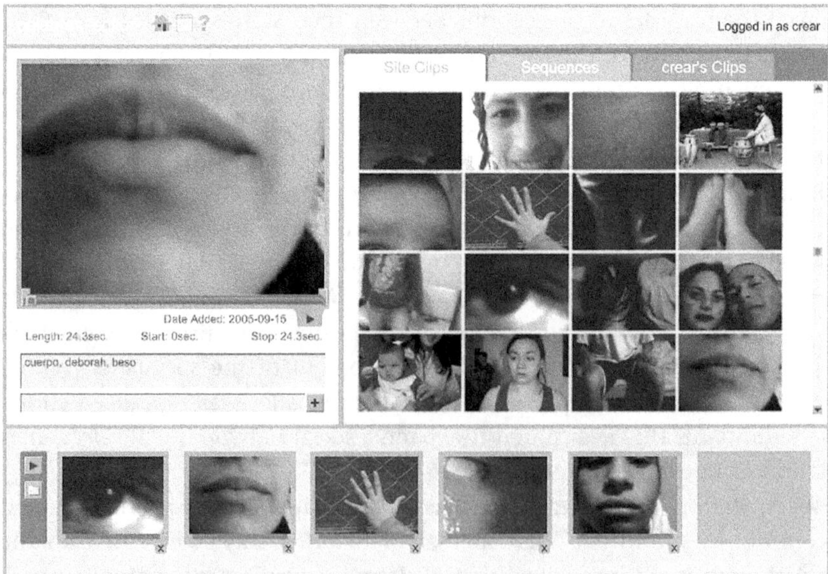

(b)

Figure 8.9

Sharon Daniel, *Palabras,* 2006–2007. Software tools and interfaces that helped technologically disenfranchised communities to represent themselves in the knowledge economy. Images from the project Web site. *a:* Home page. *b:* Editor.

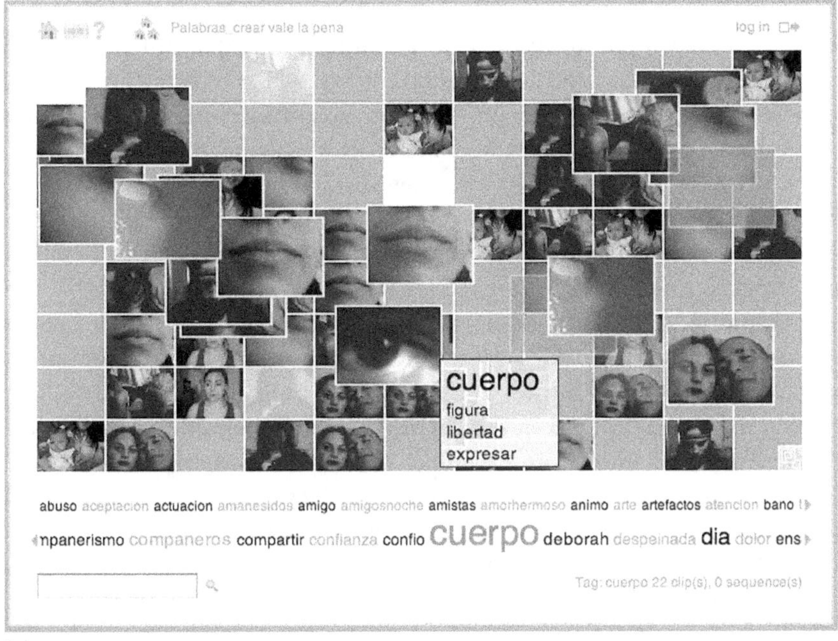

(c)

Figure 8.9 (continued)
c: Tag browser.

California at Santa Cruz redesigned the interfaces. Much of the design was implemented and tested with groups in Buenos Aires, but the students graduated before the new version could be completed and launched to the public. As she puts it: "I think it did and still could serve a productive function for specific communities, but it would really require an organization to take it over at this point to keep it moving forward."[74]

She has developed projects with women inmates in California state prisons (*Public Secrets* and *Improbable Voices*) and with the staff and patients at the Casa Segura, a HIV prevention clinic near her former home in Oakland, California (*Need_X_Change*). In the last five years, she has been recording conversations with injection drug users to make a database of audio interviews called *Blood Sugar*.

Can artists effect social change by creating situations in which other people make art? There is often a tradeoff between working close to home and not making much impact and moving beyond where the stakes may be higher. Among disenfranchised groups, there is more room in which to make a difference. When artists sign objects created with groups of nonartists, however, they can be accused of instrumentalizing the communities they aim to empower, bringing to mind the stereotype in which a high-profile New York art star is flown to an inner-city neighborhood to spend the day producing a collaborative artwork with a specific sited community.[75] Many collaborate with local outreach groups in their own communities (Sharon Daniel began *Need_X_Change* when she lived near Casa Segura).

No matter how sincere an artist is, community outreach brings with it connotations of social work's ethos of poverty management and charity's parade of rich benefactors. These questions need to be addressed before they disqualify all artists who seek to collaborate with communities outside their own. One way to counter moral arguments of this kind is to be part of the community, but community does not necessarily follow ethnic, racial,[76] or class lines.

Indigenous Australian new media artist, activist, and curator Jenny Fraser heralds a new kind of "digital native" who does not wait for others to define the communities to which she belongs. She self-identifies as a member of both the global movement that links up aboriginal groups on several continents and the international new media art community and moves fluently from Yugambeh country in South East Queensland[77] to the Banff New Media Institute in the Canadian Rockies. Fraser sees her curating activities as "an act of sovereignty and emancipation" and a means of restitution.[78] Among the exhibitions she has organized, *The Other APT* (2006) in Brisbane was an alternative to the fifth Asia Pacific Triennial, featuring artworks by Australia-based artists of different cultural backgrounds.[79]

Yet these attempts at mapping communities depend on one artist-instigator, which can cause a bottleneck when artworks have to transit via this person to be published or exhibited. And extension or even just survival depends on the capacity of that person to pursue the project. This has worked in somewhat localized situations: for example, Thomas Beller continues to supervise his New York neighborhood, even from New Orleans where he lives part of the year.

Another approach to turning spectators into producers is to refuse to play the artist in the first place. Self-taught programmer and software critic Jo Walsh has conceived and built the infrastructure for a number of other artists' mapping projects. Walsh was initially interested in the bottom-up approach used in artificial life and recommendation systems.[80] In programming, this means building a program by cobbling together many small specialized ones that communicate among themselves. Walsh defines her project *spacenamespace* as "a kind of *collaborative mapping* project. It consists of geographical models which are represented as RDF graphs. You can wander round them, like a MUD or MOO, with a bot interface which you can use to create and connect new places." Elsewhere she notes "it is an experiment in *gonzo geographical data collection*, with location grid data extrapolated from and converted between different sources on the Internet, and new connections made between them." It allows collaborative filtering and mapping by providing "a scheme for semantic web identification of places."[81]

She began by creating software applications to run automated tasks on the Internet. These programs, called *bots*, perform simple, repetitive tasks much faster than a human being. *Chatterbots* emulate humans, allowing people to ask questions in ordinary English to which the program responds using pattern-matching techniques. An *IRC bot* connects to a teleconferencing system, Internet Relay Chat, as a client, appearing to other users as one of them.[82] IRC bots may lurk in the background of a conversation channel, commenting on participants' remarks. Infobot, for instance, "listens to people chatting, and if it sees something it identifies as a factual statement—'X is Y' or 'X are Y'—then it records it in its memory, and if it sees something like a question to which it knows the answer— 'what is X?' or just 'X?'—then it parrots its answer."[83]

"To me," says Walsh, "a map is just a pretty picture of information. The underlying model is what I want to get at. The bots are a way of allowing humans to be able to contribute their own 'mental models' to the map. When the model improves—which is what the *OpenStreetMap* project is about—the bot can serve as a guide and a proxy."[84]

She went from programming chatterbots for IRC discussion forums to building tools for spatial annotation. Her first bots were autonomous; each one had a "brain" in a text file or a database and its own grammar and language containing "conversational triggers" to allow it to interact with humans. She connected several bots together so they could offer each other suggestions and share information on their "backchannel" using a simple common grammar:[85]

> I was looking for ways in which bots could share information that was richer, and also share the contents of their brains over the Web, in some kind of XML format. Talking to people about this, I was pointed at RDF, the Resource Description Framework which is the graph model for expressing concepts and logical relations, with an XML syntax for carrying it around.[86]

Starting with a Web-based "brain" that could pull up (and add to) a model in RDF/XML, she wrote a little bot. It had "a simple grammar that would take human requests and convert them into requests to the Web-based 'brain' and then interpret the results back into human form."[87]

To test the interactions, she started where she was, making an object to represent her room, and then moved outward, connecting the room to her flat and the flat to the street. Connecting her street to the next, she arrived at the local Underground station. To connect her model to the rest of London via the Tube network, she found a Web site with a model of its 273 stations that she could easily scrape.[88] The next step involved making models of streets in the vicinity of Underground islands that she was familiar with. At this time, friends started exporting the addresses and grid references that they gathered for their online *Open Guide to London*[89] in RDF/XML. This meant that she could add it to her bot model, which had become a project on its own, *Mudlondon*.

Mudlondon was both a model of London and a bot that could communicate with humans using several instant messaging languages.[90] The model could be explored like a MUD and augmented through the bot interface. The bot let human correspondents tag locations with geodata; add comments, images, and hyperlinks; create new spaces; and connect them up. One could move freely from the real world to the MUD and elsewhere on the Internet via pointers to other Web sites. When I discovered Walsh's work in 2003, her text-based multiplayer virtual world had already gone offline.

Inspired by her project, Wilfried Hou Je Bek created a language of description that enabled people to "take the psychogeographical imprint" of a neighborhood, town, or room. He called it *PML* (Psychogeographic MarkUp Language). By using concepts borrowed from the Semantic Web, he aimed to create a generalizable language allowing one to make statistical maps of users' subjective impressions.

Dressed in all the buzz words of the time, *PML* was touted as a "psychogeographical content management system" and also "a protocol that contains unified metadata about urban space recorded during psychogeographical drifts." According to one's point of view, it could become "a knowledge base on urban environments . . . an engine that, after being fed certain parameters, generates new psychogeographical drifts.[91] It could be "datamined to show never before suspected patterns in the urban fabric . . . [or] used to transform a mass of subjective data into an objective representation," and above all, it could "be fired up into a new mythology for urban space."[92]

PML objects were modeled as *psychogeograms*: "the diagrammatic representation of both informational, physical & emotive aspects of urban space."[93] To create visualizations using *PML* tags, he learned the basics of Java. Tags like *open*, *closed*, *crowded*, or *empty* allowed walkers to evaluate the atmosphere of a street. Distinctions in the urban fabric could be located to create a *bolagram* (boundary map).

Architects from the Atelier Rijksbouwmeester used *PML* to annotate the Hofkwartier, a neighborhood under reconstruction in Dordrecht. Their annotations were visualized in a *psychogeogram* displayed on Hou Je Bek's *Social Fiction* Web site. Extending the principle of situationist ambiance maps, *PML* proposed a group appreciation by aggregating all the individuals' data to chart collective subjectivity. Presented in a manner that was at once serious and parodic, *PML* reappropriated methods of statistical analysis, much as Russian artists Komar and Melamid had used opinion polls ordered from professionals to determine the parameters of their *Most Wanted Paintings*.[94] Both Walsh's *Mudlondon* and Hou Je Bek's *PML* are notable, not so much in what they actually accomplished as in what they made imaginable. In this sense, they can be considered milestones.

Linking the Maps

Jo Walsh sees the semantic web as the most efficient way of linking maps. It can be used "to connect up the edges, to help point directions out of the network via things on the edge, as well as draw coherence out of the structures in the core."[95] As a member of different groups, she recognized possibilities for convergence. In 2005, she saw "a 'radical geek movement' in the offing" that she aspired to ground "with other people's concerns" by organizing "'Open Knowledge Forums,' in particular about the geodata access issue which is seriously hampering the development of grassroots locative projects in the UK; the ideal is to socialize our problems and solutions to people working for NGOs and local government organizations, who may share our concerns and possibly participate in or support our projects."[96]

Today, this way of thinking continues to inform the open-source, free-software, copyleft movements. In their quest for autonomy, many artists prefer to use and develop tools that are available to all. For them, the simple possibility of walking wherever one wills is already a potent political message, walking being the most basic way of "reclaiming the streets." They program with pencil and paper or develop networked cartographic systems within which users can share skills and knowledge. Wilfried Hou Je Bek's pedestrian supercomputer is emblematic of that aspiration. "Do it!" was Jerry Rubin's call for action in 1968,[97] and although it long survived as little more than an advertising slogan, it has regained some of its former resonance. When "Do it yourself" segues into "Do it ourselves" or "Do it with others," each pedestrian is a potential cartographer. When all the maps are effectively linked up and the datasets accessible to the general public, now actively involved in producing its own location-based data, other problems arise. Dealing with these problems and searching for "ways through" will be the object of this book's last chapter.

9 Mapping "Ways Through"

What happens when we connect the maps? For the most part, the projects and tools of collaborative cartography draw connections among sources of information. This has not prevented cartographers from being accused of taking a superior, godlike view of whatever they are mapping.[1] Do people map something to gain knowledge of it and ultimately power over it? This is certainly true of artist-activists who map contemporary capitalism. Even those who put mapping tools into the hands of other people create systems that function as meta-maps. These systems can become means of control.

Online collaboration can sustain projects like *OpenStreetMap* or *Wikipedia*, but it also empowers extremists, ultranationalists, proponents of conspiracy theories, paramilitary organizations, religious fundamentalists, and hysterical fringe groups.

The Trouble with Linking the Maps

Networked databases can enrich maps with precise, regularly updated information from a wide range of sources. Photographs and GPS tracks can be linked with other data. The next step is the large-scale integration of information gleaned from contemporary forms of surveillance.

Using technologies that were developed by companies in Western countries, the Chinese are developing the Golden Shield program, which enables surveillance. Shenzhen, one of China's fastest-growing cities, is a test for the booming homeland security industry. Reporting in 2008, Naomi Klein saw the Shenzhen program as a harbinger of things to come in Europe and America. Through the collaboration of governments and corporations like Honeywell, IBM, and General Electric, these tools will be linked "in a massive, searchable database of names, photos, residency information, work history, and biometric data."[2] Some entrepreneurs are improving camera resolution and facial-recognition software, while others are developing the ambient intelligence of radio frequency identification tags.[3] The police will be able to track Chinese citizens thanks to "national ID cards with scannable computer chips and photos that are instantly uploaded to police databases and linked to their holder's personal data."[4] Using this information to identify sources of political unrest, the government will be able to nip dissent in the bud before it blooms into another Tiananmen Square.[5]

Predators in the West have an easier task. In an age of self-broadcasting, millions of people willingly share private information on social networking sites. Many camera phones automatically geotag photographs without the knowledge of the photographer. When the image files are uploaded to the Web, the information is made available to anyone who is curious enough to consult the metadata. In this way, data made available by individuals themselves can be mined by identity thieves, Big Brother governments, e-marketers, or spiritual mappers.[6]

Today surveillance technologies are at the heart of most online and many offline experiences. Much has been written about the shift from the disciplinary regime (that Michel Foucault theorized in *Discipline and Punish*)[7] to the control society (defined by Gilles Deleuze). According to Deleuze, "Foucault has brilliantly analyzed the ideal project of these environments of enclosure, particularly visible within the factory: to concentrate; to distribute in space; to order in time; to compose a productive force within the dimension of space-time whose effect will be greater than the sum of its component forces."[8] Foucault focused on the highly refined forms of discipline used by modern institutions (factories, schools, hospitals, prisons). To individuate bodies so they could perform differentiated tasks, Foucault showed that building design was based on Jeremy Bentham's Panopticon. Bentham's plan for a model prison allowed guards at the top of a central tower to observe inmates in their cells below while remaining unseen by the prisoners. Bentham claimed that inmates would be less likely to break rules if they believed they were being watched and could incur punishment.[9]

Today, the situation has changed. "We are in a generalized crisis in relation to all the environments of enclosure—prison, hospital, factory, school, family," wrote Deleuze in 1989. What he calls "the new forces knocking at the door . . . are the *societies of control*, which are in the process of replacing disciplinary societies." The "new monster" uses "ultrarapid forms of free-floating control" to break down older forms of solidarity.[10] The ubiquitous corporation has replaced the factory floor where the assembly lineswere located in space and time:

> The factory constituted individuals as a single body to the double advantage of the boss who surveyed each element within the mass and the unions who mobilized a mass resistance; but the corporation constantly presents the brashest rivalry as a healthy form of emulation, an excellent motivational force that opposes individuals against one another and runs through each, dividing each within. [Today the] . . . numerical language of control is made of codes that mark access to information, or reject it. . . . Individuals have become *"dividuals"* and masses, samples, data, markets, or *"banks."*[11]

This permeation of control into every aspect of our lives can have long-term repercussions. Today, citizens are filmed by innumerable closed-circuit television cameras, and as more and more of our daily activities—including phone calls, email messages, and credit-card purchases—become precisely quantifiable and date-stamped, they leave traces in databases.

By using data on the movement of millions of individuals that were made available to them by a mobile phone company, network scientists have developed an algorithm that can calculate people's probable movements based on their previous travel patterns.[12] Whether this predictability is evidence of scientific progress or an assault on our privacy, we must come to terms with it. In this final chapter, we take a look at various "ways through" that have been charted by artists.

Surveillance, Control, (Mis)Trust

Closed-circuit television has often been used as a surveillance device, and many of the earliest works of video art involve deconstructing surveillance (or some aspect of it) to expose its underpinnings. *Wipe Cycle* (1969) by Ira Schneider and Frank Gillette showed a battery of video monitors that juxtaposed prerecorded material and live images of gallery visitors. Bruce Nauman's *Video Surveillance Piece: Public Room, Private Room* (1969–1970) consists of two rooms, each containing a video camera and a monitor: the private room could be viewed on the monitor in the public room and vice versa.[13]

One of Yoko Ono's film scores, *Film No. 4 (Rape, or Chase)* (1968), stipulated that "a cameraman will chase a girl on a street with a camera persistently until he corners her in an alley, and, if possible, until she is in a falling position." The resulting film *Rape* (John Lennon and Yoko Ono, 1969) was made from a candid recording by cameraman Nic Knowland. Ono was not present for the shooting, but she says that after looking at the footage, she "kept pushing him to bring back better material."[14] Overcoming an initial reluctance, Knowland and his film crew finally spotted a young Hungarian woman, an illegal immigrant who appeared to speak no English.[15] The crew started filming her in a cemetery, pursued her relentlessly in the street, refusing to speak with her in spite of her attempts at communication, finally trapping her in her own apartment.

In an attempt to understand whether ordinary people would follow immoral orders, as many had in Nazi Germany, social psychologist Stanley Milgram measured the willingness of experiment participants to obey an authority figure who instructed them to perform acts contrary to their personal moral beliefs. He found that many were willing to administer what they believed were painful electric shocks on innocent people. In a sense, the presence of a camera modifies the behavior that it purports to document, and professional cameras tend to bestow authority on the person behind the lens. Their power of intimidation is increased when the victim is an illegal immigrant. Knowland, a pacifist, was aware that his camera was inflicting psychological torture on a particularly vulnerable victim, and yet he and his film crew pursued their subject to create a sexually charged film that seems to revel in predatory violence.

Vito Acconci's two-channel video *Remote Control* (1971) shows how harm can be done with the victim's consent and even active collaboration. Two performers, Acconci and Kathy Dillon, are locked in separate rooms that are equipped with video monitors and cameras. Dillon's room contains a length of rope, and Acconci tries to persuade her to tie herself up with the rope, alternately cajoling and pleading with her. "The tension between resist and submit is mesmerizing," writes Barbara London: "This stress is the sticky flypaper of reality TV which invariably has a boss-person getting a subordinate to do something objectionable. However, no one gets terminated in *Remote Control*. The action plays out like a ballet. When the female sighs and complies, the male happily prances about, and when she rebels, he walks around forlornly."[16]

Gazing Back

A recent approach involves gazing back at the increasing number of people whose job it is to watch other people. The term *sousveillance* was coined by Steve Mann as a response to the increasing level of surveillance in our societies. Derived from the French *surveillance*, it means, he writes, "watchful vigilance from underneath."[17]

In Mann's view, everything has a simple explanation. A balance of power among divergent viewpoints creates equilibrium, while imbalance leads to unrest, riots, and violence. The true causes of terrorism are oppression, bad foreign policy, and secrecy. Secret organizations lack the feedback mechanisms that are found in a home thermostat.[18] The thermostat actively controls heat in the home to maintain an optimal temperature, and when the room (or homeland) gets too hot, it cuts off or reduces the heat. In the absence of a thermostat, the heat will continue to increase until it sparks off a fire—or an explosion of terrorism.

Today there is an imbalance: governments and corporations carry on secret operations while employing Big Brother surveillance methods to keep the rest of us in line. To restore the balance, Mann proposes that ordinary people should reverse this surveillance: "Rather than tolerating terrorism as a feedback means . . . an alternative framework would be to build a stable system to begin with, e.g., a system that is self-balancing. Such a society may be built with sousveillance (inverse surveillance) as a way to balance the increasing (and increasingly one-sided) surveillance."[19]

Mann himself was one of the first to practice sousveillance. In 1994, he invented a device called the wearable wireless webcam or Wearcomp, a small eyepiece that transformed its wearer into a cyborg. For two years, he wore it nearly all the time, taking it off only to swim, shower, or sleep. The device was connected to the Internet and allowed online viewers to see the world through Mann's eyes. And what he (and they) saw were more and more cameras eyeing him back.

The Web documentary *Shooting Back* (1995) shows Mann wearing an EyeTap (sunglasses equipped with a hidden camera) as he walks into stores and searches for the surveillance cameras that are filming him. When employees blame the presence of surveillance cameras on their superiors, he takes out his own camera and films them, much to their discomfort.[20]

Governments and private corporations use security systems that are inspired by Bentham's Panopticon. To discourage shoplifting, stores install both decoy and real cameras behind smoked glass domes and mirrors. Because customers do not know whether or not they are being filmed, they censor their behavior. In one experiment, Mann walked into a store with several conference attendees who all carried bags with smoked domes on their sides. Some of the bags contained webcams that transmitted the performance back to the conference.[21]

If sousveillance is, to a certain extent, just more surveillance, as Mann notes, it does "destroy the monopoly on surveillance."[22] In this era of one-upmanship, another arms race might be in the offing.

Another of Mann's projects was called *Invisibility Suit: Street Theater of the Absurd* (2001). Worn on the back like a sandwich board, a computer display shows output from a camera worn in front so that people can "see right through" the wearer. Here, the wearer turns his back into a window to show people what is in front of him. When agents of surveillance in stores question him about it, the wearer claims it is an "invisibility suit to provide privacy and protection from their surveillance cameras."[23] For the *3rdi* (2010–2011), a work referencing both Steve Mann and Stelarc, Iraqi American artist Wafaa Bilal had a camera surgically attached to the back of his head to record what it sees for one year, beginning in 2010. The photos were transmitted to his server by a cell phone, one per minute, and displayed as a live stream in an installation at the Mathaf Arab Museum of Modern Art in Qatar.[24]

The dangers of unregulated surveillance devices are multiplied with the expansion of the Internet. Michael Naimark was shocked to discover that a camera placed in a public space could be made to observe private spaces. When it is connected to the Internet, no one knows how many viewers can be watching anonymously: "Laws and conventions acceptable for a single live gaze do not scale for remote multiple ones."[25]

Inspired by the *Archimedes Project* (2001), in which activists at the Group of Eight economic summit in Genoa, Italy, used mirrors to focus sunlight on police helicopters, tanks, and eyes,[26] Naimark explored "camera zapping" by aiming a laser pointer directly into the lens of a video camera: "The tiny beam neutralized regions of the camera sensor far larger than the actual size of the beam. Properly aimed, it could block a far-away camera from seeing anything inside of a large window." This work, he writes, has "divided my artist colleagues into those who see [it as] a new activist tool and those who liken it to burning canvasses. Indeed, is an antitool a tool? Then there's the question of releasing potentially useful information to criminals and terrorists."[27]

Is it possible to control representations of ourselves? We can decide to avoid cameras, pay only in cash, or not to care. Naimark notes that "Whatever alternative or optimal approaches may exist, it's clear that 'depresentation' is as fundamental a force as re-presentation as we approach the brave new world of massive databases and cameras everywhere. Camera zapping may provide a robust metaphor for these deeper issues."[28]

What *Do* I See?

In New York, closed-circuit surveillance cameras were first installed in the 1970s in Times Square to deter organized crime. Their number multiplied in the 1990s as part of former Mayor Rudy Giuliani's zero tolerance for crime and drugs. After the attacks on the World Trade Center in 2001, 1,500 more cameras were installed in the subways and in Brooklyn and the Bronx.[29] An effective way to communicate concerns about surveillance is to chart the location of closed-circuit TV cameras on an online map and make the information public. *ISee* is a route-finder that was developed by the Institute for Applied Autonomy (IAA) in 2001 to enable users to plot "paths of least surveillance" so they can move through public space without being filmed by unregulated surveillance cameras. Users click on a city map to set the starting point for their journeys (an icon marks the spot) and then click again to define a destination. *ISee* generates "the safest 'path of least surveillance' between these two places."[30]

The IAA collaborated with the Surveillance Camera Players and the New York American Civil Liberties Union to set up a database locating surveillance devices in Manhattan's public places. The application they built reveals the biases inherent to these systems. Using simple visualization tools, the group showed that surveillance cameras, ostensibly installed to protect inhabitants of neighborhoods considered unsafe (like Chinatown), were placed not in residential areas but in shopping districts. Their locations reveal that they serve mainly the interests of business owners.[31]

Geographer-artist Trevor Paglen's specialty is countersurveillance of the military. In the past ten years, he has accumulated images of highly secret American government operations in remote places. He photographs military installations and aircraft from afar with a high-power telephoto lens. Using Federal Aviation Authority flight-tracking data, he monitors the paths of ordinary planes with blocked tail numbers and charts the movements of cargo planes, fighters, bombers, trainers, transports, and spy planes to reveal the physical contours of the military-industrial complex.

He has exhibited photographs, lists of code names designating active classified military programs, and applications that map flight data from unmarked military

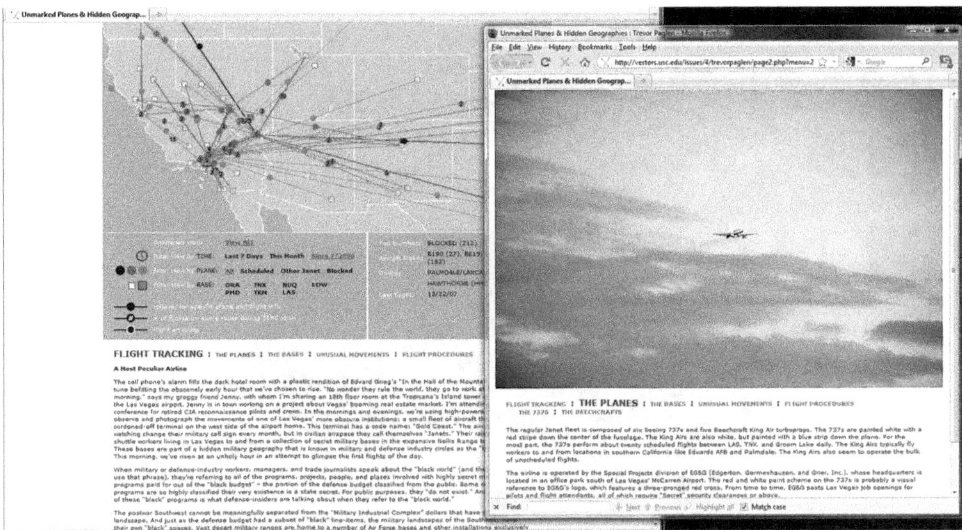

Figure 9.1

Trevor Paglen, *Unmarked Planes and Hidden Geographies*, 2006. Web site. This site maps a fleet of military aircraft that use the call-sign Janet when they operate in civilian airspace.

aircraft. He has written about clandestine military prisons like the Salt Pit in Afghanistan; collected patches, emblems, and insignia used by the workers involved in secret projects; led expeditions to observe military sites in the desert; and visualized the orbits of classified American spacecraft.[32]

Unmarked Planes and Hidden Geographies (2006) maps the comings and goings of a fleet of military aircraft that use the call-sign Janet when they operate in civilian airspace (figure 9.1). The Janets shuttle workers to and from remote military installations in the Southwest and undertake support operations for other obscure activities. Because they operate under the guise of a civilian organization, their flight plans must be filed with the Federal Aviation Administration and made publicly available. *Unmarked Planes* uses these public data sources to map the covert operations, places, and personnel known in military and defense-industry parlance as the "black world."[33]

For the project *Terminal Air*, Paglen worked with the Institute for Applied Autonomy to make mapping software that tracks CIA aircraft flights in near real time and saves this information in a database (figure 9.2). This application explores the network of government agencies and private contractors that are involved in transporting suspected terrorists to secret locations for interrogation and torture as part of the Central Intelligence Agency's "extraordinary rendition" program. He and John Emerson mapped *Selected CIA Aircraft Routes, 2001–2006* derived from FAA and Eurocontrol Flight Logs for *An Atlas of Radical Cartography*.[34] Except for a few place names that are

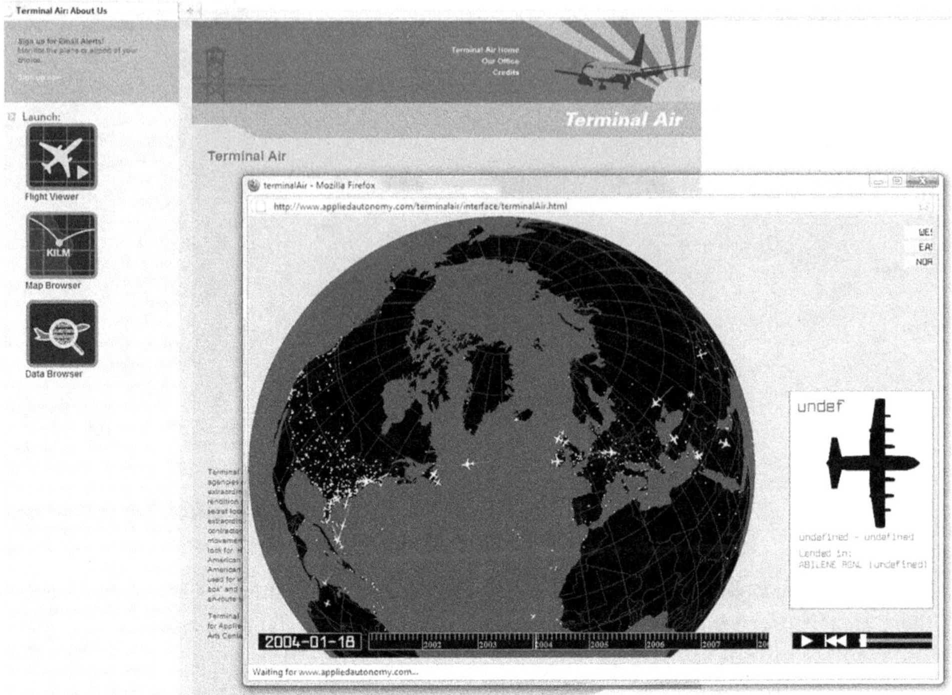

Figure 9.2

Trevor Paglen and the Institute for Applied Autonomy, *Terminal Air*, 2006–2007. Mapping software and Web site. This application tracks CIA aircraft flights that are involved in transporting suspected terrorists to secret locations for interrogation and torture.

not usually thought of as tourist destinations (Guantanamo Bay) and the list of plane-owning companies in the upper right corner, the map could be the air route atlas from any airline magazine.

Playing (for) the Cameras

Other artists-activists use humor to resist incorporation into the control society. These projects are often underpinned by extensive research. The New York Surveillance Camera Players joined forces in 1996 "to present a specially designed series of famous dramatic works of the modern period for the entertainment, amusement, and moral edification of the surveilling members of the law enforcement community."[35]

Inspired by situationist theories of *détournement*, the informal group began performing in front of publicly installed, police-watched surveillance cameras on December 10, 1996, when they presented their version of Alfred Jarry's play *Ubu roi*, exactly one hundred years after its first performance. Because the law prohibits surveillance cameras from capturing sound, the characters mimed their parts, and the titles and dialogs were displayed on hand-lettered posters resembling the placards carried by demonstrators in a protest march. This performance successfully reached its core audience when officers from the New York City police department shut it down.

Since then, the Players have performed adaptations of George Orwell's novel *1984* in the subway (the police arrived during the Room 101 torture scene) and Wilhelm Reich's *The Mass Psychology of Fascism* in front of a privately owned (and surveilled) fragment of the Berlin Wall for an audience of bemused passers-by. They have mapped camera locations (fourteen maps in New York), led walks through well-watched neighborhoods, and maintained an online encyclopedia that details legal rulings, histories, technical descriptions, and profiles of major investors and users of surveillance technology.[36] Their approach is didactic. According to Bill Brown:

> The plays that we started out doing were opaque. The relationship [of] Jarre or Becket or Poe to the surveillance cameras was not clear. So we jettisoned any play that wasn't specifically referring to the cameras because it took up valuable time in explaining it, so that ultimately meant that once we scripted George Orwell's *1984*, the only place to go there after was scripting our own plays. In addition, the signboards always show an icon of a surveillance camera so that people never have any doubt whatsoever about what we're doing.[37]

Participants in the Players' Sunday walking tours learn why surveillance endangers every citizen's constitutional right to privacy, as well as practical skills, including how to identify cameras, how they work, and what improvements can be expected as more and more public money is spent on pattern recognition software and smart technology.

Intrigued by the two-tone police sirens that can be heard at any hour of the day or night in Paris, the duo HeHe (Heiko Hansen and Helen Evans) built their own (reverse) surveillance system that can be installed on private balconies. *Siren Shield* (2008–), siren-recording open-source software, analyzes the ambient sound in real time (figure 9.3). When it detects the frequency of a siren announcing the arrival of a police vehicle (in France, the notes D and A alternate every half second), it sets off a webcam.

In June 2009, a giant rotating beacon occupied the front room at the Ars Longa Gallery in Paris, while in the back, video projections showed footage of "crime scenes" both real and fictive. "*Siren Shield* software can also be used to monitor sirens on the digital television network," notes Heiko Hansen. "The thousands of videos captured, both of real police cars in Paris and Geneva alongside fictional fragments of police series, sitcoms, films, classical orchestras and cartoons from television, are remixed in the exhibition space with the SIREN MIXER software. The installation is completed with a giant rotating police warning light and mock police badges to wear that are adorned with a custom insignia."[38] And visitors are left to find their way among digital reflections and simulacra.

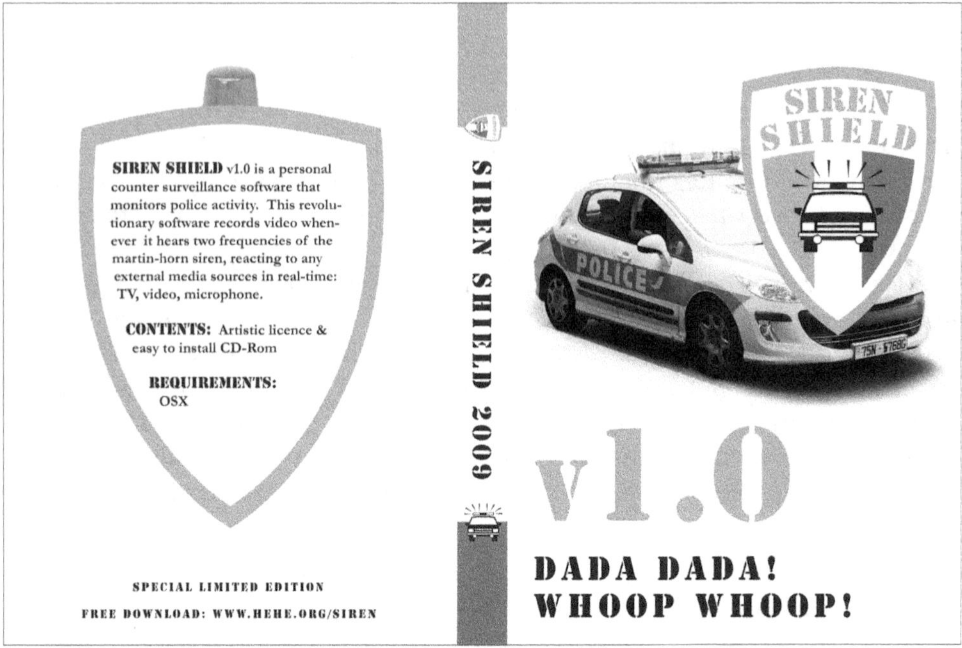

(a)

(b)

Figure 9.3

HeHe (Heiko Hansen and Helen Evans), *Siren Shields*, 2008–ongoing. Siren Shield v1.0 is a personal counter surveillance software that monitors police activity. This software is freely available for download. A webcam is controlled by siren-recording open-source software that analyzes the ambient sound in real time. When it detects a siren of an approaching police vehicle, it sets off the webcam. *a:* Brochure. *b:* Webcams equipped with *Siren Shield* can be installed on balconies.

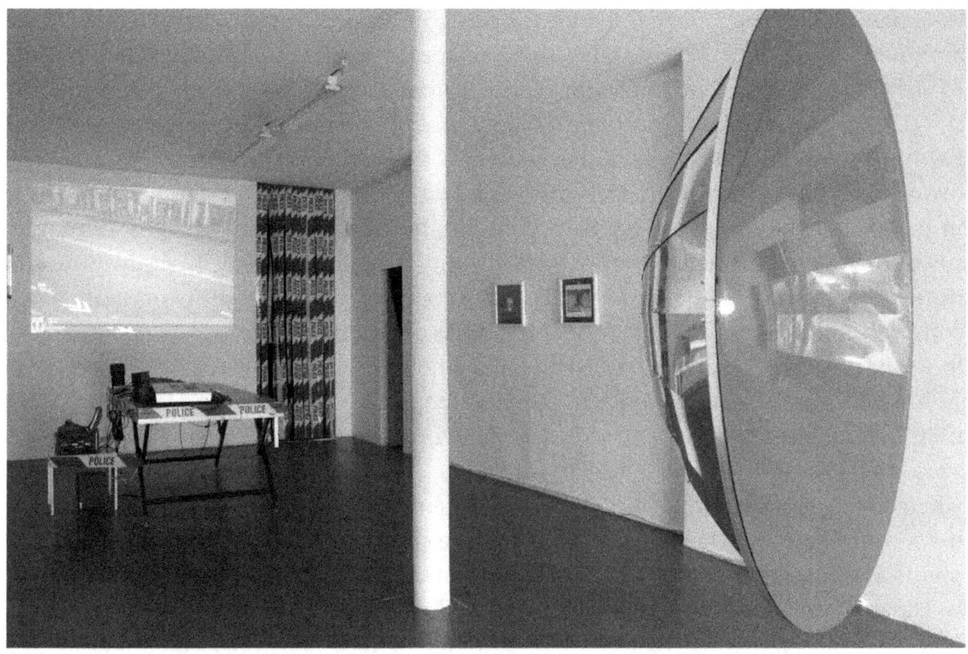

(c)

Figure 9.3 (continued)
c: Exhibition view at Ars Longa Gallery in Paris, June 2009.

Wile E. Coyote and the Roadrunner

During the same period, other artists focused on the dataprints that people leave as they move around with cell phones, take the subway, or use credit cards. Unlike footprints in the sand, these tracks can be permanent, as any victim of identity theft discovers.

In 2002, the two Italian artists known as the zero-ones (0100101110101101.org) carried a GPS transmitter everywhere they went, which captured track data and uploaded it to a remote server via cell phone. The data were then visualized on a Web site where viewers could follow the artists in real time. This work, called *VOPOS*, an allusion to the national police of the former German Democratic Republic (*Volkspolizei*, also known as the VP or VoPo). The artists saw it as "a criticism of the potential of the GPS: who uses the coordinates it provides, and what does the electronic profile that can be deduced from them reveal?" As a "planned collection of comprehensive, person-specific data," it was the second part of their *Self-Surveillance System for Complete Digital Transparency Project* called *Glasnost*. It had begun with *life_sharing* (2001), turning the hard drive of their computer into a Web server, thus making publicly available their private emails, project sketches, and software.[39]

Hasan Elahi has a personal reason for being interested in state surveillance. In the aftermath of September 11, 2001, this Bangladeshi-born American became a suspect in the war on terror. Returning from a trip abroad in June 2002, he was detained by the U.S. Immigration and Naturalization Service[40] at Detroit Metropolitan Airport and held for questioning because he had rented a storage locker in Tampa, Florida. The owners had reported that an Arab man had fled on September 12 and left explosives in the locker. The explosives were never found, but Elahi's origins brought him under suspicion. After repeated interrogations by the Federal Bureau of Investigation and nine polygraph tests, he proved his innocence by demonstrating mastery of "a common culture—the ability to quote the lyrics of country songs, or talk about college football, the sort of things a terrorist would find very hard to fake."[41]

After this harrowing experience, he began to leave a deliberate electronic paper trail, first for his FBI agent and then for the whole world, fixing the ephemera of his successive journeys like Peter Pan trying to trap his shadow. His cell phone posts his whereabouts to a real-time online map. By systematically using a credit card, snapping his surroundings as others might punch a time clock, he has built an archive of documents and images that attest to his movements.

Hasan Elahi's *Tracking Transience: The Orwell Project* (2002–present) has been exhibited in various versions (figure 9.4). I saw it first in 2004. It was a simple looped projection that showed a sequence of interchangeable airport waiting zones, people movers, and gates with overlaid titles, like EWR, DTW, AMS and SIN. Over time, the installations have grown more elaborate, with banks of plasma screens showing images sorted thematically in gridded series that echo the classification schemata of Bernt and Hilla Becher. Only, here, the steel factories have been replaced by contemporary service industries.

It would be difficult to track Elahi using the information he has posted to his Web site. With its lush graphics and animated panoramic interface, the site abounds in sensory overload. Too much information kills the information, and viewers begin to wonder whether the project is a way of escaping notice. The information is there, but the pictures need contextualizing to make sense: they lack even basic captions to anchor them. Airport corridors look alike the world over. What can we infer from seeing the contents of a meal tray if we have no way of distinguishing yesterday's supper from a six-year-old lunch? The archives are not searchable, and the site is off-limits to the Wayback Machine. Someone who controls his public image to this extent has become nearly invisible.

In a world where more and more ordinary people use smart phones with GPS service, post home videos on YouTube, and geotag photos on Facebook, what distinguishes Elahi's project? Ironically, through his handmade form of self-surveillance, he realizes Andy Warhol's dream of becoming a machine. By systematically picturing details of his environment, he aesthetizes surveillance. Steve Mann and Wafaa Bilal both automate the process by creating prostheses, but Elahi, like Tehching Hsieh punching his time clock, keeps pressing the shutter button.

In today's commodity culture, where inherited identity and traditions no longer hold sway, marketers and advertisers offer consumers a common identity through the products that they buy and use. "Liz Taylor drinks Coke, and just think, you can drink Coke, too. A Coke is a Coke and no amount of money can get you a better Coke than the one the bum on the corner is drinking."[42] Andy Warhol famously said, so Hasan Elahi, the quintessential "painter of modern life," buys camera equipment at B&H "just like you and me." His credit-card purchases and familiarity with contemporary branding shows him to be one of us (consumers) and not one of them (terrorists).

For his study using mobile phone records to predict people's movements, Albert-László Barabási asked Elahi to provide him with information as to his whereabouts over several months.[43] As a contemporary flâneur who has learned to "be away from home and yet to feel at home anywhere; to see the world, to be at the very center of the world, and yet to be unseen of the world,"[44] Elahi consistently eluded his pursuers.

It may be too soon to tell if this will become an all-encompassing project like *OPALKA 1965 / 1 – ∞*, Roman Opalka's meditation on time, begun in 1965 and completed only with the artist's death in 2011. For the time being, transience continues to be tracked at a dizzying pace. Elahi's personal Web page used to carry an epigraph:

> Wile E. Coyote did finally catch the Roadrunner,
> but then he held up a sign: "What do I do now?"[45]

Inside Out: Remapping Private and Public

How many wireless video camera systems have been sold to monitor babies' sleep? Michelle Teran notes that "people place cameras on what they want to protect. Perhaps this is a desire, as Bachelard describes, to return to the original shell of early childhood. . . . A sheltered being gives perceptible limits to his shelter."[46] Yet when parents install nanny cams for security, they are also leaving the door open to anyone equipped with a cheap receiver to stalk them in their living rooms.[47]

Michelle Teran's performance *Life: A User's Manual* (2003–2006) reflects on this other aspect of surveillance technology (figure 9.5). She borrowed her title from George Perec's spatially organized novel. "I imagine a Parisian building with its facade removed," wrote Perec in a preliminary project statement, "so that from the ground floor to the attic, all the rooms that are on the front are instantly and simultaneously visible."[48] Inspired by a Saul Steinberg drawing, the novel moves from one apartment to the next, gathering their occupants' stories. Radio waves traverse walls invisibly, virtually removing facades. Here, participants use a video scanner to capture live views that are broadcast inadvertently by users of wireless surveillance devices: in a sense,

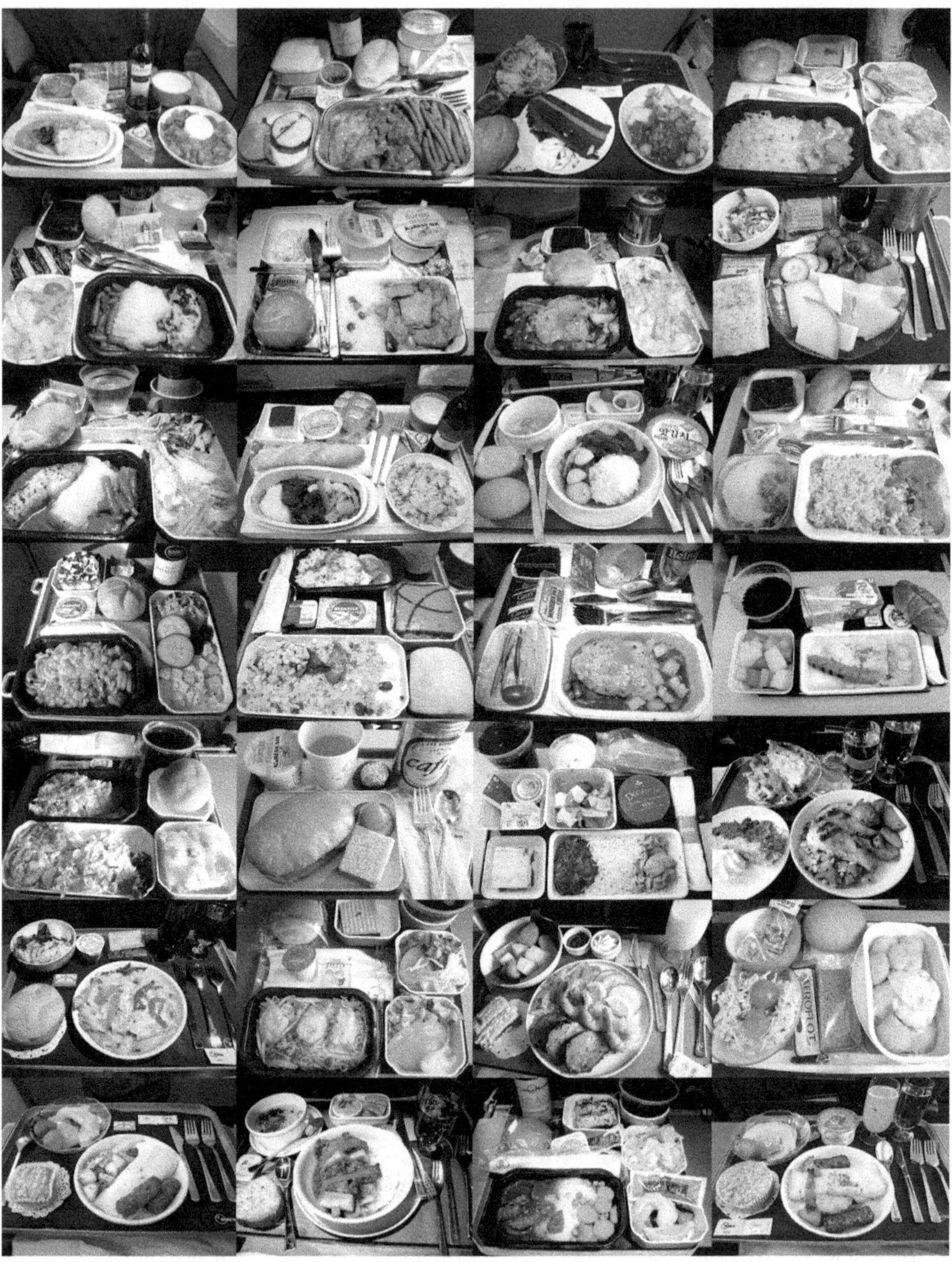

(a)

Figure 9.4

Hasan Elahi, *Tracking Transience: The Orwell Project*, 2002–ongoing. Website and photographic installations. After becoming a suspect in the war on terror, the artist proved his innocence by demonstrating mastery of a common culture. His electronic paper trail captures the ephemera of his successive journeys. *a:* Airline meal trays.

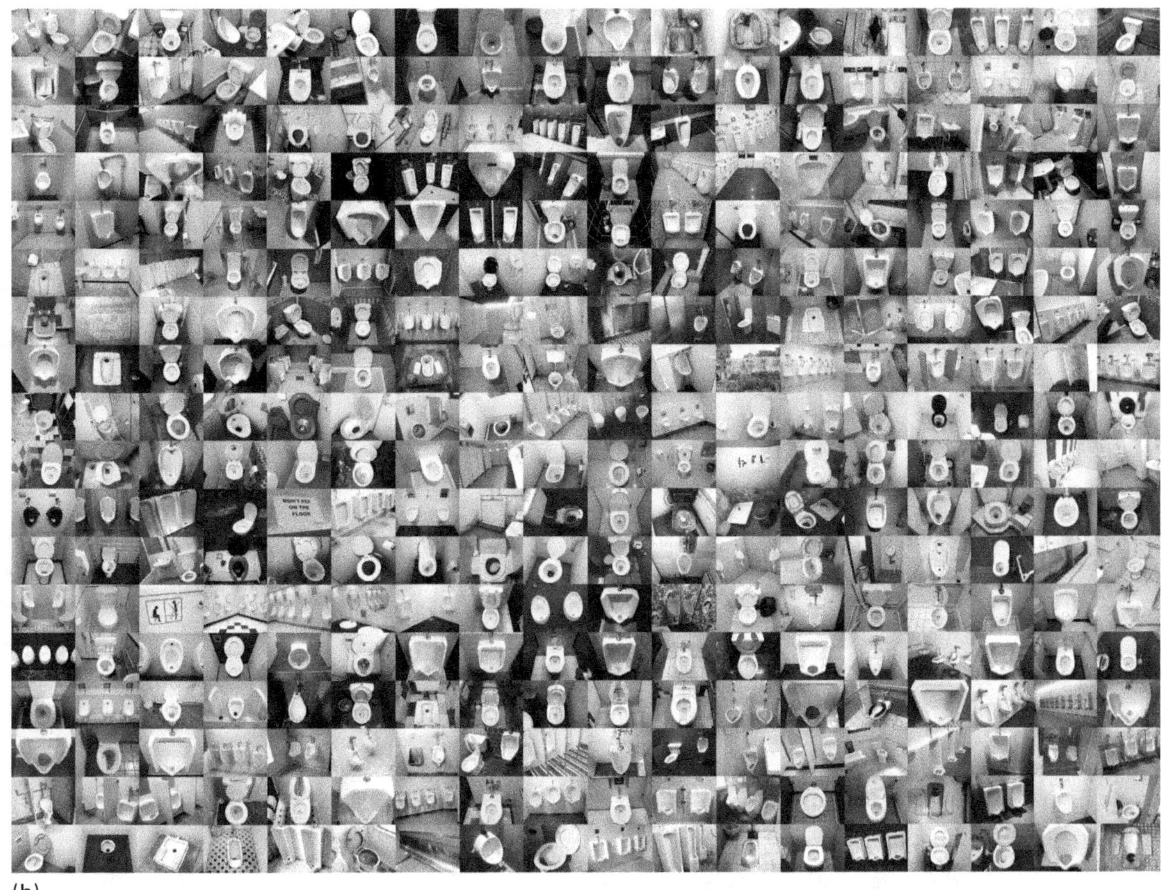

(b)

Figure 9.4 (continued)
b: Restroom fixtures.

the rooms describe themselves automatically in real time. Teran has staged performance walks in Brussels, Amsterdam, Berlin, Linz, and Montreal to explore "the hidden stories captured by private wireless CCTV streams and how they intersect with the visible world around us."[49] In the video of the 2005 Berlin walk, a woman in black pulls a rolling video-suitcase, on the front of which a vignette window shows an indistinct black and white image. She moves her wrist so that the device strapped to it can pick up nearby video streams: a high-angle view of a supermarket aisle is replaced by a shot of an open window seen from inside looking out. Elsewhere, the suitcase became a backpack (Montreal) or a street vendor's cart piled up with television monitors (Linz).

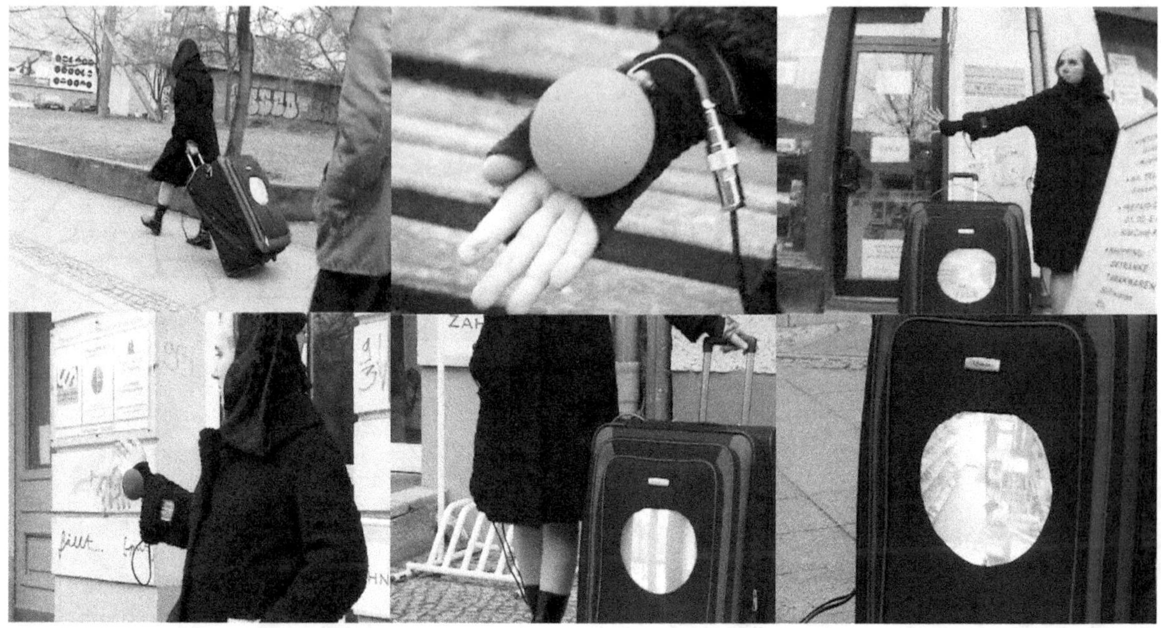

(a)

(b)

Figure 9.5

Michelle Teran, *Life: A User's Manual*, 2003–2006. Performance. Participants in performance walks in Berlin, Montreal, and Linz capture live views that were broadcast inadvertently by users of wireless surveillance devices. How do the hidden stories captured by private wireless CCTV streams intersect with the visible world around us? *a:* In Berlin, the images were visible on a monitor from inside a rolling suitcase. *b:* In Montreal, the suitcase became a backpack.

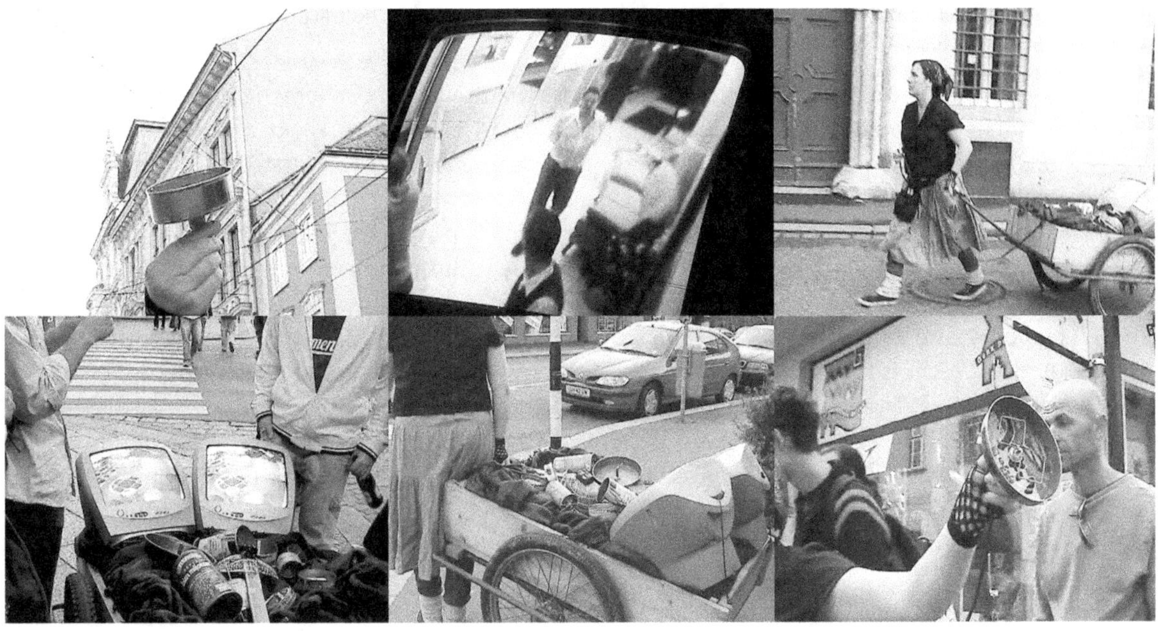

(c)

Figure 9.5 (continued)
c: In Linz, a street vendor's cart is piled up with television monitors.

In Teran's work, activities that take place within the monitored rooms are revealed to a handful of participants as they unfold. This project questions the limits between public and private space as they are traditionally defined—inside (a home or a business) and outside (the street). These limits shift when people film their interiors and post their videos on the Web. Teran taps into private video streams but does not rebroadcast the footage she captures.

Others operate radical transfers of so-called private information into the public sphere. In 1983, Sophie Calle used an address book she found on the street as the basis for a series of articles that appeared in the French daily newspaper *Liberation.* By conducting phone interviews with the people listed in the address book, she published a *portrait en creux* of its owner (a man she had never met) and thus exposed him to public scrutiny. In 2008, Raphaël Meltz, a journalist for the French newspaper *Le Tigre* mined the Web and social networks for user-contributed information to produce a data portrait of a person chosen at random:

Happy Birthday, Marc. On December 5, 2008, you'll be celebrating your twenty-ninth birthday. You don't mind if we call each other *tu,* do you, Marc? It's true that you don't know me. But I know you very well. You have the (mis)fortune to be *Le Tigre*'s first Google portrait. A very simple column: take an anonymous person and describe his life using all the traces that he left voluntarily or involuntarily on the Internet.[50]

Meltz wanted to warn people that they expose themselves to danger when they reveal intimate information on social media sites. Popular sites like Flickr and Facebook belong to private companies: users have almost no control over what those sites do with their information.

This kind of violent breach of ordinary people's privacy to make a point recalls John Lennon and Yoko Ono's film *Rape*. After their film premiered on Austrian TV in March 1969, Lennon offered this interpretation: "We are showing how all of us are exposed and under pressure in our contemporary world. This isn't just about the Beatles. What is happening to this girl on the screen is happening in Biafra, Vietnam, everywhere." Twenty years later, Ono gave it a more personal twist: "A lot of my works have been a projection of my future fate. It frightens me. It simply frightens me. I don't want to see *Rape* now. I haven't seen the *Rape* film in a long time, but just thinking about the concept of it frightens me because now I'm in that position, the position of the woman in the film."[51]

Stalking My Shadow

Hasan Elahi practices self-surveillance, putting his information online for any potential controller to watch. His FBI agent may or may not take him up on the offer. In contrast, self-initiated surveillance reappropriates the other's gaze. One of the earliest instances was Sophie Calle's *The Shadow* (1981) (discussed in chapter 4). Calle led her unwitting private-detective collaborator through Paris to all her favorite haunts. Then, after receiving the detective's report on her movements, she exhibited it and her own account side by side, along with candid photographs of the detective taken by a third person. This pursuit was carried out in 1981 before the advent of sophisticated means of digital tracing used today. The same protocol took on new resonance twenty years later when Calle's gallery owner hired a private detective to follow her once again.

In Britain, Manu Luksch and Jill Magid have renewed the genre. Both took advantage of European Union directives that give ordinary citizens access to personal data held in computer databases to make artworks using surveillance footage, with very different results.

Manu Luksch's *Faceless* (2002–2007) is a fifty-minute "science fiction fairytale" that is made entirely from video footage recovered under the United Kingdom's Data Protection Act, which allows any individual filmed by a CCTV recording system in a public place to obtain a copy of the footage (figure 9.6). Its scenario was inspired by the legal obligation for the faces to be erased to protect the privacy of third parties.

Luksch's film shows a society much like our own that has lost its memory: "an eerily familiar city, where the reformed RealTime calendar has dispensed with the past and the future, freeing citizens from guilt and regret, anxiety and fear. Without memory

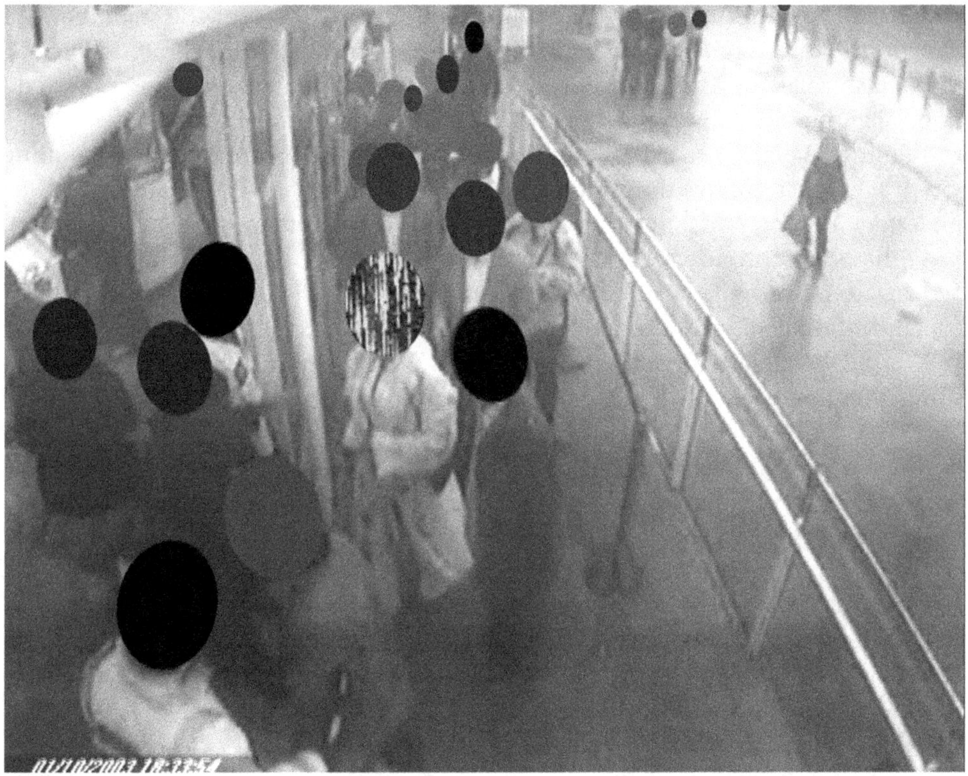

Figure 9.6
Manu Luksch, *Faceless,* 2002–2007. Video on DVD, 50 minutes. Video footage was recovered under the United Kingdom's Data Protection Act and complied with a legal obligation for faces to be erased to protect the privacy of third parties.

or anticipation, faces have become vestigial—the population is literally faceless. Unimaginable happiness abounds—until a woman recovers her face." The time-travel theme and emphatic voiceover text recall Chris Marker's 1962 classic *La jetée*. Luksch's film inveighs against the tyranny of time management, which regiments our lives and hampers our freedom to wander, daydream, or just waste time. "RealTime orients the life of every citizen. Eating, resting, going to work, getting married—every act is tied to RealTime. And every act leaves a trace of data—a footprint in the snow of noise."[52]

She began using closed-circuit television as a medium after the Data Protection Act was extended in 1998 to include these recordings. *Faceless* was produced under the rules of her "Manifesto for CCTV Filmmakers," which forbids using any other camera: "Why bring in additional cameras, when much private and public urban space is already covered from numerous angles?"[53] Because CCTV systems do not record sound, another rule requires the filmmaker "to establish a set of rules for the soundtrack (if any) of the movie—for example, prohibiting field recordings."[54] This procedure recalls the Danish collective Dogme 95, which aimed to purify filmmaking by refusing additional lighting and postproduction and special effects. For Luksch, this was time-consuming. She notes that hers "was a rather tedious production method, requiring lots of stamina to survive the multiple paper wars and not that 'cheap' after all."[55] She undertook it to make a point: viewers should make use of their rights.

With its synchronized choreography, low-tech visual imagery, and transitions evoking technical glitches in surveillance footage, Luksch's film oscillates between experimental cinema and music video. It often has the look and feel of 1960s structural cinema by calling attention to the broadcast's physical substance (visual noise and conflicting time code stamps).

Controller and Guardian Angel

London may have the world's largest population of surveillance cameras, but many of them are aging. As Luksch points out, they give such poor image quality that they are unable to serve their purpose—recognizing individual faces. Other cities are catching up. In 2004, with its 242 strategically placed cameras and its sixty-monitor video wall with cutting-edge touch screen technology, Citywatch (Merseyside Police and Liverpool City Council) was the largest video surveillance system in England, employing six full-time operators and a supervisor.

In 2004, Jill Magid spent thirty-one days—"one cycle of CCTV memory"—in Liverpool, where she performed in camera-watched places, dressed in a bright red trench coat. Every day, she wrote a letter to her anonymous observer, replete with details of her clothing, movements, surroundings—and feelings.

Surveillance footage is stored for thirty-one days, and if it is not requested as evidence, it is erased. To gain access to the recordings, Magid submitted thirty-one letters as subject-access request forms, and these forms make up her book *One Cycle of Memory in the City of L* (2004), "an intimate portrait of the relationship between herself, the police and the city."

To recover footage from the camera owners, Manu Luksch had to convince them to comply with the then little-known law. Operators often refused to deliver the data requested, offering up instead a "sorry litany of malfunctioning equipment, erased tapes, lost letters, and sheer evasiveness."[56] In contrast, Magid focused from the outset on infiltrating the institution, persuading the staff at Citywatch to collaborate in making the artwork. She notes that "the presence of so many cameras turned the city into a movie set with 242 cameramen."[57] To stage her videos, she would call the control room, requesting that the person on duty film her in particular places. She says she wanted to "engage the system on an intimate, personal level and for that, access is required."[58]

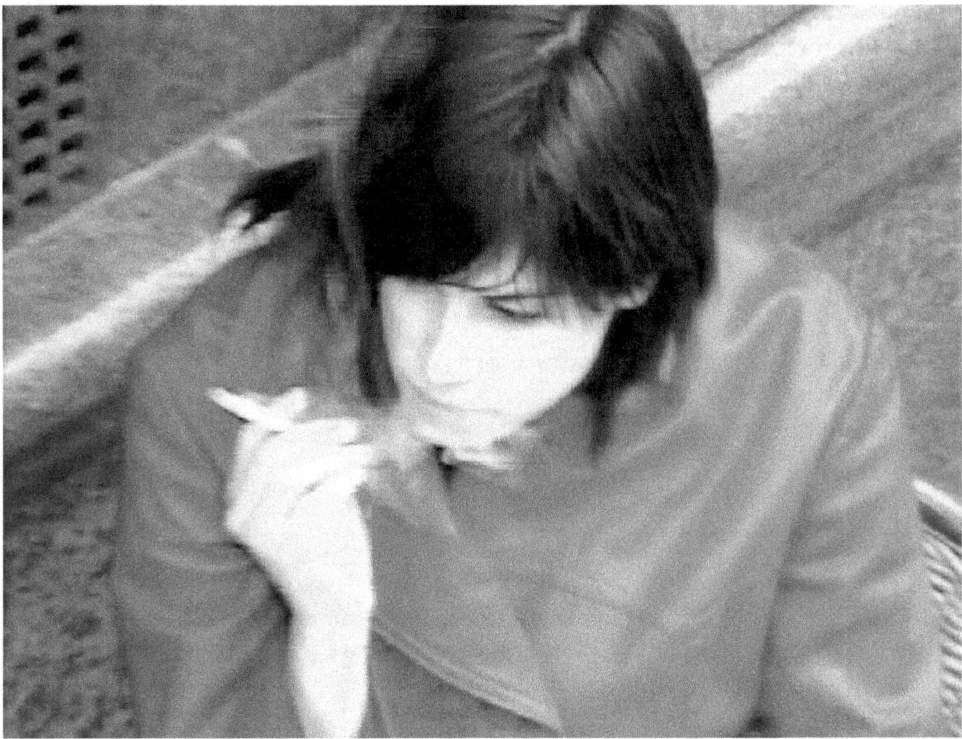

Figure 9.7
Jill Magid, *Trust (Evidence Locker)*, 2004. DVD, edited CCTV footage and audio, 18 minutes. The artist spent thirty-one days in Liverpool performing in a red trench coat. She wrote a daily letter to an anonymous observer and once asked him to guide her through a busy pedestrian area with her eyes closed. Video still © Jill Magid. Courtesy of the artist and Yvon Lambert Paris, New York.

Evidence Locker (2004) is a multimedia installation, including DVDs edited from police recordings, a sound piece, a novella, and a Web site (figure 9.7).[59] The title of the piece comes from the storage lockers in which CCTV footage retained as evidence is kept for seven years. Magid uses technology to automatically control access: as a third-party witness, the Web viewer can read the diary only by having the letters mailed individually to an email account, one per day for thirty-one days. The letters are all addressed to an unnamed observer (who could be any one of the six staff members). In them, she notes her impressions of Liverpool; relates events, outings, and dreams (going out in the snow without pants or shoes); describes people on the street (an Indian man in a big hooded coat who lurches toward her to stop her from being hit by a car); makes coy remarks ("I don't think I always want to tell you where I am."); and asks impertinent questions ("They told me that sometimes you drive around at night in a van and film people. You make a history of everyone you see so that you can remember them later. Do you remember them? Or do you forget them because you film them?").[60]

As the days progress, the tone becomes more familiar and bantering. The letters report dialogs and meetings with her distant observer. She often stops in at the control room and makes appointments to look at her footage in the review suite:

I called you before I left Rodney, at 6:34 p.m. and told you I was going out.
You asked where.
Water Street.
Should I follow you?
You can. I just wanted to let you know I was going out.
How long should I follow you?
Just as far as you want to.
I would follow you to the end of the world.
Motorcycle and all?
Would you like that?
Yes.
Then I will. Don't talk to any strange men. . . .
You found me at 8:49 p.m. on the bottom of Bold. You began to follow and then rang me on my phone. I tried not to smile, but you asked me to, so I did.
I thought you were out for the night.
No. I have work to do
That's all right.
Are you going to walk me home?
I will get you there safely.[61]

Although the observer has power over the woman he watches, he is not completely in control: the cameras are not allowed to film "spaces of privacy." This allows sessions of hide and seek, with Magid moving in and out of his view. As the game develops, it becomes clear that more often than not, the woman calls the shots. We are a long way from *Rape*.

Magid is often very directive, telling her observer: "I still need to show you Godard's *Le Mépris* since you have not seen it. I have selected parts of the film for you. Then you will know how to follow me like the camera follows her."[62] One day, she asks him to guide her through a busy pedestrian area with her eyes closed, creating an exercise in dependence, collaboration and trust. The video *Trust* (2004) shows Magid advancing hesitantly, veering slightly left and right as directed. At one point, still following instructions, she moves three steps to the side and then backs up to sit on a bench in a remotely controlled maneuver that is not unlike parking a car. The soundtrack consists of the controller's side of their phone conversation. In addition to his detailed instructions, he describes the reactions of passers-by, even explaining his own moves as he zooms in and changes cameras, knowing that his subject would be viewing the footage later. Several times he tells "Jill" how she looks to him, noting "that's a good shot" or "you look quite peaceful."

In the current context, where the rapid expansion of surveillance cameras adds to the climate of insecurity fostered by digital technologies, the word *trust* sounds out of place if not absurd. Acconci's wheedling in *Remote Control* comes to mind here: he controls his victim with her own consent, evoking situations in which hostages become devoted to their captors.[63] Here, since the whole project was undertaken at Magid's behest, that reference is turned on its head.

Extimacy

"Self-surveillance is a way of seeing myself, via technology, in a way I could not otherwise," says Magid. "I use a system or a technology as my mirror. The type of reflection I face is specific to the tool I am using. Who I appear to be in that reflection is unfamiliar. The process of coming to recognize myself as I appear there is what I call my work."[64] This is not true only of video imagery. Esther Polak notes that self-observation is inherent to GPS tracking: "Someone else can observe you and control your movements. You're looking at the display, the representation of yourself in the world."[65]

Michelle Teran sees the images made by her suitcase as informational *doppelgängers*, which reveal aspects of the *Unheimliche*. Invoking Schelling's definition, Freud wrote: "everything is *unheimlich* that ought to have remained secret and hidden but has come to light."[66] The theme of the double also carries a certain ambivalence (one's shadow can also be the shadow of death).

Jill Magid's remark evokes what Serge Tisseron calls "the desire for extimacy," the wish to expose a part of our intimacy so as to gain recognition by others. It is a way of discovering ourselves through the gaze of our peers, and we are careful to choose whose gaze we want to engage.[67] In *Evidence Locker*, Magid poses the question of reciprocity. Whereas Sophie Calle remains aloof—her "shadow" remains a shadow; she does not ask him to comment on her account—Magid allows her observer to move her.[68] It is significant that the video *Trust* adopts his point of view, yet we hear only his side of the conversation: we see what he saw and hear what she heard. We could take this to reflect male dominance (like children, women are to be seen and not heard), but here, it is tempered by the inverse and equally one-sided point of view given in the letters. There, we hear only the woman's voice.

The element of mutual trust is important. The controller respects the artist, and he willingly participates in her project. Magid herself has nothing of the anti-surveillance activist who is locked into a binary script. To begin with, she assumes her interlocutor is capable of appreciating the camera work in a Godard film. In this, both depart from categorical stances, allowing art to take place in the world, not outside it or above it.

Regaining Agency: Shifting Lines of Force

"Lines for Which Millions Have Died"

Globalization has brought down some barriers and erected others. The easier it is for goods to circulate, the harder it is for people to do so. Borders tell stories of occupation and exile. "Frontiers are lines," wrote Georges Perec: "Millions of people have died because of these lines. Thousands have died because they weren't able to cross them: survival would have meant crossing a simple river, a small hill, a calm forest: on the other side was Switzerland, the neutral country, the free zone."[69]

Whatever their shape or size, fences tend to bring to the fore the boundaries that separate them from us, either by keeping them in (behind bars) or out (of the fortress under siege). For their project *The Measured Wall* (1984), Philipp J. Bösel and Burkhard Maus photographed every inch of the Berlin wall, a barrier that cut into the flesh of the city, making wounds that even now have not all healed. After the wall was destroyed in 1989, people began dreaming of a world without borders, but although some fences came tumbling down, many others were being erected. Now they separate the affluent from their less well-off neighbors, contain rebellion, restrain both felons and dissidents in high-security prisons, and fragment occupied territories.

In 1997, the InSite Biennial took place in the border region between Tijuana, Mexico, and San Diego, California. Invited to participate, Francis Alÿs used his artist's fee to travel from Tijuana to San Diego without crossing the U.S.-Mexican border. He traveled south through Latin America to Chile, crossing over to Australia, then moving north up the Pacific Rim area, through Hong Kong, back over to Alaska and then heading south to Vancouver and Los Angeles, before reaching San Diego five weeks later. This performance, presented in postcard form, showed an inverted mirror image that contrasted the permeability of borders for contemporary globe-trotting artists with the impermeability of the barrier erected to prevent prospective immigrants from entering the United States.

In 2000, Heath Bunting often with Kayle Brandon crossed the borders between countries in Europe on foot, without passports or visas, and created *BorderXing Guide* (2000–2001) (figure 9.8). They arrived over land, traversing rivers, mountains, and tunnels. It was the first in a series of *BorderXing* projects, during which the duo gathered data concerning clandestine border crossing. The result of this research, the *BorderXing Guide,* demonstrates how borders work. The attractive splash page entices Web travelers to enter, but like prospective immigrants, we soon discover that our credentials do not give us access. The site is visible only from certain, static Internet Protocol addresses that are deemed worthy of trust. Rather than overcoming physical barriers, as many people had hoped, here the Internet works to enforce them.[70]

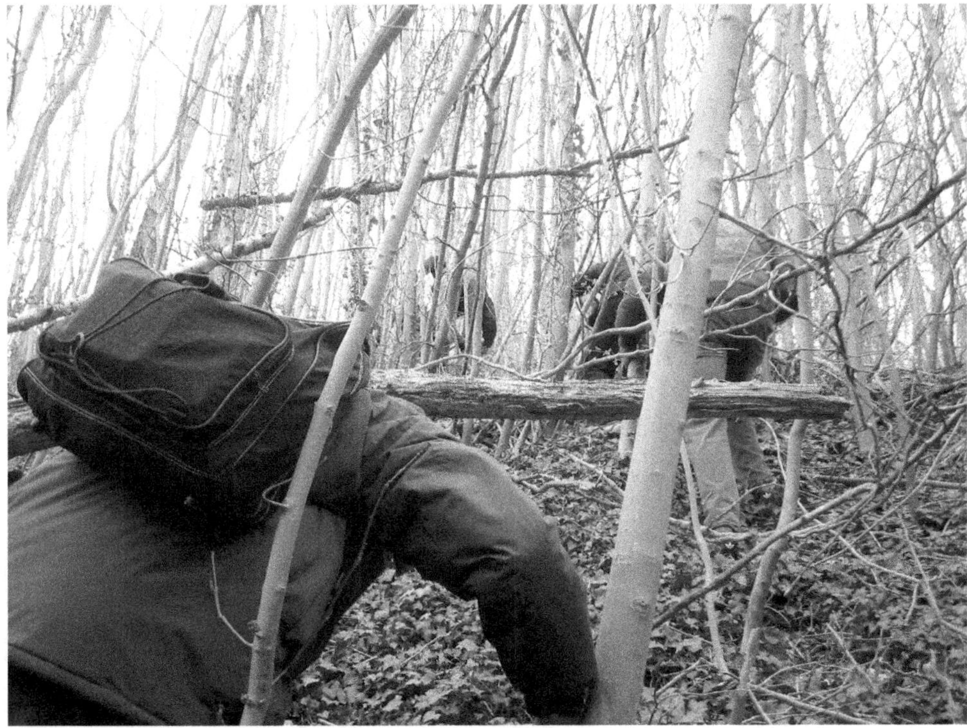

Figure 9.8
Heath Bunting, *BorderXing*, 2000–2008. Multimedia project. Heath Bunting crossed twenty-four borders between countries in Europe on foot, without passport or visa, to gather data on clandestine border crossing. Here, a *BorderXing* workshop between Belgium and the Netherlands.

Translation for Borders

Antoni Muntadas began the project *On Translation* in 1995: "the world we live in is a totally translated world, everything is always filtered by some social, political, cultural and economic factor by the media, of course, by context and by history."[71] For Jacques Rancière, we are all translators because we translate what is given to us in terms of our own experience. We learn by translating one type of knowledge into another, building incrementally on what we already know.[72]

Fear, too, can be learned. Muntadas's recent work focuses on how fear develops. *On Translation: Fear/Miedo* (2003–2005) took place on either side of the border between the United States and Mexico. He interviewed inhabitants of Tijuana and San Diego and broadcast those conversations on television. He redesigned covers for books containing the words *terrorism* or *fear* in their titles, converting them into stark red letters on a black background and positioning them on a grid. Another piece showed suburban houses protected by fences and security alarm systems. He plastered gallery walls with media headlines in black type in which keywords like *fear* and *panic* were written in red: "Fear of foreigners roils Iowa," "Survey fuels recession fears," "Executives Confront Computer Fears," "Muslim leaders fear backlash," "Job cuts spark fear in Hollywood."

In 2006, after the deaths of prospective immigrants in Ceuta and Melitta brought fortress Europe to the attention of the media, Muntadas focused on the border between Spain and Morocco. Like the Rio Grande, the Straits of Gibraltar are viewed as a gate to the prosperous north. Both borders see traffic in drugs and human beings. One separates two countries, and the other separates two continents with different religious cultures. *On Translation: Miedo/Jauf* (2007–2010) is "a choral interpretation" based on interviews that Muntadas conducted on both sides of the Mediterranean. He sees it as "an attempt to perceive and understand hope in a continent 'forgotten' by the Western world."[73] Both works deal with the complex relationship of attraction and repulsion that links the global south and north. For affluent northerners, the south is a tourist destination, both exotic and threatening, and the north continues to attract candidates who seek a better life despite the dangers awaiting them.

Hundreds of immigrants die each year crossing the border between Mexico and the United States. Some lose their way in the desert and collapse from thirst and heat exhaustion. An artist collective known as the Electronic Disturbance Theater / b.a.n.g. Lab[74] has developed *Transborder Immigrant Tool* (2007–2011), a cell phone application designed to help immigrants find resources and reduce the number of these deaths (figure 9.9). Ricardo Dominguez calls it a "mobile Statue of Liberty" as it "repurposes inexpensive used mobile phones that have GPS antennae . . . to guide 'the tired, the poor,' the dehydrated—citizens of the world—to water safety sites."[75] The project originated in Brett Stalbaum's *Virtual Hiker* (2004), an algorithm that produces computationally derived paths from data in a way that allows them to be followed through the actual world.[76] The navigation system looks like a compass: visual symbols and vibrations signal the location of water stations that were set up by humanitarian organizations and snippets of poetry.

The artists developed the project in stages, mapping the border area, writing code, and walking south into Mexico and then back north into the United States. On June 4, 2011, as part of *Political Equator 3*, artist Marlène Ramírez-Cancio officially walked the *Transborder Immigrant Tool* from San Diego into Tijuana.

The project received media attention when the artists were accused of encouraging illegal immigration, and Dominguez, an associate professor at the University of California at San Diego, was investigated for misuse of research funds. His colleagues wrote in their letter of support: "*Transborder Immigrant Tool,* was developed at CALIT2 as an 'affective' tool, designed to encourage discussion and dialog over the mounting number of deaths suffered by undocumented workers crossing into the US. . . . While

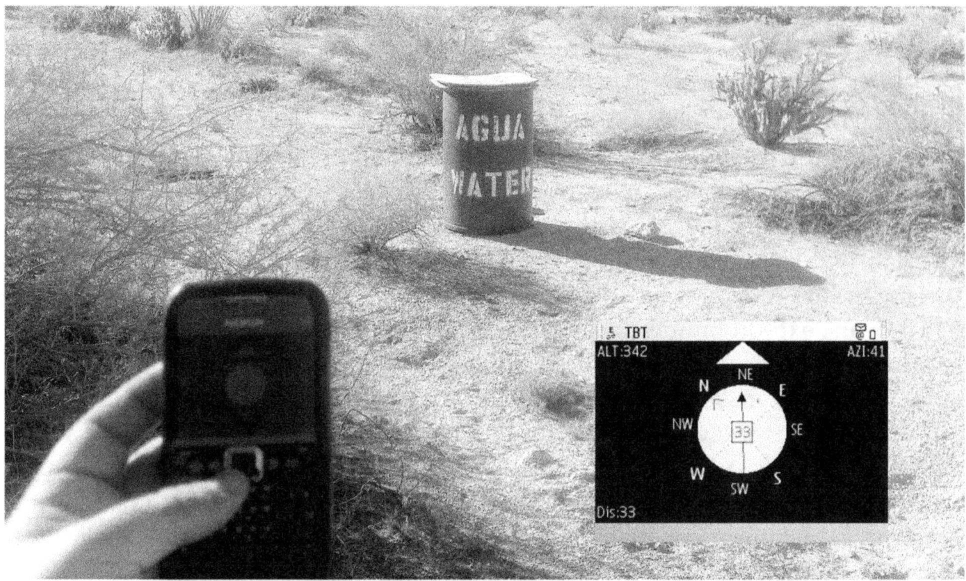

Figure 9.9
Electronic Disturbance Theater / b.a.n.g. Lab, *Transborder Immigrant Tool*, 2007–2011. Cell phone application. This cell phone application helps immigrants when they cross the border between Mexico and the United States. This image shows a screenshot directing users to a water cache in the Anza Borrego Desert. Photograph: Brett Stalbaum.

the *Tool* employs a form of 'Global Positioning System' software, it might be more accurately described as an 'ideological' positioning system, revealing points of tension and contradiction in the current debate over undocumented labor in this country. How do we value human life? Is it a universal good, or does our responsibility for the survival of others depend on their legal status or nationality?"[77] Africans also die in the desert when traveling northward toward Europe: a typical news story from 2010 notes that "Twelve African nationals trying to illegally enter Europe have died from thirst and hunger in the Algerian desert."[78]

Florian Schneider compares the educator to a coyote who helps undocumented immigrants to cross the border from one nation state to another: "Etymologically, in Greek and Latin *pedagogue* or *educator* means 'drawing out' or 'pulling out' and refers to an ancient Greek practice: a family slave called 'pedagogue' used to walk the child from the private house to a place of learning. Rather than the teacher, who was supposed to have and transmit knowledge, the pedagogue was the person who accompanied the student to the place where the teacher imparted it."[79] The artists in this chapter all have something of the coyote.

Stalkers and Coyotes

The group Stalker has been organizing walks since 1995, when most of its members were architecture students. They spent four days walking around the periphery of Rome, taking photographs and keeping a diary. This, to them, was what architects should be doing. Their name was inspired by the Andrei Tarkovsky film, *Stalker* (1979), in which the title character guides two clients to a wilderness site known as The Zone: although potentially dangerous, it is capable of fulfilling a person's innermost desires. The Italian group designated itself as a collective guide (stalker) taking people across the border into forbidden areas.

Their first expedition was documented in an artists' book.[80] There, they depict the landscape they encountered in the outskirts of Rome—fields, power plants, chain fences, squatters' makeshift camps, a highway under construction, an accumulation of wooden boards and worn tires, and a tufa plateau straight out of Monument Valley. Since then, Stalker has taken people on walks through "urban voids," crossing Rennes, Milan, Miami, and Berlin to propose "a reverse reading" of the architectural network. Rather than building urban blocks, they document the marginal, nonfunctional zones that separate them.[81]

The Appia–Egnatia is an ancient Roman road that was built to connect Rome and Constantinople. In the last century, it has been taken by millions of refugees moving from their homelands toward western Europe. To preserve the heritage of these scattered communities, Stalker/ON (Osservatorio Nomad) created *Egnatia: A Path of Displaced Memories* (2002–2005). In Istanbul, Athens, Rome, and Paris, starting points or final destinations of journeys along the Egnatia, the group established open spaces called "agencies" in collaboration with groups like the Atelier d'Architecture Autogéré[82] in Paris, to gather stories and foster intercultural exchange. In Paris, this led to the research project *Mobile Geographies*, which studied immigrant communities' creative ways of using space in the La Chapelle area where 35 percent of the population is foreign-born.

I participated in a *Mobile Geographies* workshop at ECObox in February 2005 that was organized by Constantin Petcou and Doina Petrescu (AAA) and Béatrice Rettig (Borderphonics) with Lorenzo Romito and Peter Lang from Stalker/ON (figure 9.10).[83] AAA employs "urban tactics" to encourage city dwellers to take charge of unused spaces. In 2002, the group obtained temporary use of two lots owned by the Réseau Ferré de France. With students from the University of Sheffield, neighborhood residents, and pupils from a local school, they built a prototype garden in the courtyard of the Halle Pajol using recycled pallets, gravel, and plastic bottles. ECObox was born. To adapt the garden to a completely mineral field, a flexible, modular system was designed that allowed participants to create surface plots of different sizes that were defined by rows of stacked pallets. Each family built its own plot and the path leading to it.[84] Other residents participated in setting up a mobile urban kitchen[85] and a temporary radio/media broadcasting unit in the indoor studio space.

To preserve urban biodiversity, the group hosted microevents, including concerts, debates, film showings, art and technology workshops, crafts studios, a banquet, and a GPS *Movies* session with Liliane Terrier and Daniel Sciboz. While I was there, Béatrice Rettig, Jean-Baptiste Bayle, and a group of residents used secondhand turntables and electronic equipment to remix music in the studio.

The locale was a former warehouse behind the Gare du Nord. In true Stalker tradition, we began with a walk to explore the interstices of La Chapelle, a neighborhood that was far more porous than the ones I later visited on Paris's left bank.[86] These patches of resistance to urbanization represent what sociologists call "the reserve of 'availability' of a city": "La Chapelle is an area that, because of its history and its geographical position—an 'urban island' isolated from the great railway influences Gare du Nord and Gare de l'Est—still retains a significant number of industrial wastelands and vacant lots, awaiting future real estate transactions."[87]

Planting the Map: "Trees Make Time Tangible"

Natalie Jeremijenko began using new technologies in the hope of effecting social transformation, a "delusion" that she says still "drives" her now. Quoting Hippocrates—"the greater part of the soul lays outside the body, treatment of the inner requires treatment of the outer"—she contends that the notion of health needs redefining: for her, when "it's external, it's shared, we can do something about it."[88] To this end, she founded the Environmental Health Clinic at New York University, where "impatients" are given prescriptions for changes they can make to improve the environment. The clinic prescribes "medicines" such as *RX Upshoes* (springs affixed to high heels to make them into "a high-powered pedestrian vehicle that lifts you higher and gets you where you're going faster"), "fallout shelters for the climate crisis" (an urban agriculture rooftop facility that takes carbon dioxide from the building and supplies oxygen instead), and *NoPark* (planted in "no parking" spaces to intercept pollutants before they enter the harbor, these engineered micro landscapes "prevent storm water runoff, use foliage to stabilize the soil, and . . . provide a durable low maintenance surface cover") (figure 9.11).

Other projects use mapping techniques to revisit the nature/nurture debate. For Natalie Jeremijenko's landmark *OneTrees* (1998–present), twenty genetically identical trees were planted in different San Francisco Bay Area neighborhoods to form a networked map that was literally rooted in the territory (figure 9.12). In 1998, she had the Burchell Nursery in Modesto, California, micropropagate in culture a thousand clones of a fruitless walnut tree: "The idea for doing it came out of the question we all ask: why do they look like that?," she explains, "asked at a time when the human

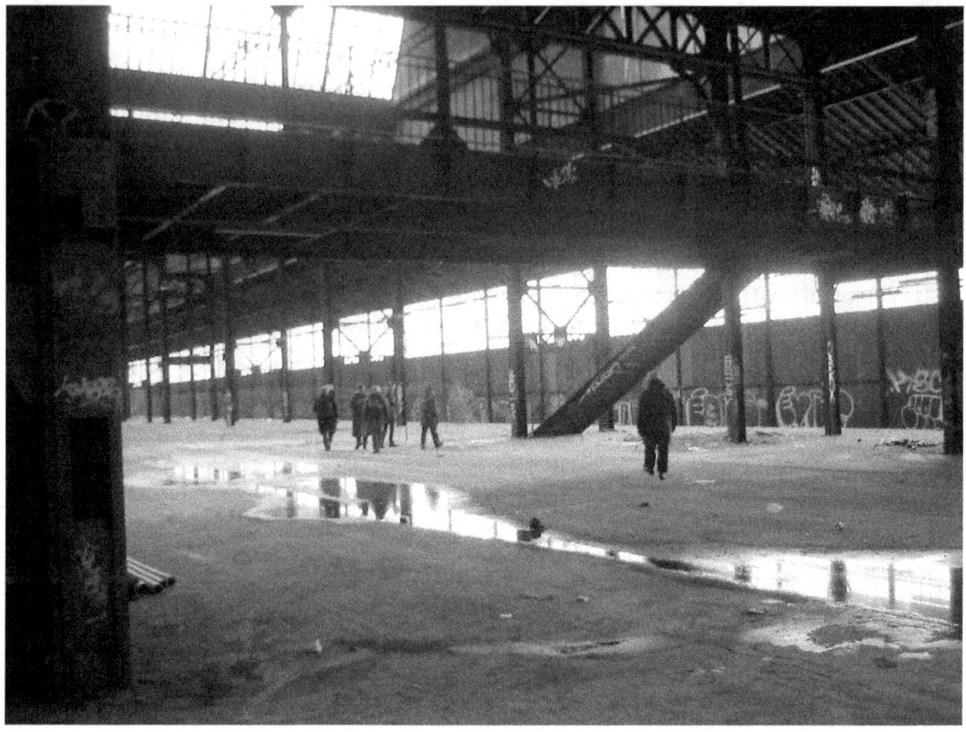

(a)

Figure 9.10
Atelier d'Architecture Autogérée Stalker/ON and Borderphonics, *Mobile Geographies*, 2005. *a:* Walk in the La Chapelle neighborhood of Paris. Participants explore an abandoned warehouse.

genome was being announced—and with it the implication, and the actual assertion, that genes are the code of life"[89]:

> Trees have always posed this question . . . and when you see them all leaning in synchronized swimming sameness along a road you suddenly recognize the effects of the shadows of the buildings and the thousands of independent little decisions that each sprouting bud has made: will I go this way or that? and as each has decided to go with the sunnier option . . . you see huge trees aggregating these decisions into a massive leaning structure poised like a ballerina in an impossible arabesque. Trees make time tangible.[90]

The trees themselves are of the paradox variety, a hybrid of the native California walnut tree crossed with the English walnut. Faster-growing and more vigorous than its parents, the paradox is an ideal urban tree since it produces no fruit to drop on people's heads or pollen to make them sneeze.[91]

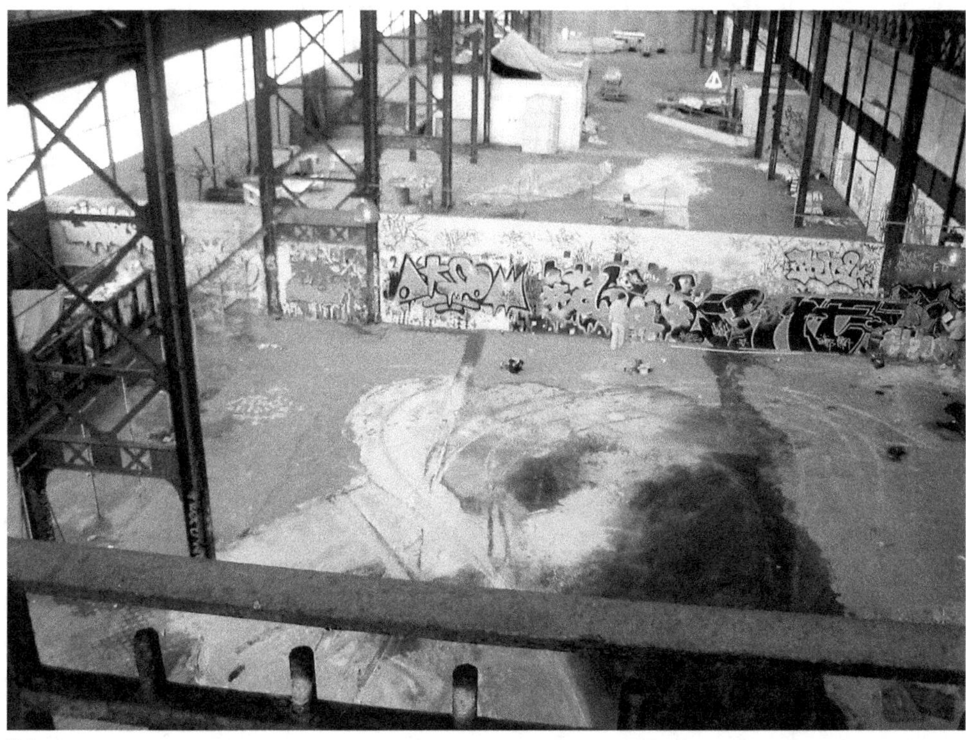

(b)

Figure 9.10 (continued)
b: Traces of squatters' presence in the city's interstices. Photographs: Karen O'Rourke.

When the plantlets were first exhibited together at Yerba Buena Center for the Arts in San Francisco, each in a sterile, individually sealed cup, they were already showing differences in branching patterns, numbers of leaves, and internodal lengths. Although they have the same genetic material, they are individually engaged in complex forms of interaction with their environment. Like continually evolving open-source code, genetic information contains a large measure of indeterminacy. Had the tree been cloned by taking a cutting of mature tissue, the variation in the plantlets would have been less.

After the seedlings had time to develop, Jeremijenko and a group of volunteer tree stewards planted twenty pairs in various places around the Bay Area so that residents of these areas could witness the processes. As living databases, the trees reveal environmental change over decades and centuries, which helps chart slow environmental changes.

The pairs of trees were experimentally injected into different biotopes. Because they have the same genes, they "render the social and environmental differences to which

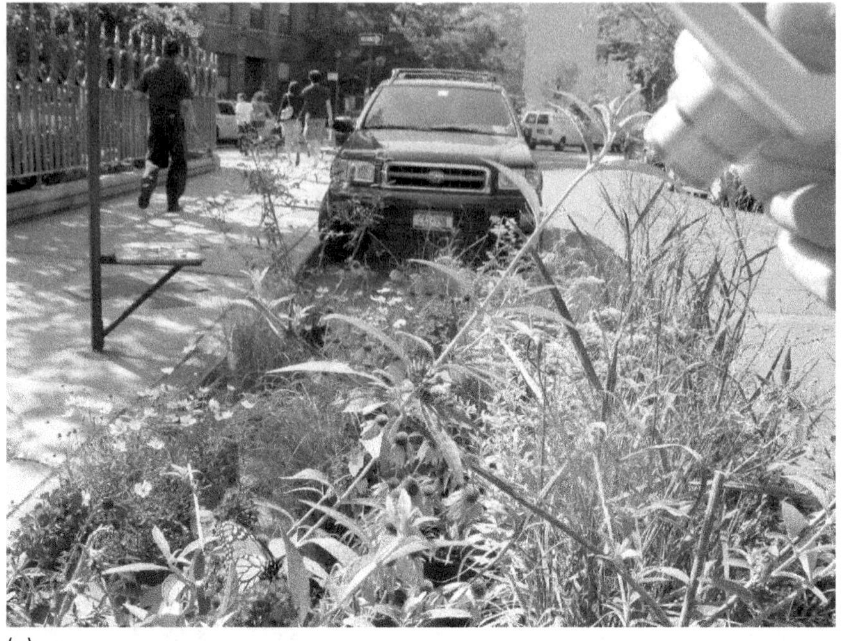

(a)

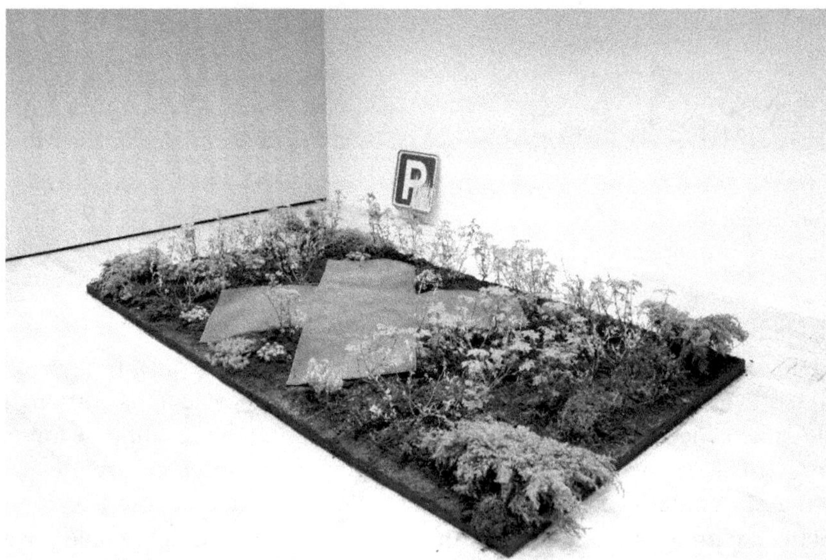

(b)

Figure 9.11

Natalie Jeremijenko and the Environment Health Clinic, *NoPark*, 2008 ongoing. *a:* Engineered microlandscapes planted in "no parking" spaces intercept urban pollutants before they enter the harbor. *b:* Engineered microlandscapes exhibited in Iceland at Gallery 100°/Orkuveitan showing the subarctic ecology involved for the first *NoPark* subsequently installed at the Reykjavík pond. With thanks to Producer/Curator: Lanie Yamamoto and the Reykjavík Department of Transportation.

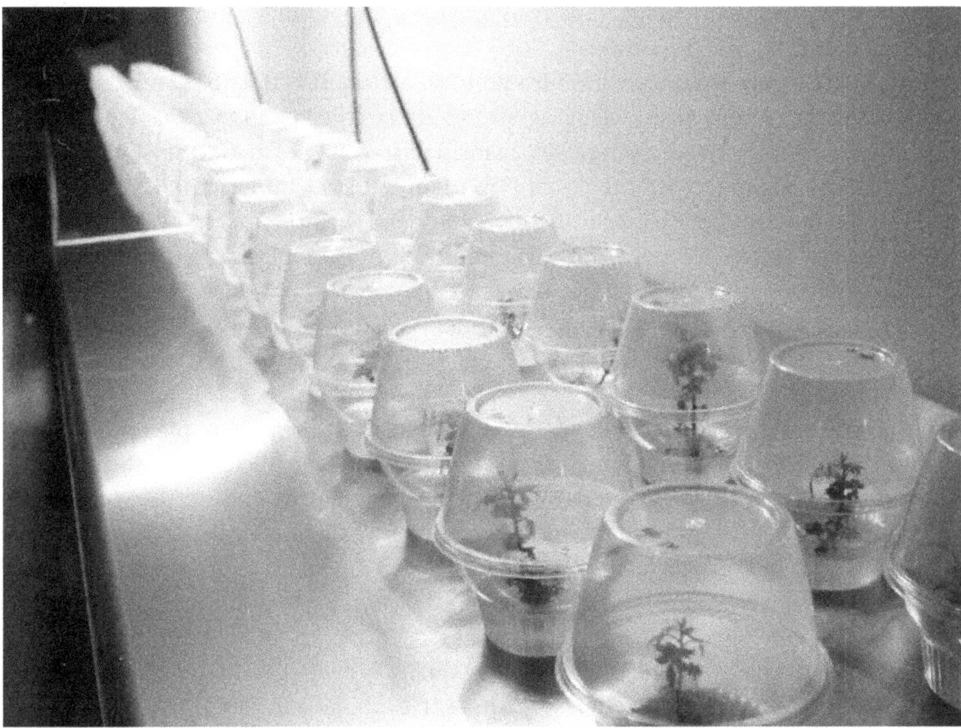

Figure 9.12
Natalie Jeremijenko, *OneTrees*, 1998–ongoing. Twenty genetically identical trees were planted in various San Francisco Bay Area neighborhoods to form a networked map that was rooted in the territory. One thousand plantlets were exhibited at Yerba Buena Center for the Arts in sterile, individually sealed cups.

they are exposed."[92] Soil conditions, for instance, are essential to plant life. In areas where the soil is a mixture of sand and bay sludge, trees die. Economic conditions count, too. The neighborhoods with abundant and healthy plant life are often wealthy, whereas economically depressed areas tend to accumulate industrial waste and depleted soil.[93] Planting the saplings in pairs allows people to observe individual differences. Even in the same environment, trees, like siblings, may develop differently.

Works like *OneTrees* are public experiments that pose the kind of questions that scientists, experts, and political policy makers ask and give nonspecialists the chance to see the evidence for themselves. How will the trees adapt to their environment over time? How will they modify it? Will they provide shade or crowd out smaller plants? Will they become beloved landmarks like the thousand-year-old olive trees in southern France, around which highways are built? When volunteers participate in the experiment by planting a tree or taking care of one, they see how the experiment was set up, participate in its organization, view the results, and draw their own conclusions.

This offers a powerful motivation for political action. It is not about artists empowering others but about acknowledging all people as equals and as capable of poking around and finding out for themselves. Instead of standing by helplessly while experts disagree, they acquire experience, enabling them to better understand issues and difficulties that are inherent to scientific research.[94] For this to happen, bystanders must participate in the experiment, however modestly. Just looking at the trees is not enough: the back story informs the experiment. To be meaningful, observation needs to take place over a significant period of time.

Road Mapping

Each of Natalie Jeremijenko's projects "places evidence in the public sphere that would otherwise only be available to particular experts, as a strategy to change the structure of participation."[95] This can be done in other ways. For example, the Milan-based architecture collective Multiplicity has mapped border devices in Palestine and exhibited the results in Europe.

Time has displaced place in our perception of distance. We no longer think in terms of miles or kilometers but hours and minutes. "Time-space compression" designates "processes that so revolutionize the objective qualities of space and time," writes David Harvey, "that we are forced to alter, sometimes in quite radical ways, how we represent the world to ourselves." These processes seem to accelerate the experience of time and reduce the significance of distance: "a strong case can be made that the history of capitalism has been characterized by speed-up in the pace of life, while so overcoming barriers that the world sometimes seems to collapse in upon us."[96]

Israeli regulations seem to have spared Palestinians this acceleration. The 1993 Oslo Accords created the Palestinian Authority and divided West Bank territories into three zones: zone A is under Palestinian military and administrative control, zone B under Israeli military control and Palestinian administrative control, and zone C under Israeli military and administrative control. To travel from one settlement to another in zone C, Israelis can use the bypass roads that link the colonies while avoiding Palestinian villages. Palestinians traveling from one part of zone A to another part of zone A must go through the B or C zones, where direct roads have been closed to traffic and checkpoints bar access to anyone without a special pass issued by the Israeli government. For a Palestinian, the hundred-kilometer trip from Jenin to Hebron on the West Bank can take up to fourteen hours.

The Israeli newspaper *Ha'aretz* published a map of the checkpoints in February 2002: "No fewer than twenty-four permanent checkpoints block the way from Jenin to Hebron, and that doesn't count the 'breathing sieges,' 'surprise' checkpoints, and various trenches dug across the roads to prevent cars from traveling."[97] Before the

Intifada, checkpoints were located mainly along the green line between Israel and the occupied territories to prevent terrorists from entering the country. Now they are erected to defend settlers who live outside of Israel. The map shows that the border zigzags deep into the territories, splitting them into archipelagos of islands and preventing Palestinians from communicating with each other. The author notes that, even from the viewpoint of Israeli officials, these checkpoints are counterproductive. As symbols of Israeli occupation, they fuel Palestinian resentment.

In 2003, Multiplicity set out to measure with their European Union passports "the density of border devices in the area surrounding Jerusalem." On January 13, they traveled with an Israeli citizen between the colonies of Kiriat Arba and Kudmin on Highway 60, and the next day, they accompanied a person holding a Palestinian passport from Hebron to Nablus. The "extraordinary entanglement of zones, borders, and control points" they discovered was shown in the installation *Solid Sea 03: The Road Map*: "The two routes both start and end in the same latitude; at some points they overlap. Their traveling times, however, are profoundly different. It took the Israeli traveler around one hour to move between the two latitudes, while it took the Palestinian five and half hours."[98]

The title also could be read as an ironic allusion to the Bush-era peace plan. Multiplicity's *Road Map* is didactic. Shown in adjacent rooms in a layout conceived as a metaphor for the left and right brain hemispheres,[99] it consisted of video footage and maps showing the two taxi routes with place and time information for each leg of the journey. On the yellow Israeli path, all the checkpoints bypassed are noted with corresponding time stamps, while the green, Palestinian itinerary shows all the places where the road was closed and where passengers had to wait in line at a checkpoint, leave their taxi, and cross the border on foot. To be effective, this work depends on the authority of the images and annotated maps coupled with the conventions of time stamping.

In another mapping project, Till Roeskens's *Videomappings: Aida, Palestine* (2008), residents of a Palestinian camp east of Jerusalem draw maps on paper as they recount their ordinary itineraries. We see only the lines that emerge on the map. Roeskens notes that he was inspired by Henri-Georges Clouzot's 1956 Le Mystère Picasso (The Mystery of Picasso), in which the artist at work was filmed through a glass pane. The maps recall the itineraries that pedestrians drew for Stanley Brouwn, except that here they are accompanied by stories that situate them, and these are subtitled in several languages. Like the lines, the voices sometimes waver. A woman recounting the beginnings of the camp in 1950 draws tents while naming family members who died as martyrs. Another shows the labyrinthine route that she must follow to take her daughter to the hospital for regular checkups. The stories culminate with that of a woman who saw the Israeli separation wall built in one day, surrounding her house and isolating it from the rest of the camp to reassure tourists who visit Rachel's tomb nearby.

As Paul Virilio notes, "Territory and movement are linked. For instance, territory is controlled by the movements of horsemen, of tanks, of planes, and so on." Virilio's research on "the logic and impact of speed, necessarily implies the study of the organization of territory. Whoever controls the territory possesses it. This ownership is not primarily about laws and contracts but first and foremost a matter of movement and circulation."[100]

Raja Shehadeh's book *Palestinian Walks* recounts six excursions in the countryside surrounding his hometown of Ramallah between 1978 and 2006. A *sarha* resembles a situationist *dérive*: "A man going on a sarha wanders aimlessly, not restricted by time and place, going where his spirit takes him to nourish his soul and rejuvenate himself. . . . Going on a sarha implies letting go. It is a drug-free high, Palestinian-style."[101] Here lies the paradox at the heart of his book. What Palestinian today can wander in these hills where, in defiance of international law, Israelis continue to build settlements, segregated highways, checkpoints, and concrete walls?

Shehadeh describes his itineraries through the "dry and stony" hills interwoven with the concerns of his walking companions and their back stories. The walks were chosen for their historical resonance. They show how, over a period spanning four decades, the West Bank landscape in which he grew up has been disfigured by the poured concrete of settlements and roads dug deep into the hills. From a few small enclaves, the settlers are rapidly deploying throughout what was slated to become the Palestinian state. Today, even Ramallah is under siege, with "the yellow lights of these illegal outposts creating an illuminated noose around the city."[102]

The subtitle of Shehadeh's book is *Forays into a Vanishing Landscape*. Each walk/chapter shows a different stage in his life and in the occupation of Palestine. The different layers coexist in a bucolic setting where hikers can pick up unexploded missiles or come under fire by Palestinian police who use the slope as a practice range. The same valley evokes events from different times. Six years after being shot at, he and a Palestinian Dutch friend were hiking back from examining dinosaur footprints when they heard dogs barking and they suddenly were surrounded by a group of armed men in military fatigues. Shehadeh was suspected of kidnapping a foreigner.

Elsewhere, overcome by vertigo, he is helped up a steep cliff by a rifle-toting Israeli soldier. In the last walk, a young Israeli settler preparing a *nergila* encountered near a stream hesitates between using his rifle and offering the stranger a smoke. "I came to realize that the biography of these hills was in many ways my own, the victories and failures of the struggle to save this land also mine," says Shehadeh. "I wanted to preserve in words what was quickly being destroyed."[103]

Raja Shehadeh sees art as a means of liberation. For many years, as a lawyer and founder of the human rights organization Al-Haq, he fought to expose the myth-making and legal distortions used by Israeli administrators to take over land that belonged to his Palestinian clients. Now he writes. His first memoir was therapeutic, after the murder of his father in 1985 went unpunished. The Oslo accords in 1993 "buried my truth," he wrote, denying the many legal battles that had been waged to maintain Palestinian land rights. Only the military struggle was acknowledged "for bringing us to this 'peace.'"[104]

Shehadeh, who studied law in Great Britain, wrote his book in English, quoting Thackeray, Mark Twain, and Robinson Jeffers. With his first memoir, *Strangers in the House*, he discovered that writing was also "an exercise of power, capable of moving people, changing perception and mobilizing forces in new directions."[105]

Knowing one's environment by walking it could become the foundation for a common culture. Shehadeh notes that Palestinian villagers do not feel that they have time for recreational walking, but walking is a form of conviviality. He and his companions discuss politics and exchange stories as they scramble up hills and amble through valleys. Like shared meals in Mediterranean cultures, an afternoon spent walking together is a way of connecting with others, taking care both of oneself and each other.

Conclusion

In Jorge Luis Borges's story "The Garden of Forking Paths,"[1] the narrator's great-grandfather Ts'ui Pên "renounced worldly power in order to write a novel . . . and to construct a labyrinth in which all men would become lost." Ts'ui Pên was murdered before he could finish his novel, and what remained of it, "an indeterminate heap of contradictory drafts," made no sense at all: "in the third chapter the hero dies, in the fourth he is alive." The labyrinth was never found. As it turns out, the labyrinth and the book were one and the same, the forking taking place "in time, not in space":

> In all fictional works, each time a man is confronted with several alternatives, he chooses one and eliminates the others; in the fiction of Ts'ui Pên, he chooses—simultaneously—all of them. He creates, in this way, diverse futures, diverse times which themselves also proliferate and fork.

Like Ts'ui Pen's labyrinth, my "map larger than the territory" turned out to be a book. It is an attempt to map some of the mappings I have encountered, to chart the paths that appeared on the way and what happened when one or more artists followed them. Unlike Ts'ui Pên, however, whose labyrinth was a maze with many branching corridors, here I have proposed only one of many possible through-paths for mine.

The Art of Alter-Mapping: Context

For alternative mapping efforts to thrive, they need to build on previous experiences, even though most artists' projects have a limited shelf life. Artists, critics, and historians look back at earlier periods and rescue forgotten predecessors, which can be an effective way to forge a new tradition in which to locate contemporary works. But they can do so only if the predecessors are findable. A book can be a way of preserving a trace of ephemeral works, mapping landmarks against which new art can be measured.

For this to happen, there needs to be a meaningful way of connecting them. Although a lot of linking has been facilitated by the advent of the Internet, it is at best only partial, creating clusters here and there. Researchers in network science[2] have called our attention to the fact that a great portion of the Web remains uncharted by search engines, with many areas isolated from the main nerve centers. Networks tend to self-organize according to power laws in which new nodes link to the most popular, well-connected hubs. If individual nodes are not connected to from "the mainland," they remain islands or at best archipelagos, which spawn isolated, niche communities.

A Map for Listening

Several artists' projects allude to the Australian Aboriginal songlines as a kind of ideal map. Can the system of Dreaming tracks offer a pertinent model for a network of alternative mappings? Paths across the land, through the sky, and even underground mark routes that were followed by each group's totemic ancestor during the Dreamtime. These routes are reactualized in songs, stories, dances, and paintings. Aboriginal culture also offers the model of a dynamic tradition, evolving and adapting to conditions of globalization. Western observers have sometimes misunderstood the concept of the Dreamtime, imagining that the mythical landscape was shaped once and forever at some past time, when in fact it invites new paths and experiences. Each Aboriginal painting renews the basic design, without ever copying it in the same way, "resetting it so it becomes ALIVE," writes Barbara Glowczewski: "Since every painting is a fragment of territory and a story, it can be infinitely connected with others, just as the meetings between mythical heroes are virtually infinite. The paintings are open both on their borders and between the elements that compose them."[3] They have no beginning and no end, and one can always extend the space between two sites to let a new story emerge.

Could this approach scale to a globalized map of maps? Can a bottom-up, pedestrian map emerge that borrows from both the songlines and contemporary meshworks? It does not need to be as uniform as more top-down models. It must only be readable by all while preserving the idiosyncrasies of member projects.

This map will be able to listen to, amplify, and adapt other sounds, images, and texts as a video performance artist (VJ) does. In the preceding pages, I have proposed an interface that is based on short personal, experiential texts and images. This kind of media formatting can be counterbalanced by allowing users to design their own interfaces.

This map will take into account experiences in both physical geographical space, including walks, performances, objects, and environments that are located in the world and in the virtual space of Internet. Can we trace paths between existing nodes and networks, as possible destinations or entry points? Link up the major metamapping projects from these past few years, both local and global?

Jeremy Hight has a similar project. He calls it "modulated mapping": "The map can be active, malleable, open source fed, and even, in a sense, intelligent and able to adapt."[4]

The map actively searches for other maps. Objects can be built and placed on the map, guaranteeing an afterlife for ephemeral projects. Preserved and rebuilt, they can be experienced in new forms that are difficult to imagine at the outset.

Maps and Trajectories

Every day, I discover instances of walking and mapping to place on this map. Mélanie Perrier's performative devices and microactions happen at the intersection of performance, dance, and video, and Yolande Harris's sonic navigations use GPS. Sabrina Biokou-Sellier is knitting GPS signals to track conversations engaged in while walking, while Marie-Isabelle Ribes maps a distributed *doppelganger* for a defunct Chilean village in the Atacama desert. Tisha Mukarji made a thirty-day walk "from Køge in the direction of Berlin, while pushing a piano (yes, a piano; I constructed a trolley to push it)": "It ended up in a series of photographs with the trolley in front of signposts along the way as well as a series of line drawings that are maps without geographical coordinates. *Une carte sans repère.*"[5]

All along the book's trajectory, there were branching byways (artists' footwear, art centered on mobility, borders, intercultural exchange) that would have taken us too far afield from my intent. Without following them up, I could not place them on my map. To pursue the path of this book to its culmination, I promised myself that I could later go back and explore these forkings. Next time, they can be main thoroughfares.

In conclusion, let us turn to Richard Long for the last word. "If you undertake a walk," he says, "you are echoing the whole history of mankind, from the early migrations out of Africa on foot that took people all over the world. Despite the many traditions of walking—the landscape walker, the walking poet, the pilgrim—it is always possible to walk in new ways."[6] The same can be said of mapping.

Notes

Preface

1. A few years ago, Lev Manovich used Borges's image to describe online "indexes and the data they index." Now, he wrote, the map is even greater in size than the territory that it represents. Lev Manovich, *The Language of New Media* (Cambridge: MIT Press, 2001), 225.

2. Warren Weaver, "Rockefeller Report on Science and Complexity" (1958), quoted in Jane Jacobs, *The Death and Life of Great American Cities* (New York: Random House, 1961), 433.

3. Alison Sant, "Redefining the Basemap," *Intelligent Agent* 6, no. 2 (2006), http://www.intelligentagent.com/archive/Vol6_No2_interactive_city_sant.htm.

Introduction

1. Michel de Certeau, *L'invention du quotidien: I. Arts de faire* (Paris: Gallimard, coll. Folio, 1980, 1990), *The Practice of Everyday Life* , trans. Steven Rendall (Berkeley: University of California Press, 1984), 91–92.

2. No matter how limited in area. Chombart de Lauwe's study, *Paris et l'agglomération parisienne* (1952), cited by Guy Debord in "Théorie de la dérive," *Les Lèvres Nues* 9 (November 1956), reprinted in *Internationale Situationniste* 2 (December 1958), "Theory of the Derive," in *International Anthology*, ed. and trans. Ken Knabb (Berkeley: Bureau of Public Secrets, 1981, 2006), http://www.bopsecrets.org/SI/2.derive.htm, showed the restrained perimeter in which people live: "he diagrams all the movements made in the space of one year by a student living in the 16th Arrondissement. Her itinerary forms a small triangle with no significant deviations, the three apexes of which are the School of Political Sciences, her residence and that of her piano teacher." Today's Chombart de Lauwe would be Albert-László Barabási, who has used data sets obtained from mobile phone companies to study the patterns in users' everyday movements. Albert-László Barabási, *Linked: How Everything Is Connected to Everything Else and What It Means for Business, Science, and Everyday Life* (Cambridge: Perseus, 2002). He claims that it is possible to predict people's everyday comings and goings with more than 80 percent accuracy. See chapter 9.

3. Tim Ingold, "Footprints through the Weather-World: Walking, Breathing, Knowing," in *Making Knowledge: Explorations of the Indissoluble Relation Between Mind, Body and Environment*, ed. T. H. J. Marchand (Oxford: Wiley-Blackwell, 2011), 121–122.

4. Maurice Merleau-Ponty, *Phenomenology of Perception* (Paris: Gallimard, 1945), transl. Colin Smith (London: Routledge, 1962, 2005).

5. Fredric Jameson, *Postmodernism or, The Cultural Logic of Late Capitalism* (Durham, NC: Duke University Press, 1991), 51, 54.

6. Debord, "Theory of the Dérive" (in English), http://www.bopsecrets.org/SI/2.derive.htm.

7. Ibid.

8. This paragraph follows de Certeau's account in *The Practice of Everyday Life,* 120–121.

9. Pierre Janet, *L'évolution de la mémoire et la notion du temps* (Paris: Chahine, 1928), 284–287, cited in de Certeau, *The Practice of Everyday Life,* 221 n. 12.

10. As atlases used to be called. See de Certeau, *The Practice of Everyday Life,* 120–121.

11. With reference to anthropologist Clifford Geertz's method of describing an event in its cultural context for outsiders to understand. See Clifford Geertz, "Thick Description: Toward an Interpretive Theory of Culture," *The Interpretation of Cultures: Selected Essays* (New York: Basic Books, 1973), 3–30.

Chapter 1

1. "Là où la carte découpe, le récit traverse." Michel de Certeau, *L'invention du quotidien.* Tome 1. *Arts de faire* (Paris: Gallimard, coll. Folio, 1980, 1990), *The Practice of Everyday Life*, trans. Steven Rendall (Berkeley: University of California Press, 1984), 129.

2. Lewis Mumford, *The City in History: Its Origins, Its Transformations, and Its Prospects* (New York: Harcourt, Brace and World, 1961).

3. Ibid.

4. Ibid., 486.

5. Constant (Nieuwenhuis), "Another City for Another Life," *Internationale Situationniste* 3 (December 1959) (Dutch section of the Situationist International), trans. Paul Hammond, http://notbored.org/another-city.html.

6. Robert Moses, quoted in Joel Kotkin, "Get Used to It: Suburbia's Not Going Away, No Matter What Critics Say or Do," *American Enterprise* (January 1, 2005): 32–37.

7. Bill Owens, *Suburbia* (San Francisco: Straight Arrow Press, 1972).

8. "Orléans-la-Source," *Wikipedia*, http://fr.wikipedia.org/wiki/Orl%C3%A9ans-la-Source. "Retour à La Source: les premières années d'un quartier orléanais," Le portail des archives de la ville d'Orléans, http://archives.orleans.fr/article.php?laref=139&titre=retour-a-la-source-les-premieres-annees-d-un-quartier-orleanais.

9. Rectorat de l'Académie d'Orléans, http://www.ac-orleans-tours.fr/rectorat/documentation/archives/zep.htm.

10. Celestine Bohlen, "France Braces for More Violence a Year after Riots," http://www.bloomberg.com/apps/news?pid=20601085&sid=awF7fWcbR0xw&refer=europe.

11. Wilfried Hou Je Bek provided me with photocopies of the annotated maps.

12. Lénaïg Bredoux, "Licenciée pour solidarité," *L'Humanité*, October 26, 2006.

13. When we learn to identify wildflowers or trees, we begin to recognize plants that we never noticed before. Esther Polak makes a similar remark about birdwatching in chapter 7.

14. Wilfried Hou Je Bek, "Language/Psychogeonamics and Where to Go Next," 2004, http://web.archive.org/web/20041114142739/http://www.socialfiction.org/psychogeography/psychogeonamics.html.

15. Patrick Beurard-Valdoye, *Les noms perdus, des sources aux pertes de la Meuse,*(La Souterraine: La Main courante, 1996).

16. As Raja Shehadeh notes in his introduction to *Palestinian Walks: Forays into a Vanishing Landscape* (New York: Scribner, 2007), xx. See chapter 9.

17. Barbara Glowczewski, "The Paradigm of Indigenous Australians: Anthropological Phantasms, Artistic Creations and Political Resistance," in Géraldine Le Roux and Lucienne Strivay, eds., *The Revenge of Genres: Australian Contemporary Art* (Paris: Diff' Art / Aïnu Éditions, 2007), 84.

18. This is how the Arunta, a group from central Australia, can repeat extremely long traditional tales. Olive M. Pink, "Spirit Ancestors in a Northern Aranda Horde Country," *Oceania* 4, no. 2 (December 1933): 176–186, quoted in Kevin Lynch, *Image of the City* (Cambridge: MIT Press, 1961), 127.

19. Both definitions from *Webster's New World College Dictionary* (Cleveland: Wiley, 2010).

20. Peter Suber, *The Paradox of Self-Amendment, A Study of Law, Logic, Omnipotence, and Change,* appendix 3, http://www.earlham.edu/~peters/writing/psa (original work published by Peter Lang Publishing, New York, 1990).

21. Wilfried Hou Je Bek, email interview with the author, February 28, 2005, published in French translation as "Questions à Wilfried Hou Je Bek" in *Art++*, ed. David-Olivier Lartigaud (Orleans: Editions HYX, 2011), 293–302. He situates his experiments within the British tradition of peripatetic writers.

22. Henry de Bearn, André Conord, Mohamed Dahou, Guy-Ernest Debord, Jacques Fillon, Patrick Straram, and Gil J. Wolman, "Response to the question: 'Does thought enlighten both us and our actions with the same indifference as the sun, or what is our hope, and what is its value?,'" signed in the name of the *Lettrist International*, in *La Carte d'après nature* (June 1954), in *Not Bored!*, trans. Nick Tallet, 29 (1998), http://www.notbored.org/la-carte.html.

23. Guy Debord, "Introduction à une critique de la géographie urbaine," *Les Lèvres Nues* 6 (Brussels, September 1955), "Introduction to a Critique of Urban Geography," trans. Ken Knabb, *Situationist International Anthology* Berkeley: Bureau of Public Secrets, 1995 (original work published in 1981), http://www.bopsecrets.org/SI/urbgeog.htm.

24. De Bearn et al., "Response to the question," http://www.notbored.org/la-carte.html.

25. Guy Debord, "Exercise in Psycho-Geography," *Potlatch* 2 (June 29, 1954), http://www.notbored.org/exercise.html.

26. Ralph Rumney, quoted in Phil Baker, "Review of *Psychogeography," Fortean Times* (October 2007), http://www.forteantimes.com/reviews/books/736/psychogeography.html; Iain Sinclair, *Lights Out for the Territory* (London: Penguin, 2003) (original work published in 1997), 54; Iain Sinclair, *London Orbital* (London: Penguin, 2002), 204 (he notes that "I couldn't help reading the Dante spirals as models for a celestial M25") (see chapter 3); Rebecca Solnit, *Wanderlust* (London: Verso, 2002):180–181; Wilfried Hou Je Bek, "Do-It-Yourself Urbanism: Psychogeography, Generosity, Serendipity and Turriphilia," in *Archilab 2004: La ville à nu* (The Naked City), catalog (Orléans: HYX, 2004). Walpole's architectural experiment, Strawberry Hill, became the setting for his tongue-in-cheek ghost story, *The Castle of Otrante*. Merlin Coverley, *Psychogeography* (London: Pocket Essentials, 2006): 32.

27. De Quincey quoted by Guy Debord,"Préface 'pour un livre projeté par Ralph Rumney'"(September 1957), *Guy Debord Œuvres*, édition établie et annotée par Jean-Louis Rançon en collaboration avec Alice Debord (Paris: Gallimard, 2006), 333; "Psychogeographical Venice," trans. NOT BORED! *NOT BORED*! no. 41 (2009), http://www.notbored.org/psychogeographical-venice.html.

28. Charles Baudelaire, *Constantin Guys: Le peintre de la vie moderne* (Geneva: La Palantine, not dated), http://fr.wikisource.org/wiki/Le_Peintre_de_la_vie_moderne, "The Painter of Modern Life," trans. P. E. Charvet, in *Baudelaire: Selected Writings on Art and Artists* (Cambridge: Cambridge University Press, 1981), 399–400. Work first published in 1863. Translation first published by Penguin Books in 1972.

29. Charles Baudelaire, "Les Foules" (The Crowds), *Le spleen de Paris: Petits poèmes en prose* (Paris, 1869). Translation at http://www.theflaneur.co.uk/lesfoules.html.

30. Walter Benjamin, "The Paris of the Second Empire in Baudelaire" (1938), in *The Writer of Modern Life: Essays on Charles Baudelaire*, ed. Michael Jennings trans. Harry Zohn (Cambridge: Belknap Press of Harvard University Press, 2006), 46–133. Rebecca Solnit found no mention of this practice in nineteenth-century literature.

31. Baudelaire, "The Painter of Modern Life", in Charvet, 420. See also Louis Aragon. *Le paysan de Paris*, Paris: Gallimard (coll. Folio), 1972 (original publication in 1926), André Breton, *Nadja*, Paris, Gallimard, 1962 (original publication in 1928), Philippe Soupault, *Les Dernières Nuits de Paris*, Paris, Gallimard, coll. "L'Imaginaire", 1997. (Original publication in 1928).

32. Jean-Michel Mension, *La Tribu*, interviews with G. Berréby and F. Milo (Paris: Allia, 1998), 108–111.

33. Guy-Ernest Debord, "Théorie de la dérive," *Les Lèvres Nues* 9 (November 1956), reprinted in *Internationale Situationniste* 2 (December 1958), "Theory of the Derive," in *Situationist International Anthology*., ed. and trans. Ken Knabb (Berkeley: Bureau of Public Secrets, 1981 2006), http://www.bopsecrets.org/SI/2.derive.htm.

34. Ibid. (in English), http://www.bopsecrets.org/SI/2.derive.htm.

35. Michèle Bernstein, "*Dérive* by the Mile," *Potlatch* 9–11 (August 17–31, 1954), http://www.notbored.org/derive-by-the-mile.html. One wonders if today's low-cost Vélib' bicycles are conducive to drifting. Like Bernstein's taxis, they can be picked up and left in stations all over Paris.

36. Here they were greatly influenced by Chombart de Lauwe, cited in Debord, "Critique of Urban Geography," http://www.bopsecrets.org/SI/urbgeog.htm. Thierry Paquot declares: "The study *Paris et l'agglomération parisienne* (1952), edited under the leadership of Paul-Henry Chombart de Lauwe (1913–1998), constitutes the first great work in the field of social urban anthropology. This incomparable research is now a reference work, presenting at the same time snapshots of Paris and an experimentation of new methodological tools (aerial views, districts' monographs, 'dynamic' cartography—that is to say making connections between different parameters—unstructured interviews, research-action, commented bibliographies, etc.)." Thierry Paquot, "A Sociologist in Paris," *Espaces et sociétés*, 103 (2000), http://www.espacesetsocietes.msh-paris.fr/103/resumes_eng.html.

37. Debord, "Critique of Urban Geography," http://www.bopsecrets.org/SI/urbgeog.htm.

38. Guy Debord, "Two Accounts of the Dérive," *Les Lèvres Nues* 9 (November 1956), trans. Thomas Y. Levin, http://www.cddc.vt.edu/sionline/presitu/twoaccounts.html.

39. Debord, "Theory of the Drift."

40. Debord, "Two Accounts." Ralph Rumney maintained that drifts could often arise out of necessity. Proponents disdained proper jobs. Michèle Bernstein supported herself and Guy Debord by composing crossword puzzles for newspapers. They were unwelcome in some of the more expensive bars at Saint Germain-des-Près because they did not keep buying drinks. So the psychogeographical maps also had a practical purpose. Ralph Rumney, *Le consul: Entretiens avec Gérard Beréby* (Paris: Éditions Allia, 1999).

41. Although the creation of the Situationist International in 1957 coincided with the beginning of the end of unitary urbanism, I follow scholarly practice in using the term *situationist* to refer also to the members of the Lettrist International to not confuse them with the better-known lettrists Isidore Isou and Maurice Lemaître, who were not situationists.

42. Ivan Chtcheglov (using the pseudonym Gilles Ivain), "Formulaire pour un urbanisme nouveau" (October 1953), *Internationale Situationniste* 1 (June 1958), "Formulary for a New Urbanism," in *Situationist International Anthology*, trans. and ed. Ken Knabb (Berkeley: Bureau of Public Secrets, 1995), http://www.bopsecrets.org/SI/Chtcheglov.htm.

43. Ibid.

44. Constant, "Another City for Another Life," *Internationale Situationniste* 3 (December 1959), trans. Paul Hammond, in the Dutch section of *Situationist International Anthology*, ed. Ken Knabb (Berkeley: Bureau of Public Secrets, 1995), http://www.bopsecrets.org/SI/3.constant.htm. *New*

Babylon was "a provocative name," as Henri Lefebvre notes, "since in the Protestant tradition Babylon is a figure of evil. New Babylon was to be the figure of good that took the name of the cursed city and transformed itself into the city of the future." Henri Lefebvre, "Henri Lefebvre on the Situationist International" (1983), interview conducted and translated by Kristin Ross, *October* 79 (Winter 1997, http://www.notbored.org/lefebvre-interview.html.

45. Chtcheglov, "Lettres de loin" ("Letters from afar, " my translation), http://debordiana.chez.com/francais/is9.htm#lettres.

46. Lefebvre, "Henri Lefebvre on the Situationist International."

47. Ibid.

48. In an email message to the author, December 13, 2004.

49. Wilfried Hou Je Bek, "Algorithmic Psychogeography," 2002, http://web.archive.org/web/20020207142455/http://www.socialfiction.org/psychogeography/algoeng.htm.

50. Ibid.

51. A tongue-in-cheek take on HTML, XML, and so on.

52. Wilfried Hou Je Bek, email interview with the author (February 28, 2005).

53. *Gutai* means "embodiment" or "concrete."

54. The flyer is reproduced in *Dada,* catalog of the exhibition (Paris: Centre Pompidou, 2005), 858; Jacques-Yves Conrad, *Promenade surréaliste sur la colline de Montmartre* (Paris: University of Paris III, Sorbonne Nouvelle Center for the Study of Surrealism, 2007). http://melusine.univ-paris3.fr/Association/Conrad.htm.

55. This and a mock trial of reactionary writer Maurice Barrès held later in the year fueled the falling out between Tristan Tzara and future surrealists André Breton and Francis Picabia. Hans Richter, *Dada: Art and Anti-art* (London: Thames & Hudson, 2004), 183–185.

56. "DADA: Cities," National Gallery of Art, http://www.nga.gov/exhibitions/2006/dada/cities/index.shtm.

57. The original cap was stolen in Germany but soon was replaced by another hat. See Christel Hollevoet, "Wandering in the City," *The Power of the City: The City of Power* (New York: Whitney Museum, 1972), 35. In the 1970s, Filliou seemed to favor berets.

58. Maxa Zoller, "The Cinematic Body," http://www.no-w-here.org.uk/index.php?cat=1&subCat=docdetail&id=187.

59. Georges Perec, *Tentative d'épuisement d'un lieu parisien,* Paris: Christian Bourgois, 1982.

60. Georges Perec, *Espèces d'espaces* (Paris: Éditions Galilée, 1974), 13 (my translation).

61. Ibid., 14.

62. Ibid., 21.

63. Ibid., 87. The sequence of chapters in his novel *La vie mode d'emploi* is determined by a similar chess figure called the "knight's tour," in which a knight stops on every square of the chessboard only once.

64. Jacques Roubaud, "Sonnet Walking: New York and after, 29 Fevrier – 15 Mars 2000," *Po&Sie* 92 (2nd trimester 2000): 90–103; Véronique Montémont, *Jacques Roubaud: L'amour du nombre* (Lille: Presses Universitaires du Septentrion, 2004), 202.

65. Adrian Piper, *Talking to Myself: The Ongoing Autobiography of an Art Object* (Hamburg: Hossmann, 1974), 14, reprinted in *Out of Order, Out of Sight*, Vol. 1, *Selected Writings in Meta-Art 1968–1992* (Cambridge: MIT Press, 1996).

66. See Hollevoet, "Wandering in the City," 51.

67. Or diffusion of responsibility in large groups. The 1964 case triggered research studies and attempts to find solutions to this problem. Yet in April 2010, a homeless man, stabbed while defending a woman being attacked by a knife-wielding assailant, bled to death on a Queens sidewalk as more than twenty pedestrians walked by.

68. Hsieh spent an entire year locked inside a cage, another punching a time clock every hour. The outdoor project took place from September 26, 1981 to September 26, 1982.

69. President Reagan signed the Economic Recovery Tax Act into law on August 13, 1981. This law amended the Internal Revenue Code "to encourage economic growth through reduction of the tax rates for individual taxpayers". Public Law 97-34, 97th Congress. The full text of the law: http://www.scribd.com/doc/61986150/Economic-Recovery-Tax-Act-of-1981-PL-97-34.

70. Tehching Hsieh, "Tehching Hsieh—One Year Performance, 1980–1981 (Time Clock Piece)," video posted to YouTube by Foundation for Art and Creative Technology (FACT) Liverpool (2010), http://www.youtube.com/watch?v=90izVR2Kip0.

71. Tehching Hsieh in Adrian Heathfield and Tehching Hsieh, *Out of Now. The Lifeworks of Tehching Hsieh* (London/Cambridge: the Live Art Development Agency and MIT Press, 2009), 160. The only exception was when he was arrested by the police, an event that was documented on videotape. Ibid., 44–45.

72. As Adrian Heathfield notes, in ibid., 40.

73. Tehching Hsieh, Ibid., 334.

74. He spent another year tied by an eight-foot rope to fellow artist Linda Montano. Both shaved their heads, and as in previous works, the beginning and end of the performance were duly attested by witnesses. According to their official statement, "We will stay together for one year and never be alone. We will be in the same room at the same time, when we are inside. We will be tied together at the waist with an 8 foot rope. We will never touch each other during the year. The performance will begin on July 4, 1983, at 6 p.m., and continue until July 4, 1984, at 6 p.m.," Ibid., 230–233.

75. "Like Franz Kafka says, you have to take an ax" to the frozen sea in "people's hearts." Tehching Hsieh, quoted in Deborah Sontag, "A Caged Man Breaks Out at Last," *New York Times*, March 1, 2009.

76. A case could also be made for a feminist interpretation. The dark laces that bind Hatoum's white ankles recall the neck choker worn by Édouard Manet's reclining nude, *Olympia* (1863). The heavy boots (similar to those worn by police officers and skinheads) bring to mind Nancy Sinatra's song "These Boots Are Made for Walking" (1966), with its refrain "one of these days these boots are going to walk all over you."

77. Barely audible on the tape, the remark was highlighted by Hatoum when she presented the work at the Centre Pompidou in January 2008.

78. http://www.ramblers.org.uk/Campaigns+Policy/campaign_home_old.

79. In the United Kingdom, the Vagrancy Act 1824 makes it an offense to sleep on the streets or to beg. Donna Landry, "Radical Walking," *Open Democracy*, 2001, http://www.opendemocracy.net/ecology-climate_change_debate/article_465.jsp.

80. Ibid.

81. Ewen Chardronnet, "History of Unitary Urbanism and Psychogeography at the Turn of the Sixties," Lecture notes for Art+Communication Festival, Riga, May 2003, http://semaphore.blogs.com/semaphore/2008/02/history-of-unit.html.

82. *Grève* means both "bank" (it is near the banks of the Seine river) and "strike."

83. Michelangelo Pistoletto, "The Minus Objects," *Michelangelo Pistoletto,* exhibition catalog (Genoa: Galleria La Bertesca, 1966), republished on Michelangelo Pistoletto's official Web site http://www.pistoletto.it/eng/testi/minus_objects.pdf.

84. See the artist's Web site at http://www.webnetmuseum.org/html/fr/expo-retr-fredforest/textes_critiques/textes_divers/note_de_synthese_fr.htm (my translation). It prefigures the media subversion pranks of activist groups like ®TMark, the Institute of Applied Autonomy, and the Yes Men.

85. Fred Forest, email message to the author, March 1, 2010. When I asked about the repercussions of contemporary events, he mentioned that the Brazilian police had questioned him about the acronym MIR (the acronym of a Chilean revolutionary movement) that someone had scrawled on one of the signs.

86. Hakim Bey, *T.A.Z.: The Temporary Autonomous Zone, Ontological Anarchy, Poetic Terrorism* (New York: Autonomedia, 1985), http://www.hermetic.com/bey/taz_cont.html.

87. Characteristic actions include closing Camden High Street to motor traffic for an afternoon in the spring of 1995 and organizing a street party at a busy crossroads on Upper Street in Islington in the summer of 1995, with music and an improvised sandpit for children to play in. Reclaim the Streets Web site, http://rts.gn.apc.org.

88. "Reclaim the Streets," *Do or Die: Voices from the Ecological Resistance* 6 (1997): 1–10, http://www.eco-action.org/dod/no6/rts.htm. Both Wilfried Hou Je Bek and Ewen Chardronnet belonged

to a smaller, transnational Association of Autonomous Astronauts that participated in the 1999 Carnival against Capitalism. See Ewen Chardronnet, "History of Unitary Urbanism, and Psychogeography at the Turn of the Sixties."

89. Julian Priest, "About the State of Wireless London," 2004, http://informal.org.uk/people/julian/publications/the_state_of_wireless_london.

90. David Garcia and Geert Lovink, "The ABC of Tactical Media," March 2002, http://project.waag.org/tmn/frabc.html.

91. Critical Art Ensemble Web site, http://www.critical-art.net/TacticalMedia.html.

92. Brown is a member of the Surveillance Camera Players who are discussed in chapter 9.

93. Originally founded by Ralph Rumney at the meeting of the first Situationist International in 1957.

94. The work of these artists is studied in detail by Thierry Davila, *Marcher, Créer. Déplacements: Rêveries, dérives dans l'art de la fin du 20e siècle* (Paris: Éditions du Regard, 2002).

95. Maspero was criticized by Guy Debord when, as a publisher, he censored texts to prevent them from being banned. Debord coined the term *masperize*.

96. François Maspero and Anaïk Frantz, *Les passagers du Roissy-Express* (Paris: Le Seuil, 1990), *Roissy Express: A Journey through the Paris Suburbs,* trans. Paul Jones (London: Verso, 1994); François Bon, *Paysage Fer* (Iron Landscape) (Lagrasse: Verdier, 2000); Philippe Vasset, *Un livre blanc* (A Blank Book) (Paris: Fayard, 2007).

97. Sinclair, *Lights Out for the Territory*, 4.

98. Debord, "Théorie de la dérive."

99. Stewart Home, "How I Discovered America," *Infopool* #6, 2002. http://www.stewarthomesociety.org/art/america.htm.

Chapter 2

1. Maurice Merleau-Ponty, *Phénoménologie de la perception* (Paris: Gallimard, 1945), *Phenomenology of Perception*, trans. Colin Smith (New York: Humanities Press, 1962), viii.

2. Jean-Jacques Rousseau, *Les confessions* (1781), trans. J. M. Cohen (London: Penguin Books, 1953), 382.

3. Joakim Garff, *Søren Aabye Kierkegaard: A Biography*, trans. B. Kirmmse (Princeton: Princeton University Press, 2005).

4. François Plas, Éric Viel, and Yves Blanc, *La marche humaine: Kinésiologie dynamique, biomécanique et pathomécanique*, 3rd ed. (Paris: Masson, 1979) (original work published in 1975).

5. "Researchers at the Kennedy Krieger Institute in Baltimore, Maryland, found that there are separate adaptable networks controlling each leg and there are also separate networks controlling leg movements, e.g., forward or backward walking. . . . The combined results demonstrate there

are distinct brain modules responsible for right/forward, right/backward, left/forward and left/backward walking. Most significantly, these modules can be individually trained." "New Research Discovers Independent Brain Networks Control Human Walking," *Nature Neuroscience*, August 7, 2007, http://multivu.prnewswire.com/mnr/bastian/29010 and http://www.kennedykrieger.org/overview/news/new-research-discovers-independent-brain-networks-control-human-walking.

6. John Dewey, *Art as Experience* (New York: Perigee Books, 2005), 16 (original work published in 1934). In her song "Walking and Falling" (1981), Laurie Anderson calls attention to their relation.

7. Anna Halprin, *Parades and Changes, Intensive Care*, Catalogue, Centre Pompidou, Festival d'Automne, 2004.

8. In the midtwentieth century, Ludwig Wittgenstein (in his second period), J. L. Austin, Gilbert Ryle, H. L. A. Hart, Peter Strawson, and John R. Searle turned away from traditional philosophical problems and specialized jargon to examine the ways words were used in ordinary language. In much the same way, choreographers refused the stylistic dictates of modern dance to explore everyday pedestrian movement.

9. Yvonne Rainer, "Some Retrospective Notes on a Dance for 10 People and 12 Mattresses Called Parts of Some Sextets" (1965), in *Happenings and Other Acts*, ed. Mariellen R. Sandford (London: Routledge, 1995), 166.

10. W. J. T. Mitchell, "Golden Memories: Interview with Sculptor Robert Morris," *ArtForum* (April 1994): http://findarticles.com/p/articles/mi_m0268/is_n8_v32/ai_16109620/?tag=rbxcra.2.a.22. On the influence of Forti, see also Robert Morris, "Interview: Robert Morris," by Simon Grant, *Tate Etc.*14 (Autumn 2008), http://www.tate.org.uk/tateetc/issue14/morris.htm.

11. Between thirty-four and eighty-four participants, according to the score.

12. Steve Paxton, score for *Satisfyin' Lover*, reproduced in Sally Banes, *Terpsichore in Sneakers: Post-modern Dance* (Middletown, CT: Wesleyan University Press, 1987), 74. Asimina Chremos felt that the semiformal stagings of *Past Forward* transformed process-oriented pieces into products: "There are rather clear parameters for how to walk, stand, sit, climb on the Huddle, Scramble, etcetera. A certain amount of self-conscious decorum seems to be called for that doesn't seem authentic to the original spirit of the work." Asimina Chremos, "White Oak Diary," *Dance Insider*, Flash Notes, November 21, 2000, http://web.archive.org/web/20060317034329/http://www.danceinsider.com/f2006/f0217_2.html. Her idea of authenticity is contradicted by Paxton's score.

13. Organized by Mikhael Baryshnikov's White Oak Dance Project.

14. Asimina Chremos, "White Oak Diary," http://web.archive.org/web/20060317034329/http://www.danceinsider.com/f2006/f0217_2.html.

15. Touchdown Dance, http://www.touchdowndance.co.uk/graphic/contact_improvisation.html.

16. Steve Paxton, quoted in Elizabeth Zimmer, "Contact Improvisation Comes of Age," *Dance Magazine* (June 2004): http://findarticles.com/p/articles/mi_m1083/is_6_78/ai_n6143404.

17. The ladder was suspended at an angle from a water tower. In the photograph of the performance, no wires or pulleys are visible.

18. *Walking on the Wall* (1971) was performed indoors at the Whitney Museum of American Art. Brown and her fellow dancers, supported by harnesses that were suspended from the ceiling, walked around the walls. *Set and Reset* (1983) was a solo version of *Walking on the Wall.*

19. Trisha Brown, quoted in Graham Watts, "Review of Trisha Brown Dance Company, *Man Walking Down the Side of a Building,*" May 2006, London, Tate Modern, in *Ballet Magazine* (September 2006), http://www.ballet.co.uk/magazines/yr_06/sep06/gw_rev_trisha_brown_0506.htm.

20. "Although gravity eventually wins, it does so only on Trisha Brown's terms and in her own time. Brown herself observed that the dancer's powerful body undergoing this simple everyday motion, illustrated "'the paradox of one action working against another . . . gravity working one way on the body . . . a naturally walking person in another way.'" Watts, "Review." Watts evokes another performance, *Spiral* (1974–1975), in which "Carmen Beuchat, Sylvia Palacios and Trisha Brown strapped themselves to ropes which spiraled around trees and pillars. During their performances (lasting only a matter of 15 to 30 seconds) the three dancers walked around the pillars, hanging out into space, parallel to the floor."

21. Tom Johnson, "Changing the Meaning of Static," *Village Voice,* September 7, 1972, quoted in Edward Strickland, "Minimalism T (1992)," *Writings on Glass: Essays, Interviews, Criticism,* ed. Richard Kostelanetz and Robert Flemming (Berkeley: University of California Press, 1997), 114.

22. "Reconstitutions of Gestures made by Christian Boltanski between 1948 and 1954," 1970.

23. In 1988, when Joan Simon remarked that the phrase "a direct statement on how the artist lives, works, and thinks" could be applied to any number of Nauman's works, Nauman responded: "There was also the idea that if I was in the studio, whatever I was doing was art. Pacing around, for example." Bruce Nauman, "Breaking the Silence," interview with Joan Simon, reprinted in *Please Pay Attention Please: Bruce Nauman's Words. Writings and Interviews,* ed. Janet Kraynak (Cambridge: MIT Press, 2005), 322–323. In 1968 and 1969, he worked in a studio in Southampton, Long Island, New York. It was lent to him by Roy Lichtenstein and Paul Waldman on the condition that he not use tape or tacks on the walls. To make his videos and his corridor pieces, he built his own freestanding walls in the middle. See Joan Simon, "Bruce Nauman: The Matter in Hand," *Tate,* June 1, 1998, http://www.speronewestwater.com/cgi-bin/iowa/articles/record.html?record=628.

24. "The camera lies on its side and registers for an hour everything that happens in the studio. The actor, Nauman himself, moves back and forth through the space with stiffened legs, disregarding the logic of a straight line. This method suggests the pages of description found in [Samuel Beckett's novel] *Molloy* in which the protagonist stumbles forward on stiffened legs without bending a knee or stopping." Gijs van Tuyl, "Human Condition / Human Body," in *Bruce Nauman: Image/Text 1966–1996,* exhibition catalog (London: Hayward Gallery, 1998), 69. In the works of both Beckett and Nauman, says van Tuyl, "gravity exerts its pull everywhere, though not always visibly. As with all human beings, the groundward tug effects or exerts (as an accidental by-product) shapeliness, grace and balance, even as it deforms those things, pulling them

into disorganization, flatness or comic indistinction." Ibid., 60–75. See also Marcia Tucker, "PheN-AUMANology," in *Bruce Nauman: Image/Text 1966–1996*, exhibition catalog (London: Hayward Gallery, 1998), 82–87, and Willoughby Sharp, "Interview with Bruce Nauman," in *Bruce Nauman: Image/Text 1966–1996*, exhibition catalog (London: Hayward Gallery, 1998), 88–97.

25. Samuel Beckett, *Molloy* (1951), trans. Samuel Beckett and Patrick Bowles, in *Three Novels: Molloy, Malone Dies, The Unnamable* (New York: Grove Press, 1995). See chapter 5 on wayfinding.

26. Bruce Nauman, in Willoughby Sharp, "Nauman Interview," *Arts Magazine* (March 1970), reprinted in *Bruce Nauman*, exhibition catalog (London: Hayward Gallery, London, 1998), 88–97.

27. Bruce Nauman, "Setting a Good Corner," Interview, *Art 21*, http://www.pbs.org/art21/artists/bruce-nauman.

28. Cindy Nemser "A Conversation with Eva Hesse," *Artforum* 8, no. 7 (May 1970), reprinted in *Eva Hesse*, ed. Mignon Nixon (Cambridge: MIT Press, 2002), 11.

29. Samuel Beckett, *Collected Shorter Plays of Samuel Beckett* (London: Faber and Faber, 1984), 291. It was created for German television and broadcast on October 8, 1981, performed at http://ftvdb.bfi.org.uk/sift/title/326964. S. E. Gontarski notes that "since the figures always turn left, not only at the centre but at all the corners also, the pattern is that of the damned in the *Inferno. Quad* is indeed a sinister piece." S. E. Gontarski, "'Quad I & II': Beckett's Sinister Mime(s)," *Journal of Beckett Studies* 9 (Spring 1983): 137–138.

30. John Dewey, *Art as Experience* (New York: Perigee Books, 2005), 2 (work originally published in 1934).

31. Robert Filliou (1970) "Interview," quoted in *Robert Filliou: Génie sans talent, exhibition catalog* (Villeneuve d'Ascq: Musée d'Art Moderne Lille Métropole, 2003), back cover.

32. Dewey, *Art as Experience*, 10.

33. Available at http://www.max-neuhaus.info/soundworks/vectors/walks.

34. Dewey, *Art as Experience*, 54–55.

35. All quotations from the tapescript of *Her Long Black Hair* courtesy of the artist and the Public Art Fund, New York.

36. William Alex and Elizabeth Barlow, *Frederick Law Olmsted's New York* (1972), quoted in Robert Smithson, "Frederick Law Olmsted and the Dialectical Landscape," *Robert Smithson: The Collected Writings*, ed. Jack D. Flam (Berkeley: University of California Press, 1996), 165. Smithson uses the expression "urban blight."

37. This stance has had a long history, from Gordon Matta-Clark at Fresh Kills to Francis Alÿs and Gabriel Oroszco's meanderings in the 1990s. Even the waste manager who moves through forty years of American history in Don DeLillo's 1997 novel *Underworld* is something of a rag picker.

38. Dewey, *Art as Experience*, 36.

39. Ibid., 37. Today we often use the word *closure* to denote "a feeling of completeness." According to *Wiktionary*, it is "the experience of an emotional conclusion, usually to a difficult period," http://en.wiktionary.org/wiki/closure. *Merriam Webster Online* uses the word for both the experience and the thing that causes it: "an often comforting or satisfying sense of finality <victims needing closure>; *also* : something (as a satisfying ending) that provides such a sense." http://www.merriam-webster.com/dictionary/closure.

40. Dewey, *Art as Experience*, 42. Conversely, a drift (*dérive*), as Debord defined it, would be *an* experience. The drift that he recounted (see chapter 1) is *an* experience, a whole. It is written up, there is plot development, and the high points and low points are identified. The experience is complete. At the end, we cross the border into everyday life again.

41. Dewey, *Art as Experience*, 16.

42. Ibid., 56.

43. Ibid., 58.

44. Ibid., 58.

45. Janet Cardiff and Mirjam Schaub, *Janet Cardiff: The Walk Book* (Vienna: Thyssen-Bornemisza Art Contemporary in collaboration with Public Art Fund, 2005), 79.

46. Ibid., 4–5.

47. Ibid.

48. Ibid., 19.

49. Tom Eccles, "Comments," in Cardiff and Schaub, *Janet Cardiff: The Walk Book*, 46–47.

50. Ibid., 33.

51. In an email message to the author, August 20, 2008.

52. Central Park was built on the site of Seneca Village, which was inhabited by African-American freed slaves and Irish immigrants. A 1997 show called "Before Central Park: The Life and Death of Seneca Village" at the New York Historical Society demonstrated the fallacy of "the ideology long reflected in histories of Central Park, that it was a "wasteland" inhabited by "squatters" living in "shanties." This notion facilitated the eviction of the 1,600 residents displaced from the park site, including those who lived in Seneca Village, which was situated on the park's west side, from the Great Lawn to Central Park West, between 82d and 88th Streets." Douglas Martin, "A Village Dies, A Park Is Born", *New York Times,* January 31, 1997, http://www.nytimes.com/1997/01/31/arts/a-village-dies-a-park-is-born.html.

53. Robert Smithson, "Frederick Law Olmsted and the Dialectical Landscape," in *Robert Smithson: The Collected Writings*, ed. Jack D. Flam (Berkeley: University of California Press, 1996), 164.

54. Ibid., 165.

55. Ibid., 160.

56. Ibid., 165.

57. Frederick Law Olmsted, "The Spoils of the Park" (1882), quoted in Ibid., 157. The Parc des Buttes-Chaumont was built on the site of a landfill (a depleted gypsum quarry that had been used as a garbage dump).

58. Smithson, "Frederick Law Olmsted and the Dialectical Landscape," 170.

59. Ibid.

60. Cardiff and Schaub, *Janet Cardiff: The Walk Book.*

61. In 1938, audiences were used to hearing dire news from abroad (in Spain, cities were being bombed from the air), but this disaster was closer to home. Orson Welles's dramatization was made more plausible by what sounded like live news reports and interviews with eyewitnesses and experts.

62. The first audio guide was a twenty-pound reel-to-reel tape recorder used by Valentine Burton in 1957 to record his visit to a museum in the company of a curator. Jennifer Fisher, "Speeches of Display: The Museum Audioguides of Sophie Calle, Andrea Fraser and Janet Cardiff," *Parachute: Contemporary Art Magazine,* 94 (April 1, 1999), 24–31.

63. Ibid.

64. http://www.hamish-fulton.com/hamish_fulton_v01.htm.

65. Heath Bunting, quoted in Kayle Brandon and Heath Bunting, "Interview with Kayle Brandon and Heath Bunting," interview by Mark Dunhill and Tamiko O'Brien, March 2004, Collaborative Arts, http://collabarts.org/?p=81. See chapter 3.

Chapter 3

1. *Wikipedia,* http://en.wikipedia.org/wiki/Protocol_(natural_sciences).

2. Sol LeWitt, "Paragraphs on Conceptual Art," *Artforum* 5 No 10 (June 1967): 79–83.

3. Roubaud often maps out walks following a series of locations in which he has placed memories. On the *ars memoriae,* see chapter 5. Jacques Roubaud, *Le grand incendie de Londres, récit avec incises et bifurcations, 1985–1987* (Paris: Seuil, 1989), *The Great Fire of London: A Story with Interpolations and Bifurcations,* trans. Dominic Di Bernardi (Elmwood Park, IL: Dalkey Archive Press, 1991), 98–99; Jean-Jacques Thomas, "Swing Troubadour: Roubaud's Self-portrait," *The Great Fire of London by Jacques Roubaud: A Casebook,* ed. Peter Consenstein (Urbana-Champaign, IL: Dalkey Archive Press, 2003 http://www.dalkeyarchive.com/book/?GCOI=15647100788640&fa=details.

4. "My first work made by walking, in 1967, was a straight line in a grass field, which was also my own path, going 'nowhere.' In the subsequent early map works, recording very simple but precise walks on Exmoor and Dartmoor, my intention was to make a new art which was also a

new way of walking: walking as art. Each walk followed my own unique, formal route, for an original reason, which was different from other categories of walking, like travelling. Each walk, though not by definition conceptual, realised a particular idea. Thus walking—as art—provided an ideal means for me to explore relationships between time, distance, geography and measurement." Richard Long, 2000, http://www.richardlong.org.

5. Richard Long, "Richard Long: No Where," interview with Colin Kirkpatrick, Piers Arts Centre, Orkney, July 8, 1994, http://www.speronewestwater.com/cgi-bin/iowa/articles/record.html?record=293.

6. Ibid.

7. La Monte Young, "Draw a Straight Line and Follow It," interview, in Richard Kostelanetz, *The Theater of Mixed-Means: An Introduction to Happenings, Kinetic Environments and Other Mixed-Means Presentations* , 2nd ed. (New York: Dial, 1980) (original work published in 1968). Republished as Richard Kostelanetz "Conversation with La Monte Young" in La Monte Young and Marian Zazeela, *Selected Writings*, (Munich: Heiner Friedrich, 1969), 44.

8. Long, "Richard Long: No Where."

9. Long, http://www.richardlong.org.

10. See chapter 5 on the Australian aboriginal people and rhythm.

11. Discussed in chapter 9. Kayle Brandon and Heath Bunting, "Interview with Kayle Brandon and Heath Bunting," *Collaborative Arts* (March 2004), http://collabarts.org/?p=81.

12. Ibid. See http://irational.org/heath/d-fence; cf. J. Lillemose, in Susanne Ackers, Inke Arns, Matthew Fuller, Francis Hunger, Jacob Lillemose, and Darija Simunovic, *The Hartware Guide to Irational.org* (Frankfurt am Main: Revolver Books, 2006), 22. A play on words: defense (budget) cuts (or defensive cuts?).

13. Iain Sinclair, *Lights Out for the Territory* (London: Penguin 2003) (original work published in 1997), 1.

14. Ibid., 3.

15. Ibid., 11.

16. Email message from the artist to the author, November 14, 2011. My translation.

17. Julio Cortázar and Carol Dunlop, *Los autonautas de la cosmopista o Un viaje atemporal Paris-Marsella* (Barcelona: Muchnik, 1983), *Autonauts of the Cosmoroute*, trans. Anne McLean (London: Telegram, 2008), 35–36. They traveled by van from one rest stop to the next (it is forbidden to walk on the motorway itself), but most of their time was spent on the ground. Virtually all the artists considered here have used motor vehicles, trains, and even planes to travel to and from the sites of their walks.

18. Iain Sinclair, *London Orbital* (London: Penguin, 2002), 31, 37, 125.

19. Ibid., 16.

20. Ibid., 3, 11.

21. Ibid., 34.

22. Ibid., 82.

23. Ibid., 7.

24. Ibid.

25. Jane Jacobs, *The Death and Life of Great American Cities* (New York: Random House, 1961), 259.

26. Laurent Tixador, *L'inconnu des grands horizons* (Nantes: Éditions Michel Baverey, 2003), 57.

27. Ibid., 61.

28. Ibid., 8.

29. Marina Abramović and Ulay, *The Lovers: The Great Wall Walk*, film, BBC, 1988; Marina Abramović and Ulay, *The Lovers: The Great Wall Walk* (Amsterdam: Stedelijk Museum, 1989), 36, 35.

30. Marina Abamović, quoted in Zoe Kosmidou, "Transitory Objects: A Conversation with Marina Abramović," *Sculpture Magazine* 20, no. 9 (November 2001), http://www.sculpture.org/documents/scmag01/nov01/abram/abram.shtml.

31. Hans-Ulrich Obrist, "Obrist/Abramović/Chaitin Interview," Kitakyushu, Japan, July 2001, in *HuO: Hans-Ulrich Obrist: Interviews* (Milan: Charta/Fondazione Pitti Immagine Discovery, 2003), 29–44.

32. Marina Abramović, in Kosmidou, "Transitory Objects," http://www.sculpture.org/documents/scmag01/nov01/abram/abram.shtml.

33. François Maspero and Anaïk Frantz, *Les passagers du Roissy-Express* (Paris: Le Seuil, 1990), 158 (my translation).

34. Ibid., 203–204.

35. Ibid., 23.

36. Ibid., 297.

37. Ibid., 307.

38. Long, "Richard Long: No Where."

39. Sinclair, *London Orbital*, 3.

40. Ibid., 7

41. *Meniscus: Excursions to the Millennium Dome*, London, 1999.

42. Iain Sinclair, "A Circular Story," *The Guardian*, October 25, 2003, http://www.guardian.co.uk/books/2003/oct/25/featuresreviews.guardianreview27.

43. Sinclair, *London Orbital*, 44.

44. Even so, the book was five years in the making, a long time in our speed-obsessed era (although in keeping with the pace of the walk itself).

45. Laurent Malone and Christine Breton /LMX, "L'agence de documentation sur les mutations urbaines," *ICHIM 04 Conference Proceedings* (Berlin: ICHIM, 2004), 8, http://ichim.org.

46. "Ecological transects are used to describe changes in habitat over some gradient such as a change in topography or distance from a water body." *Wikipedia,* http://en.wikipedia.org/wiki/Transect.

47. *Wikipedia,* http://en.wikipedia.org/wiki/Transect_(urban) and http://newurbannetwork.com/article/transect-applied-regional-plans.

48. See my article Karen O'Rourke, "The Artist's Book and Photography: The Example of Michael Snow's *Cover to Cover,*" *Revue Française d'Etudes Américaines* 8 (1979): 215–224.

49. Self-published by Ruscha in 1966.

50. A tongue-in-cheek allusion to the annual French cross-country bicycle race. In French *tour* can also refer to the circumference of a circle as in the expression *tour de taille* ("waist length").

51. Heath Bunting and Kayle Brandon, *Tour de Fence,* ed. Gerrit Gohlke (Berlin: Künstlerhaus Bethanien, 2003), 5.

52. Ibid.

53. *Wikipedia,* http://en.wikipedia.org/wiki/Bricolage.

54. Guy-Ernest Debord and Gil J. Wolman, "A User's Guide to Détournement" (1956), in *Situationist International Anthology*, ed. and trans. Ken Knabb (Berkeley: Bureau of Public Secrets, 1995) (original work published in 1981). See chapter 8.

55. Kristian Gravenor, "Segregation Fence to Live On," *Montreal Mirror*, November 8, 2001, http://www.montrealmirror.com/ARCHIVES/2001/110801/news3.html.

56. He has received a number of commissions from the Tate Gallery, the Arts Council, the Banff Institute, and others. http://irational.org/cgi-bin/cv2/temp.pl.

57. http://www.e-flux.com/shows/view/5106 consulted February 11, 2008.

58. André Rouillé, "L'art entre choses et expérience," *Paris-Art.com* no. 319, June 10,2010, http://www.paris-art.com/art-culture-France/l-art-entre-choses-et-experiences/Rouille-Andre/319.html; André Rouillé, "Visibilité paradoxale de l'art," *Paris-Art.com*, no. 226, November 25, 2010, http://www.paris-art.com/art-culture-France/visibilite-paradoxale-de-l-art/rouille-andre/336.html. See Jacques Rancière, *Le partage du sensible* (Paris: La Fabrique Éditions, 2000), *The Politics of Aesthetics*, trans. Gabriel Rockhill (London: Continuum, 2006).

59. Maspero and Frantz, *Les passagers du Roissy-Express*, 20.

60. Ibid.,12.

61. Ibid., 18.

62. Pierre Bourdieu, editor, *La misère du monde* (Paris: Le Seuil, 1993).

63. Thomas McEvilley, "Great Wall Talk," in Abramović and Ulay, *The Lovers,* 77.

64. Tixador and Poincheval, *L'inconnu des grands horizons.*

65. Ibid., 41.

66. Paul Ardenne, "In utero terrae," in Laurent Tixador and Abraham Poincheval, *Horizon moins vingt* (Paris: Isthme Éditions, 2006).

67. Anna Halprin, *Parades and Changes, Intensive Care,* catalogue (Paris: Centre Pompidou / Festival d'Automne, 2004).

68. Morton Subotnick, "Je me souviens de Parades and Changes," in Anna Halprin, *Parades and Changes, Intensive Care,* catalogue (Paris: Centre Pompidou / Festival d'Automne, 2004).

69. Cortázar and Dunlop, *Autonauts,* 61.

70. Ibid., 62. Their unswerving adherence to their rules contrasts with Tehching Hsieh, who allowed himself an occasional minor deviation from the rule. He notes that "a little bit of damage is good for the system." but too much would make the work "collapse," Adrian Heathfield and Tehching Hsieh, *Out of Now: The Lifeworks of Tehching Hsieh (*London/Cambridge: Live Art Development Agency and MIT Press, 2009), 328.

71. Young, "Draw a Straight Line and Follow It."

72. Maspero and Frantz, *Les passagers du Roissy-Express,* 24.

73. Sinclair, *London Orbital,* 3.

74. Ibid., 69.

75. Richard Long notes that "At the heart of my work is the fact that I make it myself. I have the pleasure of walking and being in these places and making these works in the landscape. It's also a question of realizing particular ideas, too. So let's say I have a certain idea about the symmetry of time and places, I can actually carry it out personally by walking that idea. In other words, there's no point in getting somebody else to do it." Richard Long, "Interview with Richard Long," interview by Robert Ayers, *ArtInfo* (June 28, 2006), http://www.artinfo.com/news/story/18221/richard-long/?page=2.

Chapter 4

1. Robert Morris, "The Present Tense of Space," *Continuous Project Altered Daily: The Writings of Robert Morris,* 175–209 (Cambridge: MIT Press, 1993).

2. Bruce Altshuler, "Art by Instruction and the Pre-History of *Do It,*" in Hans Ulrich Obrist, ed., *Do It,* exhibition catalog (New York: Independent Curators Incorporated, 1997). The idea of art as a diagram goes back to the temples of antiquity and the cathedrals of the Middle Ages. See

Bill Viola, "Will There Be Condominiums in Data Space?," *Video* 80, no. 5 (1982): 36–41, reprinted in Noah Wardrip-Fruin and Nick Montfort, *New Media Reader*, 465–470 (Cambridge: MIT Press, 2003). I return to these questions later.

3. "It was a geometry book, which he had to hang by strings on the balcony of his apartment in the rue Condamine; the wind had to go through the book, choose its own problems, turn and tear out the pages. Suzanne did a small painting of it, '*Marcel's Unhappy Readymade*.' That's all that's left, since the wind tore it up. It amused me to bring the idea of happy and unhappy into readymades, and then the rain, the wind, the pages flying, it was an amusing idea." Marcel Duchamp, in Pierre Cabanne, *Entretiens avec Marcel Duchamp* (Paris: Belfond, 1967), *Dialogues with Marcel Duchamp* (London: Thames and Hudson, 1971; repub. Da Capo Press, 1987), 61.

4. André Breton, in Michel Sanouillet, *Dada à Paris* IV (Paris: Pauvert, 1965), 443.

5. Tristan Tzara, "Pour faire un poème dadaïste," *Littérature* 15 (July 1920), *Dada manifeste sur l'amour faible et l'amour amer*, 8, in *Oeuvres complètes* vol.1 (Paris: Flammarion, 1975), 382.

6. Tristan Tzara was also one of the authors, with Jean Arp and Walter Serner, of the passage in the *Dada Almanac* from 1920 that allegedly inspired Moholy-Nagy: "the good painter was recognized, for instance, by the fact that he ordered his works from a carpenter, giving his specifications on the phone." Richard Huelsenbeck, ed., *The Dada Almanac* (London: Atlas Press, 1993), 95. Perhaps his goal was to protest against the elitist notion of art practice as a separate sphere that was reserved for specialists and to encourage ordinary people to write poetry, but if this is true, the ironic tone of the text would not be appropriate. Peter Bürger sees it as an invitation extended to anyone and everyone to make art: "Given the avant-gardiste intention to do away with art as a sphere that is separate from the praxis of life, it is logical to eliminate the antithesis between producer and recipient. It is no accident that both Tzara's instructions for the making of a Dadaist poem and Breton's for the writing of automatic texts have the character of recipes. This represents not only a polemical attack on the individual creativity of the artist; the recipe is to be taken quite literally as suggesting a possible activity on the part of the recipient. The automatic texts also should be read as guides to individual production. But such production is not to be understood as artistic production, but as part of a liberating life praxis. This is what is meant by Breton's demand that poetry be practiced (*pratiquer la poesie*)." Peter Bürger, *Theory of the Avant-Garde*, trans. Michael Shaw (Manchester: Manchester University Press, 1984), 53.

7. Krisztina Passuth, *Moholy-Nagy* (London: Thames and Hudson, 1985), 31–32. Moholy-Nagy later declared it was so simple that "I might even have done it over the telephone!," and so came into being his "telephone pictures." Passuth, *Moholy-Nagy*, 33, 394.

8. Wilfried Hou Je Bek, "Algorithmic Psychogeography" (2002), http://web.archive.org/web/20020207142455/http://www.socialfiction.org/psychogeography/algoeng.htm.

9. John Cage, *Silence: Lectures and Writings*, 2nd ed. (London: Marion Boyars, 1978), 35 (original work published in 1961).

10. John Cage, "An Autobiographical Statement" (1989), *Southwest Review* (1991), http://newalbion.com/artists/cagej/autobiog.html.

11. John Cage, *Indeterminacy: New Aspect of Form in Instrumental and Electronic Music. Ninety Stories by John Cage, with Music,* John Cage, reading; David Tudor, music, Folkways FT 3704, 1959, reissued as Smithsonian/Folkways CD DF 40804/5, 1992. See Eddie Kohler, http://www.lcdf.org/indeterminacy/index.cgi.

12. Cage, *Silence,* 260.

13. "The audience were given programs and three stapled cards, which provided instructions for their participation: 'The performance is divided into six parts. . . . Each part contains three happenings which occur at once. The beginning and end of each will be signaled by a bell. At the end of the performance two strokes of the bell will be heard. . . . There will be no applause after each set, but you may applaud after the sixth set if you wish.' These instructions also stipulated when audience members were required to change seats and move to the next of the three rooms into which the gallery was divided." Paul Schimmel, "Leap into the Void: Performance and the Object," in Paul Schimmel and Kristine Stiles, eds., *Out of Actions: Between Performance and the Object, 1949–1979* (Los Angeles: Museum of Contemporary Art, 1998), 61f. In activities carried out in "everyday life," Allan Kaprow relinquished the kind of creative control that he maintained in his happenings. These works could take the form of a mutual agreement or pact. For example, one time he and a friend decided "to do something nice for each other. And that nice event was to clean each other's kitchen floors. And so we arranged to trade keys, only it was decided that the way to do this event was going to be a little unusual. Instead of the usual mops and cleanser, we were going to use Q-tips and spit. Without going into it too deeply, what happened there was an apparently obsessive act, but one that was decided upon, not compelled. Both of us had the freedom to stop." Allan Kaprow, "Interview with Allan Kaprow," interview with Robert C. Morgan, *Journal of Contemporary Art* 4, no.2 (1991): 56–69, http://www.jca-online.com/kaprow.html.

14. Schimmel, "Leap into the Void: Performance and the Object."

15. Benesh movement notation uses abstract symbols based on figurative representations of the human body for the aesthetic and scientific study of all forms of human movement. Like Western music notation, Benesh notation uses a five-line staff that reads from left to right with bar lines to mark the passage of time. The five lines of the staff coincide with the head, shoulders, waist, knees, and floor (from top to bottom). Other signs designate the dimension and quality of the movement. A number of other systems exist, such as DanceWriting, which was developed by Valerie Sutton in 1972 and evolved into the International Movement Writing Alphabet (IMWA), an ordered set of symbols that can be used to record movement and gesture. Various specialized subsets of IMWA exist for writing movements of sign languages, dance choreography, classic mime, ice skating, and gymnastics. The IMWA currently has over 27,000 symbols. Each has a unique ID number that contains information about the category, group, symbol, variation, fill, and rotation. It uses eight categories—hand, movement, face, head, upper body, full body, space, and punctuation.

16. The location of the symbol on the staff defines the body part that it represents. The center line of the staff represents the center line of the body, and symbols on the right or left represent the right or left side of the body. The staff is read from bottom to top, and the length of a symbol defines the duration of the movement.

17. The categories of effort are space (direct or indirect), weight (strong or light), time (sudden or sustained), and flow (bound or free). These forms of notation do not deal with macro patterns. They are particularly suited to a certain type of movement or dance style and are not universal (they are not adapted for notating non-Western forms of dance). Because they aim at being complete, they take a long time to learn.

18. Robert Ellis Dunn, unpublished notes, March 30, 1980, quoted in Sally Banes, *Democracy's Body: Judson Dance Theatre, 1962–1964* (Durham: Duke University Press, 1993), 3.

19. Robert Ellis Dunn, interview, May 16, 1980, quoted in ibid., 7.

20. "The score consists of 10 sheets of paper and 12 tranparencies. The sheets of paper have drawings of 6 differentiated (in thickness and texture) curved lines. 10 of the transparencies have randomly distributed points (the amounts of points on the transparencies are 7, 12, 13, 17, 18, 19, 22, 26, 29, and 30). Another transparency has a grid, measuring two by ten inches, and the last one contains a straight line (10¾ inch). By superimposition the performer creates a structure from which a performance score can be made." http://www.johncage.info/workscage/fontana.html.

21. Ouvroir de Littérature Potentielle (Workshop of Potential Literature) was founded in 1960 by writer Raymond Quenneau and mathematician François Le Lionnais as a subcommittee of the Collège de Pataphysique (the science of imaginary solutions, according to Alfred Jarry). Its members included Georges Perec, Italo Calvino, and Jacques Roubaud.

22. Faced with the complexity of the modern media landscape, members of Fluxus developed "a taste for simplicity" through practices that Dick Higgins called Intermedia—"an art which is based on the underlying images that an artist has always used to make his point." Happenings, event pieces, and mixed media films helped Fluxus artists to find a new way of looking at things: "We do not ask any more to speak magnificently of taking arms against a sea of troubles; we want to see it done. The art which most directly does this is the one which allows this immediacy, with a minimum of distractions." Dick Higgins, "Statement on Intermedia," in *Dé-coll/age* 6, ed. Wolf Votstell (Frankfurt/New York: Typos Verlag/Something Else Press, 1967), http://www.artpool.hu/Fluxus/Higgins/intermedia2.html.

23. Ken Friedman, "Forty Years of Fluxus," http://www.artnotart.com/fluxus/kfriedman-fourty-years.html. An early version of this article was first published in 1989 as "Fluxus and Company," in *The Fluxus Reader* (New York: Wiley, 1998).

24. Yoko Ono, *Grapefruit: A Book of Instructions by Yoko Ono* (New York: Simon and Schuster, 1970).

25. Ibid.

26. James Robert Brown, *Stanford Encyclopedia of Philosophy*, http://plato.stanford.edu/entries/thought-experiment.

27. This is an excerpt from a January 1966 lecture that Yoko Ono gave at Wesleyan University. Quoted in Lucy Lippard, *Six Years: The Dematerialization of the Art Object from 1966 to 1972* (New York: Praeger, 1973), http://www.artnotart.com/fluxus/yono-lecture.html.

28. Unattributed text in *Potlatch* 1 (June 22, 1954), translation at http://www.notbored.org/game-of-the-week.html. Christel Hollevoet makes this comparison in her article "Wandering in the City," *The Power of the City: The City of Power* (New York: Whitney Museum, 1992), 35.

29. Yoko Ono's January 1966 lecture at Wesleyan University. See note 27.

30. "The most conspicuous of the mannerisms into which Painterly Abstraction has degenerated is what I call the 'Tenth Street touch' (after East Tenth Street in New York), which spread through abstract painting like a blight during the 1950s. The stroke left by a loaded brush or knife frays out, when the stroke is long enough, into streaks, ripples, and specks of paint. . . . What turned this constellation of stylistic features into something bad as art was its standardization, its reduction to a set of mannerisms, as a dozen, and then a thousand, artists proceeded to maul the same viscosities of paint, in more or less the same ranges of color, and with the same 'gestures,' into the same kind of picture." Clement Greenberg, "Post-Painterly Abstraction," catalog essay (Los Angeles: Los Angeles County Museum of Art, 1964), http://www.sharecom.ca/greenberg/ppaessay.html.

31. Sol LeWitt, "Paragraphs on Conceptual Art," *Artforum*5 no. 10 (June 1967): 79.

32. Sol LeWitt, 2000, quoted in http://www.sfmoma.org/about/press/press_news/releases/72.

33. Sidra Stich, *Yves Klein* (Stuttgart: Cantz Verlag, 1994), 173–177.

34. Artists had employed assistants and had their works fabricated before. Here, artists had works built to counter the myth of the artist's individual genius—to separate idea and crafted object. It is beyond the scope of this chapter to deal with the labor conditions that are involved in making contemporary art. On the role of artists' assistants, see Wade Saunders, "Making Art, Making Artists," *Art in America* (January 1993): http://allanmccollum.net/allanmcnyc/Wade_Saunders_all.html.

35. Calvin Tomkins, *Off the Wall* (Harmondsworth: Penguin, 1981), 71, 269.

36. Jan van der Marck, "Introduction," *Art By Telephone*, LP record (Chicago: Museum of Contemporary Art, 1969). http://www.ubu.com/sound/art_by_telephone.html .

37. Lucy Lippard, quoted in Wade Saunders, "Not Lost, Not Found: Bill Bollinger," *Art in America* 88, no. 3 (March 2000): 104–117, 143–144.

38. Altshuler, "Art by Instruction and the Pre-History of *Do It*," 29.

39. Ibid., 28.

40. "When an artist uses a conceptual form of art, it means that all of the planning and decisions are made beforehand and the execution is a perfunctory affair." LeWitt, "Paragraphs on Conceptual Art." See chapter 3.

41. LeWitt's wall drawings were (and still can be) carried out by others who follow his directions. After reducing his vocabulary to basic shapes, colors, and lines, he could give instructions such as these: "Three concentric arches. The outside one is blue; the middle red; and the inside one is yellow." *Wall Drawing 579*, November 1988. It was presented in a retrospective exhibition at

the Massachusetts Museum of Contemporary Art (Mass MoCA). http://www.massmoca.org/lewitt/walldrawing.php?id=579.

42. Adachiara Zevi, *Sol LeWitt Critical Texts* (Rome: Editrice Inonia, 1994), 95.

43. http://www.myartspace.com/blog/2008/04/art-space-talk-vito-acconci.html.

44. Vito Acconci, "Shelley Jackson talks with Vito Acconci," interview, 2006, http://www.believermag.com/issues/200612/?read=interview_acconci.

45. Ibid.

46. Ibid.

47. Ibid.

48. Sophie Calle, *Doubles jeux. Livre IV. A suivre* (Nimes: Actes Sud, 1998), 38.

49. So much so that we are reminded of Dashiell Hammett's behaviorist stories from the 1930s.

50. He used himself as a guinea pig: "I began by using my own person. I realized that I had to focus on myself—it became 'I' and 'me' . . . but there are other people in the world. So later I focused on how do I concentrate on him/her, or how do I concentrate on you while you concentrate on me? I think that it all began with that notion of movement, in that you move through the page, you move within yourself, you move within a space and back and forth. Gradually it becomes clear that you /the people are in a space. The question then is how to react to a space." http://www.designboom.com/eng/interview/acconci.html.

51. Calle, *Doubles jeux. Livre IV. A suivre*, 53.

52. Sophie Calle, *M'as-tu vue?*, exhibition catalogue (Paris: Editions du Centre Pompidou / Xavier Barral, 2003): 79.

53. When the rules are written in an unambiguous language to be performed by a computer, it is also known as software art. Software art generally is any artwork that uses concepts.

54. Lee Walton, *City System* (New York: City System, 2003). The original booklet is available on Walton's Web site, http://www.leewalton.com/work/projects/city_systems/index.html.

55. Kevin Lynch, *The Image of the City* (Cambridge: MIT Press, 1960), 129. One of Allan Kaprow's small scale "activities" from the late 1980s "required a participant to carry cinder blocks, one at a time, up five flights of stairs, then down again. The number of blocks corresponded to the carrier's age." David Antin, quoted in Holland Cotter, "Allan Kaprow, Creator of Artistic 'Happenings,' Dies at 78," *New York Times*, April 10, 2006, http://www.nytimes.com/2006/04/10/arts/design/10kaprow.html?_r=1&scp=2&sq=Allan+Kaprow&st=nyt.

56. Unless otherwise noted, Walton's remarks come from an email interview with the author, September 21, 2007.

57. Lee Walton, *City System* (New York: City System, 2003), 16.

58. Ibid., 5.

59. Such as the hypnotic therapy of Milton Erickson.

60. This, too, distorted our perception of *Ping!* predicated on the overlay of network and physical space.

61. Ivan Chtcheglov, "Formulary for a New Urbanism," http://www.bopsecrets.org/SI/Chtcheglov.htm.

62. See Gregory Bateson's theory of the double bind in "Toward a Theory of Schizophrenia," *Steps to an Ecology of Mind: Collected Essays in Anthropology, Psychiatry, Evolution, and Epistemology* (Chicago: University of Chicago Press, 1999) (original work published in 1972).

63. Kate Armstrong, email message to the author, September 21, 2007.

64. Ibid.

65. Kate Armstrong, "Ping!" Tapescript (2003, unpublished document).

66. Ibid.

67. Natalie Jeremijenko, founder of the Bureau of Inverse Technology (BIT), http://tech90s.walkerart.org/nj/transcript/nj_09.html.

68. It may be a bit pretentious to compare these passages to the "Chinese encyclopedia," the *Celestial Empire of Benevolent Knowledge* that was imagined by Jorge Luis Borges and quoted by Michel Foucault in the introduction to *The Order of Things: An Archaeology of Human Sciences* (New York: Vintage, 1994). They are strange but not excessively so to anyone familiar with Chtcheglov's visionary text. Nevertheless, many artists appreciate Borges's animal categories, which range from "a) belonging to the Emperor, b) embalmed" to "m) having just broken the water pitcher, n) that from a long way off look like flies" (ibid., xv.). The passage has been understood as relativizing the Western schemas of classification because Foucault wrote: "This book first arose out of a passage in Borges, out of the laughter that shattered, as I read the passage, all the familiar landmarks of thought—*our* thought, the thought that bears the stamp of our age and our geography—breaking up all the ordered surfaces and all the planes with which we are accustomed to tame the wild profusion of existing things and continuing long afterwards to disturb and threaten with collapse our age-old definitions between the Same and the Other" (ibid., xv).

69. Kate Armstrong, email message to the author, September 21, 2007.

70. "It is not, of course, a traditional relationship with site specificity. It is more like a critical or experiential framework that is activated and applied to any place or time, becoming specific the way any idea becomes specific—by being applied to a certain context. Its relationship to place becomes almost like a subject matter, like the work is a set of ideas that implicate different cities when applied to those cities." Kate Armstrong, ibid.

71. First published in the French news magazine *Le Nouvel Observateur* in July 1967.

72. Lee Walton has carried out similar negotiations. One summer day in 2003, he purchased a thirty-five-pound weight from Copeland's Sports on Fourth Street and Market Street in downtown

San Francisco, carried the weight six and a half miles to another Copeland's Sports, and simply returned it. *35 Pounds*, San Francisco, 2003.

73. It was part of an exhibition/workshop program entitled "En marche," organized by Mélanie Perrier at the Université Paris 1 on April 1, 2009.

74. Thomas de Quincey, *Confessions of an English Opium Eater* (Teddington: Echo Library, 2006), 72–73.

75. Simon Sadler, *The Situationist City* (Cambridge: MIT Press, 1998), 88.

76. Philippe Vasset, *Un livre blanc* (Paris: Fayard, 2007).

77. Wilfried Hou Je Bek published a series of "release notes" for the project *.Walk* at frequent intervals during 2003 and 2004 on his Social Fiction Web site (http://www.socialfiction.org). This Web site has gone offline. Excerpts from the *.Walk* project (release notes) can be found at http://runme.org/feature/read/+dot-walk/+31 and on http://rhizome.org/discuss/view/6655.

78. Ibid.

79. Wilfried Hou Je Bek, "The Technology Will Find Uses for the Street on Its Own" (originally published in 2003 on the socialfiction.org Web site), Cryptoforestry blog at http://cryptoforest.blogspot.fr/2010/11/technology-will-find-uses-for-street-on.html.

80. Wilfried Hou Je Bek, "*.Walk* release note #4." No longer available online. Copy in the author's archives dated September 11, 2003.

81. Wilfried Hou Je Bek, interview with the author, 2005 (published in French). Karen O'Rourke, "Questions à Wilfried Hou Je Bek," *Art++*, edited by David-Olivier Lartigaud (Orléans: Editions HYX, 2011), 292–299. Florian Cramer sees *.Walk* as "romantic deconstruction of computing and its concealed metaphysics of architecture." Florian Cramer, http://www.runme.org/feature/read/+dot-walk/+31.

82. Hou Je Bek interview (2005).

83. A player from Seattle wrote: "I had a definite heart-stopping moment when my concerns suddenly switched from desperately trying to escape, to desperately hoping that the runner chasing me had not been run over by a reversing truck (that's what it sounded like had happened)." Blast Theory, http://www.blasttheory.co.uk/bt/work_cysmn.html.

84. See http://www.blasttheory.co.uk/bt/work_rider_spoke.html.

85. http://www.blasttheory.co.uk/bt/work_yougetme.html.

86. Daniel Wetzel, "I Try to Speak about Reality," in Helgard Haug, Stefan Kaegi, and Daniel Wetzel, "Interview with Patrice Blaser," 29 January 2004, http://www.rimini-protokoll.de/website/en/article_2572.html.

87. Rimini Protokoll, diary entry for October 25, 2004, "Here the city has expanded without any plan," in notes from the diary of Rimini Protokoll in Calcutta and Berlin, Part 1, trans. Sabita Dhar. No longer available online.

88. Stefan Kaegi, email to the author, September 5, 2008.

89. Wetzel, "I Try to Speak about Reality."

90. Stefan Kaegi, email to the author.

91. As Stefan Kaegi noted in a talk at La Villette on February 19, 2010.

92. Stefan Kaegi, email to the author.

93. Ibid.

94. See chapter 6.

95. http://humanchess.typepad.com/project/2004/04/how_to_play_hum.html.

96. http://humanchess.typepad.com/lowereastside.

97. Did monarchs ever play human-scale chess using real people in which at each move, an actual fight would take place? Whichever player survived took over the spot. Note that this connotation is intentional. Sharilyn Neidhardt also plays in a band with the facetious name "Weapons of Mass Destruction."

98. Daniel Wetzel, "I Try to Speak about Reality,"

99. Richard Long, in Sean O'Hagan, "One Step Beyond," *The Observer*, May 10, 2009, http://www.guardian.co.uk/artanddesign/2009/may/10/art-richard-long.

100. Another borderline case is *Tour de Fence*, in which one part is a classic shaped walk that is carried out by two performers according to a predesigned figure (*D'Fence Cuts*). The other part begins with a group of fence climbers who scramble up Bristol's finest fences. We do not know how they arrived at their selection of fences, their classification of techniques, or even what sort of overall plan the climbers followed.

Chapter 5

1. Till Roeskens, "Comment aller chez Krimhilde" in *Rafraîchir l'écran* (Refreshing the Screen), curated by Julien Maire, *Livraison* 5 (Strasbourg: Rhinocéros, 2005).

2. The way of Saint James. Later, maps were drawn to describe a territory by combining information culled both from observation and received traditions. See Michel de Certeau, *The Practice of Everyday Life*, trans. Steven Rendall (Berkeley: University of California, 1984), 120–121.

3. Kevin Lynch, *The Image of the City* (Cambridge: MIT Press, 1960), 3. The following paragraphs present Lynch's thesis.

4. http://www.documentsdartistes.org/artistes/roeskens/repro6-5.html.

5. See W. H. Matthews, *Mazes and Labyrinths: A General Account of Their History and Development* (Charleston: Forgotten Books, 2008) (original work published by Longman's, Green and Co. in 1923).

6. "At one sole glance, one can discern both the Cartesian layout of the so-called labyrinth at the Botanical Gardens and the following warning sign: NO PLAYING IN THE LABYRINTH. There could be no more succinct summary of the spirit of this entire civilization. The very one that we will, in the end, bring down." See "Ariadne Unemployed," *Potlatch* 9–11 (August 17–31, 1954), http://www.notbored.org/ariadne.html. Guy-Ernest Debord, "Projet pour un labyrinthe éducatif," December 8, 1956. In *Guy Debord Œuvres,* 284.

7. Ibid.

8. Constant Nieuwenhuys, "*New Babylon*: A Nomadic Town," in *New Babylon* exhibition catalog (The Hague: Haags Gemeetenmuseum, 1974), http://www.notbored.org/new-babylon.html.

9. Submitted to SPUR, the German section of Situationist International, in 1960. See Simon Sadler, *The Situationist City* (Cambridge: MIT Press, 1998), 7 n. 18.

10. Constant, "*New Babylon.*"

11. Ibid.

12. By Daniel Spoerri, Jean Tinguely, Robert Rauschenberg, Martial Raysse, Niki de Saint-Phalle, and Per Olof Ultveld.

13. Museum of Modern Art, https://www.moma.org/interactives/exhibitions/2009/inandout/timeline.html.

14. Rauschenberg's pieces were not discarded. Denys Riout, *Qu'est-ce que l'art moderne?* (Paris: Gallimard, 2000), 441–442. See also Marie Escorne, "Le labyrinthe dans les arts du XXe siècle. Les arts du XXe siècle dans le labyrinthe," *Amaltea, Revista de mitocritica* 1 (2009): 253.

15. Catherine Grenier, "Robert Morris and Melancholy: The Dark Side of the Work," in *Robert Morris 1961–1994: Catalogue du MNAM*, ed. Catherine Grenier (Paris: Centre Georges Pompidou, 1995), 316.

16. Robert Morris, "Simon Grant Interviews Robert Morris" (December 1, 2011), http://www.tate.org.uk/context-comment/articles/simon-grant-interviews-robert-morris. "I want to fashion a conceptual, mental, psychological and physical space. I want to make a world within which I alone move amongst my objects. Reading Wittgenstein's remarks in the *Tractatus* that 'I am my world (The microcosm),' my heart skips a beat. I make a 50-foot long plywood *Passageway,* which narrows as it curves. Two arcs of a circle converging. I wedge my body between the narrowing walls, which curve ahead and out of sight. I am suspended, embraced and held by my world. I listen to the faint sound of the hidden mechanical heartbeat I have installed over the ceiling of *Passageway.* There is nothing to look at here in this curving space which diminishes to zero. In this blind space whatever constitutes the 'I' of my subjectivity evaporates and I think of that other remark of Wittgenstein: 'The subject does not belong to the world: rather, it is a limit of the world.'" Ibid. Elsewhere, the scrawled "Fuck you, Bob Morris" is attributed to Yvonne Rainer. Julie H. Reiss notes that Morris was more authoritarian about spectator participation than Allan Kaprow was. Julie H. Reiss, *From Margin to Center: The Spaces of Installation Art* (Cambridge: MIT Press, 2001).

17. "Simon Grant Interviews Robert Morris," http://www.tate.org.uk/context-comment/articles/simon-grant-interviews-robert-morris.

18. Since then he has created spaces such as the vast *Lyon Labyrinth*, onto which he projected video recordings of performances from the 1960s (*Arizona, Site, Waterman Switch*). When video was added, the labyrinth became a sort of metaphysical architecture and "constituted a maze in time as well as space that was characteristic of the artist's investigations." See Anne Dagbert, "Robert Morris," *Artforum International,* September 1, 2000: http://findarticles.com/p/articles/mi_m0268/is_1_39/ai_65649503.

19. Ilya Kabakov, "'*The Corridor (My Mother's Album)*,' 1988," *The Text as the Basis of Visual Expression* (Oktagon: Cologne, 2000), 369.

20. Ilya Kabakov, *Installations, 1983–1995* (Paris: Editions du Centre Pompidou, 1995. The photographs of the coastal city of Berdyansk were taken by the artist's uncle, a professional photographer. See Rachel Taylor's description at http://www.tate.org.uk/servlet/ViewWork?workid=138&tabview=text.

21. Kabakov, *Installations, 1983–1995.*

22. Garcia Rossi, Le Parc, Morellet, Yvaral, Sobrino, and Stein.

23. Letter written by GRAV to Jean Leering. Cf. explanations by Maïté Vissault. Archives Frank Popper: http://www.archivesdelacritiquedart.org/uploads/dossiers_archive/pdf/5/26_Popper.pdf (my translation).

24. Bruce Nauman: "Stairway" (Art 21 Interview with Bruce Nauman), http://www.art21.org/texts/bruce-nauman/interview-bruce-nauman-stairway. "The way the property runs, you can never see the whole thing at one time. . . . Because there is no regular rhythm to going up and down, you have to take each step and watch it. And so it requires you to pay quite a lot of attention, even more down than up, because it's a little less comfortable going down. But nothing is so abrupt that it totally catches you off guard. But you can feel yourself, your body, kind of measuring where your foot has to go at each step. You can't ever quite find a rhythm and it makes you very aware of yourself. . . . You're now a participant in the work. You're very aware as you walk up or down that your body has to make an adjustment at each step. And so you have to figure when you can change your weight and where your foot is going to be placed and how high you step or how far down you step. And nothing is so great that you have to struggle with it, but everything is a little bit of an adjustment. So you're kept a little off-balance all the time, adjusting yourself. . . . I'm hoping people can exercise a little more choice [than rats in his rat maze]. And there's no reward at the end of this one, except getting to the end." Ibid.

25. See Doug Hall and Sally Jo Fifer, *Illuminating Video: An Essential Guide to Video Art* (San Francisco: Aperture/Bay Area Video Coalition, 1990), 186.

26. Dan Graham, interview by Eric de Bruyn, in Gloria Moure, ed., *Dan Graham* (Barcelona: Fundacio Antoni Tapies, 1998), 203.

27. *Two-Way Mirror Hedge Labyrinth*, 1989–1993, San Diego, in *New Labyrinth for Nantes*, 1992–1994, Nantes, mirrors, glass, and ivy. For the Minneapolis Sculpture Garden, he built *Two-Way Mirror Punched Steel Hedge Labyrinth*, 1994–1996, a large (508 in. × 206 5/16 in. × 90 in.) geometric maze with walls that are made of both transparent and reflective surfaces and that juxtapose

industrial and natural materials—stainless steel, glass, and arborvitae. See Walker Art Center, Minneapolis, 1998, http://collections.walkerart.org/item/object/7673. Another pavilion, *Two-Way Mirror Curved Hedge Zig-Zag Labyrinth*, 1996, was made of glass, steel, arborvitae nigra (7½ feet high with a radius of 15 feet) and was designed for the plaza of the Middlebury College Center for the Arts, Middlebury, Vermont. http://www.middlebury.edu/arts/campus/artexhib/dan_graham_two_way_mirror. Rooftops are at the Dia Center in New York and the San Francisco Museum of Modern Art.

28. "—so maybe virtual reality will lead itself to the next development." Conversation before a live audience at the Institute of Contemporary Art, London, March 1992, first published by the ICA in 1994, reprinted in Dan Graham and Alexander Alberro, *Two-Way Mirror Power* (Cambridge: MIT Press, 1999), 153.

29. Jean-Pierre Balpe, "Poétiques," http://poetiques.blogg.org/date-2005-06-10-billet-168369.html; Maurice Benayoun, http://www.benayoun.com/projet.php?id=20.

30. Alexander Trevi, Pruned blog, http://pruned.blogspot.com/2010/05/labyrinth-of-ikea.html. "Show rooms seem to flow endlessly into other show rooms, never toward an exit. Countless bounds but boundless. The same corner sofa with the taste-affirming Swedish appellation is passed by a dozen times. On the thirteenth pass, comes overwhelming desire, mortgage payments be damned." Ibid.

31. Yoko Ono, 1965, quoted in Christine Macel, *Jeppe Hein*, trans. Charles Penwarden (Paris: Éditions du Centre Pompidou, 2005), 34.

32. Yoko Ono, interview in *Anna* magazine, Helsinki, May 1999, quoted on the artist's Flickr page, http://www.flickr.com/photos/yokoonoofficial/2891959205.

33. Marcel Brion, quoted in Macel, *Jeppe Hein*, 42.

34. Quoted in Lynch, *The Image of the City*, 182 n. 8.

35. Sigmund Freud, *The Complete Letters to Wilhelm Fliess (1887–1904)*, ed. Joseph M. Masson (Cambridge: Belknap Press, 1985), 365.

36. The earliest known treatise, *Rhetorica ad Herennium,* develops a theory of artificial memory that "includes backgrounds and images." Backgrounds are "complete and conspicuous" scenes—"for example, a house, an intercolumnar space, a recess, an arch, or the like. An image is, as it were, a figure, mark, or portrait of the object we wish to remember; for example, if we wish to recall a horse, a lion, or an eagle, we must place its image in a definite background." To be able to stimulate the memory, these "active images" ("imagines agentes") must strike the imagination. Unusual, obscene, odd, grotesque, or violent images are "strong and sharp and suitable for awakening recollection": "if we set up images that are not many or vague, but doing something; if we assign to them exceptional beauty or singular ugliness; if we dress some of them with crowns or purple cloaks, for example, so that the likeness may be more distinct to us; or if we somehow disfigure them, as by introducing one stained with blood or soiled with mud or smeared with red paint, so that its form is more striking, or by assigning certain comic effects to our images, for that, too, will ensure our remembering them more readily." It is best to arrange the

background scenes in logical series to be able to summon them up in the right order. [Cicero], *Rhetorica ad Herennium*, trans. Harry Caplan (Cambridge: Loeb Classical Library, 1954), III,xxii, 209.

37. Simonides of Ceos, a poet of the fifth century BCE, is said to have discovered this method. According to a story told by Cicero, Simonides's patron, Scopas, reproached him at a banquet for devoting too much time to praising Castor and Pollux in a panegyric celebrating Scopas's victory in a chariot race. Scopas paid him only half the fee they had agreed on, suggesting that he ask the twin gods for the remainder. Shortly afterward, Simonides was told that two young men wished to speak to him, and after he left the banquet hall, the roof fell in and crushed Scopas and his guests. During the excavation of the rubble, Simonides was asked to identify those who had been killed. He remembered all of the guests' positions (*loci*) at the table and therefore was able to identify them for burial. After thanking Castor and Pollux for paying their half of the fee by saving his life, Simonides used this experience to develop the "memory theater" or "memory palace"—an art of memory that was widely used in antiquity: "He inferred that persons desiring to train this faculty (of memory) must select places and form mental images of the things they wish to remember and store those images in the places, so that the order of the places will preserve the order of the things, and the images of the things will denote the things themselves, and we shall employ the places and the images respectively as a wax writing-tablet and the letters written upon it." Marcus Tullius Cicero, *De oratore*, II, lxxxvi, 351–354, trans. E. W. Sutton, completed with an introduction by H. Rackham, Loeb Classics Edition (London: Heinemann, 1942). On the interpretation of these texts, see Frances Yates, *The Art of Memory* (London: Pimlico, 2001), 17–41 (original work published by Routledge and Kegan Paul in 1966). In addition to Cicero and the anonymous author of Ad Herennium, we owe a third author, Quintilian, the "clear directions about how to go through the rooms of the house." Ibid. 38.

38. Rob M. Kitchin, "Cognitive Maps: What Are They and Why Study Them?," *Journal of Environmental Psychology* 14 (1994): 1–19.

39. Tom Vanderbilt, "Cerebral Cities," in *ELSE/WHERE: MAPPING—New Cartographies of Networks and Territories*, ed. Janet Abrams and Peter Hall (Minneapolis: University of Minneapolis Design Institute, 2006), 176–183.

40. He went on to suggest that it was not. Maurice Merleau-Ponty, *Phénomenologie de la perception* (Paris: Gallimard, 1945), trans. Colin Smith, *Phenomenology of Perception* (London: Routledge, 1962, 2005), 77.

41. Mélodie Gonzales, email message to the author, July 30, 2008.

42. E. C. Tolman, "Cognitive Maps in Rats and Men," *Psychological Review* 55, no. 4 (July 1948): 189–208. 194.

43. Lynch, *The Image of the City*, 47.

44. Districts were, in Lynch's words, "medium-to-large sections of the city . . . recognizable as having some common identifying character." ibid., 47–48.

45. Ibid., 47.

46. Scott Snibbe, "Boundary Functions," http://www.snibbe.com/projects/interactive/boundaryfunctions.

47. Ibid.

48. From the catalog of works owned by the FRAC (regional collections of contemporary art).

49. Jeppe Hein, quoted in Anna McCarthy, "Focus on Jeppe Hein," *Houghton Hall Education Newsletter* (January 2009): 3.

50. Robert Morris, "Notes on Sculpture, Part 2," *Continuous Project Altered Daily* (Cambridge: MIT Press, 1993), 15.

51. GRAV, quoted in Macel, *Jeppe Hein*, 33.

52. Jan L. Souman, Ilja Frissen, Manish N. Sreenivasa, and Marc O. Ernst, "Walking Straight into Circles," *Current Biology* 19, no. 18 (August 20, 2009): 1538–1542.

53. David Lewis, "The Way of the Nomad," in *From Earlier Fleets: Hemisphere—An Aboriginal Anthology* (1978), 78–82, cited in David Turnbull, *Maps Are Territories, Science Is an Atlas: A Portfolio of Exhibits*, (Chicago: University of Chicago Press, 1989), 52–53.

54. Lynch, *The Image of the City*, 124.

55. "All [their] words for 'country' . . . are the same as the words for 'line.'" Bruce Chatwin, *The Songlines* (New York: Vintage Classics, 1998), 57 (original work published in 1987). Tim Ingold prefers the term *meshwork* to describe their intersecting paths. Tim Ingold, *Lines: A Brief History* (London: Routledge, 2007), 80. Elsewhere, Chatwin refers to them as "the labyrinth of invisible pathways which meander all over Australia and are known to Europeans as 'Dreaming-tracks' or 'Songlines'; to the Aboriginals as the 'Footprints of the Ancestors' or the 'Way of the Law.' Aboriginal Creation myths tell of the legendary totemic being who wandered over the continent in the Dreamtime, singing out the name of everything that crossed their path—birds, animals, plants, rocks, waterholes—and so singing the world into existence." Chatwin, *The Songlines*, 2

56. Dreaming tracks can move underground, above ground, or into the air in the case of birds. The songlines crossed the whole continent, even the wilderness of Wollemi National Park, which is one of the roughest landscapes in Australia and is where in 2003 archeologists discovered a cluster of sites of rock art. Shaun Hooper, a Wiradjuri man and a leader of the project, explains, "All across Australia there's pathways that people could use to move about the country. As long as you knew the protocol and the proper ceremonies associated with each place, you could use those pathways." James Woodford, "Songlines across the Wollemi," *Sydney Morning Herald*, September 27, 2003, http://www.smh.com.au/articles/2003/09/26/1064083186183.html.

57. The bark paintings help children to "put a map in their heads," writes David Lewis, who reminds us of our own abstract maps: "The map diagrams on Sydney suburban trains are quite as abstract as anything drawn by Aborigines." Lewis, "The Way of the Nomad," 53.

58. The fact that people from oral cultures talk continually may also have some bearing on their extraordinary feats of navigation. Katherine Milton notes that "tropical rain forest Indians talk

endlessly, a characteristic I believe reflects the importance of the oral transmission of culture." Katherine Milton, "Civilization and Its Discontents," *Natural History* (March 1992): 39, cited in Denis Wood, *The Power of Maps* (New York: Guildford Press, 1992), 44. David Lewis makes the same remark about the Australian Aborigine groups that he traveled with. Lewis, "The Way of the Nomad," quoted in Turnbull, 53.

59. Turnbull notes that "David Lewis's example . . . shows that relative spatial location is indeed preserved. . . . It is accomplished through the telling of a myth that 'connects' the salient features of the landscape in the way the travelers experienced them. In other words, the bark painting can be read as a map only if you have a thorough understanding of the forms of life of Aboriginal culture. Likewise, European maps are not autonomous. They can only be read through the myths that Europeans tell about their relationship to the land." Turnbull, *Maps Are Territories*, exhibit 9. In recent history, the Aboriginal painter Shorty Lungkarta Tjungurrayi created a series of water paintings that depict actual sources of water in his county. He knew these places south of Lake MacDonald from memories and ancestral stories. Fred Myers, "The Power of Papunya Painting," *Australian Aboriginal Art Magazine* (March 2009): 45.

60. Lewis, "The Way of the Nomad."

61. Guy Deutscher, "Does Your Language Shape How You Think?," *New York Times*, August 26, 2010, http://www.nytimes.com/2010/08/29/magazine/29language-t.html?pagewanted=all. Deutscher cites research by John Haviland and Stephen Levinson that shows that Guugu Yimithirr uses cardinal directions to describe space.

62. Barbara Glowczewski,"The Paradigm of Indigenous Australians: Anthropological Phantasms, Artistic Creations, and Political Resistance," in Géraldine Le Roux and Lucienne Strivay, eds., *La revanche des genres: Art contemporain australien* (Paris: Diff Art / Aïnu Éditions, 2007), 96.

63. Barbara Glowczewski, "Lines and Criss-Crossings: Hyperlinks in Australian Indigenous Narratives," *Media International Australia* 116 (2005): 24–35.

64. Ibid.

65. Henri Lefebvre, *La production de l'espace*, 4th ed. (Paris: Anthropos, 2000), 72 *The Production of Space*, trans. Donald Nicholson-Smith (London: Blackwell, 1991), 59 (original work published in 1974).

66. Louis Althusser, "Ideological State Apparatuses," in *Lenin and Philosophy* (New York, 1972), quoted in Frederic Jameson, *Postmodernism or, The Cultural Logic of Late Capitalism* (Durham, NC: Duke University Press, 1991), 51.

67. Ibid., 51, see also 415.

Chapter 6

1. Henri Lefebvre, *La production de l'espace*, 4th ed. (Paris: Anthropos, 2000), 102–103, *The Production of Space*, trans. Donald Nicholson-Smith (London: Basil Blackwell, 1991) (original work published in 1974).

2. Thierry Davila, *Marcher, créer. Déplacements, flâneries, dérives dans l'art de la fin du 20e siècle* (Paris: Éditions du Regard, 2002), 63–64.

3. Alÿs's first *Leak* performance was created for the twenty-fourth São Paulo Biennial in 1995. The films were made by Julien Devaux. On a similar walk between two museums in Stockholm, Alÿs, wearing a blue sweater, dropped a loose thread of yarn, gradually unraveling the pullover as he made his way across the city (*The Loser / The Winner*, 1998).

4. Francis Alÿs, press release for his exhibition *Sometimes doing something poetic can become political and sometimes doing something political can become poetic*. David Zwirner Gallery, New York, February 2007.

5. Marc Tuters and Kazys Varnellis note that this term "is derived from the locative noun case in the Latvian language, which indicates location." Marc Tuters and Kazys Varnellis, "Beyond Locative Media," http://networkedpublics.org/locative_media/beyond_locative_media.

6. Jo Walsh, email interview with the author, March 15, 2005.

7. Ben Russell, "TCM Online Reader Introduction," *TCM Online Reader*, http://web.archive.org/web/20060720212044/http://locative.net/tcmreader/index.php?intro;russell.

8. Tuters and Varnellis, "Beyond Locative Media."

9. Stephen Wilson, "Excerpt from Proposal 'Potential Contributions of the Arts to Research Agendas in Ubiquitous Computing and Gesture Recognition,'" http://userwww.sfsu.edu/~swilson/papers/wilson.ubi.gesture.html; Anne Galloway, "Intimations of Everyday Life: Ubiquitous Computing and the City," *Cultural Studies* 18, nos. 2–3 (2004): 384–408.

10. Mark Weiser, "The Computer for the 21st Century," *Scientific American* 265, no. 3 (1991): 3–11.

11. Ibid., 4.

12. Ibid.

13. Simon Faithfull walked along the Greenwich meridian in a recent project.

14. Steve Mann, "Sousveillance: Inverse Surveillance in Multimedia Imaging," *Proceedings of the Twelfth Annual ACM International Conference on Multimedia* (New York: ACM, 2004), 620–627; Steve Mann, "Existential Technology: Wearable Computing Is Not the Real Issue!," *Leonardo* 36, no. 1 (2003): 19–25; Steve Mann, Jason Nolan, and Barry Wellman, "Sousveillance: Inventing and Using Wearable Computing Devices for Data Collection in Surveillance Environments," *Surveillance and Society* 1, no. 3 (July 2003): 331–355.

15. Volker Grassmuck, "Explorations into the Realms of Possibility: Sketches on the work of Masaki Fujihata," in *Small Fish*, ed. Kiyoshi Furukawa, Masaki Fujihata, and Wolfgang Münch, digital arts edition (Karlsruhe: ZKM, Ostfildern, 1999), 42f. At the time, wireless Internet service was rare, so most data gathered in the field had to be taken back to the computer lab to be processed and uploaded.

16. A more precise reading, made by averaging the results, was mapped inside the installation. Laura Kurgan sums up the project: "Taking advantage of a then newly operational network of 24 Global Positioning Satellites, this installation recorded the traces, and presented in real time, an attempt to inhabit the unruly and disorienting spaces of satellite mapping system." Laura Kurgan and Xavier Costa, eds., *You Are Here: Architecture and Information Flows* (Barcelona: Museu D'Art Contemporani, 1995).

17. Stephen Wilson, "The Telepresent," http://userwww.sfsu.edu/%7Eswilson/art/telepresent/telepresent.html.

18. In an email message to the author, September 30, 2010. The student may have been inspired by Bureau of Inverse Technology's *Suicide Box* from 1996.

19. Marcel Mauss, "Essai sur le don: Forme et raison de l'échange dans les sociétés archaïques" (1902–1903) (first published in *l'Année Sociologique*, seconde série, 1923–1924). Digital edition: Jean-Marie Tremblay, Feb. 17, 2002. http://classiques.uqac.ca/classiques/mauss_marcel/socio_et_anthropo/2_essai_sur_le_don/essai_sur_le_don.pdf.

20. The only direct benefit that they receive from peers building on their work is an enhanced reputation. Warren Hagstrom, "Gift Giving as an Organizing Principle in Science," in *Science in Context: Readings in the Sociology of Science*, ed. Barry Barnes and David Edge (Cambridge: MIT Press, 1982). It can also gain one what Pierre Bourdieu called "cultural capital." See Pierre Bourdieu, "Les trois états du capital culturel," *Actes de la Recherche en Sciences Sociales* 30 (1979): 3–6.

21. "Gift cultures are adaptations not to scarcity but to abundance. They arise in populations that do not have significant material-scarcity problems with survival goods. We can observe gift cultures in action among aboriginal cultures living in ecozones with mild climates and abundant food. We can also observe them in certain strata of our own society, especially in show business and among the very wealthy. Abundance makes command relationships difficult to sustain and exchange relationships an almost pointless game. In gift cultures, social status is determined not by what you control but by *what you give away*. Thus the Kwakiutl chieftain's potlach party. Thus the multi-millionaire's elaborate and usually public acts of philanthropy. And thus the hacker's long hours of effort to produce high-quality open-source code." Eric A. Raymond, "Homesteading the Noosphere," http://catb.org/~esr/writings/homesteading/homesteading.

22. Wilson, "The Telepresent."

23. Stephen Wilson in an email message to the author, September 30, 2010.

24. http://www.aimglobal.org/technologies/RFID/what_is_rfid.asp.

25. Eduardo Kac in an email message to the author, August 31, 2010.

26. Ju Row Farr explains their choice: "It's about a sense of living now, in the moment. I'm not quite sure apart from commercially what the value of recording is. . . . in our work it doesn't feel like drawing a line is meaningful. Every time you go to the theatre or to a club to have a live experience, it's always different. . . . Sometimes the positions on the map are being recorded, but it's strictly for us to learn, and we don't offer it to the members because seeing the trail doesn't

suit the piece of work." Ju Row Farr, interview with Andrea Urlberger, http://www.ciren.org/ciren/laboratoires/Paysage_Technologique/art/blast/index.html.

27. From the Future Applications Lab (Viktoria Institute) and PLAY Studio (Interactive Institute).

28. Lalya Gaye, Margot Jacobs, Ramia Mazé, and Daniel Skoglund, "Sonic City," http://www.viktoria.se/fal/projects/soniccity.

29. This must be done discreetly to avoid getting in the way of what the user wants to do. Lalya Gaye, "Mapping New Media to Physical Urban Space: Strategies and Challenges for Everyday Creativity," PLAN:ICA workshop, London, UK, February 2005, http://www.viktoria.se/%7Elalya/texts/Gaye_PLAN_ICA.pdf.

30. Composed of artist Natacha Roussel, designer Michel Panouillot, and electronic engineer Michael Roy. Jumpsuit design by Jeanne Laurent. http://www.digitalarti.com/fr/blog/natacha_roussel/interact_wearing.

31. Their further claim that these two types of locative media "correspond to two archetypal poles winding their way through late twentieth-century art, critical art, and phenomenology" is debatable. Tuters and Varnellis, "Beyond Locative Media."

32. Jeremy Wood, *Writing over the Earth*, GPS drawing, http://www.gpsdrawing.com.

33. Ibid.

34. Jeremy Wood, post on the Synapse discussion list, July 25, 2008. http://list.synapse.net.au//pipermail/elist/2008-July/000150.html.

35. Wood also makes prints, maps, and sculptures that he exhibits in art galleries. Jeremy Wood, http://www.gpsdrawing.com. The custom software, GPSograph, was developed for the project by Hugh Pryor. Alex Garfitt developed an online database for the management and viewing of GPS and GIS data.

36. Teri Rueb, email message to the author, November 15, 2011.

37. Ibid.

38. Rueb's *Choreography* had a budget of about $700. The custom software was written by In Choi, an undergraduate computer science student at the University of Maryland, Baltimore. Ibid.

39. Of the four hundred people who responded to the public call, sixty were invited to participate. Rebecca Ross, "Perils of Precision," in *ELSE/WHERE: MAPPING—New Cartographies of Networks and Territories*. ed. Janet Abrams, and Peter Hall (Minneapolis: University of Minnesota Design Institute, 2006), 184–186.

40. "A GPS tracking unit is a device that uses the Global Positioning System to determine the precise location of a vehicle, person, or other asset to which it is attached and to record the position of the asset at regular intervals. The recorded location data can be stored within the tracking unit, or it may be transmitted to a central location data base, or internet-connected computer, using a cellular (GPRS), radio, or satellite modem embedded in the unit. This allows

the asset's location to be displayed against a map backdrop either in real-time or when analysing the track later, using customized software. Such systems are not new; amateur radio operators have been operating their free GPS-based nationwide realtime Automatic Packet Reporting System (APRS) since 1982." http://en.wikipedia.org/wiki/GPS_tracking.

41. The coordinates were sent via general packet radio service (GPRS). The Waag society developed software to fetch these data and project them in the exhibition space using a beamer. In 2009, the artist published a detailed technical description on the project Web site, http://realtime.waag.org.

42. A runner who was training for the marathon ran the same path over and over again, reinforcing his accumulated miles while thickening the lines that defined his route. http://realtime.waag.org.

43. Jean-François Augoyard, *Step by Step, Everyday Walks in a French Urban Housing Project* , trans. D. A. Curtis (Minneapolis: University of Minnesota Press, 2007), 19.

44. Esther Polak, "Elastic Mapping: Implications of a GPS Drawing Robot in Times of Locative Media," Paper presented at the Fifteenth International Symposium on Electronic Art (ISEA 2009), Belfast. http://www.elasticmapping.net/PolakISEA-ElasticMappping.pdf. In 2009, seven years later, she built a Web site showing their archived traces.

45. Ibid., 1.

46. As Rebecca Ross notes, "Living and mapping become dynamically linked." Ross, "Perils of Precision," 186.

47. See the Sense*able* City Lab Web site, http://senseable.mit.edu.

48. Produced by the Invisible Dynamics program at the San Francisco Exploratorium. See http://cabspotting.org/index.html. Project Websites: In Transit: http://cabspotting.org/projects/intransit and Fly Cab: http://cabspotting.org/projects/flycab.

49. Michel de Certeau, *L'invention du quotidien. Tome I. Arts de fair* (Paris: Gallimard, coll. Folio, 1980, 1990), *The Practice of Everyday Life*, trans. Steven Rendall (Berkeley: University of California Press, 1984), 117–118.

50. Ibid., xxii.

51. This was true of my own "A Map Larger Than the Territory," as noted in the preface. Several online projects were baptized *Songlines*—including Marc Tuters and Karlis Kahlins's GPS map in Utrecht and Jim Naurekas's *New York Songlines* (see chapter 8).

52. De Certeau, *L'invention du quotidien*, 120–121.

53. Drew Hemment, Locative Arts, http://www.drewhemment.com/2004/locative_arts.html.

54. To let users discover some things for themselves, not all hot spots were marked on the map. Jeremy Hight, "Narrative Archeology," *Streetnotes* (Summer 2003), http://www.xcp.bfn.org/hight.html.

55. Drew Hemment, Locative Arts, http://www.drewhemment.com/2004/locative_arts.html.

56. Teri Rueb, http://www.terirueb.net/trace/index.html.

57. Galloway, "Intimations of Everyday Life."

58. The project was led by Proboscis (Giles Lane with Alice Angus, John Paul Bichard, and Nick West) in collaboration with a number of firms and the public mapping agency Ordnance Survey. http://proboscis.org.uk.

59. "Public Authoring in the Wireless City," http://urbantapestries.net; About Mass Observation, http://www.massobs.org.uk/index.htm.

60. "Look around you: what is happening, what has happened, what could happen? Plot your experience, be it a newsstand or a daydream. What is closer, the past or the future? Map the places you miss, map the plots you imagine." *PDPal* presentation, http://www.o-matic.com/play/pdpal.

61. Steve Dietz, who commissioned the project for the Walker, explains how it worked for the lambda user: "When users log onto the *PDPal* website, their city or personal map is displayed, and it can also be visualized alongside the cities of other *PDPal* users and, eventually, filtered according to various criteria—the ratings and attributes entered when making a map. Users can connect with other users whose home places are near theirs in order to see how they imagine the shared neighborhood. Or they can filter the maps by keywords used when entering data, creating what the artists refer to as a 'communicity' out of everyone's personal city, without losing access to the personal and the individual. Everyone's individual maps can be combined and recombined, so that *PDPal* effectively image-maps the city without the intervention of an authority. Steve Dietz, "Mapping the Urban Homunculus," in *ELSE/WHERE: MAPPING*, ed. Janet Abrams, and Peter Hall (Minneapolis: University of Minnesota Design Institute, 2006), 203, 205.

62. http://nearfuturelaboratory.com/projects/pdpal.

63. "While the categories for mapping are relatively preconfigured, the prescription of certain categories or metatags also allows a more effective mapping of all the contributions." Christiane Paul, "Digital Art / Public Art: Governance and Agency in the Networked Commons," *First Monday*, special issue 7, *Command Lines: The Emergence of Governance in Global Cyberspace* (2006). These problems are addressed at greater length in chapter 8.

64. "Public Authoring," http://urbantapestries.net.

65. See the artists' individual sites. Scott Paterson's is at http://www.sgp-7.net/index2007.shtm?k=works.

66. Many projects have similar aims, among them Warren Sack and Michael Dales's *Street Stories* (version 2.0, 2004), which aimed to design "new places of community for the network society through the creation of a new practice and technology of place-based storytelling"; *Passing Glances: Ambient Interludes from the Dublin Cityscape* (2003–2004), an MIT Media Lab project that "invites people to use SMS messaging on their cell phones to post images or video to a public display board. Display boards in different cities would be connected to one another.

The system intelligently draws in other imagery to support the content of what users posted to the board"; Andrea Wollensak's *Memory Markers* (2004), which uses "GPS to create site-specific artwork of Saint-Lo, France resulting in cartographic drawings, specific waypoints and related narratives."

67. In a blog post at http://nearfuturelaboratory.com/2008/04/28/mapping-without-terrain.

68. Dietz, "Mapping the Urban Homunculus."

69. The *[murmur]* Web site is at http://murmurtoronto.ca/about.php.

70. Shawn Micallef, quoted by Caitlin O'Donovan, "Murmurings: An interview with members of the [murmur] collective," *Year 01* 12 (2003), http://www.year01.com/archive/forum/issue12/caitlin.html.

71. "It's difficult to say how we control the negotiation between story and space. I want to say it's not our place to determine what fits and what doesn't—and leave it up to the story itself to make its own case. Sometimes it will be an uncomfortable (discomforting) fit—stories about great happenings in wonderful buildings that are now parking lots might spark a lot of dissonance within the listener. . . . Much like story curation itself, a good fit occurs when people can relate to the story and the space itself, and perhaps think differently about it from then on. If the story is such that a person can run their hand along a façade or ruin, walk through portholes and passages described in stories or relate physically with elements of the story—well, we could hardly ask for a better experience." Shawn Micallef, quoted in O'Donovan, ibid., http://www.year01.com/archive/forum/issue12/caitlin.html.

72. Nathan Alderman, "Using Cell Phones as Neighborhood Tour Guides," *J-Lab New Voices* (December 27, 2004): http://www.j-newvoices.org/site/story_spotlight/using_cell_phones_as_neighborhood_tour_guides.

73. Kris Scheuer, "Listening to the Murmur in the Junction," *My Town Crier*, October 13, 2008, http://www.mytowncrier.ca/viewthread.php?action=printable&tid=12329.

74. See http://www.geelongcity.vic.gov.au/connectingidentities/research.html.

75. "*Connecting Identities* has brought together artists, community members, cultural organisations and local government through workshops, exhibitions and events to build connection and strengthen local identity." http://www.geelongcity.vic.gov.au/connectingidentities. No public project is exempt from manipulation, however. Politicians may be tempted to use it to mask unresolved problems, and local business owners welcome the publicity it gives them.

76. Tuters and Varnellis, "Beyond Locative Media" (see chapter 3 for a definition of *détournement*).

77. Jo Walsh notes that "artists and academics have been used as cheap corporate R&D for locative services offerings; the heavy involvement of Urban Tapestries with HP, Orange, and France Telecom always made me recoil from their project. Artists can be very ingenuous with regards to the motivations of corporate support for this kind of practise." Jo Walsh, email interview with the author, March 5, 2005.

78. Robert Smithson quoted in "Earth" Symposium at White Museum, Cornell University, in *Robert Smithson: The Collected Writings*, ed. Jack D. Flam (Berkeley: University of California Press, 1996), 181.

79. "Core Sampling (Mining)", Britannica Online Encyclopedia http://www.britannica.com/EBchecked/topic/137466/core-sampling.

80. As part of the exhibition *Art on the Harbor Islands*, curated by Carole Anne Meehan at the Institute of Contemporary Art in Boston, June 23 to October 8, 2007.

Chapter 7

1. *Life* magazine published Mili's photos of skater Carol Lynne's figures. Mili's best-known photograph of Picasso was taken in a darkened room while the artist crouched and drew a nearly life-sized centaur in the air. Mili developed the technique of strobe photography with engineer Harold Edgerton at MIT. See Pablo Picasso and Gjon Mili, *Picasso's Third Dimension*, photos and text by Gjon Mili (New York: Triton Press, 1970).

2. The third element was the name: "Or there may be a relation which consists in the fact that the mind associates the sign with its object; in that case the sign is a *name*." Charles Sanders Peirce, "One, Two, Three: Fundamental Categories of Thought and of Nature" (1885), *Writings of Charles S. Peirce, A Chronological Edition*, ed. Peirce Edition Project, vol. 5, *1884–1886*, ed. Christian J. W. Kloesel et al. (Bloomington: Indiana University Press, 1981–), 5:245.

3. Peirce, "Logical Tracts, No. 2," in ibid., vol. 4, *1879–1884*, 4:447.

4. Bertolt Brecht, quoted in Walter Benjamin, "Little History of Photography," in Michael Jennings et al., *The Work of Art in the Age of Its Technological Reproducibility and Other Writings on Media* (Cambridge: Belknap Press of Harvard University Press, 2008), 293. Brecht's remark was reportedly made after seeing a photograph of the interior of the Krupp factory by Renger-Patzsch. Krupp's factories made steel, ammunition, and armaments. AEG's factories made electrical equipment.

5. Patrick Keiller, *London* (film soundtrack, 1994).

6. Ibid.

7. Ibid.

8. Today the resident population is about 7000, and about 316,700 people work there. http://www.cityoflondon.gov.uk/business/economic-research-and-information/statistics/Pages/default.aspx.

9. Keiller, *London* (soundtrack).

10. "The Future of Landscape: Patrick Keiller," interview by Andrew Stevens, *3:AM* magazine, July 14th, 2010. http://www.3ammagazine.com/3am/the-future-of-landscape-patrick-keiller.

11. Guy Debord, "Introduction à une critique de la géographie urbaine," *Les Lèvres Nues* 6 (Brussels, September 1955), "Introduction to a Critique of Urban Geography," trans. Ken Knabb,

Situationist International Anthology (Berkeley: Bureau of Public Secrets, 1995; original work published in 1981). http://www.bopsecrets.org/SI/urbgeog.htm.

12. Nick Relph and Oliver Payne, *Driftwood* (film soundtrack, 1999).

13. The word *Montmartre* is thought to be derived from Latin for either *mons martyrium* (martyrs' mountain) or *mons mercurei et mons martis* (mountain of Mercury and Mars).

14. Rémy Viard, on the soundtrack of *Un pointillé sur une carte* (Marie Preston, 2007).

15. Nam June Paik, Barbara and Peter Moore, and Yoshi Wada.

16. This project recalls a 1980 project in which Sophie Calle asked people from the Bronx to take her to places in their neighborhood that had particular meaning for them. She then photographed the places and transcribed their stories.

17. The title is a play on words. In French, *sans* (without) and *cent* (one hundred) are pronounced the same way. It also alludes to Max Ernst's collage novel *La femme 100 têtes.*

18. Marie Preston, "L'objet fort de la collaboration," *Mecca Nouement* (Créteil: Le Credac, 2011). My translation.

19. In 2010, a French entrepreneur commercialized Eyenimal VideoCam, "a miniature camera that allows you to enter the skin of your favorite animal." See *Écrans*, July 9, 2010, http://www.ecrans.fr/Faudrait-chat-voir,10364.html.

20. In fact, Clark was alluding to the expression "an elephant in our living room," which refers to the collective denial of a problem that is too big to be ignored.

21. See Bill Viola, "Will There Be Condominiums in Data Space?," *Video* 80, no. 5 (1982): 36–41, reprinted in *New Media Reader*, ed. Noah Wardrip-Fruin and Nick Montfort (Cambridge: MIT Press, 2001), 467.

22. See the project Web site at http://www.field-works.net.

23. Drew Hemment, "Locative Arts," http://www.drewhemment.compdf/locativearts.pdf.

24. Masaki Fujihata, "Landing Home in Geneva," *Field Works*, http://www.field-works.net.

25. Jean-Louis Boissier, "Masaki Fujihata: Poétique de la carte, du panorama et du miroir (virtuels)," http://www.mobilisable.net/2008/?page_id=130 (my translation). Boissier uses the expression "preneur de vues" (literally, "view taker").

26. Masaki Fujihata, quoted in Jean-Louis Boissier, "Three *Mobilisable* Works," http://www.mobilisable.net/2008/?page_id=130.

27. Sciboz presented these works at the Ninth Workshop and Symposium on Space and the Arts in May 2005. See Michael Hohl, "Space: Planetary Consciousness and the Arts, Yverdon-les-Bains, CH," http://www.hohlwelt.com/en/conferences/plancon.html.

28. Andrea Urlberger, "Paysages technologiques: Théories et pratiques autour du GPS," 2007, http:www.ciren.org/ciren/laboratoires/Paysage_Technologique/index.html.

29. "Double jeu, rencontres autour du numérique et des arts de la piste". A prototype for a DVD was later shown at the exhibition *Jouable* (Playable).

30. Each team was filmed by another camera from across the street to produce a documentary on the making of the work.

31. On the Web site of the Foundation Beelddiktee (Image Dictation), which she set up to raise money for her projects.

32. http://milkproject.net/en/index.html.

33. A commodity chain is "a functionally integrated network of production, trade, and service activities that covers all the stages in a supply chain, from the transformation of raw materials, through intermediate manufacturing stages, to the delivery of a finished good to a market." Jean-Paul Rodrigue, "Commodity Chains and Freight Transportation," J.-P. Rodrigue et al., *The Geography of Transport Systems*, Hofstra University, Department of Global Studies & Geography, 2009, http://people.hofstra.edu/geotrans/eng/ch5en/conc5en/ch5c3en.html.

34. Tracy Ore's class on the sociology and politics of food was held at Saint Cloud State University, Minnesota: http://web.stcloudstate.edu/teore/Food/FoodPolitics.htm. *How Stuff Is Made* at http://howstuffismade.org uses wiki software but, as a university-based project, must maintain standards of evidence that are overseen by academics. A recent addition is *WikiChains*, which was founded by geographer Mark Graham in 2010 "to encourage ethical consumption and transparency in commodity chains." *WikiChains* aims to leverage popular support from Internet users around the world to document all manner of commodity chains using text, images, sounds, and videos (but not yet GPS). http://www.oii.ox.ac.uk/research/projects/?id=75.

35. The discussions were also filmed and posted on the project blog so that Polak's activities could be followed simultaneously in Europe. Esther Polak, interview with Annet Dekker, November 2008, for the catalog of Transmediale 2009, *Deep North*, http://www.beelddiktee.nl/projects/GPS-projects/nomadM/Trans-catalog-eng.htm. She also conducted a workshop in Brazil.

36. Ibid.

37. This was the way the project was presented in March 2010 at the Electrosmog festival. The project is documented on the Nomadic Milk Web site at http://nomadicmilk.net/full.

38. Esther Polak, Artist statement, Amsterdam, 2005, http://www.beelddiktee.nl/projects/GPS-projects/milk/Artist-statement-EP-eng.htm.

39. Ibid.

40. Esther Polak, "Elastic Mapping: Implications of a GPS Drawing Robot in Times of Locative Media," Paper presented at the Fifteenth International Symposium on Electronic Art (ISEA 2009), Belfast, August 29, 2009, http://www.beelddiktee.nl/tekst/ISEA-abstract-eng.htm.

41. Ibid.

42. Ibid.

43. Lev Manovich, "Understanding Hybrid Media," www.manovich.net/DOCS/hybrid_media_pictures.doc.

44. Ibid.

45. Unless otherwise noted, all quotations from Ruiz Guttiérrez are from email exchanges with the artist on December 11 and 14, 2010.

46. Project description available at http://www.elsewhere.name.

47. Charles Baudelaire, "Les Fenêtres," *Le Spleen de Paris (Petits Poèmes en prose) La Fanfarlo*, ed. David Scott and Barbara Wright (Paris: Flammarion, 1987), 155. My translation.

48. Claude Lévi-Strauss, *Anthropologie structurale, deux* (Paris: Plon, 1973), 396–397 (my translation). Ruiz Guttiérrez says this reference was not intentional on her part.

Chapter 8

1. Sharon Daniel and Karen O'Rourke, "Mapping the Database: Trajectories and Perspectives," *Leonardo* 37, no. 4 (2004): 286–296.

2. "Each Songline will follow a single pathway, whether it goes by one name or several; the streets go from river to river, while the avenues stop at 59th Street, which is my upper limit for the time being. . . . at most intersections you can click on one of the arrows to turn the corner and explore a new Songline. Many of the addresses noted are simply the ordinary shops, restaurants, and apartment buildings that you would pass if you were walking along a Manhattan street." Jim Naurekas, *New York Songlines*, http://www.nysonglines.com. He contends that "an oral culture uses song as the most efficient way to remember and transmit large amounts of information; the Web is our technological society's closest equivalent." Ibid.

3. Georges Perec, "Approches de quoi?," in *L'infra-ordinaire* (Paris: Le Seuil, 1989): 12 (my translation).

4. At the same time, the New Museum had a show that explored the cultural diversity of the Bowery (Counter Culture). An online archive was devoted to artists who lived there (Bowery Artists Tribute), and the group Place Matters created an online tour (Marking Time on the Bowery). http://www.placematters.net/files/flash/bowery/bowery.swf.

5. It is one of several art and science projects that make up Invisible Dynamics, an interdisciplinary program at the San Francisco Exploratorium that studied the Bay area and was initiated by Peter Richards and Susan Schwartzenberg.

6. Cris Benton, "Artist's Statement: Salt Pond Aerials," blog entry, November 12, 2008, http://arch.ced.berkeley.edu/hiddenecologies/?page_id=431.

7. Cris Benton, "Layers of Time," blog entry, November 12, 2005, http://arch.ced.berkeley.edu/hiddenecologies/?page_id=70.

8. A recent issue of *Carnets du Paysage* was devoted to odology, the study of routes: a science initiated by Kurt Lewin and John Brinckerhoff Jackson, who saw it as a fertile direction for future investigation. *Les Carnets du Paysage* 11 (Autumn–Winter 2004).

9. http://www.re-title.com/exhibitions/archive_FondationCartierpourlartcontemporain4659.asp. The exhibition was designed by the architects Diller, Scofidio, and Renfro in collaboration with Mark Hansen, Laura Kurgan, and Ben Rubin.

10. Paul Virilio, "Terre natale: Ailleurs commence ici. Conversation entre Raymond Depardon et Paul Virilio," *Terre natale: Ailleurs commence ici*, eds. Paul Virilio, Raymond Depardon, Diller, Scofidio, and Renfro, Mark Hansen, Laura Kurgan, and Ben Rubin, (Arles: Actes sud, Paris : Fondation Cartier, 2009), 14.

11. Ibid.

12. The exhibition benefited from the participation of François Gemenne, a researcher and professor of migratory movement that is linked to climate change. He is affiliated with Sciences Po (Centre d'Études et de Recherché Internationales) and the University of Liege (Centre d'Études de l'Ethnicité et des Migrations). See his essay, "Repères," Ibid., 126–139.

13. Using the same technology, notes the artist, as the military in Baghdad. http://shadowsfromanotherplace.net. See Paula Levine, *Shadows from Another Place: Transposed Space*, http://paulalevine.net/essays/shadows/shadows.pdf.

14. http://thewall.name.

15. In a similar way, the collaborative project *You Are Not Here*, "a platform for urban tourism mash-ups," brought Gaza to the streets of Tel Aviv in 2007 and 2009 and Baghdad to the streets of New York in 2006. *You Are Not Here: A Dislocative Tourism Agency* proposed a downloadable map and audiotour. As in *[murmur]*, passers-by might also stumble onto "You Are Not Here" signs in the street, with a telephone number to call the "Tourist Hotline" portal and listen to the tour. It was created by a multidisciplinary team including Thomas Duc, Kati London, Dan Phiffer, Andrew Schneider, Ran Tao, and Mushon Zer-Aviv.

16. The train trip: http://www.nogovoyages.com/attractionsperipheriquesbyRER.html A description of the attractions: http://www.nogovoyages.com/attractionsperipheriques.html.

17. http://www.nogovoyages.com/hypnorama_bus.html.

18. http://www.nogovoyages.com/utopiafactoryabraxas.html and http://www.nogoland.com/recent/utopia-factory-abraxas-2010.

19. http://www.nogovoyages.com/wikiforest.html.

20. Ibid.

21. Guy Debord and Gil J. Wolman, "Mode d'emploi du détournement" *Les Lèvres Nues* 8 (May 1956): Reprinted in *Guy Debord Œuvres*, 221–229, "A User's Guide to *Détournement*," (trans. Ken Knabb) http://www.bopsecrets.org/SI/detourn.htm.

22. "The lot is based on 1996 statistics. It shows the whole year's statistics compressed into one day. It shows the relative frequency of crime by place and by hour," notes Wilson. http://userwww.sfsu.edu/~netart/crimezy/mapzy.html.

23. Stamen Design has created an interactive map of crimes in Oakland called Oakland Crimespotting to inform ordinary people about crime in their neighborhood. Their map shows violent crimes, property crimes, and "quality of life" crimes. http://oakland.crimespotting.org.

24. The SOM is a kind of artificial neural net that displays emergent properties when applied to large data sets.

25. The map could be consulted on the Internet. Clicking on an object allowed online viewers to see its properties and its attached stories and to compare it to its neighbors. Museum visitors and Web surfers could add comments and stories to any object from anywhere in the world. George Legrady, "Pockets Full of Memories," *Visual Communication* (2002), http://www.mat.ucsb.edu/%7Eg.legrady/glWeb/publications/publ_art/textpfom.html. Several years later, in an expanded and redesigned version of the installation, visitors could track object movement over time or display the textual descriptions. See Legrady's Web site at http://www.mat.ucsb.edu/~g.legrady/glWeb/Projects/projectslist.html.

26. George Legrady's project *Blink* (2006–2007) demonstrates the process of self-organization in a vast matrix of eyes that open and close according to their neighbors' behaviors. Each eye statistically evaluates in real time what its immediate neighbors are doing and adjusts its behavior accordingly. The overall pattern oscillates between states of stability where all eyes imitate their neighbors and states of transitional disruption. The movements are dynamically calculated in real time using the Ising mathematical model, which describes phase transitions between ordered and a disordered states. The latter takes place when the eyes observe their neighbors, shifting continually in the absence of a clear overall pattern to follow.

27. The first two take the most recent additions to the database, using appropriate algorithms either to place large images randomly and fill in blank spaces with smaller ones (Cell_Bin) or to highlight new photos with a yellow frame and surround them with randomly selected images from Flickr that share common tags (Cell_Clusters). The third, Cell_Burst, shows most recent contributions bursting open like fireworks, first with their tags and then with related Flickr images, while Cell_Finale throws all the images in the database onto the screen randomly and repeatedly like the final bouquet of a fireworks display. The project was updated to include sonification (by Christopher Jette) in 2010. http://www.mat.ucsb.edu/g.legrady/glWeb/Projects/celltango/cell.html.

28. George Legrady, quoted in Cate McQuaid, "Can You See Me Now?," *Boston Globe*, October 9, 2009.

29. George Legrady, interview with Sarah Smerch, http://bhjournal.com/issues/Vol6_2/george_legrady.php. He has written several academic articles dealing with the results.

30. Other works in the series include "Frozen Feelings," based on the *World Emotion Maps* and described by the artist as "deflated emotional distortions of the globe. The Frozen Feelings are

3D snapshots of the world's emotions. Digitally carved into different kinds of materials," http://www.benayoun.com/projet.php?id=29.

31. Maurice Benayoun, email message to the author, September 2, 2010. Other examples include the "Emotion vending machine" in the form of a beverage vending machine. Consumers can choose three from a range of nine emotions (such as fear, joy, and ecstasy) updated in real-time. When a choice is made, the machine browses the Internet and displays the result in the shape of words that represent the three emotions and sounds that are composed by Jean-Baptiste Barrière. Consumers can record their unique, real-time audiovisual emotional cocktails on a USB flash drive.

32. *Hidden Ecologies* was initially meant to incorporate data that were gathered by other people, but to date the Web site shows Benton and Lanier to be the only active participants.

33. In most volatile map interfaces, users are free to save their own itineraries on their own computers, but to guarantee their privacy, they are not automatically added to the database. With the recent proliferation of invasive user profiling, inadvertent participation is on the rise.

34. "What's This?" *Mr Beller's Neighborhood*, http://mrbellersneighborhood.com/what.

35. Quoted in Matthew Mirapaul, "Today's Publishing: Better by the Book or by the Web?," *New York Times*, February 4, 2002, http://www.nytimes.com/2002/02/04/books/arts-online-today-s-publishing-better-by-the-book-or-by-the-web.html?pagewanted=all&src=pm.

36. In an email message to the author, January 2010.

37. As Beller says, "We tend to put about three up at once, every week. 'We' is me and the managing editor, who is the person who runs things, receives all the submissions, chooses, edits. I hover in the background, offering notes, attending to publishing issues, and soliciting writers. Right now the managing editor is Jean Paul Cativiela. There have been two others. All are very interesting writers." Email to the author, January 2010.

38. Mirapaul, "Today's Publishing." Members of the "Story of the Week" mailing list receive headlines and teasers for newly published articles.

39. In an email message to the author, January 2010.

40. Ibid.

41. Two anthologies of stories from the Web site have been published in paper editions—*Before and After: Stories from New York* (2002) and *Lost and Found: Stories from New York (2)* (2009).

42. Steve Zeitlin, "City of Memory," *Voices, the Journal of New York Folklore* 34 (Fall–Winter 2008), http://www.nyfolklore.org/pubs/voic34-3-4/downstate.html.

43. Jake Barton, quoted in Christina Ray, Glowlab blog, http://www.christinaray.comlab2/artist_project.php?project_id=115&artist_id=5. Barton has realized other works based on this theme. At the first Psy-Geo-Conflux in May 2003, he showed an immersive sound and video work called *New York Observers*, a documentary in which New York's "living landmarks"—street vendors, building superintendents, and police officers—recount their observations.

44. Hal Sirowitz, "Sitting behind Cybill Shepherd," http://mrbellersneighborhood.com/2010/02/sitting-behind-cybill-shepherd.

45. Christine Nieland, "And Bingo Was Her Name," http://mrbellersneighborhood.com/2010/02/and-bingo-was-her-name.

46. At most, they could add threads in Urban Tapestries. See chapter 7.

47. The project Web site, now offline, detailed their plan: "Step 1–Collect GPS data, Step 2–Normalise and Synthesise Data into Real Shapes, Step 3–Annotate Shapes with Real-World Semantics, Step 4a–Annotate Completed Map with Civic and Historic Information, Step 4b–Find Partner Organisations to Contribute to, and Back, the Project, Step 5–Give Everything Away."

48. In a message to the Locative mailing list on March 16, 2005, Saul Albert evokes the high-quality geodata collected by Bunting for a "skateboarder's map of Bristol." He notes that "Jo Walsh made a reinterpretation of that data and made a great feature annotation system and GPS trace layer." Bunting was reportedly offering the free data "as a prize for an urban orienteering challenge."

49. http://locate.irational.org/bristol_map and http://locate.irational.org/cgi-bin/bristol_map/bristol_map.pl, respectively.

50. M. Haklay and P. Weber, "OpenStreetMap: User-Generated Street Maps," *IEEE Pervasive Computing, IEEE Computer Society, and IEEE Communications Society* 7, no. 4 (2008): 12–18.

51. http://wiki.openstreetmap.org/wiki/SF_Press_Release.

52. Developed by Michal Migurski of Stamen Design, http://walking-papers.org.

53. Based on its simple idea, *OpenStreetMap* has federated more than a hundred thousand users and groups in countries on seven continents. According to *OpenStreetMap*'s engine, as of July 28, 2009, it had 139,963 users, 983,790,201 uploaded GPS points, 393,752,740 nodes, and 30,831,360 ways.

54. These points are made about Wikipedia by Aaron Swartz, "Why (Some) Wikis Work," http://www.aaronsw.com/weblog/whywikiswork.

55. On *Wikipedia*, see Clay Shirky, *Here Comes Everybody: The Power of Organizing without Organizations* (New York: Penguin, 2008).

56. Haklay and Weber, "*OpenStreetMap*: User-Generated Street Maps." According to the project's wiki, it mobilizes open-source software tools. Some were designed expressly for *OpenStreetMap*: Osmarender is a rule-based rendering tool for generating scalable vector graphics (SVG) images of *OpenStreetMap* data. Others have been adapted: Mapnik, the open-source map renderer, was used to render the main slippy map layer.

57. "The Open Street Map. What's possible when geographic information is shared?" *Assignment Zero. Crowdsourcing Maps*. Nate Olson interviews Steve Coast via email, May 12–21, 2007. http://web.archive.org/web/20070713172458/http://zero.newassignment.net/filed/steve_coast_intro_and_q.

58. Muki Haklay, "How Good Is Volunteered Geographical Information? A Comparative Study of *OpenStreetMap* and Ordnance Survey Datasets," *Environment and Planning B* 37, no. 4 (2010): 682–703, doi:10.1068/b35097. There is also a geographic imbalance in the number of geotagged articles on *Wikipedia*: Small towns in the United States often receive extended descriptions, whereas much larger cities in Africa and South America are *terra incognita*. As problems like these are raised, the *Wikipedia* community looks for solutions, which has led to the creation of a wiki project devoted to "countering systemic bias."

59. http://www.mappingforchange.org.uk.

60. Bruno Latour, *Reassembling the Social: An Introduction to Actor Network Theory* (Oxford: Oxford University Press, 2005).

61. Andy Feehan, "Mark Lombardi: In Memoriam," 2000. http://web.archive.org/web/20000823221456/http://www.pierogi2000.com/memorial/lombardm.html.

62. Massimiliano Gioni, ed., *Get Lost: Artists Map Downtown New York* (New York: New Museum, 2007). Brian Holmes, "Cartography of Excess. Bureau d'Études and Multiplicity," http://brianholmes.wordpress.com/2012/02/23/cartography-of-excess (originally published in March 2002).

63. Walter Benjamin, "The Author as Producer" (1934), *The Work of Art in the Age of Its Technological Reproducibility, and Other Writings on Media*, ed. Michael W. Jennings, Brigid Doherty, and Thomas Y. Levin (Cambridge.: Belknap Press of Harvard University Press, 2008), 86.

64. Bertolt Brecht, "The Radio as an Apparatus of Communication" (1932), *Brecht on Theater*, trans. and ed. Jon Willett (New York: Hill and Wang, 1964).

65. Benjamin, "The Author as Producer."

66. Ibid., 89.

67. Some took up to ten years. Luca Cerizza, *Alighiero e Boetti: Mappa* (London: Afterall Books, 2008), 35.

68. Ibid., 75.

69. Daniel and O'Rourke, "Mapping the Database." This was also true of my own *A Map Larger Than the Territory*.

70. "While the "personal computer" provides a gateway to the Internet where communities can evolve, regardless of distance, the 'community computer' is intended not to bypass but to strengthen and empower communities of place." Ibid.

71. She worked with members of the nongovernmental organization Crear Vale la Pena.

72. In our era of ubiquitous user participation, *Palabras* does not allow contributions from online visitors.

73. Sharon Daniel, *Palabras*, http://palabrastranquilas.ucsc.edu.

74. In an email to the author, September 5, 2010.

75. Hal Foster, "The Artist as Ethnographer," in *The Return of the Real* (Cambridge: MIT Press, 1996): 171–204.

76. In March 1992, Chicago-based organizers invited African American artist Renee Green to create a collaborative artwork with a local community. They had defined a community and a theme that they thought would interest her—inner-city racial conflict—but Green wanted to explore the architectural legacy of Frank Lloyd Wright. Miwon Kwon, *One Place after Another: Site-Specific Art and Locational Identity* (Cambridge: MIT Press, 2004), 140–141.

77. She interviewed older members of her extended family for the Web documentary *Unsettled* (2007) and learned to speak their language. Born in Mareeba, Far North Queensland, Fraser is a Murri. http://www.cybertribe.culture2.org/theotherapt/jenny.html.

78. "My personal commitment to giving back to the community includes founding cyberTribe—an online art gallery that features the works of Indigenous Artists internationally." Jenny Fraser, "The Word: Aboriginal New Media Arts—A Real Cultural Practice?" http://www.thenaica.org/edition_nine/word/newmedia/newmedia.htm. She also founded the Blackout Collective in 2002.

79. According to Fraser, "the *Other APT* explores issues for Australia's Native peoples and our role in the Asia Pacific Region and also deals with the issues of migration of our neighbors including the importance of Place, Legend, Identity, Politics, and Mutual Respect in the interest and importance of open Art Dialogue." http://www.cybertribe.culture2.org/theotherapt/jenny.html. The *Other APT* was shown in the 2008 Sydney Biennial as an artwork with Fraser listed as the artist, which raises questions about the roles of artist and curator that have been hotly debated since the 1960s.

80. She now considers these systems inadequate as filters for information because they are subject to power laws.

81. Unless noted otherwise, all quotes from Jo Walsh come from an email interview I conducted with her on March 5, 2005. Jo Walsh, "Questions à Jo Walsh," interview with Karen O'Rourke, *Art ++*, ed. David-Olivier Lartigaud (Orléans: Hyx, 2011).

82. http://tools.ietf.org/html/rfc1459. *Wikipedia* explains: "IRC is a form of real-time Internet text messaging (chat) or synchronous conferencing. It is mainly designed for group communication in discussion forums, called channels." http://en.wikipedia.org/wiki/Internet_Relay_Chat. See also http://en.wikipedia.org/wiki/IRC_bot and http://en.wikipedia.org/wiki/Internet_bot.

83. Jo Walsh, email interview March 5, 2005. Infobot was programmed by Kevin Lenzo in 1995.

84. Ibid.

85. They also work like recommendation systems, using collaborative filtering. According to Jo Walsh, "The first bots I wrote were all 'standalone.' They'd have their little brains in text files or databases, understand their own 'little languages' or grammars, which were 'conversational triggers' for programmed interactions with a human. I started looking for ways to connect different bots together so that each one specialized in a particular domain and they could offer suggestions to each other. . . . 'Infobot' is a classic of this genre." Ibid.

86. Ibid.

87. Ibid.

88. Automatically extract information.

89. Earle Martin and Kake Pugh. "OpenGuides™ is a network of free, community-maintained wiki guidebooks to places around the world." http://openguides.org.

90. The protocols Jabber (now XMPP), AIM, and IRC.

91. Wilfried Hou Je Bek, "Psychogeographical Markup Language (PML)" http://web.archive.org/web/20041204062411/http://socialfiction.org/psychogeography/PML.html.

92. Wilfried Hou Je Bek, "Cracking the Urban Cheat Code: +A Practical Account of How to Do It," September 2003, http://web.archive.org/web/20030908183123/http://www.socialfiction.org/psychogeography/psychogeogram.html.

93. Ibid.

94. http://awp.diaart.org/km/intro.htm.

95. "Machine-readable graph descriptions of social/organizational networks can be connected up with simple inference techniques. I've done in the past a bit of work with Mute on building simple tools which allow people to write their own vocabularies to express relations between things in organizational maps—an attempt to automate the production of visualizations such as the power-mapping work done by Bureau d'Etudes and to externalize and make sharable the thinking processes that go into designing the 'language' with which the map is written. These tools are unfinished, but I use them a lot to help myself understand the dynamics of different networks that I am connected to. The vocabularies are different for each specialist domain, each group, and mappings between them can be established differently by different interpreters." Jo Walsh, interview with the author, March 5, 2005.

96. Ibid.

97. Jerry Rubin, *Do It! Scenarios of the Revolution* (New York: Simon & Schuster, 1970). See also the series of exhibitions curated by Hans Ulrich Olbrist.

Chapter 9

1. See Coco Fusco's incendiary article, "Questioning the Frame," *In These Times*, December 16, 2004, http://www.inthesetimes.com/article/1750, and various rebuttals.

2. Naomi Klein, "China's All-Seeing Eye," *Rolling Stone* 1053 (May 2008): http://www.naomiklein.org/articles/2008/05/chinas-all-seeing-eye.

3. See chapter 6 and Rob van Kranenburg, *The Internet of Things: A Critique of Ambient Technology and the All-Seeing Network of RFID* (Amsterdam: Institute of Network Cultures, 2007).

4. Klein, "China's All-Seeing Eye."

5. Ibid.

6. Spiritual mapping is an initiative that was spearheaded by Reverend Thomas Muthee. Citing a 1999 article in the *Christian Science Monitor*, Jo Walsh attempts to define it: "A team of the devout researches and annotates spaces meeting with disapproval—non-conforming churches, vendors of magic supplies, family planning clinics, gay bars. Thus is gathered 'the strategic information necessary for effective intercessory "smart prayer" deployment,' and warfare (in the form of cluster prayer bombardment) is carried to the territorial spirits. . . . mappers play with the language of military planners, and pronounce 'strategic level spiritual warfare' on the genius locii." Jo Walsh, Mapping Hacks Blog, October 27, 2008, http://web.archive.org/web/20090105184246/http://mappinghacks.com/2008/10/27/thought-for-the-day.

7. Michel Foucault, *Surveiller et punir: Naissance de la prison*, (Paris: Gallimard, 1975), trans. Alan Sheridan, *Discipline and Punish: the Birth of the Prison*, (New York: Random House, 1977); Jeremy Bentham, *The Panopticon Writings*, ed. Miran Bozovic (London: Verso, 1995).

8. Gilles Deleuze, "Post-scriptum sur les sociétés de contrôle," *L'autre journal* (May 1990): reprinted in *Pourparlers 1972–1990* (Paris: les Éditions de Minuit, 1990), p. 240–247. "Postscript on the Societies of Control," trans. Martin Joughin *October* 59 (Winter 1992): 3–7.

9. Foucault, *Surveiller et punir*; and Bentham, *The Panopticon Writings*.

10. Deleuze, "Post-scriptum sur les sociétés de contrôle."

11. Ibid.

12. Albert-László Barabási, *Bursts: The Hidden Pattern behind Everything We Do* (New York: Dutton, 2010).

13. Michael Auping, "Sound Thinking," *Artforum* (January 2005): 158–161.

14. Yoko Ono, "Yoko Ono," interview with Scott MacDonald, in *A Critical Cinema 2: Interviews with Independent Filmmakers* (Berkeley: University of California Press, 1992), 139–156. Ono's score *Film No. 4 (Rape, or Chase)* was reprinted in Scott MacDonald, *Screen Writings: Scripts and Texts by Independent Filmmakers* (Berkeley: University of California Press, 1995), 22.

15. James Hoberman, *Vulgar Modernism: Writing on Film and Other Media* (Philadelphia: Temple University Press, 1991), 185–187. Although ordinary people today are more used to being filmed, illegal immigrants are just as vulnerable as they were in 1969.

16. http://www.newmedia-arts.be/cgi-bin/show-oeu.asp?ID=150000000039650&lg=GBR.

17. Steve Mann, "Sousveillance," 2002, http://wearcam.org/sousveillance.htm.

18. Ibid.

19. Ibid.

20. See http://eyetap.org/wearcam/shootingback/shootingback.html and Steve Mann, "Wearable Computing: A First Step Toward Personal Imaging," *IEEE Computer* 30, no. 2 (February 1997): 25–32.

21. Ibid. and Steve Mann (with Hal Niedzviecki), *Cyborg: Digital Destiny and Human Possibility in the Age of the Wearable Computer* (Toronto: Doubleday Canada, 2001).

22. See http://eyetap.org/wearcam/shootingback/shootingback.html, and Mann, "Wearable Computing."

23. Steve Mann, Jason Nolan, and Barry Wellman, "Sousveillance: Inventing and Using Wearable Computing Devices for Data Collection in Surveillance Environments," *Surveillance & Society* 1, no. 3 (2003): 355. A series of projects realized by Mann and his students in 2001 using "conspicuously concealed cameras" are documented at http://www.wearcam.org/adwear/index.htm.

24. Although part of the device had to be surgically removed after it was rejected by the artist's body, he has continued the experiment with a camera strapped to the back of his head. See the project Web site at http://www.3rdi.me.

25. See the project page on Naimark's Web site at http://www.naimark.net/projects/zap/howto.html.

26. http://rtmark.com/archimedes.html.

27. http://www.naimark.net/projects/zap/howto.html.

28. Ibid.

29. "Surveillance Camera Players: Ten-Year Report," December 10, 2006, SCP Web site, http://www.notbored.org/10-year-report.html.

30. http://www.appliedautonomy.com/isee/info2.html.

31. Institute for Applied Autonomy, "Tactical Cartography," in L. Mogel and A. Baghat, eds., *Atlas of Radical Cartography* (Los Angeles: Journal of Aesthetics, Protest Press, 2007), 34.

32. See Paglen's Web site at http://www.paglen.com/pages/projects.htm.

33. Trevor Paglen, "Unmarked Planes and Hidden Geographies: Author's Statement," *Vectors Journal* 2, no. 2 (Winter 2007), http://www.vectorsjournal.org/projects/index.php?project=59.

34. Trevor Paglen, quoted in Lize Mogel and Alexis Bhagat, eds., *An Atlas of Radical Cartography* (Los Angeles: Journal of Aesthetics, Protest Press, 2007).

35. http://www.notbored.org/10-year-report-long.html.

36. Ibid.

37. Erich W. Schienke and Bill Brown, "Streets into Stages: An Interview with Surveillance Camera Players' Bill Brown," *Surveillance and Society* 1, no. 3 (2003): 361.

38. In an email to the author, August 2009.

39. Vera Tollmann, "The World in One's Pocket? The Net Project 'VOPOS' by the Italian Group 0100101110101101.org," trans. Tim Jones, http://www.springerin.at/dyn/heft_text.php?textid=1191&lang=en.

40. The U.S. Immigration and Naturalization Service became part of the Department of Homeland Security in March 2003.

41. Ethan Zuckerman, "Tracking Hasan Elahi," October 19, 2006, http://www.worldchanging.com.

42. Andy Warhol, *The Philosophy of Andy Warhol: (From A to B and Back Again)* (New York: Harcourt Brace Jovanovich, 1975; Harvest edition, 1977), 100–101.

43. Barabási, *Bursts*.

44. Charles Baudelaire, *Constantin Guys: Le peintre de la vie moderne* (Geneva: La Palantine, n.d.) (my translation), http://fr.wikisource.org/wiki/Le_Peintre_de_la_vie_moderne.

45. http://web.archive.org/web/20040714122350/http://elahi.rutgers.edu.

46. Quoted in Michelle Teran's project description at http://www.ubermatic.org/life.

47. The camera is intended to send its video signal to a nearby base station so that it can be viewed on a computer or a television. But its signal can be intercepted from more than a quarter mile away by off-the-shelf electronic equipment (video-sniffing). See John Schwartz, "Nanny-Cam May Leave a Home Exposed," *New York Times*, April 14, 2002. Video sniffing is illegal in England.

48. George Perec, *Espèces d'espaces* (Paris: Éditions Galilée, 1974), 57–58.

49. Michelle Teran's project description at http://www.ubermatic.org/life.

50. Raphaël Meltz, "Marc L***," *Le Tigre* 28 (November 2008): http://www.le-tigre.net/Marc-L.html (my translation).

51. Yoko Ono, "Yoko Ono," interview with Scott MacDonald, in *A Critical Cinema 2*, 151.

52. Manu Luksch and Mukul Patel, "Faceless: Chasing the Data Shadow," 2007, http://www.ambienttv.net/2007/faceless/chasingthedatashadow2007.pdf.

53. Manu Luksch and Mukul Patel, "Manifesto for CCTV Filmmakers," 2004, http://www.ambienttv.net/content/?q=dpamanifesto.

54. Ibid.

55. Seda Gürses, Michelle Teran and Manu Luksch, "A Trialogue on Interventions in Surveillance Space: Seda Gürses in Conversation with Michelle Teran and Manu Luksch," *Surveillance and Society* 7, no. 2 (2010): 165–174.

56. Luksch and Patel, "Faceless: Chasing the Data Shadow," 2007.

57. Jill Magid, quoted in Geert Lovink, "Surveillance, Performance, Self-Surveillance: Interview with Jill Magid," Institute of Network Cultures Weblog. (October 29, 2004), http://networkcultures.org/wpmu/weblog/2004/10/29/surveillance-performance-self-surveillance.

58. Jason Oddy, "An Outsider's Guide to Getting Inside Places Only Insiders Normally Get to Go," *Art on Paper* 13, no. 5 (May–June 2009): 58–71.

59. http://www.evidencelocker.net.

60. Jill Magid, *One Cycle of Memory in the City of L* (Liverpool: FACT, 2004). Letter dated Friday, January 30, 2004, Day 2.

61. Ibid. Letter dated Monday, February 2, 2004, Day 5.

62. Ibid. Letter dated Saturday, February 7, 2004, Day 10.

63. In 1974, heiress Patricia Hearst was kidnapped by a guerrilla group called the Symbionese Liberation Army and eventually espoused her captors' cause and participated in a bank robbery. This paradoxical behavior has been explained in evolutionary terms: bride kidnapping contributes to the survival of the species (the abduction of the Sabine women is part of the founding myth of Rome).

64. Jill Magid, quoted in Lovink, "Surveillance, Performance, Self-Surveillance: Interview with Jill Magid." For her work, I prefer the term *self-initiated surveillance* to *self-surveillance.*

65. Esther Polak, interview with Andrea Urlberger, February 8, 2007, in *Paysage technologique: Théories et pratiques autour du Global Positioning System*, http://www.ciren.org/ciren/laboratoires/Paysage_Technologique/art/polak/index.html.

66. Sigmund Freud, "The Uncanny" (1919), *The Standard Edition of the Complete Psychological Works of Sigmund Freud*, ed. and trans. James Strachey, vol. 17 (London: Hogarth, 1953), 219–252.

67. Serge Tisseron, *L'empathie au cœur du jeu social* (Paris: Albin Michel, 2010), 56–61.

68. Her public persona, the narrator of her text.

69. Perec, *Espèces d'espaces*, 100. See Tim Ingold, *Lines: A Brief History* (London: Routledge, 2007), 81. My translation.

70. Tate Gallery Web site, http://www2.tate.org.uk/intermediaart/borderxing.shtm.

71. Antoni Muntadas, in an interview with Michèle Cone, "*Translating Muntada,s*" *Artnet Magazine*, June, 2005. http://www.artnet.com/Magazine/features/cone/cone6-9-05.asp.

72. Jacques Rancière, *Le maître ignorant: Cinq leçons sur l'émancipation intellectuelle* (Paris: Fayard, 2004) (original work published in 1987).

73. Antoni Muntadas, "Construction of Fear" (October 2007), http://www.gabriellemaubrie.com/web.php?mode=article&id=55.

74. EDT/b.a.n.g. lab (Bits.Atoms.Neurons.Genes): Ricardo Dominguez, Brett Stalbaum, Amy Sara Carroll, Micha Cárdenas, Jason Najarro, Elle Mehrmand, and Diana Le.

75. Ricardo Dominguez, "On Electronic Civil Disobedience: Interview with Ricardo Dominguez," *Reclamations* blog, January 17, 2012, http://www.reclamationsjournal.org/blog/?ha_exhibit=interview-with-ricardo-dominguez.

76. Brett Stalbaum, http://www.youtube.com/watch?v=pWYXa7ftvVk. The project was published on Source Forge in 2004 at http://virtualhiker.sourceforge.net.

77. Faculty Letter of Support for Ricardo Dominguez, Visual Arts Department, University of California at San Diego, http://va-grad.ucsd.edu/~drupal/node/1492. Calit2 is the California Institute for Telecommunications and Information Technology.

78. According to AFP, cited by Google news August 15, 2010, http://www.google.com/hostednews/afp/article/ALeqM5j-hSOD5E5rkM_pJyjBySYM023nHg.

79. Florian Schneider, "Collaboration," February 17, 2007, http://summit.kein.org/node/190.

80. Stalker, *Attraverso i territori attuali / A travers les territoires actuels* (Paris: Jean-Michel Place, 2000).

81. "ON/Stalker > osservatorionomade > Italy," Archilab 2004 Press release, http://www.archilab.org/public/2004/en/textes/stalker.htm.

82. In English, Studio for Self-Managed Architecture.

83. Among the participants were Jean-Baptiste Bayle (Borderphonics), Myriam Rambach (Bordercartograph), Wilfried Hou Je Bek, and Laurent Malone, who had been walking with Stalker. See Urban Radio, http://ecoboxvirtuel.free.fr/radio.

84. http://www.osservatorionomade.net/egnatia/sito%20egnatia/parigi.html.

85. http://www.rhiz.eu/artefact-30362-en.html.

86. The 15th arrondissement explored with Ici-Même (see chapter 4).

87. Constantin Petcou and Doina Petrescu, "Au rez-de-chaussée de la ville," *Multitudes* 20 (Spring 2005), http://multitudes.samizdat.net/Au-rez-de-chaussee-de-la-ville.

88. She opposes it to an "internal, genetically predetermined or individualized" approach. Natalie Jeremijenko, "The Art of the Eco-Mind Shift," TED talk, http://www.ted.com/talks/natalie_jeremijenko_the_art_of_the_eco_mindshift.html.

89. Natalie Jeremijenko, in an email message to the author, August 23, 2010.

90. Ibid.

91. Natalie Jeremijenko, *OneTrees*, an information environment, project timeline http://www.nyu.edu/projects/xdesign/onetrees/timeline/index.html. About the cloning process, see http://www.nyu.edu/projects/xdesign/onetrees/clones/index.html.

92. Natalie Jeremijenko, "*One Trees*: An Information Environment," http://www.nyu.edu/projects/xdesign/onetrees/description/index.html.

93. "San Francisco's environmental variation is dramatic, but in addition to microclimates, the Bay Area also has highly balkanized social contexts," Jeremijenko said. "The economic difference between east and west Palo Alto, for instance, is greater than the difference between some countries." Natalie Jeremijenko, quoted in Zahid Sardar, "Natalie Jeremijenko's Trees Aren't Simply Decorative: They Can Be Read Like a Social Register," *San Francisco Chronicle*, Saturday, October 23, 2004.

94. http://www.nyu.edu/projects/xdesign/mainmenu/notes_trees.html.

95. Ibid.

96. David Harvey, *The Condition of Postmodernity: An Enquiry into the Origins of Cultural Change* (Cambridge: Blackwell, 1990), 240, 242–247.

97. Akiva Eldar, "Checkpoints in the Territories—and Jerusalem," *Haaretz*, February 21, 2002, http://www.haaretz.com/print-edition/features/checkpoints-in-the-territories-and-jerusalem-1.52324.

98. http://www.multiplicity.it. Multiplicity, Exhibition Web site, Center for Contemporary Image, Geneva, http://www.attitudes.ch/expos/multiplicity/road%20map_gb.htm. The Road Map is part of the border-device research, a project developed by Multiplicity with Domus Academy, Milano, and the Berlage Institute, Rotterdam. I saw it at the Musée d'Art Moderne de la Ville de Paris.

99. See Hans-Ulrich Obrist, "Collectifs de recherche et pratique curatoriale: Nouveaux territoires de l'art," interview with Cécilia Bezzan, *L'art même* 23 (2004), http://www2.cfwb.be/lartmeme/no023/pages/page5.htm.

100. Paul Virilio, "Ctheory Interview with Paul Virilio: The Kosovo War Took Place in Orbital Space," with John Armitage, trans. Patrice Riemens, October 18, 2000, http://www.ctheory.net/articles.aspx?id=132.

101. Raja Shehadeh, *Palestinian Walks: Forays into a Vanishing Landscape* (New York: Scribner, 2007), 2.

102. Ibid.

103. Raja Shehadeh, "Interview with Raja Shehadeh," with Mark Thwaite, http://www.bookdepository.com/interview/with/author/raja-shehadeh.

104. Shehadeh, *Palestinian Walks*, 123. The negotiators wanted the world to recognize the Palestinian Liberation Organization: "Political expediency blinded them to the war of annihilation that Israel was waging against all Palestinians inside and outside the Occupied Territories." Ibid., 118.

105. Raja Shehadeh, *Strangers in the House* (London: Profile Books, 2002), 238.

Conclusion

1. Jorge Luis Borges, "El jardin de senderos que se bifurcan" (1941), *El jardin de senderos que se bifurcan* (Buenos Aires: Sur, 1941), "The Garden of Forking Paths," trans. Donald A. Yates, in *Labyrinths: Selected Stories & Other Writings*, ed. Donald A. Yates and James E. Irby (New York: New Directions, 1964), 19–29 Reprinted in Noah Wardrip-Fruin and Nick Montfort, *The New Media Reader* (Cambridge: MIT Press, 2003), 30–34.

2. See Albert-László Barabási, *Linked: How Everything Is Connected to Everything Else and What It Means for Business, Science, and Everyday Life* (Cambridge: Perseus, 2002).

3. Barbara Glowczeswki, *Yapa: Aboriginal Painters from Balgo and Lajamanu* (Paris: Galerie Baudoin Le Bon, 1991).

4. Jeremy Hight, "NeMe: Rhizomatic Cartography: Modulated Mapping and the Spatial Net," May 5, 2009, http://www.neme.org/991/rhizomatic-cartography.

5. In an email to the author, August 31, 2010.

6. Richard Long, quoted in Sean O'Hagen, "One Step Beyond," *The Observer*, May 10, 2009, http://www.guardian.co.uk/artanddesign/2009/may/10/art-richard-long.

Bibliography

Abramović, Marina, and Ulay. *The Lovers: The Great Wall Walk*. Amsterdam: Stedelijk Museum, 1989.

Abrams, Janet, and Peter Hall, eds. *ELSE/WHERE: MAPPING—New Cartographies of Networks and Territories*. Minneapolis: University of Minnesota Design Institute, 2006.

Ackers, Susanne, Inke Arns, Matthew Fuller, Francis Hunger, Jacob Lillemose, and Darija Simunovic. *The Hartware Guide to Irational. org*. Frankfurt am Main: Revolver Books, 2006.

Altshuler, Bruce. "Art by Instruction and the Pre-History of *Do It*." In *Do It,* exhibition catalogue, edited by Hans Ulrich Obrist. New York: Independent Curators Incorporated, 1997.

Aragon, Louis. *Le paysan de Paris*. Paris: Gallimard, 1972. (Original work published in 1926.)

Archilab 2004 festival and exhibition, *The Naked City*. Orléans: Editions HYX, 2004.

Ardenne, Paul. "In utero terrae." In *Horizon moins vingt*, edited by Laurent Tixador and Abraham Poincheval. Paris: Isthme Éditions, 2006.

Ardenne, Paul. *Un art contextuel*. Paris: Flammarion, 2002.

"Ariadne Unemployed," *Potlatch* 9–11 (August 17–31, 1954). Translated by notbored.org. http://www.notbored.org/ariadne.html.

Arns, Inke. "Social Technologies: Deconstruction, subversion, and the utopia of democratic communication" *Media Art Net,* http://www.medienkunstnetz.de/themes/overview_of_media_art/society.

Augé, Marc. *Un ethnologue dans le métro*, Paris, Hachette, 1987. Ed. Coll. Pluriel, 2001.

Augé, Marc. *Non-lieux: Introduction à une anthropologie de la sur-modernité*, Paris: Le Seuil, 1992. *Non-places: Introduction to an Anthropology of Supermodernity*. Translated by John Howe. London: Verso, 1995.

Augoyard, Jean-François. *Step by Step: Everyday Walks in a French Urban Housing Project*. Translated by D. A. Curtis. Minneapolis: University of Minnesota Press, 2007. (Original title *Pas à pas*)

de Balzac, Honoré. *Théorie de la démarche (Theory of Walking)*. Pandora, 1978.

Banes, Sally. *Democracy's Body: Judson Dance Theater, 1962–1964*. Durham: Duke University Press, 1993.

Banes, Sally. *Terpsichore in Sneakers: Postmodern Dance*. Middletown, CT: Wesleyan University Press, 1987.

Barabási, Albert-László. *Bursts: The Hidden Pattern behind Everything We Do*. New York: Dutton, 2010.

Barabási, Albert-László. *Linked: How Everything Is Connected to Everything Else and What It Means for Business, Science, and Everyday Life*. Cambridge: Perseus, 2002.

Bateson, Gregory. Toward a Theory of Schizophrenia. In *Steps to an Ecology of Mind: Collected Essays in Anthropology, Psychiatry, Evolution, and Epistemology*. Chicago: University of Chicago Press, 1999. (Original work published in 1972)

Baudelaire, Charles. *Constantin Guys: Le peintre de la vie moderne*. Geneva: La Palantine, not dated.

Baudelaire, Charles. "Les Foules" (The Crowds). *Le spleen de Paris: Petits poèmes en prose*. Paris, 1869.

Beckett, Samuel. *Collected Shorter Plays of Samuel Beckett*. London: Faber and Faber, 1984.

Beckett, Samuel. *Molloy*. In *Three Novels: Molloy, Malone Dies, The Unnamable*. Translated by Samuel Beckett and Patrick Bowles. New York: Grove Press, 1995. (Original work published in 1951)

Benjamin, Walter. "The Author as Producer" (1934). *The Work of Art in the Age of Its Technological Reproducibility and Other Writings on Media*, edited by Michael W. Jennings et al. Cambridge: Belknap Press of Harvard University Press, 2008.

Benjamin, Walter. "Little History of Photography" (1931). Translated by Edmund Jephcott and Kingsley Shorter. In *The Work of Art in the Age of Its Technological Reproducibility and Other Writings on Media*, edited by Michael W. Jennings et al., 274–298. Cambridge: Belknap Press of Harvard University Press, 2008.

Benjamin, Walter. "The Paris of the Second Empire in Baudelaire" (1938). Translated by Harry Zohn. In *The Writer of Modern Life: Essays on Charles Baudelaire*, edited by Michael W. Jennings, 46–133. Cambridge: Belknap Press of Harvard University Press, 2006.

Bentham, Jeremy. In *The Panopticon Writings*, edited by Miran Bozovic. London: Verso, 1995.

Bernstein, Michèle. "Dérive by the Mile," *Potlatch* 9–11 (August 17–31, 1954), http://www.notbored.org/derive-by-the-mile.html.

Bernstein, Michèle. *Tous les chevaux du roi* (All the King's Horses), Paris, Buchet-Chastel, 1960, republished by Allia, 2004.

Beurard-Valdoye, Patrick. *Les noms perdus: Des sources aux pertes de la Meuse*. La Souterraine: La Main Courante, 1996.

Bey, Hakim. *T.A.Z.: The Temporary Autonomous Zone, Ontological Anarchy, Poetic Terrorism,* 1985, Autonomedia, http://hermetic.com/bey/taz_cont.html.

Boissier, Jean-Louis. "Masaki Fujihata: Poétique de la carte, du panorama et du miroir (virtuels)." http://www.mobilisable.net/2008/?page_id=130.

Bon, François. *Paysage Fer* (Iron Landscape). Lagrasse: Verdier, 2000.

Borges, Jorge Luis. "El jardin de senderos que se bifurcan." "The Garden of Forking Paths." In *Labyrinths: Selected Stories & Other Writings,* edited by Donald A. Yates and James E. Irby. Translated by Donald A. Yates. New York: New Directions,1964. Reprinted in *The New Media Reader,* edited by Noah Wardrip-Fruin and Nick Montfort, 30–34. Cambridge: MIT Press, 2003. (Original work published in 1941)

Bourdieu, Pierre, ed. *La misère du monde.* Paris: Le Seuil, 1993.

Bourdieu, Pierre. *Les règles de l'art.* Paris: Le Seuil, 1992.

Brandon, Kayle, and Heath Bunting. "Interview with Kayle Brandon and Heath Bunting." Interview by Mark Dunhill and Tamiko O'Brien, March 2004, *Collaborative Arts,* http://collabarts.org/?p=81.

Breton, André. [1928]. *Nadja.* Paris: Gallimard, 1962.

Bunting, Heath, and Kayle Brandon. In *Tour de Fence,* edited by Gerrit Gohlke. Berlin: Künstlerhaus Bethanien, 2003.

Cabanne, Pierre. *Entretiens avec Marcel Duchamp.* Paris: Belfond, 1967. *Dialogues with Marcel Duchamp.* London: Thames and Hudson, Da Capo Press, 1987. (Original work published in 1971)

Cage, John. *Indeterminacy: New Aspect of Form in Instrumental and Electronic Music. Ninety Stories by John Cage, with Music.* John Cage, reading; David Tudor, music. Folkways FT 3704, 1959. Reissued as Smithsonian/Folkways CD DF 40804/5, 1992.

Cage, John. *Silence: Lectures and Writings.* 2nd ed. London: Marion Boyars, 1978. (Original work published in 1961)

Calle, Sophie. *Doubles jeux. Livre IV. A suivre.* Nimes: Actes Sud, 1998.

Calle, Sophie. *M'as-tu vue? Exhibition Catalogue.* Paris: Éditions du Centre Pompidou / Xavier Barral, 2003.

Cardiff, Janet, and Mirjam Schaub. *Janet Cardiff: The Walk Book.* Vienna: Thyssen-Bornemisza Art Contemporary in collaboration with Public Art Fund, 2005.

Chardronnet, Ewen. "History of Unitary Urbanism and Psychogeography at the Turn of the Sixties," Lecture notes for Art+Communication Festival, Riga, May 2003, http://semaphore.blogs.com/semaphore/2008/02/history-of-unit.html.

Chatwin, Bruce. *The Songlines.* New York: Vintage Classics, 1998. (Original work published in 1987)

Chremos, Asimina. "White Oak Diary," *Dance Insider*, Flash Notes, November 21, 2000, http://web.archive.org/web/20060317034329/http://www.danceinsider.com/f2006/f0217_2.html.

Chtcheglov, Ivan. (Pseudonym Gilles Ivain). "Formulaire pour un urbanisme nouveau" (October 1953), *Internationale Situationniste* 1 (June 1958), "Formulary for a New Urbanism," in *Situationist International Anthology*, translated and edited by Ken Knabb. Berkeley: Bureau of Public Secrets, 1995, http://www.bopsecrets.org/SI/Chtcheglov.htm.

Chtcheglov, Ivan. "Lettres de loin." http://debordiana.chez.com/francais/is9.htm#lettres ("Letters from afar," my translation).

Cicero. *Rhetorica ad Herennium*. Translated by Harry Caplan. Cambridge: Loeb Classical Library, 1954.

Cone, Michèle. " Translating Muntadas." Interview with Antoni Muntadas. *Artnet Magazine*. June, 2005. http://www.artnet.com/Magazine/features/cone/cone6-9-05.asp.

Cortázar, Julio, and Carol Dunlop. *Los autonautas de la cosmopista: o Un viaje atemporal Paris-Marsella*. Barcelona: Muchnik, D.L., 1983. *Autonauts of the Cosmoroute*. Translated by Anne McLean. London-Berkeley: Telegram, 2008.

Coverley, Merlin. *Psychogeography*. London: Pocket Essentials, 2006.

Daniel, Sharon, and Karen O'Rourke. "Mapping the Database: Trajectories and Perspectives." *Leonardo* 37, no. 4 (2004): 286–296.

Davila, Thierry. *Marcher, créer: Déplacements, rêveries, dérives dans l'art de la fin du 20e siècle*. Paris: Éditions du Regard, 2002.

de Bearn, Henry, André Conord, Mohamed Dahon, Guy-Ernest Debord, Jacques Fillnon, Patrick Straram, and Gil J. Wolman. "Response to the Question: 'Does thought enlighten both us and our actions with the same indifference as the sun, or what is our hope, and what is its value?'" Signed in the name of the Lettrist International in *La Carte d'après nature* (June 1954). Translated by Nick Tallett in *Not Bored!* 29 (1998), http://www.notbored.org/la-carte.html.

Debord, Guy. "Exercise in Psycho-Geography." *Potlatch* 2 (June 29, 1954). http://www.notbored.org/exercise.html.

Debord, Guy. "Introduction à une critique de la géographie urbaine." *Les Lèvres Nues* 6 (1955). "Introduction to a Critique of Urban Geography." In *Situationist International Anthology*, edited and translated by Ken Knabb. Berkeley: Bureau of Public Secrets, 1981, 2006.

Debord, Guy. "Préface pour un livre projeté par Ralph Rumney." In *Guy Debord Œuvres*, édition établie et annotée par Jean-Louis Rançon en collaboration avec Alice Debord, 332–335. Paris: Gallimard, 2006. (Original work published in 1957)

Debord, Guy. "Projet pour un labyrinthe éducatif" (1956). In *Guy Debord Œuvres*, 289.

Debord, Guy. "Psychogeographical Venice." Translated by notbored.org. *NOT BORED*! 41 (2009). http://www.notbored.org/psychogeographical-venice.html.

Debord, Guy. "Théorie de la dérive." *Les Lèvres Nues* 9 (November 1956), reprinted in *Internationale Situationniste* 2 (December 1958). "Theory of the Drift." In *Situationist International Anthology*, edited and translated by Ken Knabb. Berkeley: Bureau of Public Secrets, 1981, 2006.

Debord, Guy. "Two Accounts of the Dérive." *Les Lèvres Nues* 9 (November 1956). Translated by Thomas Y. Levin, http://www.cddc.vt.edu/sionline/presitu/twoaccounts.html.

de Certeau, Michel. *L'invention du quotidien I: Arts de faire*. Paris: Gallimard, coll. Folio, 1980, 1990. *The Practice of Everyday Life*. Translated by Steven Rendall. Berkeley: University of California Press, 1984.

De Quincey, Thomas. "Confessions of an English Opium-Eater" (1821). Teddington: Echo Library, 2006.

Deleuze, Gilles. "Post-scriptum sur les sociétés de contrôle," *L'autre journal* (May 1990). "Postscript on the Societies of Control." Translated by Martin Joughin." *October* 59 (Winter 1992): 3–7.

Dewey, John. *Art as Experience*. New York: Perigee Books, 2005. (Original work published in 1934)

Dietz, Steve. Mapping the Urban Homunculus. In *ELSE/WHERE: MAPPING—New Cartographies of Networks and Territories*, edited by Janet Abrams and Peter Hall, 200–205. Minneapolis: University of Minnesota Design Institute, 2006.

Escorne, Marie. "Le labyrinthe dans les arts du XXe siècle. Les arts du XXe siècle dans le labyrinth." *Amaltea, Revista de mitocritica* 1 (2009): 253–265.

Fisher, Jennifer. "Speeches of Display: The Museum Audioguides of Sophie Calle, Andrea Fraser, and Janet Cardiff." *Parachute: Contemporary Art Magazine* 94 (April 1, 1999): 24–31.

Foucault, Michel. *The Order of Things: An Archaeology of Human Sciences*. New York: Vintage, 1994. (Original work published as *Les mots et les choses* in 1966).

Foucault, Michel. *Surveiller et punir. Naissance de la prison*. Paris: Gallimard, 1975. *Discipline and Punish. The Birth of the Prison*. Translated by Alan Sheridan. New York: Vintage, 1977.

Freud, Sigmund. *The Complete Letters to Wilhelm Fliess (1887–1904)*. Ed. Joseph M. Masson. Cambridge: Belknap Press, 1985.

Freud, Sigmund. "The Uncanny" (1919), *The Standard Edition of the Complete Psychological Works of Sigmund Freud*. vol. 17. Translated and edited by James Strachey, 219–252. London: Hogarth, 1953.

Friedman, Ken. "Forty Years of Fluxus." http://www.artnotart.com/fluxus/kfriedman-fourtyyears.html.

Fusco, Coco. "Questioning the Frame," *In These Times*, December 16, 2004. http://www.inthesetimes.com/article/1750.

Galloway, Anne. "Intimations of Everyday Life: Ubiquitous Computing and the City." *Cultural Studies* 18 (2–3) (2004): 384–408.

Garcia, David, and Geert Lovink. "The ABC of Tactical Media," March 2002. http://project.waag.org/tmn/frabc.html.

Garff, Joakim. *Søren Aabye Kierkegaard: A Biography*. Translated by B. Kirmmse. Princeton: Princeton University Press, 2005.

Geertz, Clifford. "Thick Description: Toward an Interpretive Theory of Culture." In *The Interpretation of Cultures: Selected Essays*, 3–30. New York: Basic Books, 1973.

Gioni, Massimiliano, ed. *Get Lost: Artists Map Downtown New York*. New York: New Museum, 2007.

Glowczewski, Barbara. "Lines and Criss-Crossings: Hyperlinks in Australian Indigenous Narratives." *Media International Australia* 116 (2005): 24–35.

Glowczewski, Barbara. "The Paradigm of Indigenous Australians: Anthropological Phantasms, Artistic Creations and Political Resistance." In *La revanche des genres: Art contemporain australien*, edited by Géraldine Le Roux and Lucienne Strivay, 84–109. Paris: Diff' Art/Aïnu, 2007.

Glowczeswki, Barbara. *Yapa: Aboriginal Painters from Balgo and Lagamanu*. Paris: Baudoin Le Bon Editeur, 1991.

Gontarski, S. E. "'Quad I & II': Beckett's Sinister Mime(s)." *Journal of Beckett Studies* 9 (Spring 1983): 137–138.

Graham, Dan. In *Two-Way Mirror Power: Selected Writings by Dan Graham on his Art*, edited by Alexander Alberro. Cambridge: MIT Press, 1999.

Grenier, Catherine, ed. *Robert Morris 1961–1994: Catalogue du Musée National d'Art Moderne*. Paris: Centre Pompidou, 1995.

Gürses, Seda, Michelle Teran, and Manu Luksch. "A Trialogue on Interventions in Surveillance Space: Seda Gürses in Conversation with Michelle Teran and Manu Luksch." *Surveillance & Society* 7 (2) (2010): 165–174.

Haklay, M., and P. Weber. "*OpenStreetMap:* User-Generated Street Maps." *IEEE Pervasive Computing/ IEEE Computer Society / IEEE Communications Society* 7, no. 4 (2008): 12–18.

Halprin, Anna. *Parades and Changes, Intensive Care*. Catalogue. Paris: Centre Pompidou / Festival d'Automne, 2004.

Harvey, David. *The Condition of Postmodernity: An Enquiry into the Origins of Cultural Change*. Cambridge: Blackwell, 1990.

Heathfield, Adrian, and Tehching Hsieh. *Out of Now: The Lifeworks of Tehching Hsieh*. London/ Cambridge: Live Art Development Agency and MIT Press, 2009.

Hemment, Drew. "Locative Arts." 2004. http://www.drewhemment.com/pdf/locativearts.pdf.

Higgins, Dick. "Statement on Intermedia." http://www.artpool.hu/Fluxus/Higgins/intermedia2.html.

Hight, Jeremy. "Narrative Archeology" *Streetnotes* (Summer 2003). http://web.archive.org/web/20110409234138/http://www.xcp.bfn.org/hight.html.

Hight, Jeremy. "NeMe: Rhizomatic Cartography: Modulated Mapping and the Spatial Net," May 5, 2009, http://www.neme.org/991/rhizomatic-cartography.

Hollevoet, Christel. *"Wandering in the City": The Power of the City, The City of Power*. New York: Whitney Museum, 1992.

Home, Stewart. "How I Discovered America." *Infopool* 6 (2002), http://www.stewarthomesociety.org/art/america.htm.

Hou Je Bek, Wilfried. "Algorithmic Psychogeography." 2002. http://studio.berkeley.edu/070707/texts/ALGORITHMIC%20PSYCHOGEOGRAPHY.pdf.

Hou Je Bek, Wilfried. "Cracking the Urban Cheat Code + A Practical Account of How to Do It," September 2003, http://web.archive.org/web/20030908183123/http://www.socialfiction.org/psychogeography/psychogeogram.html.

Hou Je Bek, Wilfried. "Do-It-Yourself Urbanism: Psychogeography, Generosity, Serendipity and Turriphilia." In *Archilab 2004: La ville à nu* (The Naked City). Catalog. Orléans: HYX, 2004.

Hou Je Bek, Wilfried. "Language/Psychogeonamics and Where to Go Next." 2004. http://web.archive.org/web/20041114142739/http://www.socialfiction.org/psychogeography/psychogeonamics.html.

Hou Je Bek, Wilfried. "Questions à Wilfried Hou Je Bek. Un entretien par Karen O'Rourke." In *Art++*, edited by David-Olivier Lartigaud, 293–302. Orléans: Editions HYX, 2011.

"Independent Brain Networks Control Human Walking." *Science Daily* (Aug. 14, 2007). http://www.sciencedaily.com/releases/2007/08/070807135759.htm.

Ingold, Tim. "Footprints through the Weather-World: Walking, Breathing, Knowing." In *Making Knowledge: Explorations of the Indissoluble Relation between Mind, Body and Environment,* edited by T. H. J. Marchand. Oxford: Wiley-Blackwell, 2011. doi: 10.1002/9781444391473.ch6.

Ingold, Tim. *Lines: A Brief History*. London: Routledge, 2007.

Institute for Applied Autonomy. "Tactical Cartography." In *Atlas of Radical Cartography*, edited by L. Mogel and A. Baghat, 29–38. Los Angeles: Journal of Aesthetics, Protest Press, 2007.

Jacobs, Jane. *The Death and Life of Great American Cities*. New York: Random House, 1961.

Jameson, Fredric. *Postmodernism or, The Cultural Logic of Late Capitalism*. Durham, NC: Duke University Press, 1991.

Jeremijenko, Natalie. "The Art of the Eco-Mind Shift," TED talk, http://www.ted.com/talks/natalie_jeremijenko_the_art_of_the_eco_mindshift.html.

Kabakov, Ilya. *Installations, 1983–1995*. Paris: Editions du Centre Pompidou, 1995.

Kaprow, Allan. "Interview with Allan Kaprow," interviewed by Robert C. Morgan. *Journal of Contemporary Art* 4 (2) (1991): 56–69.

Kitchin, Rob M. "Cognitive Maps: What Are They and Why Study Them?" *Journal of Environmental Psychology* 14 (1994): 1–19.

Klein, Naomi. "China's All-Seeing Eye," *Rolling Stone* 1053 (May 2008): http://www.naomiklein.org/articles/2008/05/chinas-all-seeing-eye.

Knabb, Ken, ed. and trans. *Situationist International Anthology.* Berkeley: Bureau of Public Secrets, 1995. (Original work published in 1981)

Kosmidou, Zoe. "Transitory Objects: A Conversation with Marina Abramović." *Sculpture Magazine* 20, no. 9 (November 2001). http://www.sculpture.org/documents/scmag01/nov01/abram/abram.shtml.

Kostelanetz, Richard, and Robert Flemming, eds. *Writings on Glass: Essays, Interviews, Criticism.* Berkeley: University of California Press, 1997.

Kotkin, Joel, "Get Used to It: Suburbia's Not Going Away, No Matter What Critics Say or Do." *American Enterprise,* January 1, 2005.

Kurgan, Laura, and Xavier Costa, eds. *You Are Here: Architecture and Information Flows.* Barcelona: Museu D'Art Contemporani, 1995.

Kwon, Miwon. *One Place after Another: Site-Specific Art and Locational Identity.* Cambridge: MIT Press, 2004.

Landry, Donna. "Radical Walking." *Open Democracy.* 2001. http://www.opendemocracy.net/ecology-climate_change_debate/article_465.jsp.

Lefebvre, Henri. "Henri Lefebvre on the Situationist International." Interview conducted and translated by Kristen Ross, *October* 79 (Winter 1997). http://www.notbored.org/lefebvre-interview.html.

Lefebvre, Henri. *La production de l'espace.* 4th ed. Paris: Anthropos, 2000. *The Production of Space.* Translated by Donald Nicholson-Smith. London: Basil Blackwell, 1991. (Original work published in 1974)

Lewis, David. "The Way of the Nomad." In *From Earlier Fleets: Hemisphere—An Aboriginal Anthology.* Cited in David Turnbull, *Maps Are Territories, Science Is an Atlas: A Portfolio of Exhibits,* 52–53. Chicago: University of Chicago Press, 1989.(Original work published in 1978)

LeWitt, Sol. "Paragraphs on Conceptual Art." *Artforum* 5 (10) (June 1967): 79–83.

Lippard, Lucy R. *Six Years: The Dematerialization of the Art Object from 1966 to 1972.* New York: Praeger, 1973.

Long, Richard. "Interview with Richard Long." Interview by Robert Ayers. *ArtInfo* (June 28, 2006), http://www.artinfo.com/news/story/18221/richard-long/?page=2.

Long, Richard. "Richard Long: No Where." Interview with Colin Kirkpatrick. July 8, 1994. Piers Arts Centre, Orkney. http://www.speronewestwater.com/cgi-bin/iowa/articles/record.html?record=293.

Lovink, Geert. "Surveillance, Performance, Self-Surveillance: Interview with Jill Magid," Institute of Network Cultures Weblog. (October 29, 2004), http://networkcultures.org/wpmu/weblog/2004/10/29/surveillance-performance-self-surveillance.

Luksch, Manu, and Mukul Patel. "Faceless: Chasing the Data Shadow," 2007. http://www.ambienttv.net/2007/faceless/chasingthedatashadow2007.pdf.

Luksch, Manu, and Mukul Patel. "Manifesto for CCTV Filmmakers," 2004. http://www.ambienttv.net/content/?q=dpamanifesto.

Lynch, Kevin. *The Image of the City*. Cambridge: MIT Press, 1960.

Macel, Christine. *Jeppe Hein*. Translated by Charles Penwarden. Paris: Éditions du Centre Pompidou, 2005.

Magid, Jill. *One Cycle of Memory in the City of L*. Liverpool: FACT, 2004.

de Maîstre, Xavier. *Voyage autour de ma chambre*. Paris: José Corti, 1984.

Malone, Laurent, and Christine Breton / LMX. "L'agence de documentation sur les mutations urbaines." *ICHIM 04 Conference Proceedings*. Berlin: ICHIM, 2004. http://ichim.org.

Malone, Laurent, and Dennis Adams. *JFK*. Marseille: éditions LMX, 2002.

Mann, Steve. "Continuous lifelong capture of personal experience with EyeTap." Keynote address, ACM International Multimedia Conference, Proceedings of the 1st ACM workshop on Continuous archival and retrieval of personal experiences (CARPE 2004), New York, New York, Oct. 15, 2004, 1–21.

Mann, Steve. "Existential Technology: Wearable Computing Is Not the Real Issue!" *Leonardo* 36 (1) (2003): 19–25.

Mann, Steve. "Sousveillance," 2002, http://wearcam.org/sousveillance.htm.

Mann, Steve. "Sousveillance: Inverse Surveillance in Multimedia Imaging." *Proceedings of the Twelfth Annual ACM International Conference on Multimedia*. New York: ACM, 2004.

Mann, Steve. "Wearable Computing: A First Step Toward Personal Imaging." *IEEE Computer* 30 (2) (February 1997): 25–32.

Mann, Steve, Jason Nolan, and Barry Wellman. "Sousveillance: Inventing and Using Wearable Computing Devices for Data Collection in Surveillance Environments." *Surveillance & Society* 1 (3) (July 2003): 331–355.

Manovich, Lev. *The Language of New Media*. Cambridge: MIT Press, 2001.

Manovich, Lev. "Understanding Hybrid Media." http://manovich.net/articles.

Maspero, François, and Anaïk Frantz. *Les passagers du Roissy-Express*. Paris: Le Seuil, 1990. *Roissy Express: A Journey through the Paris Suburbs*. Translated by Paul Jones. London: Verso, 1994.

Meltz, Raphaël. "Marc L***," *Le Tigre* 28 (November 2008). http://www.le-tigre.net/Marc-L.html.

Merleau-Ponty, Maurice. *Phénoménologie de la perception*. Paris: Gallimard, 1945. *Phenomenology of Perception*. Translated by Colin Smith. New York: Humanities Press, 1962.

Mitchell, W. J. T. "Golden Memories: Interview with Sculptor Robert Morris," *ArtForum* (April 1994).

Mogel, Lize, and Alexis Bhagat. *An Atlas of Radical Cartography*. Los Angeles: Journal of Aesthetics, Protest Press, 2007.

Montémont, Véronique. *Jacques Roubaud: L'amour du nombre*. Lille: Presses Universitaires du Septentrion, 2004.

Morris, Robert. "Interview: Robert Morris." Interviewed by Simon Grant. *Tate Etc.*14, Autumn 2008, http://www.tate.org.uk/tateetc/issue14/morris.htm.

Morris, Robert. "Notes on Sculpture, Part 2." In *Continuous Project Altered Daily: The Writings of Robert Morris*. Cambridge: MIT Press, 1993.

Morris, Robert. "The Present Tense of Space." *Continuous Project Altered Daily: The Writings of Robert Morris*, 175–209. Cambridge: MIT Press, 1993.

Moure, Gloria, ed. *Dan Graham*. Barcelona: Fundacio Antoni Tapies, 1998.

Multiplicity. *U. S. E.—Uncertain States of Europe*. Milan: Skira, 2003.

Mumford, Lewis. *The City in History: Its Origins, Its Transformations, and Its Prospects*. New York: Harcourt, Brace and World, 1961.

Nauman, Bruce. "Breaking the Silence." Interview with Joan Simon. Reprinted in *Please Pay Attention Please: Bruce Nauman's Words. Writings and Interviews*, edited by Janet Kraynak, 317–338. Cambridge: MIT Press, 2005.

Nauman, Bruce. *Bruce Nauman: Image/Text, 1966–1996*. London: Hayward Gallery, 1998.

Nauman, Bruce. "Setting a Good Corner," Interview, *Art 21*, http://www.pbs.org/art21/artists/bruce-nauman.

Naurekas, Jim. *New York Songlines*, http://www.nysonglines.com.

Nemser, Cindy. "A Conversation with Eva Hesse." In *Artforum* 8, no. 7 (May 1970), reprinted in *Eva Hesse*, edited by Mignon Nixon, 1–24. Cambridge: MIT Press, 2002.

"New Research Discovers Independent Brain Networks Control Human Walking." *Nature Neuroscience* (August 2007). http://multivu.prnewswire.com/mnr/bastian/29010.

Nieuwenhuis, Constant. "Another City for Another Life." *Internationale Situationniste* 3 (December 1959). Translated by Paul Hammond. http://notbored.org/another-city.html.

Obrist, Hans-Ulrich. "Obrist/Abramović/Chaitin Interview." Kitakyushu, Japan, July 2001. *HuO: Hans-Ulrich Obrist: Interviews*, 29–44. Milan: Charta / Fondazione Pitti Immagine Discovery, 2003.

Oddy, Jason. "An Outsider's Guide to Getting Inside Places Only Insiders Normally Get to Go." *Art on Paper* 13 (5) (May–June 2009): 58–71.

O'Hagen, Sean. "One Step Beyond," *The Observer*, May 10, 2009,.http://www.guardian.co.uk/artanddesign/2009/may/10/art-richard-long.

Ono, Yoko. *Film No. 4 (Rape, or Chase)*. In *Screen Writings: Scripts and Texts by Independent Filmmakers*, edited by Scott MacDonald. Berkeley: University of California Press, 1995.

Ono, Yoko. *Grapefruit: A Book of Instructions*. New York: Simon & Schuster, 1970.

Ono, Yoko. "Yoko Ono." Interview with Scott MacDonald. In *A Critical Cinema 2: Interviews with Independent Filmmakers*, 139–156. Berkeley: University of California Press, 1992.

O'Rourke, Karen. "The Artist's Book and Photography: The Example of Michael Snow's *Cover to Cover*." *Revue Francaise d'Etudes Americaines* 8 (1979): 215–224.

O'Rourke, Karen. "Dérives programmées [promenades assistées par ordinateur]." In *Art++*, edited by David-Olivier Lartigaud, 258–279. Orléans: Editions HYX, 2011.

O'Rourke, Karen. "Questions à Jo Walsh." In *Art++*, edited by David-Olivier Lartigaud, 280–291. Orléans: Editions HYX, 2011.

O'Rourke, Karen. "Questions à Wilfried Hou Je Bek." In *Art++*, edited by David-Olivier Lartigaud, 292–299. Orléans: Editions HYX, 2011.

Owens, Bill. *Suburbia*. San Francisco: Straight Arrow Press, 1972.

Paglen, Trevor. "Unmarked Planes and Hidden Geographies: Author's Statement," *Vectors Journal* 2 (2) (Winter 2007), http://www.vectorsjournal.org/projects/index.php?project=5924.

Paglen, Trevor. "Mapping Ghosts: Visible Collective talks to Trevor Paglen." In *An Atlas of Radical Cartography*, edited by Lize Mogel and Alexis Bhagat, 39–50. Los Angeles: Journal of Aesthetics, Protest Press, 2007.

Passuth, Krisztina. *Moholy-Nagy*. London: Thames and Hudson, 1985.

Peirce, Charles Sanders. "One, Two, Three: Fundamental Categories of Thought and of Nature." In *Writings of Charles S. Peirce, A Chronological Edition, 1884–1886*, vol. 5, edited by Peirce Edition Project with Christian J. W. Kloesel et al. Bloomington: Indiana University Press, 1981. (Original work published in 1885)

Perec, Georges. *Espèces d'espaces*. Paris: Galilée, 1974.

Perec, Georges. *Tentative d'épuisement d'un lieu parisien*. Paris: Christian Bourgois, 1982.

Perkins, Chris, and Martin Dodge. "The potential of user-generated cartography: a case study of the. openstreetmap project and Mapchester mapping party." *North West Geography* 8 (1) (2008): 19–32.

Petcou, Constantin, and Doina Petrescu. "Au rez-de-chaussée de la ville," *Multitudes* 20 (Spring 2005). http://multitudes.samizdat.net/Au-rez-de-chaussee-de-la-ville.

Picasso, Pablo, and Gjon Mili. *Picasso's Third Dimension*. Photos and text by Gjon Mili. New York: Triton Press, 1970.

Piper, Adrian. *Talking to Myself: The Ongoing Autobiography of an Art Object.* Hamburg: Hossmann, 1974. Reprinted in *Out of Order, Out of Sight.* Volume 1, *Selected Writings in Meta-Art 1968–1992.* Cambridge: MIT Press, 1996.

Pistoletto, Michelangelo. "The Minus Objects," *Michelangelo Pistoletto,* exhibition catalog Genoa: Galleria La Bertesca, 1966. Republished on Michelangelo Pistoletto's official Web site http://www.pistoletto.it/eng/testi/minus_objects.pdf.

Plas, François, Éric Viel, and Yves Blanc. *La marche humaine: Kinésiologie dynamique, biomécanique, et pathomécanique.* 3rd edition. Paris: Masson, 1989. (Original work published in 1975)

Polak, Esther. "Elastic Mapping: Implications of a GPS Drawing Robot in Times of Locative Media." Paper presented at the Fifteenth International Symposium on Electronic Art (ISEA 2009), Belfast, August 29, 2009.

Polak, Esther. Interview with Andrea Urlberger, February 8, 2007, in *Paysage technologique: Théories et pratiques autour du Global Positioning System.* http://www.ciren.org/ciren/laboratoires/Paysage_Technologique/art/polak/index.html.

Priest, Julian. "About the State of Wireless London," 2004, http://informal.org.uk/people/julian/publications/the_state_of_wireless_london.

Rainer, Yvonne. "Some Retrospective Notes on a Dance for Ten People and Twelve Mattresses Called Parts of Some Sextets" (1965). In *Happenings and Other Acts,* edited by Mariellen R. Sandford. London: Routledge, 1995.

Rancière, Jacques. *Le maître ignorant: Cinq leçons sur l'émancipation intellectuelle.* Paris: Librairie Arthème Fayard, 2004. (Original work published in 1987)

Rancière, Jacques. *Le partage du sensible.* Paris: La Fabrique éditions, 2000.

Raymond, Eric A. "Homesteading the Noosphere," http://catb.org/~esr/writings/homesteading/homesteading.

Reiss, Julie H. *From Margin to Center: The Spaces of Installation Art.* Cambridge: MIT Press, 2001.

Richter, Hans. *Dada: Art and Anti-art.* London: Thames & Hudson, 2004.

Riout, Denys. *Qu'est-ce que l'art moderne?* Paris: Gallimard, 2000.

Rodrigue, Jean-Paul, C. Comtois, and B. Slack. *The Geography of Transport Systems.* 2nd ed. New York: Routledge, 2009.

Roeskens, Till. "Comment aller chez Krimhilde." In *Rafraîchir l'écran (Refreshing the Screen).* Curated by Julien Maire. *Livraison 5.* Strasbourg: Rhinocéros, 2005.

Roubaud, Jacques. *Le grand incendie de Londres, récit avec incises et bifurcations, 1985–1987.* Paris: Seuil, 1989. "The Great Fire of London: A Story with Interpolations and Bifurcations." Translated by Dominic Di Bernardi. Elmwood Park, IL: Dalkey Archive Press, 1991.

Rouillé, André. "L'art entre choses et expérience," *Paris-Art.com* no. 319, June 10, 2010, http://www.paris-art.com/art-culture-France/l-art-entre-choses-et-experiences/Rouille-Andre/319.html.

Rouillé, André. "Visibilité paradoxale de l'art," *Paris-Art.com*, no. 226, November 25, 2010, http://www.paris-art.com/art-culture-France/visibilite-paradoxale-de-l-art/rouille-andre/336.html.

Rousseau, Jean-Jacques. *Les confessions (1781), The Confessions*. Translated by J. M. Cohen. London: Penguin Books, 1953.

Rumney, Ralph. *Le consul*, entretiens avec Gérard Berréby. Paris: Éditions Allia, 1999.

Sadler, Simon. *The Situationist City*. Cambridge: MIT Press, 1998.

Saunders, Wade. "Not Lost, Not Found: Bill Bollinger." *Art in America* 88 (3) (March 2000): 104–117, 143–144.

Schienke, Erich W., and Bill Brown. "Streets into Stages: An Interview with Surveillance Camera Players' Bill Brown." *Surveillance & Society* 1 (3) (2003): 356–374.

Schimmel, Paul. "Leap into the Void: Performance and the Object." In *Out of Actions: Between Performance and the Object, 1949–1979*, edited by Paul Schimmel and Kristine Stiles. Los Angeles: Museum of Contemporary Art, 1998.

Schneider, Florian. "Collaboration," February 17, 2007, http://summit.kein.org/node/190.

Sharp, Willoughby. 1998. "Interview with Bruce Nauman," *Arts Magazine* (March 1970). Reprinted in *Bruce Nauman: Image/Text 1966–1996*, exhibition catalog, 88–97. London: Hayward Gallery.

Shehadeh, Raja. "Interview with Raja Shehadeh." Interviewed by Mark Thwaite. http://www.bookdepository.com/interview/with/author/raja-shehadeh.

Shehadeh, Raja. *Palestinian Walks: Forays into a Vanishing Landscape*. New York: Scribner, 2007.

Shehadeh, Raja. *Strangers in the House*. London: Profile Books, 2002.

Shirky, Clay. *Here Comes Everybody: The Power of Organizing without Organizations*. New York: Penguin, 2008.

Simon, Joan. "Bruce Nauman: The Matter in Hand." *Tate,* June 1, 1998. http://www.speronewestwater.com/cgi-bin/iowa/articles/record.html?record=628

Sinclair, Iain. *Lights Out for the Territory*. London: Penguin, 2003. (Original work published in 1997)

Sinclair, Iain. *London Orbital*. London: Penguin, 2002.

Smithson, Robert. Frederick Law Olmsted and the Dialectical Landscape. In *Robert Smithson: The Collected Writings*, edited by Jack D. Flam, 157–171. Berkeley: University of California Press, 1996.

Smithson, Robert. "Visit to the Monuments of Passaic." In *Robert Smithson: Collected Writings*. London/New York: Verso, 2001, 2002.

Solnit, Rebecca. *Wanderlust*. London: Verso, 2002.

Souman, Jan L., Ilja Frissen, Manish N. Sreenivasa, and Marc O. Ernst. "Walking Straight into Circles. *Current Biology* 19 (18) (August 20, 2009): 1538–1542. doi:10.1016/j.cub.2009.07.053.

Soupault, Philippe. *Les Dernières Nuits de Paris*. Paris: Gallimard, 1997. (Original work published in 1928)

Stalker. *Attraverso i territori attuali / A travers les territoires actuels*. Paris: Jean-Michel Place, 2000.

Subotnik, Morton. "Je me souviens de Parades and Changes." In Anna Halprin, *Parades and Changes, Intensive Care*. Catalogue. Paris: Centre Pompidou / Festival d'Automne, 2004.

Thomas, Jean-Jacques. "Swing Troubadour: Roubaud's Self-portrait," *The Great Fire of London by Jacques Roubaud: A Casebook*, edited by Peter Consenstein. Urbana-Champaign, IL: Dalkey Archive Press, 2003. http://www.dalkeyarchive.com/book/?GCOI=15647100788640&fa=details.

Tiberghien, Gilles. *Nature, Art, Paysage*. Arles: Actes Sud/ENSP, 2001.

Tisseron, Serge. *L'empathie au cœur du jeu social*. Paris: Albin Michel, 2010.

Tixador, Laurent, and Abraham Poincheval. *Horizon moins vingt*. Paris: Isthme Éditions, 2006.

Tixador, Laurent, and Abraham Poincheval. *L'inconnu des grands horizons*. Paris: Éditions Michel Baverey, 2003.

Tollmann, Vera. "The World in One's Pocket? The Net Project 'VOPOS' by the Italian Group 0100101110101101.org." Translated by Tim Jones. http://www.springerin.at/dyn/heft_text.php?textid=1191&lang=en.

Tolman, Edward C. "Cognitive Maps in Rats and Men." *Psychological Review* 55 (4) (July 1948): 189–208.

Tucker, Marcia. PheNAUMANology. In *Bruce Nauman: Image/Text 1966–1996*, exhibition catalog. London: Hayward Gallery, 1998.

Turnbull, David. *Maps Are Territories, Science Is an Atlas: A Portfolio of Exhibits*. Chicago: University of Chicago Press, 1989.

Tuters, Marc, and Rasa Šmite, eds. *Acoustic Space: Trans-cultural Mapping*. Riga: RIXC Centre, 2004.

Tuters, Marc, and Kazys Varnelis. "Beyond Locative Media." http://networkedpublics.org/locative_media/beyond_locative_media.

Tzara, Tristan. "Pour faire un poème dadaïste." *Littérature* 15 (July 1920). *Dada manifeste sur l'amour faible et l'amour amer*, in *Oeuvres complètes*, vol.1, p. 382. Paris: Flammarion, 1975.

Urlberger, Andrea, "Janet Cardiff: Walk in my Footsteps." Cheminements, *Les carnets du paysage*, 11 (2004): 171–183.

Urlberger, Andrea. "Paysage technologique: Théories et pratiques autour du GPS." 2007. http://www.ciren.org/ciren/laboratoires/Paysage_Technologique/index.html.

Vanderbilt, Tom. "Cerebral Cities." In *ELSE/WHERE: MAPPING—New Cartographies of Networks and Territories*, ed. Janet Abrams and Peter Hall, 176–183. Minneapolis: University of Minneapolis Design Institute, 2006.

Van Kranenburg, Rob. *The Internet of Things: A Critique of Ambient Technology and the All-Seeing Network of RFID*. Amsterdam: Institute of Network Cultures, 2007.

Van Tuyl, Gijs. "Human Condition / Human Body." In *Bruce Nauman: Image/Text 1966–1996*, exhibition catalog. London: Hayward Gallery, 1998.

Vasset, Philippe. *Un livre blanc*. Paris: Fayard, 2007.

Viola, Bill, "Will There Be Condominiums in Data Space?" *Video* 80, no. 5 (1982): 36–41. Reprinted in Noah Wardrip-Fruin and Nick Montfort, eds., *New Media Reader,* 465–470. Cambridge: MIT Press, 2003.

Virilio, Paul. "Ctheory Interview with Paul Virilio: The Kosovo War Took Place in Orbital Space," with John Armitage. Translated by Patrice Riemens, October 18, 2000, http://www.ctheory.net/articles.aspx?id=132.

Virilio, Paul, Raymond Depardon, Scofidio Diller, Mark Hansen Renfro, and Laura Kurgan. In *Terre natale: Ailleurs commence ici,* edited by Ben Rubin. Arles/Paris: Actes sud and Fondation Cartier, 2009.

Walsh, Jo. Interview with Karen O'Rourke (March 15, 2005). Published in French as "Questions à Jo Walsh," in *Art++*, edited by David-Olivier Lartigaud, 280–291. Orléans: Editions HYX, 2011.

Walton, Lee. *The City System*. New York: City System, 2003.

Warhol, Andy. *The Philosophy of Andy Warhol: (From A to B and Back Again)*. New York: Harcourt Brace Jovanovich, 1975. (Reprinted by Harvest, 1977)

Weiser, Mark. "The Computer for the Twenty-first Century." *Scientific American* 265, 3, no. 3 (1991): 3–11. (Reprinted in *IEEE Pervasive Computing*, January–March, 2002, 18–25).

Wilson, Stephen. "The Telepresent," http://userwww.sfsu.edu/%7Eswilson/art/telepresent/telepresent.html.

Wood, Denis. "The Fine Line Between Mapping and Map Making." *Cartographica: The International Journal for Geographic Information and Geovisualization* 30 (4) (Winter 1993): 40–50.

Wood, Denis. *The Power of Maps*. New York: Guilford Press, 1992.

Yates, Frances A. *The Art of Memory*. London: Pimlico, 2001. (Original work published by Routledge and Kegan Paul in 1966)

Young, La Monte, and Marian Zazeela. *Selected Writings*. Munich: Heiner Friedrich, 1969.

Young, La Monte. "Draw a Straight Line and Follow It." Interview, In Richard Kostelanetz, *The Theatre of Mixed-Means: An Introduction to Happenings, Kinetic Environments and Other Mixed-Means Presentations*. 2nd ed. New York: Dial, 1980. (Original work published in 1968)

Zuckerman, Ethan. "Tracking Hasan Elahi," October 19, 2006, http://www.worldchanging.com.

Index

Note: Page numbers in *italics* indicate illustrations.

www.ingramcontent.com/pod-product-compliance
Lightning Source LLC
LaVergne TN
LVHW081257100826
845148LV00005B/895

* 9 7 8 0 2 6 2 5 2 8 9 5 5 *